Instrument Development in the Affective Domain

D. Betsy McCoach · Robert K. Gable
John P. Madura

Instrument Development in the Affective Domain

School and Corporate Applications

Third Edition

Springer

D. Betsy McCoach
John P. Madura
Department of Educational Psychology
University of Connecticut
Storrs, CT
USA

Robert K. Gable
Alan Shawn Feinstein Graduate School
Johnson & Wales University
Providence, RI
USA

ISBN 978-1-4614-7134-9 ISBN 978-1-4614-7135-6 (eBook)
DOI 10.1007/978-1-4614-7135-6
Springer New York Heidelberg Dordrecht London

Library of Congress Control Number: 2013934719

Printed on acid-free paper

Springer is part of Springer Science+Business Media (www.springer.com)

To my Siegles: Del, Jessica, and Del

D. B. M.

To my loving wife and family: Kathe, Rick, and Kathe

R. K. G.

To Whitney, Ethan (JEM) and Maeve (Maeveen)

J. P. M.

Foreword

There has been longstanding interest in affective characteristics in both educational and corporate environments. While each domain has produced its own set of theorists and researchers, the work of some, such as Bandura, has found a place in the literature of both areas. In each of these settings, theorists and researchers have agreed on the causal connections between such constructs as self-efficacy and perceived satisfaction and success, whether that success is measured by academic achievement or corporate quality and performance resulting in profitability.

Along with this interest, comes the need for the development of valid and reliable instruments to assess affective characteristics. It is clear that no matter whether your interest lies in the relationship between self-efficacy and academic success or employee satisfaction and corporate success, it is essential that the instruments used be carefully designed and tested to assure that they are measuring what they are intended to measure in a consistent manner. This work offers the theoretical perspective, modern psychometric techniques, real examples, and data needed to enable the instrument developer to produce such valid and reliable instruments.

While the development process changes very little as one goes from the educational to the corporate domain, the inclusion in this edition of specific corporate-based theories and research examples as a complement to the academic-based examples greatly enhances the relevance of this book for those of us concerned with the effects of affective variables in the workplace. For anyone involved with the development of instruments to measure these variables, this book should prove a necessary resource. With today's emphasis on quality, this book provides the road map and background to accomplish measurement with the certitude that quality demands.

Joseph W. Keilty
Former Executive, Vice-President
Quality and Human Resources
American Express Company

Preface

Over 20 years ago, Bob Gable (and Marian Wolf) authored the second edition of Instrument Development in the Affective Domain, and it quickly became a cherished book for researchers in education, business, and the social sciences who needed to create multi-item self-report instruments. Five years later, a much younger Betsy McCoach enrolled in Bob Gable's instrument design course, and it changed her life forever. Falling in love with latent variables and structural equation modeling in the fall (thanks to Dave Kenny) and the measurement of affective constructs in the spring (thanks to Bob Gable!), Betsy spent 15 years engaging in teaching, researching, and applying these techniques to the development of affective instruments. After Bob Gable retired from the University of Connecticut, Betsy continued to teach his legendary instrument design course, each year adding additional material (much to the dismay of her graduate students!). The revision of this book grew out of Betsy and Bob's respective instrument design courses and projects over the last decade, and Betsy was thrilled when Bob agreed to collaborate on a long overdue revision of the classic. In the spring of 2011, a first year graduate student entered Betsy's instrument design class, just as she had entered Bob's class a dozen years before. John developed the same passion for latent variables and instrumentation that Bob and Betsy had, and soon after, he became the third of the collaborators on this new edition of Instrument Development in the Affective Domain. Thus, this book represents three generations of Instrument Design: a professor, her mentor, and her mentee. Our goal was to capture some of the magic of the instrument design course and package it, with the hope that it will inspire you, the reader, to engage in the instrument design journey with the passion and dedication that we feel toward the subject.

Instrument design is both art and science, both qualitative and quantitative, both conceptual and methodological, both holistic and technical, driven by both substantive theories and empirical outcomes. It is this dualism that makes the study of affective instrument design such an exciting and rewarding area, and we have tried to capture this dualism within this text. The first three chapters are quite conceptual; the following four chapters are more methodological. However, throughout the book, we have maintained a very applied, very conceptual orientation to the material. Therefore, the book requires little prerequisite knowledge in statistics, although a healthy grasp of correlation and regression would certainly aid students' grasp of the contents in Chaps. 4–7.

This book is designed for use in graduate coursework in instrument design in the affective domain or as a stand-alone guide for a researcher or evaluator who needs to develop multi-item scales to measure affective traits. Given that 20 years have elapsed since the second edition of this book, this version represents a complete revision of the text. Chapter 1 provides a brief conceptual introduction to the affective domain. Chapter 2 presents an overview of measurement, scaling, and item writing techniques. Chapter 3 introduces the concept of validity and discusses issues related to collecting validity evidence-based on the content of the instrument. Chapter 4 introduces the reader to exploratory and confirmatory factor analyzes as analytic methods to probe the internal structure of the instrument. Chapter 5 presents latent class analysis, Item Response Theory, and Rasch Modeling as additional methods for examining the internal structure of the instrument. Chapter 5 also includes an introduction to measurement invariance. Chapter 6 discusses a variety of ways to buttress the validity argument for the instrument by examining relations to external variables. Chapter 7 focuses on issues related to reliability. Finally, Chap. 8 concludes with a summary of the major steps in the instrument design process.

The book outlines a systematic approach to tackle the instrument design process and provides guidance on most aspects of the process. We hope that this book provides guidance and inspiration, but no one text can cover all topics related to instrument design in a completely comprehensive fashion. Thus, in that sense, this is an introductory text for a multi-faceted topic, rather than an encyclopedic volume on all topics related to this area. Our greatest wish is that you fall in love with instrument design the way that we have and that find the process and the book enjoyable as well as informative.

D. Betsy McCoach
Robert K. Gable
John P. Madura

Acknowledgments

There are so many people who have helped make this book possible. First, we want to thank Glen Davenport, Sarah Newton, and Kristyn Michaud, who all provided much needed editorial assistance. We also want to thank Mariya Yukymenko and Melissa Eastwood, who helped gather the literature for the update and Jessica Goldstein, who helped to develop some of the material on Latent Class Analysis that we use in this book. Thank you to the University of Connecticut for granting the first author a sabbatical leave in the Spring of 2010 to work on the manuscript. Thank you also to the National Research Center on the Gifted and Talented for supporting the first author throughout this process. Of course, all opinions contained in the book represent our own, and are in no way representative of the NRCGT, IES, or the Department of Education. However, the support that they provided during this process was invaluable. Thanks also to our colleagues at the University of Connecticut- Megan Welsh, Chris Rhoads, Swami, and Jane Rogers and all of the graduate students in the Measurement, Evaluation, and Assessment program for their support throughout the process. Thank you to the best Department Chair an Educational Psychology Department could ever have—Del Siegle, for his professional and personal support. We (especially the first author) could not ask for a better Chair and boss! We are also indebted to the hundreds of students who have taken instrument design courses at the University of Connecticut over the last 20 years. Their work has both fueled and informed this revision. Thank you to Rachel McAnallen for allowing us to use an adapted version of her data for our factor analysis examples.

We wish to thank our families, who sacrificed a great deal for the sake of this book. Countless early mornings and weekends at the office have made "the book" a legendary and mythical creature at the first author's house, second only to Santa Claus. In particular, the first author wishes to acknowledge the efforts of her husband Del, who became a single parent in the mornings for the sake of the book, an even more heroic act given that he has books of his own to pen. She also wishes to thank Jessica, Del, Mom, Melissa, Nikki, Susannah, Catherine, Ann, Dave, Brandi, Megan, Mike C., John S., and everyone else who provided physical and moral support throughout this process. Finally, she wishes to thank Sally Reis, her major advisor, who has provided invaluable mentorship, both academically and personally, and who serves as her role model for pursuing a successful academic career as a mother.

Contents

Authors' Biography

Dr. D. Betsy McCoach, Ph.D., is an Associate Professor in the Measurement, Evaluation, and Assessment program at the University of Connecticut, where she teaches coursework in structural equation modeling, multilevel modeling, and instrument design. Dr. McCoach is the current Director of the *Data Analysis Training Institute of Connecticut* (DATIC), housed in the Educational Psychology Department of the Neag School of Education at UCONN. DATIC offers week-long summer workshops in advanced modeling techniques to researchers, professors, and graduate students who wish to learn to utilize techniques in their own research. Dr. McCoach co-teaches a week-long workshop (with Ann O'Connell) on hierarchical linear modeling also teaches the week-long workshop on Structural Equation Modeling. In addition, Dr. McCoach is the Founder and Program Chair of the *Modern Modeling Methods Conference*, hosted at the University of Connecticut every May.

Dr. McCoach has extensive experience in hierarchical linear modeling, and has used multilevel modeling techniques to analyze large national datasets. She and Ann O'Connell co-edited a book, *Multilevel Modeling of Educational Data*, available from Information Age Publishing. In addition, Dr. McCoach also has extensive experience in the areas of instrument design, factor analysis, structural equation modeling, and longitudinal analysis. Dr. McCoach has published over 55 peer review journal articles and 20 book chapters in the areas of quantitative research methodology, gifted education, and educational research. She has also authored, co-authored, or helped to develop dozens of affective instruments, including the *School Attitude Assessment Survey-Revised* (*SAAS-R*) and the *Challenges to Scholastic Achievement Scale* (*CSAS*). Dr. McCoach was the Founding Co-editor of the *Journal of Advanced Academics*, and she is the current Co-editor of Gifted Child Quarterly. She is an Associate Editor of *Frontiers in Quantitative Psychology and Measurement.* She currently serves on the review board for the *Review of Educational Research* (RER), and she has also served on the editorial review boards for the *American Educational Research Journal* (AERJ), the *Journal of Educational Psychology* (JEP), the *Journal of Educational Research* (JER), and the *Journal for Primary Prevention* (JPP).

Robert K. Gable, Ed.D., M.A., B.A., State University of New York at Albany, 1970/1967/1966. Gable is the Director of the Center of Research and Evaluation in the Graduate School and Former Director of the Educational Leadership Doctoral Program at Johnson & Wales University in Providence RI. He is an Emeritus Professor of Educational Psychology in the Neag School of Education at the University of Connecticut, where he taught courses in research methodology, statistics, survey development, and program evaluation from 1970 to 2000. He is a Former Director of the Bureau of Educational Research and Service at the University of Connecticut, and served as Director of research for the Leadership Research Institute consulting firm. Gable has published numerous texts, journal articles, tests, and research reports. He is the co-author of the *Postpartum Depression Screening Scale* (Beck and Gable), the *School Situation Survey* (Helms and Gable), and the *My Class Activities* survey (Gentry and Gable). He has received the Outstanding Leadership and Service award from the Northeastern Educational Research Association, an Excellence in Teaching award from the University of Connecticut Alumni Association, co-authored the 1999 "Manuscript of the Year" (Rong and Gable) in The *Journal of College and University Student Housing*, co-authored the "Best Original Research of 2012 in the *Journal of Midwifery & Women's Health*, and received "Distinguished Paper" awards in 1995 and 2011 from the Northeastern Educational Research Association.

John P. Madura began his academic career with a B.A. in Mathematics (Logic and Computability) from Boston University and completed a M.A. in History and Education from Teachers College, Columbia University in 2000. After serving in the United States Navy as a Cryptologic Officer for 5 years, John taught secondary mathematics for 4 years in Connecticut and became interested in assessment and educational measurement, particularly in the affective domain. In 2010, he entered the Measurement, Evaluation, and Assessment doctoral program at the Neag School of Education at the University of Connecticut. At the University of Connecticut, he has worked to develop affective instruments in the fields of teacher evaluation, school science achievement, and public health. His substantive research interests center on aspects of interpersonal perception that occur in school settings and impact both school achievement and teacher evaluation. His methodological research focuses broadly on connections between theory development and statistical model specification. As a result, his work focuses on factor analysis, structural equation modeling (SEM), multilevel modeling (MLM), latent growth curve modeling (LGM), model fit, model invariance theories, and mediation and moderation effects.

Chapter 1
Affective Characteristics in School and Corporate Environments: Their Conceptual Definitions

> Measure what can be measured, and make measurable what cannot be measured.
>
> Galilleo

What is an Affective Instrument and Why are We Designing One?

This book focuses on the essential theories and methods used to create self-report affective instruments. We have all taken such instruments at some point in our lives. Although there are many drawbacks to self-report instruments, they still represent one of the quickest, easiest, and most direct methods of collecting attitudinal and affective information. What do we mean by affective characteristics? The term affective refers to feelings, attitudes, or moods. In contrast to cognitive instruments, which capture people's knowledge or skills, affective instruments attempt to capture people's feelings, attitudes, or inner emotional states. In developing an affective instrument, our goal is to be able to differentiate among people in terms of the degree to which they possess a latent construct or in terms of their level on a given latent construct.

A *construct* is a trait, a concept, or a schematic idea. The dictionary defines construct as an *image*, idea, or *theory*, especially a complex one formed from a number of simpler elements. Constructs are generally latent, meaning that they cannot be observed. Instead, latent constructs must be inferred by observing behaviors that are indicators of the underlying constructs. In the social sciences, we study many latent constructs such as creativity, intelligence, motivation, academic self-concept, anxiety, etc. None of these constructs are directly observable. Instead, we infer a person's level of intelligence by collecting information on items or behaviors that are directly observable. For example, the results of IQ testing, direct observations, parent, student, and teacher interviews, and samples of student work are all concrete observable pieces of information that we could use to make an inference about a student's level of intelligence. Because we cannot directly observe intelligence, we observe behaviors and collect information, and then we make a judgment about intelligence based on those observables.

D. B. McCoach et al., *Instrument Development in the Affective Domain*,
DOI: 10.1007/978-1-4614-7135-6_1, © Springer Science+Business Media New York 2013

In this book, we focus on creating one particular type of measurement: self-report rating scales to measure affective characteristics or traits, such as attitudes, self-concept, self-efficacy, motivation, values, interests, and anxiety, etc. To do this, we create multi-item scales that allow us to measure the construct of interest and which provide scale scores, or measures for each person. We return to the principles of measurement in Chapter 2. The remainder of this chapter provides a theoretical overview of affective characteristics and their importance within school and corporate environments.

School and Corporate Environment

The Importance of the Affective Domain in Education

During the 1960s, the cognitive domain received much attention from educators as proponents and critics argued the merits and evils of behavioral objectives, often utilizing the framework for the cognitive domain suggested in the *Taxonomy of Educational Objectives, Handbook I* (Bloom 1956). In 1964, the publication of the *Taxonomy of Educational Objectives, Handbook II: The Affective Domain* (Krathwohl et al. 1964) received far less attention, in light of the debate over behavior objectives and the apparent national consensus that the primary aims of schooling were in the cognitive domain. In his article, *Assessing Educational Achievement in the Affective Domain*, Tyler (1973) discussed the growing awareness in the late 1960s and early 1970s that schools needed to attend to the affective domain when developing their learning goals and objectives.

Tyler (1973) suggested that two prevalent views explained why affective learning was not systematically planned as part of most school curricula. First, many educators felt that affective concerns such as “feelings” were not the business of the school, but rather the responsibility of the home or church. Second, affective states were natural outgrowths of learning cognitive content and did not need to be included as separate objectives (means) to be addressed during the learning process. Fortunately, during the 1970s, educators recognized that affective objectives were important as both “ends” and “means” in the overall school process, and they were no longer considered merely acceptable outgrowths of an emphasis on the cognitive domain. As a result, state-level, as well as school- and program-level, statements of goals and objectives included both cognitive and affective objectives.

In the 1980s, a strong emphasis on the cognitive domain resurfaced mainly as a result of the continual decline in standardized test scores. Calls for increased emphasis in the cognitive area rang out loudly with publication of the report by the National Commission on Excellence in Education entitled *A Nation at Risk: The Imperative for Educational Reform* (Bell 1983) and the report of the Carnegie Foundation for the Advancement of Teaching entitled *High School: A Report on Secondary Education in America* (Boyer 1983).

The passage of the *No Child Left Behind* (NCLB) act in 2001 and the issuance of the National Common Core (NCC) Standards in (2010) have heralded the most recent reemphasis on the cognitive domain. NCLB requires all public schools receiving federal funding to implement statewide standardized tests annually to all students. One of the aims of the system of standardized testing is increased accountability of schools, teachers, and administrators. Schools must show adequate yearly progress in reading and language arts, and they must administer yearly standardized achievement tests to document that progress. Supporters of the NCLB standardized testing argue that the tests are critical to determining whether schools are meeting standards. Opponents of NCLB argue that the legislation penalizes schools with difficult populations and encourages educators to "teach to the test."

The NCC standards (2010) project, led by the National Governors Association Center for Best Practices (NGA Center) and the council of chief state school officers (CCSSO), is a state-initiated effort to adopt a common set of curricular standards and assessment methods. The NCC standards, which were developed by teachers, school administrators, and content experts, provide a clear and consistent set of standards to prepare students for college and the workforce. To date, standards exist for English-language arts and mathematics. Individual states decide if they want to adopt these standards. If a state adopts the common core standards, it must also develop or adopt a common assessment system, based on the common core state standards.

Although NCLB and NCC standards focus on the cognitive domain, there is also a renewed interest on the affective domain. Even in this era of ever increasing accountability, affective outcomes continue to play an important role in the assessment of student outcomes. Anderson and Bourke (2000) argue that affective assessment should be an important aspect of school accountability programs. They believe that school accountability may actually provide a fertile new potentially frontier for affective assessment. "In most cases, neither educators nor the public seem to want accountability programs that rely exclusively on standardized academic achievement tests. Good, solid affective assessment instruments have the potential to provide data that can be incorporated into more broadly conceptualized school accountability programs" (p. 104).

Although the passage of NCLB has greatly increased the focus on school accountability and measures of student achievement over the past decade, a parallel interest in affective domain has gained prominence in educational and psychological research. Beginning largely with Salovey and Mayer (1990), researchers have increasingly embraced the notion that affective characteristics, such as "emotional intelligence," play an instrumental role in both personal growth and job success (Golman 1995; Newman et al. 2010). The effects of research in this domain can be seen in the latest national educational policy reform known as the *21st century Skills* movement (Trilling and Fadel 2009). The *21st century Skills* movement stresses the importance of non-cognitive traits such as collaboration, flexibility, adaptability, self-directed learning, and social skills as well as non-traditional cognitive skills such as creativity and technology skills (http://www.p21.org/). In *A Whole New Mind* (2005), Daniel Pink argues that it is not sufficient to simply develop the cognitive domain (left brain) to prepare students for college and the world of work. It is also necessary to consider the affective domain (right brain). He and others insist that in today's high tech global economy, right brain competencies, such as creative thinking, are just as important as left brain competencies such as critical thinking. In *Creating Innovators*, Wagner (2012) explores what parents, teachers, and employers must do to develop the competencies young people need to become innovators and why innovation is critical for success in a competitive global economy. In *Out of Our Minds: Learning to be Creative* (2012), Sir Ken Robinson presents a rational for developing creativity in education and in business. He calls for radically different approaches to developing the creative side of students to be successful in meeting the challenges of living and working in the twenty-first century. The *21st century Skills* movement reasserts the importance of considering non-cognitive variables within the educational arena.

Therefore, although the cognitive domain receives increased attention, the affective area remains firmly entrenched as an important aspect of the schooling process as well as an outcome of schooling. Bloom's (1976) adapted model of school learning, depicted in Fig. 1.1, clearly suggests that during instruction learners approach any task with prior affective entry characteristics (e.g., attitudes, self-esteem, interests, and values), as well as cognitive behaviors. The dynamic interaction between these overlapping cognitive and affective domains during the instructional process results in both cognitive learning outcomes and associated affective outcomes (Bloom). These affective outcomes help guide future feelings about the course content and issues (attitudes), feelings of personal worth and success (self-esteem), desires to become involved in various activities (interests), and personal standards (values). In fact, even the documents supporting the reauthorization of the elementary and secondary education act (ESEA) mention the importance of motivation and engagement to the development of reading skills (U.S. Department of Education 2011).

Bandura's (1977b, 1986, 1989b, 1997) research in the area of self-efficacy has added greatly to our understanding of Bloom's learner characteristics and learning

Fig. 1.1 Model of school learning, adapted from Bloom (1976)

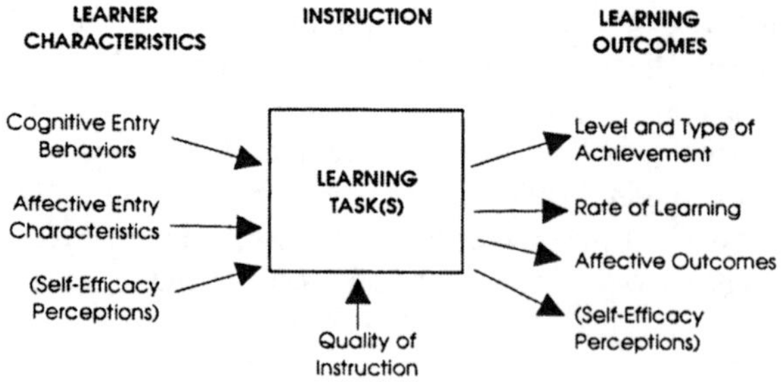

outcomes. The self-efficacy construct may be the most important affective construct described in this chapter because it addresses the interplay of the cognitive, affective, and behavioral domains. We return to self-efficacy later in the chapter.

The Importance of the Affective Domain in Corporate Settings

In the corporate setting, research on firm performance has recognized the importance of affective characteristics. For many years, *organizational climate*, a multidimensional organizational construct which encompasses such aspects as motivation, leadership, job satisfaction, and goal setting, has played a central role in corporate research due to its relationship to firm performance. Finally, Bandura's self-efficacy construct, which addresses the affective as well as the cognitive and behavioral domains, has important implications for corporate research. For example, self-efficacy theory makes an important contribution to human resources leadership development programs. Understanding the causal influence of self-efficacy beliefs on leaders' behavior is necessary for the successful development, implementation, and evaluation of leadership training programs.

The study of emotions and affect in the workplace has become an increasingly important area of research in the organizational and business-related literature. Recent studies are documenting the importance of emotions and affective characteristics in a variety of contexts such as marketing and consumer behavior. As just one example, emotional contagion, which is the tendency to experience another person's emotions (Hatfield et al. 1992), "is increasingly being recognized as a key variable affecting various aspects of organizational functioning" (Vijayalakshmi and Bhattacharyya 2012, p. 364).

Newer lines of research in business and finance are using evaluations of affective states to make predictions about future financial outcomes. For example, Mayew and Venkatachalam (2012) conducted a study in which they measured managerial affective states during earnings conference calls using vocal emotion analysis software. They concluded that measuring affective states can provide important additional information in the capital market setting. In their study, managers' emotional state predicted stock returns and future firm performance, after controlling for objective quantitative information and qualitative verbal content (Mayew and Venkatachalam 2012).

In both educational and corporate settings, the accurate assessment of affective characteristics depends upon the availability of instruments that are both theoretically based and psychometrically sound. The purpose of this text is to assist in the selection and development of such instruments.

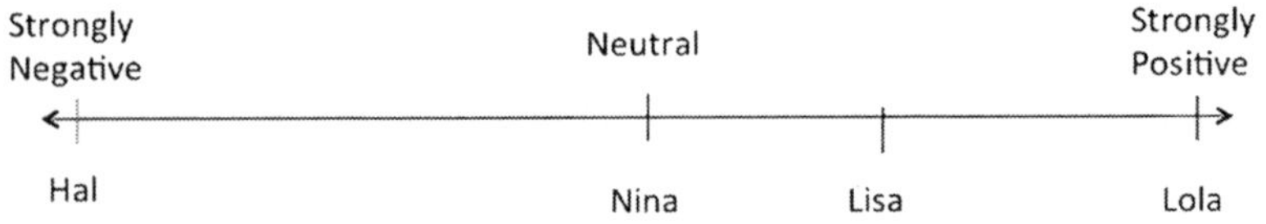

Fig. 1.2 Locations of individuals on an affective continuum

What are Affective Characteristics?

Anderson and Bourke's text entitled *Assessing Affective Characteristics in the Schools* (2000) presents an in-depth theoretical and practical discussion of affective instrument construction.[1] Human characteristics reflect "typical ways of thinking, acting, and feeling in a wide variety of situations" (Anderson and Bourke 2000, p. 4). While the first two areas reflect cognitive and behavioral characteristics, the third area reflects affective characteristics, which represent qualities that "present people's typical ways of feeling or expressing emotions" (p. 4).

According to Anderson and Bourke (2000), all affective characteristics must have three attributes: target, intensity, and direction. The *target* identifies the object, behavior, or idea at which the feeling is being directed. The *intensity* attribute refers to the degree or strength of the feeling. For example, an individual's feelings about an object could be very strong, whereas another person's could be quite mild. The *direction* attribute reflects the positive, neutral, or negative aspect of the feeling (pp. 4–5). "Love" is a very strong, positive feeling that can be directed at an object; "like" is a weaker positive feeling. Therefore, although love and like have the same direction, they differ in intensity. On the other hand, love and hate may have the same intensity but differ in direction.

Figure 1.2, adapted from Anderson and Bourke (2000, p. 5) illustrates intensity, direction, and target attributes. Imagine that the target of the affect is "statistics class." Using a hypothetical rating scale, we have measured and located three people's attitudes toward their statistics class on a continuum which specifies both the direction of the feeling (negative or positive) as well as the intensity of the feeling. The further from the midpoint a person is, the more intense his or her feelings are. The further to the right a person is, the more positive his or her feelings are; the further to the left a person is, the more negative his or her feelings are. In our example, Lola "loves" statistics: she has strong positive feelings. Lisa "likes" statistics class; she has positive feelings, but the intensity of her feelings is weaker than those of Lola. Nina is neutral about statistics; she has no direction or intensity. Hal hates statistics; he has very strong feelings, feelings that are as strong as Lola's, but they are in the opposite (negative direction).

---

[1] The authors are indebted to Anderson and Bourke (2000) for providing a clear perspective on the conceptual and operational definition of affective characteristics. Their insights greatly influenced our perspective as we crafted this chapter.

Types of Affective Characteristics

Psychologists have identified numerous constructs that reflect affective characteristics. This volume will restrict the potential list to those variables that have been shown to be correlates of actual behaviors. We begin with the construct of attitudes and move directly to a very popular and powerful construct, self-efficacy, which has been shown to be causally linked to several types of outcome behaviors in both school and corporate settings. We place considerable emphasis on the theory and application of self-efficacy research because it provides us a comprehensive understanding of the interplay of cognition, affect, and behavior. Other constructs included in the chapter are values, self-esteem, and interests. Prior to providing the mechanics how to operationally define and measure these sorts of variables, it is important to have a clear understanding of the theory underlying each construct in the context of a school or corporate setting.[2]

Attitudes

The study of attitudes, which dates back nearly a century, remains one of the core topics in social psychology (Bohner and Dickel 2011). Allport (1935), who dubbed attitude as "the most distinctive and indispensable concept in contemporary social psychology" (p. 798), defined an attitude as "a mental and neural state of readiness, organized through experience, exerting a directive or dynamic influence upon the individual's response to all objects and situations with which it is related" (p. 810). There is longstanding disagreement among social psychologists about how to best define the term attitude. In his article entitled *Attitude Measurement and Research,* Aiken stated that "attitudes may be conceptualized as learned predispositions to respond positively or negatively to certain objects, situations, concepts, or persons. As such, they possess cognitive (beliefs or knowledge), affective (emotional, motivational), and performance (behavior or action tendencies) components" (Aiken 1980, p. 2). Eagly and Chaiken (2007) define an attitude as "a psychological tendency that is expressed by evaluating a particular entity with some degree of favor or disfavor" (p. 598). This comprehensive definition also captures three essential features of attitudes: evaluation, attitude object, and tendency. "Together, these elements refer to an individual's propensity to evaluate a particular entity with some degree of favorability or unfavorability" (Eagley and Chaiken 2007, p. 583). Social psychologists have long acknowledged the multidimensional nature of attitudes and have stressed the need to restrict attitudinal

[2] Although our collective work has been done in school and corporate settings, the research that we present in this chapter and the process that we outline for measuring affective characteristics in the remainder of the book can certainly be applied in other organizational settings as well as in psychological and behavioral research.

measurement to a specified continuum (Thurstone 1928, 1946). As a result, researchers have largely focused on the evaluative dimension of the construct thus defining attitude as "the affect for or against a psychological object" (Thurstone 1931). Evaluation "encompasses the evaluative aspects of beliefs and thoughts, feelings and emotions, and intentions and overt behavior" (Eagly and Chaiken 2007, p. 583). The attitude object is the thing that is evaluated. Attitude objects are entities that can be abstract (i.e., ideologies) or concrete (i.e., the President). The term tendency is intentionally vague in that it implies neither a temporal aspect to attitudes (they could be either fleeting or permanent) nor does it specify whether the attitude is conscious. Eagley and Chaiken distinguish between attitudes, which they define as latent properties or tendencies and evaluative responses, which are influenced by attitudes and which express attitudes, but which are not, in and of themselves, attitudes (Eagley and Chaiken 2007).

The popular definition of attitudes provided by Fishbein and Ajzen is similar to that of Eagley and Chaiken. According to Fishbein and Ajzen (2010), attitudes reflect "a latent disposition or tendency to respond with some degree of favorableness or unfavorableness to a psychological object" (Fishbein and Ajzen 2010, p. 76). Fishbein and Ajzen's (1975, 2010) popular *Expectancy-Value Model* distinguishes *attitudes* from *beliefs.* Attitudes represent the individual's favorable or unfavorable evaluation (i.e., good-bad) of the target object, whereas beliefs represent the information the individual has about the object. In the expectancy value model, attitudes toward objects are determined by joining the product of the evaluation of a particular attribute associated with the target object and the subjective probability (i.e., belief) that the object has the attribute. Accordingly, the evaluation of the attribute contributes to the individual's attitude in proportion to the strength of his beliefs (see Fishbein and Ajzen 1975, pp. 222–223). Historically, the expectancy value model has provided a one of the most commonly used theoretical frameworks for understanding and measuring attitudes.

Attitudes in the School Environment

As discussed by Tyler, attitudes appropriately appear in most statements of educational objectives. In content areas such as social studies, the objectives usually pertain to "the development of objective attitudes toward alternate possible explanations of social phenomena and toward policies for dealing with social problems" (Tyler 1973, p. 5). While such an objective has a cognitive component pertaining to the recognition of objectivity in dealing with social problems, the affective (emotional) component attempts to free the student from safe, familiar views and promotes exploration of new views. Several educational programs also include statements of attitude enhancement in their objectives. Typical statements begin with the phrase, "students should develop positive attitudes toward" and end with a particular target (e.g., reading, math, science, learning, school, or teachers).

The following examples of instruments assessing attitudes within a school environment, which have resulted from the instrument design class that we teach, represent a small subsample of the ever expanding array of researcher developed measures of school-related attitudes: *School Attitude Assessment Survey-Revised* (McCoach and Siegle 2003), *Math and Me* (Adelson and McCoach 2011), *Teachers' Attitudes toward Subject Specific acceleration* (Rambo and McCoach 2012) and the *School Situation Survey* (Helms and Gable 1989).

Attitudes in the Corporate Environment

In the corporate setting, employee job satisfaction questionnaires represent one of the most common, standard assessments of attitudes. The authors of this text have participated in several employee satisfaction research studies for major corporations. In one case, the corporation gathered annual employee satisfaction data over an 8-year period for over 80,000 international employees, using surveys in 33 languages. Each year, the author provided over 3,000 breakouts of the data to report the findings (e.g., domestic, international, business units, departments, etc.). In addition to the quantitative data, reports included qualitative quotes from employees regarding obstacles faced over the past year and suggestions for addressing those obstacles. Human resource professionals feel that this line of research is extremely important and thus make substantial investments in such assessments.

Organizational researchers have also identified several attitudinal correlates of job satisfaction, such as relational maintenance and perceptions of the work environment. Waldron and Hunt (1992) examined the concept of *relational maintenance* in the workplace, where subordinates used relational maintenance strategies to enhance relationships with supervisors. Madlock and Booth-Butterfield (2012) expanded this line of research to include relational maintenance strategies among coworkers, where coworkers seek to enhance their relationships with coworkers. The researchers concluded that "the interpersonal relationships that develop in the workplace serve to fulfill coworkers' interpersonal needs for inclusion, affection, and control" (p. 27) and that coworker relational maintenance related to employee attitudes regarding job satisfaction. Similarly, Korte and Wynne (1996) found that reduced interpersonal communication between coworkers led to low levels of job satisfaction and resulted in employees leaving their jobs. Recent research has demonstrated the positive relationship between perceptions of a favorable work environment and job satisfaction (Kristof-Brown et al. 2005; Sardzoska and Tang 2012).

Are job attitudes related to job performance? For many years, researchers have examined the link between job satisfaction and other employee attitudes and job performance. Substantial research evidence has shown that positive job attitudes, such as satisfaction, are related to more positive work outcomes (Riketta 2008).

Job satisfaction is also positively related to employee retention and negatively related to employee turnover. In their study of 438 fitness club employees representing three cities in Canada, MacIntosh, and Walker (2012) reported a correlation of 0.65 ($p < 0.001$) between employee dissatisfaction and intent to leave. The satisfaction items were written in a negative direction (e.g., "In general, I do not like my job") with 1 = *strongly disagree* and 5 = *strongly agree*; intent to leave (e.g., "How often have you felt like leaving your job?" was coded 1 = *never* and 7 = *often*. Employee turnover is also strongly correlated with other negative worker behaviors such as absenteeism, lateness, drug use, and sabotage [Fisher and Locke 1992; see also Campion (1991) and Mobley (1977)]. Employee turnover is very costly. Philip estimated that the total cost of employee turnover can be as much as 1.5 times an employee's annual salary. Therefore, he concluded that investments of as much as 50% of an employee's salary in activities to eliminate turnover could actually result in monetary savings (Phillips 1990; Schlesinger and Heskett 1991). Employee turnover can also have a negative impact on customer service, further decreasing profitability (Schlesinger and Heskett 1991). Readers interested in a comprehensive review of the employee turnover literature are referred to Ongori's (2007) article, which discusses causes, sources, effects on the organization, and strategies to minimize employee turnover.

Employee attitudes can also have a direct relationship employee attitudes with customer attitudes Ulrich et al. (1991) argue that employees who share the company's values make more favorable impressions on customers, thus enhancing the firm's competitive advantage.

Organizational climate "refers to a broad class of organizational and perceptual variables that reflect individual/organizational interactions which affect individual behavior" (Hansen and Wernerfelt 1989, p. 401). Climate measures, such as organizational climate, represent an important class of attitudinal variables, and organizational climate variables have proven to be positively related to employee satisfaction and negatively related to job turnover. Hansen and Wernerfelt's (1989) study of 60 Fortune-1,000 firms found that organizational climate factors explained twice as much of the variance in profit rates than the usual economic factors did. This type of research is important to the corporate world, given the goals and activities of human resource departments, because it has demonstrated that employee-perceived, organizational climate factors can have real financial consequences. Wang and Hsieh (2012) examined the relationship of individual employee *ethical climate* perceptions and job satisfaction, and found that employees who feel their organizations are ethical will feel the organization is fair to them and "thus are more likely to reciprocate with a positive job attitude (e.g., a higher level of job satisfaction and organizational commitment)" (p. 538). Schwepker (2001) also reported that ethical climate perception and work satisfaction were positively related.

The foundation of assessment and research efforts in these important areas rests on accurate measurement of attitudes. Profiles obtained from questionnaires lacking evidence of psychometric and conceptual soundness provide both meaningless and inaccurate results. Thus, carelessly developed assessments can lead to goal statements, action plans, and policy decisions that are misguided, creating a situation analogous to ships with the wrong cargo arriving at an incorrect destination. The intent of this text is to avoid these mistakes by facilitating the development of affective questionnaires with strong psychometric properties.

Self-efficacy

In the previous section, we noted that attitudes were comprised of cognitive (beliefs), affective (evaluation), and behavioral (action) components. The interplay among these components becomes clear in the context of Albert Bandura's social cognitive theory (Bandura 1977a, b, 1982a, b, 1986, 1989a, b, 1993, 1997, 2001; Bandura et al. 1996; Pajares 1996; Schwarzer 1992). Whereas attitudes may, in fact, predispose behaviors in particular situations, Bandura argues that successfully modeled behaviors contribute to changes in attitudes. Of all the constructs described in this chapter, *self-efficacy* is perhaps the most important: it connects human motivation, thought processes, and behavior. Social cognitive theory recognizes the social origins of our thoughts and actions and the important role that cognition and thought play in human motivation, affect, and action (Bandura 1989a). Bandura (1986) defines self-efficacy as "people's judgments of their capabilities to arrange and execute courses of action required to attain designated types of performances" (p. 391). Most simply, self-efficacy can be defined as one's perception of his/her ability (i.e., confidence) to successfully perform a task or behavior. Years of research on the construct of self-efficacy indicate that those who believe they can do something are more likely to persevere and succeed than those with lower efficacy beliefs. According to Bandura and Locke (2003) "efficacy beliefs predict not only the behavioral functioning between individuals at different levels of perceived self-efficacy but also changes in functioning in individuals at different levels of efficacy over time and even variation within the same individual in the tasks performed and those shunned or attempted but failed" (p. 87).

Sources of Self-efficacy Information

People develop self-efficacy perceptions in a variety of ways. The primary sources of self-efficacy information are previous experience, physiological cues, modeling, and verbal persuasion.

Previous Experience

Previous experience (enactive attainment) is a strong source of self-efficacy information. Previous experience with mastering targeted behaviors (i.e., success influences success) could, in fact, be the most important source of self-efficacy judgments. People with high levels of self-efficacy with respect to the targeted behavior tend to view failures as situation specific, or due to a lack of effort or poor strategy (Bandura 1986, p. 399).

Physiological Cues

Another way in which individuals develop accurate self-perceptions of efficacy is self-reading or physiological cues or anxiety arousal (e.g., nervousness, sweating while attempting a particular task). Self-beliefs in capabilities regarding a particular situation, along with the cognitive ability to control aversive thoughts, determine the level of stress and anxiety arousal (Bandura 1989b; Kent 1987; Salkovskis and Harrison 1984).

Verbal Persuasion

Persuasion from others is also an important contributor to accurate self-efficacy. Often, this feedback takes the form of direct verbal feedback from others. An upward feedback system that incorporates the use of well-designed questionnaires can help provide the necessary evaluative reactions to performance that fit under Bandura's "persuasion from others" category. In such a scenario, teachers rate school principals (and immediate subordinates rate corporate managers) in order to provide accurate assessments of leader behaviors. Such upward feedback systems consist of questionnaires that assess general dimensions, such as providing leadership, managing programs, managing conflict, problem solving, demonstrating integrity, and developing teamwork. These questionnaires assess dimensions that are operationally defined by 50–70 specific observable behaviors. Some example items are:

- Sets clear goals and objectives.
- Allocates appropriate resources to support programs.
- Reacts appropriately in crisis situations.
- Encourages alternative approaches to complex problems.
- Communicates openly and honestly with others.
- Encourages individuals to work together as a team.

The ratings for these leader behaviors are attained using Likert-type response formats to quantify the *frequency* with which the leader exhibits the behavior, *agreement* that the behavior is exhibited, or *satisfaction* with the way the leader performs the behavior.

An important part of the successful incorporation of such feedback into leadership development programs is pretraining assessment with feedback to the leader profiling the ratings and periodic (e.g., 12 months) follow-up "second-generation" assessment. Changes in the targeted behaviors have implications for both the leader and the training curriculum (content and presentation). The initial feedback contributes to the leader's necessary awareness of behaviors; the second generation assessment provides crucial information regarding the success or failure of the changes in targeted behaviors. The first/second generation data also contribute to the evaluation of the overall leadership development program. Although leadership development programs in corporate settings may include first- and second-generation assessments of manager behaviors, many neglect to emphasize to the leaders the importance of their actively seeking feedback subsequent to the training.

Ashford and Tsui (1991) discuss the importance of self-regulation, grounded in the control theory (Carver and Scheier 1981), and the leader's task of minimizing the discrepancy between a goal/standard and his or her behavior, as discussed by Lord and Hanges (1987). According to Ashford and Tsui (1991), self-regulation includes three sub-processes: standard setting, discrepancy detecting, and discrepancy reducing (p. 253). Such self-regulation is consistent with the importance Bandura attributes to feedback in developing accurate perceptions of self-efficacy. The active seeking of feedback from direct reports and colleagues allows the leader to detect discrepancies between standards and behaviors. Thus, self-regulated feedback seeking becomes crucial in changing behavior to enhance leader effectiveness. In fact, interestingly, the active seeking of negative feedback (as opposed to positive feedback) from direct reports results in increased *accuracy* of the leaders' understanding of their own behaviors, as well as in increasing the *perceptions of the leaders' overall effectiveness* (Ashford and Tsui 1991). These findings are supported by Goldsmith's (1992) study of the "Top 100" executives of a "Fortune-500" company. These leaders received feedback from their direct reports, developed action plans for improving behaviors, and periodically followed up with their direct reports to check on progress and to receive further assistance. Feedback-up data for these executives received 18 months later showed significant improvement in rated leader effectiveness.

Vicarious Experience

Observation and *modeling* of successful performances of targeted behaviors during skill training can raise one's self-efficacy for performing comparable tasks (Bandura et al. 1980). The role of such vicarious experiences in developing targeted behaviors has important implications for the activities designed for leadership training programs. Building on accurate self-awareness developed through self-reading of physiological cues, feedback from others, and previous experience, the development/refinement of appropriate and new patterns of behavior (e.g., situational leadership skills) can be accomplished using competent models who successfully demonstrate the necessary behavior ("If they can do it, I can do it."). According to Bandura, a three-facet approach consisting of modeling, guided enactment (i.e., coaching/role playing), and self-directed application (Rosenthal and Bandura 1978) yields the most positive results. Successful modeling can enhance the self-beliefs of those having previous negative experiences with the targeted leadership behavior, and can offer positive reinforcement and refinements to the behaviors of those who already have confidence in their performance in the targeted skill areas. A heavy emphasis on successful skill practice (i.e., guided mastery of modeled behavior) can enhance the participants' self-efficacy for new behaviors in situations where little prior experience is available to evaluate personal competence (Bandura 1986, pp. 160–161, 400).

The *modeled behavior must also be practiced* following the training to strengthen the new skills under successful conditions. A weakness of many training programs is the lack of such follow-up activities. Participants typically attend a two-day training session, during which much information is presented, and under optimal conditions, modeling and guided role-playing activities are included. Following the training, the participants return to the work setting, essentially left on their own to successfully practice their new skills. Without periodic follow-up training and coaching/feedback, those struggling to successfully exhibit the new behaviors will have lower conceptions of self-efficacy and be less likely to continue to engage in the learned behaviors or persevere in light of continued experiences of failure. Unfortunately, this situation develops because many people engaged in leadership training place little emphasis on the third facet of Bandura's approach—namely, *self-directed practice/application.* The successful use of the new or refined behaviors contributes to the increased self-efficacy for performing the behaviors. This self-regulated practice should take place in the framework described in our earlier discussion of Ashford and Tsui's (1991) work in the area of self-regulated feedback seeking—with emphasis upon seeking negative feedback, which leads to more accurate self-perceptions and later positive ratings of leader effectiveness.

Bandura's research with mastery modeling has contributed greatly to leadership development programs. This work should be reinforced, given the critical role leaders play in the morale and productivity of an organization. Bandura reviewed Latham and Saari's (1979) work with mastery modeling techniques designed to enhance corporate manager competencies. Videotape modeling was used to demonstrate targeted skills (e.g., recognize good work, enhance interest, change work habits to enhance competence). The keys to the process were the use of guided role-playing (i.e., modeling, successful practice, and instructive feedback). In another corporate world study, improved supervisory skills developed through modeling were associated with improved organizational climate and performance (i.e., reduced absenteeism and turnover) and higher productivity (Porras et al. 1982).

Self-efficacy in the School Environment

In the school environment, several researchers contend that self-efficacy beliefs are causally related to student academic variables such as academic achievement, academic motivation, occupational interests, and career choices. Earlier in the description of Bloom's theory of school learning (see Fig. 1.1), we listed self-efficacy (e.g., academic or study skills) as a major student entry characteristic and learning outcome. Support for this position is found in Schunk's (1981) highly recommended article entitled *Self-efficacy and Academic Motivation.* In the school environment, numerous studies have established the link between self-efficacy within a given academic domain and academic achievement within that domain. Academic self-efficacy is positively correlated with grades (Richardson et al. 2012) and with more standardized measures of academic achievement (Schunk 1981). For example, Becker and Gable (2009) found general self-efficacy beliefs were related to end-of-first-term achievement (GPAs) for 194 freshmen attending an open admission for-profit career education college. Elias and MacDonald (2007) also found that academic self-efficacy beliefs predicted college academic performance, even after accounting for prior academic performance. Self-efficacy may also mediate the effect of ability on achievement. For example, Zarch and Kadivar (2006) found that mathematics ability had a direct effect on mathematics performance as well as an indirect effect via mathematics self-efficacy.

In another study of 271 undergraduate college students Brady-Amoon and Fuertes (2011) reported strong correlations between self-efficacy and self-rated abilities ($r = 0.57$, $p < 0.01$). Further, self-efficacy and self-rated abilities explained a statistically significant amount of variance in students' academic achievement measured by their GPA ($F = 9.61, p < 0.01, R^2 = 0.08$). Richardson et al. (2012) reported a comprehensive meta-analysis of 911 correlations of non-intellective constructs with academic performance found in studies conducted from 1997 to 2010. Two "motivation" constructs, academic self-efficacy (i.e., general perceptions of academic capability) and performance self-efficacy (i.e., perceptions of academic performance capability), were correlated 0.28 and 0.67 with GPAs. Both academic and performance self-efficacy were important predictors of academic success. In addition, measures of grade goal appear to partially mediate self-efficacy beliefs (Chen et al. 2000). Gender, ability, and other individual factors may influence students' self-efficacy (Lindia 1992). For example, Lindia found that males had higher interest in computers and higher levels of computer self-efficacy; higher-ability math students had higher self-efficacy scores (Lindia 1992). Finally, substantial research has examined the impact of self-efficacy beliefs on physical and mental health and health promotion behaviors (Froman and Owen 1991; Holden 1991).

In addition, teachers' self-efficacy has been linked to students' academic achievement (Caprara et al. 2006). Educators can use strategies to enhance self-efficacy (Siegle and McCoach 2007). For example, providing feedback on successful performance, helping students monitor their growth and progress, and lowering students' anxiety and stress about evaluation oriented activities such as homework, exams, and presentations promote mastery experiences and help promote self-efficacy (Richardson et al. 2012; Stock and Cervone 1990).

The educational leadership literature also has examined the importance of self-efficacy within the context of leadership development. Leithwood (1992, 1994),

Leithwood et al. (1991) and Leithwood and Jantzi (2005) have studied the role of self-efficacy in developing "transformational-leadership" behaviors of school administrators. In this framework, teachers' commitment to change is enhanced when transformational leadership promotes teachers' "capacity beliefs" (i.e., self-efficacy), a key ingredient in any school restructuring agenda (pp. 503–504). This leadership style fosters capacity development and personal commitment to organizational goals that influence self- and collective efficacies in an organization (Kurt et al. 2012). In a study of 568 French–Canadian principals and vice-principals, Trepanier et al. (2012) found that principals' self-perceptions of positive workplace relationships led to their higher levels of motivation and self-efficacy as managers, which then resulted in more frequent self-reported transformational leadership behaviors.

Bandura (2001) noted that perceived collective organizational efficacy (a group level construct) and self-efficacy beliefs (an individual level construct) are conceptually different, but share the "efficacy" construct. Kurt et al. (2012) identified relationships between perceived transformational leadership practices and teachers' sense of self-efficacy ($r = 0.23$) and with collective efficacy ($r = 0.34$). These findings are consistent with Leithwood and Jantzi (2005), who found a relationship between principal transformational leadership practices and teachers' self-efficacy beliefs. In an era of emphasis on student learning outcomes, educators who know that leadership practices are related to teachers' self-efficacy can argue the relationship between teachers' self-efficacy and student achievement. This line of reasoning provides support for the increased value of research in the area of school leadership.

Self-efficacy in the Corporate Environment

Self-efficacy provides considerable implications for corporate leadership development programs. Designers of leadership training programs need to be aware of the pervasive role of accurate self-perceptions in determining one's behavior toward personal development. People tend to avoid tasks or situations they perceive to be above their abilities, but will tend to expend more effort toward and persist longer in working to attain outcomes associated with high self-efficacy judgments (Bandura 1977a, b, 1986, 1997). People undertaking tasks that are above their capability can create functional problems for themselves as well as for their coworkers. On the other hand, accurate efficacy judgments, or even those a little above one's capability, can lead to healthy challenges and successes which contribute to personal development (Bandura 1986, pp. 393–394).

In the corporate world, Gist (1987) and Gist and Mitchell (1992) have studied the implications of self-efficacy in the context of organizational behavior and the determinants and malleability of the construct. Also, we note the comprehensive work of Den Hartog and Belschak (2012) regarding the role of transformational leadership (i.e., ability to articulate an attractive and challenging future vision, creating meaningful work situations and inspired employees) in developing employee proactive behaviors. Using Grant and Ashford's (2008) definition of proactive behavior (i.e., "anticipatory action that employees take to impact themselves and/or their environment", p. 5), Den Hartog and Belschak examined the relationship of proactive behaviors to perceptions of job autonomy (i.e., perceptions of self-determination), self-efficacy (i.e., perceived ability to successfully perform proactive behaviors; see Parker 2000), and transformational leadership. Using survey data gathered from 69 companies in The Netherlands, the researchers discussed the role of perceived job autonomy in providing employees with perceived self-determination, which enhances the employees' willingness to take responsibility for their actions and exhibit task persistence when facing obstacles. In high autonomy situations, perceptions of high transformational leadership related positively to proactive behaviors for individuals with high self-efficacy. Mathisen (2011), who studied the organizational antecedents of creative self-efficacy, concluded that when employees are given challenging tasks to develop new solutions and have job autonomy to make decisions, higher levels of creative self-efficacy were present.

Measuring Self-efficacy

"Efficacy beliefs differ in generality, strength, and level" (Bandura 2006). Because efficacy is domain specific and can even vary by task within domain, more specific measures of self-efficacy are generally more predictive than more general measures of self-efficacy. Because self-efficacy can change over time, self-efficacy is not an enduring trait. Rather, self-efficacy measures may not show a high degree of temporal stability, especially when intervening events that shape self-efficacy have occurred between the two testing occasions (Bandura 1997). Bandura (2006) provides concrete advice for measuring self-efficacy. First, because self-efficacy deals with perceived current capability, items should be stated in the present tense as "can do" statements.

As we noted in earlier sections, instruments assessing self-efficacy beliefs have been developed in several areas. For example, the *Teachers' Sense of Efficacy Scale* developed by Tschannen-Moran and Hoy (2001) contains 24-items assessing teacher self-efficacy in the following areas: Student Engagement, Instructional Strategies, and Classroom Management. Alpha reliabilities for the three scale-level dimensions ranged from 0.87 to 0.91. Erford et al. (2010) developed the *Self-Efficacy Teacher Report Scale*. This instrument contains 19 items, where teachers assess perceptions of self-efficacy of students aged 8–17 years. The following dimensions are assessed using a 3-point scale (*usually, sometimes, rarely*): Perseverance, Procrastination, Self-confidence, and Achievement efficacy. In their study, 415 teachers rated 639 students and found the alpha reliabilities for the dimension-level data to range from 0.86 to 0.91.

Values

In his book *Beliefs, Attitudes, and Values*, Rokeach (1968) argues that the concept of values is the core concept across all the social sciences. According to Rokeasch, a value is "an enduring belief that a specific mode of conduct or end-state of existence is personally or socially preferable to an opposite or converse mode of conduct or end-state of existence" (Rokeach 1973, p. 5). Clarifying the difference between an attitude and a value, Rokeach stated that an attitude refers to an organization of several beliefs around a specific object or situation, whereas a value refers to a simple belief of a very specific kind.

> This belief transcends attitudes toward objects and toward situations; it is a standard that guides *and determines action, attitudes toward objects and situations, ideology,* presentations of self to others, evaluations, judgments, justifications, comparisons of self with others, and attempts to influence others. (Rokeach 1973, p. 25)

Other writers have referred to value as "the importance or worth attached to particular activities and objects" (Aiken 1980, p. 2); "preferences for life goals and ways of life" (Nunnally 1978, p. 589); "a belief upon which a man acts by preference" (Allport 1961, p. 454); and as a "conception of the desirable—that is, of what ought to be desired, not what is actually desired—which influences the selection of behavior" (Getzels 1966, p. 98).

The Getzels, Rokeach, and Tyler see Tyler (1973) definitions of a value were summarized by Anderson and Bourke (2001) in a most informative manner as follows:

> First, values are beliefs as to what should be desired (Getzels 1966), what is important or cherished (Tyler 1973), and what standards of conduct or existence are personally or socially acceptable (Rokeach 1973). Second, values influence or guide things: behavior (Getzels); interests, attitudes, and satisfactions (Tyler); and a whole host of items, including behavior, interests, attitudes, and satisfactions (Rokeach). Third, values are enduring (Rokeach). That is, values tend to remain stable over fairly long periods of time. As such they are likely to be more difficult to alter or change than many other affective characteristics. (p. 32)

Schwartz (1992) has identified a set of 10 basic values that asserts are common across all societies. Schwartz defines values as "trans-situational goals, varying in importance, that serve as guiding principles in the life of a person or group. He theorized that basic values are organized into a coherent system that underlies and can help to explain individual decision making, attitudes, and behavior" (Schwartz et al. 2012, p. 663).

Values also possess target, direction, and intensity. According to Anderson and Bourke (2001), the targets of values tend to be ideas. However, as the definition offered by Rokeach implies, the targets could also be such things as attitudes and behavior. The direction of a value could be positive or negative (or right/wrong, important/unimportant). Finally, the intensity of values can be strong or weak, depending on the situation and the value referenced.

School Environment

Achievement values are "the incentives or purposes that individuals have for succeeding on a given task" (Wigfield 1994, p. 102). Within achievement motivation, expectancy-value theory has been the pervasive theoretical lens for examining values (Wigfield and Cambria 2010). According to the expectancy-value theory, motivation is the product of expectancy for success, and the value of the incentive (Boggiano and Pittman 1992). In other words, the value that a person places on either the task or the outcome and his perceived probability of success determine the amount of effort that he will exert attempting to successfully complete the task. The motivating potential of anticipating outcomes is largely determined by the subjective value that the person places on the attainment (Bandura 1997). Two people may hold the same belief that their behavior will result in a particular outcome, but they may evaluate the attractiveness of that outcome quite differently (Bandura 1997). The person who values the outcome or finds the outcome more attractive will be more motivated to attain the outcome. Value can somewhat compensate for low probabilities of success. People may put forth effort when they value the outcome, even when they believe that their probability of success is quite low.

Children's achievement values affect their self-regulation and motivation (Wigfield 1994) because goals influence how children approach, engage in, and respond to academic tasks (Hidi and Harackiewicz 2000). Wigfield's (1994) work in this area suggested that "when students value a task, they will be more likely to engage in it, expend more effort on it, and do better on it" (p. 102). Research also indicates that children's subjective task values are strong predictors of children's intentions and decisions to continue taking coursework in both math and English (Wigfield 1994; Wigfield and Eccles 2000). Eccles and Wigfield, two leading researchers in the field of motivation, expanded Atkinson's expectancy value model to include a variety of achievement related influences that impact individuals' expectancies and values (Wigfield 1994). In particular, they hypothesized that students' motivation to complete tasks stems from the attainment value, utility value, and intrinsic value associated with the task (Wigfield 1994), as well as with the costs associated with engaging in the task.

Attainment value is the importance students attach to the task as it relates to their conception of their identity and ideals or their competence in a given domain (Wigfield 1994). Attainment value "relates the importance individuals attach to a given task to the broader, core values they have about themselves" (Wigfield 1994). For example, students who identify themselves as athletes set goals related to their sport. Students who pride themselves on being good students seek affirmation in the form of grades or test scores. These students are motivated to attain the goals because they are associated with the students' perceptions of who they are.

Utility value is how the task relates to future goals. While students may not enjoy an activity, they may value a later reward or outcome it produces (Wigfield 1994). The activity must be integral to their vision of their future, or it must be instrumental to their pursuit of other goals. Because goals can play a key role in attaining later outcomes, educators and parents should help students see beyond the immediate activity to the long-term benefits it produces. One way to increase the value of the task is to positively reinforce students for completing the task. Extrinsic motivation is the motive to complete an activity to receive an external reward or positive reinforcement that is external to the activity itself. Extrinsic motivators include rewards such as stickers, praise, grades, special privileges, prizes, money, material rewards, adult attention, or peer admiration. Teachers should use extrinsic motivators carefully, as Lepper's over justification hypothesis suggests that providing extrinsic rewards for an intrinsically motivating activity can decrease a person's subsequent intrinsic motivation for that activity (Pintrich and Schunk 1996).

Intrinsic value often results from the enjoyment an activity produces for the participant (Wigfield 1994). When students enjoy scholastic tasks, they are intrinsically motivated to do well. Both interests and personal relevance produce intrinsic value for a student. Generally, students are intrinsically motivated to pursue activities that are moderately novel, interesting, enjoyable, exciting, and optimally challenging. When schoolwork is too easy, students become bored. However, when tasks are too difficult, students also have the potential to become frustrated and anxious (Deci and Ryan 1985).

Recent theories suggest that intrinsic and extrinsic motivation are not two opposing constructs, but rather two ends of a single motivation continuum (Alderman 1999). The intrinsic/extrinsic motivation continuum represents the extent to which actions are controlled by reward and the extent to which actions are self-determined (Alderman 1999). The more a student self-initiates and self-determines his or her actions, the more intrinsically motivated he or she is considered to be. However, students can engage in activities for both intrinsic and extrinsic rewards. According to Deci and Ryan, there are four phases of the intrinsic/extrinsic motivation continuum (Alderman 1999). During the external regulation phase, behavior is almost completely controlled by external reinforcers or punishers. During the "introjected" regulation phase, students follow rules because they should, but they have not necessarily internalized the rules or values associated with the action. In the identified regulation phase, the student accepts the rule or regulation because it is personally important for goal attainment. In integrated regulation, the student integrates and internalizes different self-determined values. A person can engage in activities to simultaneously fulfill both intrinsic and extrinsic goals.

Finally, Eccles and Wigfield stress the importance of "cost" in an individual's decision to engage in an activity. "Cost refers to how the decision to engage in one activity (e.g., doing schoolwork) limits access to other activities (e.g., calling friends), assessments of how much effort will be taken to accomplish the activity, and its emotional cost" (Wigfield and Eccles 2000). When the cost of an activity is too high, individuals may choose not to engage in that activity, even if they enjoy the activity or value the outcome of the activity.

In addition, work/career-related and human/interpersonal values play an important role in education. Work values refer to satisfactions that people desire in their future work, such as economic returns, altruism, and independence. Super's (1970) early work on the *Work Values Inventory* is an example of an instrument for assessing work-value orientations for high-school students. In a similar area, Super's *The Values Scale* (see Drummond 1988) can be used to assess intrinsic and extrinsic life/career values.

Tyler's (1973) monograph entitled *Assessing Educational Achievement in the Affective Domain* discusses the important role of values in an educational program. In this work, Tyler uses a definition of values that indicates their role in influencing interests, attitudes, and satisfactions by stating that a value is "an object, activity, or idea that is cherished by an individual which derives its educational significance from its role in directing his interests, attitudes, and satisfactions" (p. 7). Tyler argued that there are sound, esthetic, and good-health values that are appropriate as objectives of schooling. He argued that "the school should help the student discover and reinforce values that might be meaningful and significant to him/her in obtaining personal happiness and making constructive contributions to society" (Tyler 1973, p. 6).

Often, the social studies curriculum explicitly or implicitly involves the teaching of cultural values. For example, the Connecticut Social Studies standards contain objectives that require students to "explain how rules and laws help to establish order and ensure safety in one's town" (Grade 2) or "compare and contrast individual identity (e.g., beliefs, values, abilities) with that of peer group and other ethnic/cultural groups" (Grade 3).

Corporate Environment

Values surveys also can be useful in a corporate environment. The *Rokeach Value Survey* (see Vinson et al. 1977) is an instrument that assesses how important certain values are as guiding principles in one's life. Interpersonal values represent values that people consider important in their way of life, such as support, leadership, independence, conformity, and benevolence. Gordon's (1960) early work with the *Survey of Interpersonal Values* assesses these values in an instrument that is still used in the business world to assess interpersonal values during the employee hiring process.

The study of the "culture" of an organization has received much attention over the last several years (see for example, Deal and Kennedy 1982). Smircich (1983) has summarized several definitions of organizational culture as follows:

> Culture is usually defined as social or normative glue that holds an organization together (Siehl and Martin 1981; Tichy 1982). It expresses the values or social ideals and the beliefs that organization members come to share (Louis 1980; Siehl and Martin 1981). These values or patterns of belief are manifested by symbolic devices such as myths (Boje et al. 1982), rituals (Deal and Kennedy 1982), stories (Mitroff and Kilmann 1976), legends

(Wilkins and Martin 1980), and specialized language (Andrews and Hirsch 1983) (from Wiener 1988, p. 535).

Values are central to these definitions of organizational culture, because the shared set of core values, in fact, forms the operational definition of the culture. Examples of selected organizational values from companies such as American Express, Contel, Kodak, Weyerhauser, Southwestern Bell, and Texaco are as follows:

People	Treat people with respect and dignity
Customers	Listen to internal and external customers to understand and meet their needs
Quality	Create an environment that fosters a continuous quest for quality
Teamwork	Promote open communication that gives everyone a sense of personal involvement in corporate performance
Integrity	Maintain high standards of open communication where actions are consistent with words
Good citizenship	Encourage involvement in local communities

Noting that Fishbein and Ajzen (2010) discuss values as antecedents to behavior, it is important for businesses to understand and articulate their corporate values. Such shared core values influence the organization's decision making (i.e., strategy formulation and implementation), as well as its response to quickly changing business conditions and immediate crises (e.g., Johnson & Johnson's reaction to the Tylenol poison pills scare several years ago or BP's response to the 2011 massive oil spill in the southern United States). Many writers also argue that corporate values shared by employees contribute to overall organizational effectiveness. For example, consider a corporate value in the area of customer service where "satisfying customer needs" is a top priority. This value would pertain to collective efforts to meet the needs of both internal (i.e., colleagues) and external customers. Living this value with a goal of exceeding customer expectations would contribute to efficiency and productivity within the organization, which would, in turn, result in more satisfied customers and enhanced profits (see the earlier discussion of the article by Ulrich et al. 1991). Using a self-report questionnaire, Valentine et al. (2011) collected information about corporate ethical values from two separate samples: healthcare and administrative employees sales and marketing. They found perceived corporate ethical values positively related to group creativity and job satisfaction and negatively related to turnover intention. Finally, Kumar's (2012) survey research found strong correlations between perceptions of job satisfaction and the following components of perceived organizational values (Harmony, $r = 0.59$, $r^2 = 0.35$; Justice, $r = 0.62$, $r^2 = 0.38$; Progress, $r = 0.53$, $r^2 = 0.28$).

Since a value is a "standard that guides and determines action" (Rokeach 1973, p. 25), it is important to know if the company and businesses and departments within the company are indeed "walking the talk." Well-designed questionnaires administered to a large cross-section of employees, along with appropriate interview and focus-group activities, can contribute to the articulation of corporate values. Information obtained from assessments of corporate values serves as a profile of current status and sets the direction for strategic planning goal statements and action plans for developing needed change. Second generation follow-up assessments are beneficial for evaluating the efforts at change and for plotting a future course of action.

Self-concept and Self-esteem in School and Corporate Environments

Coopersmith (1967, 1989) defined self-esteem as "the evaluation which the individual makes and customarily maintains with regard to himself; it expresses an attitude of approval or disapproval, and indicates the extent to which the individual believes himself to be capable, significant, successful, and worthy" (Coopersmith 1967, pp. 4–5). In other words, self-esteem is a person's attitude toward him or herself: it is a self-judgment of a person's worth. An individual conveys information to others about his or her level of self-esteem by verbal reports and other overt expressive behavior (Coopersmith 1967). Thus self-esteem is "a global and relatively stable construct, reflecting the broad view that an individual has about him or herself."

Self-concept is a related construct that also captures people's self-perceptions. "Self-concept may be described as: organized, multifaceted, hierarchical, stable, developmental, evaluative, and differentiable" (Shavelson et al. 1976, p. 411). In addition, self-concept is seen as multidimensional: it differs across domains. The self-concept construct has received considerable attention in the school environment due to renewed emphasis on affective outcomes of education and the reported relationships between affective and cognitive measures.

Recent self-concept studies have documented the multidimensional nature of self-concept and have demonstrated the predictive power of domain specific self-concept on performance within a domain (Bong and Skaalvik 2003; Möller et al. 2011). According to Marsh and Martin (2011), in Shavelson's multidimensional, hierarchical model of self-concept, self-esteem is the global construct at the apex of the hierarchy and self-concept refers to specific components within this model. Thus, whereas self-concept consists of one's cognitive appraisals about his or her abilities in particular domains, self-esteem is more global; therefore, self-esteem comes from self-evaluations in valued domains (Hattie 1992). Therefore, a person can have high self-concept in a given domain, but that does not affect his or her self-esteem unless he or she values the domain. Conversely, it is possible to have low self-concept in a domain without it affecting a person's self-esteem of feelings of worth. For example, I could be a horrible pianist, but that does not affect my self-esteem unless I want to be a good pianist. Self-esteem is a more global construct than self-concept, and also more linked to generalized positive or negative affect. Self-concept and self-efficacy are also related constructs. However, self-concept refers to more stable self-perceptions within a domain and self-efficacy reflects a person's judgments of their personal abilities to accomplish a specific task (Bandura 1986).

As with the other affective characteristics identified in this volume, we can identify the target, direction, and intensity of self-concept. The target of self-concept is usually the domain, the direction can be positive or negative; and the intensity can range on a continuum from low to high.

Self-perceptions are formed through experiences with the environment, with important contributions coming from environmental reinforcements and significant people in one's life (i.e., self-concept is learned). Several school programs include objectives pertaining to enhancing self-concept. Typical statements read as follows: Students will develop positive feelings of self-worth. Students will evidence positive perceptions of self in relation to peers (or school achievement—i.e., academic-self or family-social relations).

The reciprocal effects model (REM) of academic self-concept (Marsh 1990) posits that prior academic self-concept in a domain influences academic achievement in that domain and that academic achievement influences academic self-concept within the domain. Marsh and Martin (2011) review the methodological, empirical, and theoretical literature on the REM and conclude that academic self-concept "are mutually reinforcing, each leading to gains in the other" (p. 73). They also present evidence that supports "the generality of the REM in developmental research, cross-cultural settings, and health and sporting domains" (p. 74).

Byrne (1990, 1996) has written extensively on creating and validating self-report measures of self-concept. Examples of self-concept and self-esteem instruments include Coopersmith's *Self-Esteem Inventory* (Coopersmith 1967, 1989; now available from Consulting Psychologists Press in children and adult forms), *Piers-Harris Children's Self-Concept Scale* (Piers and Harris 1964); and the *Tennessee Self-Concept Scale* (Fitts 1965) and *The Self-Perception Profile for Children* (Harter 1985). Currently, one of the most popular self-report measures of academic self-concept is the *Self-Description Questionnaire* (Marsh 1992a, b).

Interest

Interest measurement grew out of the early graduate-school work by Cowdery, who reported the differential interests of lawyers, physicians, and engineers (cited in DuBois 1970). On the basis of this work in the early 1900s, interest measurement became a focal point of vocational guidance personnel in the school environment through the extensive contributions of such researchers as E. K. Strong and F. Kuder. Defining interests as "preferences for particular work activities" (Nunnally and Bernstein 1994), most inventories developed during the 1900s have item content that reflects occupational and work activities and employ the "Like/Dislike" rating instructions.

Examples of popular interest inventories are the *Kuder General Interest Survey* (grades 6–12) and the *Kuder Occupational Interest Survey* (high school and beyond), available from Science Research Associates; and the *Ohio Vocational Interest Survey II* and the *Strong Interest Inventory,* available from Consulting Psychologists Press. We also note that since 1990, The Psychological Corporation's *Differential Aptitude Tests* (fifth edition) assessment has included the *Career Interest Inventory,* which addresses students' educational goals, interest in various school subjects and school-related activities, as well as in various fields of work. According to a recent meta-analysis by Nye et al. (2012) interests do relate to performance and persistence in both work and academic contexts.

Like other affective characteristics examined in this volume, interests can be described with regard to their target, direction, and intensity. The targets of interests are activities; the direction can be described as interested or disinterested; and the intensity can be labeled as high or low. Interests with high intensity would tend to lead one to seek out the activity under consideration. According to Tyler (1973), school objectives in the area of interests are quite justified when the school activity involved "can contribute to the individual's development, social competence, or life satisfaction" (p. 4). These objectives should be designed to develop interests for future learning in a wide variety of major fields of knowledge so that the student desires to pursue several activities that will assist in building a "more comprehensive and accurate picture of the world" (p. 4). Furthermore, Tyler suggests that appropriate school affective objectives in the interest area should broaden student interest to learn important things from several fields as well as deepen student interest to attend to a few special content areas. Typically, statements of educational objectives reflecting student interests read as follows: students will develop interest in listening to music. Students will develop an interest in reading.

Relationships Among Affective Characteristics

This chapter has examined the conceptual definitions of affective characteristics selected on the basis of their relevance to school and corporate environments. The characteristics are attitudes, self-efficacy, values, self-concept, and interests. In general terms, attitudes were described as feelings toward some object; self-efficacy was referred to as a self-appraisal of capability; values reflected enduring beliefs; self-concept represented perceptions of self; and interests reflected preferences for particular activities.

Clarification of the similarities and differences among the constructs was obtained through Anderson and Bourke's (2000) discussion of their target, direction, and intensity attributes. It should be emphasized that the constructs selected in this volume are clearly not independent. While many writers may disagree with respect to the criteria for taxonomy, it appears that some general statements can be offered. Values and a related value system can be considered as central to one's overall personality. Manifestations of one's values may be seen in one's interests and attitudes. Some would say that interests and attitudes are quite similar in that attitudes are targeted toward objects and that interests really reflect attitudes toward tasks or activities, whereas self-efficacy reflects a perceived ability to perform a task or activity. Clearly, one's self-concept also interacts in light of an overall value system and could be called an attitude toward self. Although, we could reframe most affective characteristics as attitudes, we will follow the lead of many writers and use different labels for the constructs in this volume. The instrument development techniques described in the remainder of this book are equally applicable to all of the constructs that we have reviewed.

In selecting an affective characteristic for measurement, instrument developers should carefully consider the theory underlying the construct. Only with a clear conceptual understanding can one proceed to create valid operational definitions (i.e., statements/items) for each affective characteristic.

References

Adelson, J. L., & McCoach, D. (2011). Development and psychometric properties of the math and me survey: Measuring third through sixth graders' attitudes toward mathematics. *Measurement and Evaluation in Counseling and Development, 44*, 225–247.

Aiken, L. R. (1980). Attitude measurement and research. In D. A. Payne (Ed.), *Recent developments in affective measurement* (pp. 1–24). San Francisco: Jossey Bass.

Alderman, M. K. (1999). *Motivation for achievement: Possibilities for teaching and learning.* Mahwah: Lawrence Erlbaum Associates.

Allport, G. W. (1935). Attitudes. In C. Murchison (Ed.), *A handbook of social psychology* (pp. 798–844). London: Oxford University Press.

Anderson, L. W., & Bourke, S. F. (2000). *Assessing affective characteristics in the schools* (2nd ed.). Mahwah: Erlbaum.

Andrews, J. A. Y., & Hirsh, P. M. (1983). Ambushes, shootouts, and knights of the roundtable: The language of corporate takeovers. In L. R. Pondy, P. Frost, G. Morgan, & T. Dandridge (Eds.), *Organizational symbolism*. Greenwich: JAI Press.

Ashford, S. J., & Tsui, A. S. (1991). Self-regulation for managerial effectiveness: The role of active feedback seeking. *Academy of Management Journal, 34*, 251–280.

Bandura, A. (1977a). Self-efficacy: Toward a unifying theory of behavioral change. *Psychological Review, 84*, 191–215.

Bandura, A. (1977b). *Social learning theory*. Upper Saddle River: Prentice Hall.

Bandura, A. (1982a). The assessment and predictive generality of self-precepts of efficacy. *Journal of Behavior Therapy and Experimental Psychiatry, 13*(3), 195–199.

Bandura, A. (1982b). Self-efficacy mechanism in human agency. *American Psychologist, 37*, 22–147.

Bandura, A. (1986). *Social foundations of thought and action: A social cognitive theory*. Upper Saddle River: Prentice Hall.

Bandura, A. (1989a). Regulation of cognitive processes through perceived self-efficacy. *Developmental Psychology, 25*, 729–735.

Bandura, A. (1989b). Human agency in social cognitive theory. *American Psychologist, 44*(9), 1175–1184.

Bandura, A. (1993). Perceived self-efficacy in cognitive development and functioning. *Educational Psychologist, 28*(2), 117–148.

Bandura, A. (1997). *Self-efficacy: The exercise of control*. New York: W. Freeman.

Bandura, A. (2001). Social cognitive theory: An agentic perspective. *Annual Review of Psychology, 52*, 1–26.

Bandura, A. (2006). Guide for constructing self-efficacy scales. In T. Urdan & F. Pajares (Eds.), *Self-Efficacy Beliefs of Adolescents* (pp. 307–337). Charlotte: Information Age Publishing.

Bandura, A., & Locke, E. A. (2003). Negative self-efficacy and goal effects revisited. *Journal of Applied Psychology, 88*(1), 87–99.

Bandura, A., Adams, N. E., Hardy, A. B., & Howells, G. N. (1980). Tests of the generality of self-efficacy theory. *Cognitive Therapy and Research, 4*, 39–66.

Bandura, A., Barbaranelli, C., Caprara, G., & Pastorelli, C. (1996). Multifaceted impact of self-efficacy beliefs on academic functioning. *Child Development, 67*, 1206–1222.

Becker, S., & Gable, R. (2009). *Self-efficacy and post-secondary first-term student achievement*. Paper presented at the annual meeting of the New England Educational Research Organization, Portsmouth.

Bell, T. H. (1983). A nation at risk: The imperative for educational reform (report of the national commission on excellence in education). *Education Week* (April 27), pp. 12–16.

Bloom, B. S. (Ed.). (1956). *Taxonomy of educational objectives, handbook 1: Cognitive domain*. New York: McKay.

Bloom, B. S. (1976). *Human characteristics and school learning*. New York: McGraw-Hill.

Boggiano, A. K., & Pittman, T. S. (1992). *Achievement and motivation: A social-developmental analysis*. New York: Cambridge University Press.

Bohner, G., & Dickel, N. (2011). Attitudes and attitude change. *Annual Review of Psychology, 62*, 391–417.

Boje, D. M., Fedor, D. B., & Rowland, K. M. (1982). Myth making: A qualitative step in OD interventions. *Journal of Applied Behavioral Science, 18*, 17–28.

Bong, M., & Skaalvik, E. M. (2003). Academic self-concept and self-efficacy: How different are they really? *Educational Psychology Review, 15*(1), 1–40.

Boyer, E. L. (1983). *High school: A report on secondary education in America*. New York: Harper & Row.

Brady-Amoon, P., & Fuertes, J. N. (2011). Self-efficacy, self-rated abilities, adjustment, and academic performance. *Journal of Counseling and Development, 89*, 431–438.

Byrne, B. M. (1990). Methodological approaches to the validation of academic self-concept: The construct and its measures. *Applied Measurement in Education, 3*, 185–207.

Campion, M. A. (1991). Meaning and measurement of turnover: Comparison of alternative measures and recommendations for research. *Journal of Applied Psychology, 76*, 199–212.

Caprara, G., Barbaranelli, C., Steca, P., & Malone, P. S. (2006). Teachers' self-efficacy beliefs as determinants of job satisfaction and students' academic achievement: A study at the school level. *Journal of School Psychology, 44*(6), 473–490.

Carver, C. S., & Scheier, M. F. (1981). *Attention and self-regulation: A control-theory approach to human behavior*. New York: Springer.

Chen, G., Gully, S. M., Whiteman, J. A., & Kilcullen, R. N. (2000). Examination of relationships among trait-like individual differences, state-like individual differences, and learning performance. *Journal of Applied Psychology, 85*, 835–847.

Coopersmith, S. (1967, 1989). *The antecedents of self-esteem*. San Francisco: Freeman.

Deal, T. E., & Kennedy, A. A. (1982). *Corporate cultures*. Reading: Addison-Wesley.

Deci, E. L., & Ryan, R. M. (1985). *Intrinsic motivation and self-determination in human behavior*. New York: Plenum.

Den Hartog, D. N., & Belschak, F. D. (2012). When does transformational leadership enhance employee proactive behavior? The role of autonomy and role breath self-efficacy. *Journal of Applied Psychology, 97*(1), 194–202.

Drummond, R. J. (1988). The values scale by Dorothy D. Nevill & Donald E. Super. *Journal of Employment Counseling, 25*, 136–138.

DuBois, P. H. (1970). *A history of psychological testing*. Boston: Ally & Bacon.

Eagly, A.H., & Chaiken, S. (2007). The advantages of an inclusive definition of attitude. Special issue: What is an attitude? *Social Cognition, 25*(5), 582–602.

Elias, S. M., & MacDonald, S. (2007). Using past performance, proxy efficacy, and academic self-efficacy to predict college performance. *Journal of Applied Social Psychology, 37*, 2518–2531.

Erford, B. T., Ducan, K., & Savin-Murphy, J. (2010). brief psychometric analysis of the self-efficacy teacher report scale. *Measurement and Evaluation in Counseling and Development, 43*(2), 79–90.

Fishbein, M., & Ajzen, I. (1975). *Belief, attitude, intention and behavior: An introduction to theory and research*. Reading: Addison-Wesley.

Fishbein, M., & Ajzen, I. (2010). *Predicting and changing behavior*. New York: Taylor & Francis.

Fisher, C. D., & Locke, E. A. (1992). The new look in job satisfaction research and theory. In C. J. Cranny, P. C. Smith, & E. F. Stone (Eds.), *Job satisfaction*. New York: Lexington.

Fitts, W. H. (1965). *A manual for the Tennessee self-concept scale*. Nashville: Counselor Recordings and Tests.

Froman, R. D., & Owen, S. V. (1991). High school students' perceived self-efficacy in physical and mental health. *Journal of Adolescent Research, 6*(2), 181–196.

Getzels, J. W. (1966). The problem of interests: A recommendation. In H. A. Robinson (Ed.), *Reading: Seventy-five years of progress*. Supplementary Monographs, (Vol. 66, pp. 97–106).

Gist, M. E. (1987). Self-efficacy: Implications for organizational behavior and human resource management. *Academy of Management Review, 12*, 472–485.

Gist, M. E., & Mitchell, T. R. (1992). Self-efficacy: A theoretical analysis of its determinants and malleability. *Academy of Management Review, 17*, 183–211.

Goldsmith, M. (1992). *The impact of feedback and follow-up on leadership effectiveness (Report No. 17)*. La Jolla: Goldsmith & Company.

Golman, D. (1995). *Emotional intelligence: Why it can matter more than IQ*. New York: Bantam Books.

Gordon, L. V. (1960). *SRA manual for survey of interpersonal values*. Chicago: Science Research Associates.

Grant, A. M., & Ashford, S. J. (2008). The dynamics of proactivity at work. *Research in Organizational Behavior, 28*, 3–34.

Hansen, G. S., & Wernerfelt, B. (1989). Determinants of firm performance: The relative importance of economic and organizational factors. *Strategic Management Journal, 10*, 399–411.

Harter, S. (1985). *The self-perception profile for children: revision of the perceived competence scale for children*. Denver: University of Denver.

Hatfield, E., Cacioppo, J. T., & Rapson, R. L. (1992). Primitive emotional contagion. In M. S. Clark (Ed.), *Emotion and social behavior, review of personality and social psychology* (Vol. 14, pp. 151–177). California: Sage.

Hattie, J. (1992). *Self-concept*. Hillsdale: Erlbaum.

Helms, B. J., & Gable, R. K. (1989). *School Situation Survey Manual*. Palo Alto: Consulting Psychologists Press, The Mindgarden.

Hidi, S., & Harackiewicz, J. M. (2000). Motivating the academically unmotivated: A critical issue for the 21st century. *Review of Educational Research, 70*(2), 151–179.

Holden, G. (1991). The relationship of self-efficacy appraisals to subsequent health-related outcomes: A meta-analysis. *Social Work in Health Care, 16*, 53–93.

Kent, G. (1987). Self-efficacious control over reported physiological, cognitive and behavioural symptoms of dental anxiety. *Behaviour Research and Therapy, 25*, 341–347.

Korte, W. B., & Wynne, R. (1996). *Telework: Penetration, potential and practice in Europe*. Amsterdam: Ohmsha Press.

Krathwohl, D. R., Bloom, B. S., & Masia, B. (1964). *A taxonomy of educational objectives, handbook II: The affective domain*. New York: McKay.

Kristof-Brown, A. L., Zimmerman, R. D., & Johnson, E. C. (2005). Consequences of individuals fit at work: A meta-analysis of person-job, person-organization, person-group, and person supervisor fit. *Personnel Psychology, 58*(2), 281–342.

Kumar, N. (2012). Relationship of personal and organizational values with job satisfaction. *Journal of Management Research, 12*(2), 75–82.

Kurt, T., Duyar, I., & Calik, T. (2012). Are we legitimate yet? A closer look at the causal relationship mechanisms among principal leadership, teacher self-efficacy and collective efficacy. *Journal of Management Development, 31*(1), 71–86.

Latham, G. P., & Saari, L. M. (1979). Application of social learning theory to training supervisors through behavioral modeling. *Journal of Applied Psychology, 64*, 239–246.

Leithwood, K. (1992). The move toward transformational leadership. *Educational Leadership, 49*(5), 8–12.

Leithwood, K. (1994). Leadership for school restructuring. *Educational Administration Quarterly, 30*(4), 498–518.

Leithwood, K. A., & Jantzi, D. (2005). Transformational leadership. In B. Davies (Ed.), *Essentials of school leadership* (pp. 31–43). Thousand Oaks: Corwin.

Leithwood, K. A., Jantzi, D., & Dart, B. (1991). *How the school improvement strategies of transformational leaders foster teacher development*. Paper presented at the Teacher Development Conference, Vancouver.

Lindia, S. A. (1992). Effects of a computer-intensive program on self-efficacy, sex-role socialization, and attitudes toward computers with sixth-grade students (Doctoral dissertation, University of Connecticut 1992).

Lord, R. G., & Hanges, P. J. (1987). A control system model of organizational motivation: Theoretical development and applied implications. *Behavioral Science, 32*, 161–179.

Louis, M. R. (1980). *A cultural perspective on organizations: The need for and consequences of viewing organizations as culture-bearing milieu*. Paper presented at the National Academy of Management, Detroit.

MacIntosh, E., & Walker, M. (2012). Chronicling the transient nature of fitness employees: An organizational culture perspective. *Journal of Sport Management, 26*, 113–126.

Madlock, P. E., & Booth-Butterfield, M. (2012). The influence of relational maintenance strategies among coworkers. *Journal of Business Communication, 49*(1), 21–47.

Marsh, H. W. (1990). The structure of academic self-concept: The Marsh/Shavelson model. *Journal of Educational Psychology, 82*(4), 623–636.

Marsh, H. W. (1992a). *Self-description questionnaire (SDQ) I: A theoretical and empirical basis for the measurement of multiple dimensions of preadolescent self-concept. An interim test manual and research monograph*. Macarthur, New South Wales: University of Western Sydney, Faculty of Education.

Marsh, H. W. (1992b). *Self description questionnaire (SDQ) II: A theoretical and empirical basis for the measurement of multiple dimensions of adolescent self-concept. A test manual and research monograph*. Macarthur, New South Wales: University of Western Sydney, Faculty of Education.

Marsh, H. W., & Martin, A. J. (2011). Academic self-concept and academic achievement: Relations and causal ordering. *British Journal of Educational Psychology, 81*(1), 59–77.

Mathisen, G. E. (2011). Organizational antecedents of creative self-efficacy. *Creativity and Innovative Management, 20*(3), 185–195.

Mayew, W. J., & Venkatachalam, M. (2012). The power of voice: Managerial affective states and future firm performance. *Journal of Finance, 67*(1), 1–44.

McCoach, D. B., & Siegle, D. (2003). Factors that differentiate underachieving gifted students from high-achieving gifted students. *Gifted Child Quarterly, 47*(2), 144–154.

Mitroff, I. I., & Kilman, R. H. (1976). On organizational stories: An approach to the design and analysis of organizations through myths and stories. In R. H. Kilman, L. R. Pondy, & D. P. Slevin (Eds.), *The management of organizational design* (pp. 189–207). New York: Elsevier-North Holland.

Mobley, W. H. (1977). Intermediate linkages in the relationship between job satisfaction and employee turnover. *Journal of Applied Psychology, 62*, 237–240.

Möller, J., Retelsdorf, J., Köller, O., & Marsh, H. W. (2011). The reciprocal internal/external frame of reference model: An integration of models of relations between academic achievement and self-concept. *American Educational Research Journal, 48*(6), 1315–1346.

National Governors Association Center for Best Practices, Council of Chief State School Officers. (2010). Common Core State Standards. Washington DC: National Governors Association Center for Best Practices, Council of Chief State School Officers.

Newman, D. A., Joseph, D. L., & MacCann, C. (2010). Emotional intelligence and job performance: The importance of emotion regulation and emotional labor context. *Industrial and Organizational Psychology, 3*(2), 159–164.

Nunnally, J. C. (1978). *Psychometric theory* (2nd ed.). New York: McGraw-Hill.

Nunnally, J. C., & Bernstein, I. (1994). *Psychometric theory* (3rd ed.). New York: McGraw-Hill.

Nye, C. D., Su, R., Rounds, J., & Drasgow, F. (2012). Vocational interests and performance: A quantitative summary of over 60 years of research. *Perspectives on Psychological Science, 7*, 384–403.

Ongori, H. (2007). A review of literature on employee turnover. *African Journal of Business Management, 1*(3), 49–54.

Pajares, F. (1996). Self-efficacy beliefs in academic settings. *Review of Educational Research, 66*(4), 543–578.

Parker, S. K. (2000). From passive to proactive motivation: The importance of flexible role orientations and role breath self-efficacy. *Applied Psychology, 83*, 835–852. doi:10.1037/00219010.83.6.835.

Phillips, D. J. (1990). The price tag on turnover. *Personnel Journal, 69*(2), 58–61.

Piers, E. V., & Harris, D. A. (1964). Age and other correlates of self-concept in children. *Journal of Educational Psychology, 55*, 91–95.

Pink, D. (2005). *A whole new mind: Moving from the information age to the conceptual age*. New York: Riverhead Books.

Pintrich, P. R., & Schunk, D. H. (1996). *Motivation in education: Theory, research, and applications*. Englewood Cliffs: Prentice Hall Merrill.

Porras, J. L., Hargis, K., Patterson, K. J., Maxfield, D. G., Roberts, N., & Bies, R. J. (1982). Modeling-based organizational development: A longitudinal assessment. *Journal of Applied Behavioral Science, 18*, 433–446.

Rambo, K. E., & McCoach, D. (2012). Teacher attitudes toward subject-specific acceleration: instrument development and validation. *Journal for the Education of the Gifted, 35*, 129–152.

Richardson, M., Abraham, C., & Bond, R. (2012). Psychological correlates of university students' academic performance: A systematic review and meta-analysis. *Psychological Bulletin, 138*(2), 353–387.

Riketta, M. (2008). The causal relation between job attitudes and performance: A meta-analysis of panel studies. *Journal of Applied Psychology, 93*(2), 472–481.

Robinson, K. (2012). *Out of our minds: Learning to be creative*. Westford: Courier Westford, Inc.

Rokeach, M. (1968). *Beliefs, attitudes, and values: A theory of organization and change*. San Francisco: Jossey-Bass.

Rokeach, M. (1973). *The nature of human values and value systems*. New York: Free Press.

Rosenthal, T. L., & Bandura, A. (1978). Psychological modeling: Theory and practice. In S. L. Garfield & A. E. Bergin (Eds.), *Handbook of psychotherapy and behavior change: An empirical analysis* (2nd ed., pp. 621–658). New York: Wiley.

Salkovskis, P. M., & Harrison, J. (1984). Abnormal and normal obsessions—A replication. *Behaviour Research and Therapy, 22*, 549–552.

Salovey, P., & Mayer, J. D. (1990). Emotional intelligence. *Imagination, Cognition and Personality, 9*(3), 185–211.

Sardzoska, E. G., & Tang, T. L. P. (2012). Work-related behavioral intentions in Macedonia: Coping strategies, work environment, love of money, job satisfaction, and demographic variables. *Journal of Business Ethics, 108*, 373–391.

Schlesinger, L. A., & Heskett, J. L. (1991). The service-driven service company. *Harvard Business Review, 69*(5), 71–81.

Schunk, D. H. (1981). Modeling and attributional effects on children's achievement: A self-efficacy analysis. *Journal of Educational Psychology, 73*(1), 93–105.

Schwartz, S. H. (1992). Universals in the content and structure of values: Theoretical advances and empirical tests in 20 countries. In M. Zanna (Ed.), *Advances in experimental social psychology* (Vol. 25, pp. 1–65). Orlando: Academic.

Schwartz, S. H., Cieciuch, J., Vecchione, M., Davidov, E., Fischer, R., Beierlein, C., et al. (2012). Refining the theory of basic individual values. *Journal of Personality and Social Psychology, 103*(4), 663–688.

Schwarzer, R. (Ed.). (1992). *Self-efficacy: Thought control of action*. Washington, DC: Hemisphere.

Schwepker, C. H. (2001). Ethical climate's relationship to job satisfaction, organizational commitment, and turnover intention in the salesforce. *Journal of Business Research, 54*(1), 39–52.

Siegle, D., & McCoach, D. B. (2007). Influencing student mathematics self-efficacy through teacher training. *Journal of Advanced Academics, 18*, 278–312.

Shavelson, R. J., Hubner, J. J., & Stanton, J. C. (1976). Self-concept: Validation of construct interpretations. *Review of Educational Research, 46*, 407–441.

Siehl, L., & Martin, J. (1981). *Learning organizational culture*. Stanford: School of Business, Stanford University.

Smircich, L. (1983). Concepts of culture and organizational analysis. *Administrative Science Quarterly, 28*, 339–358.

Stock, J., & Cervone, D. (1990). Proximal goal setting and self-regulatory processes. *Cognitive Therapy and Research, 14*, 483–498.

Super, D. T. (1970). *Manual for the work values inventory*. Boston: Houghton Mifflin.

Thurstone, L. L. (1928). Attitudes can be measured. *The American Journal of Sociology, 33*(4), 529–554.

Thurstone, L. L. (1931). The measurement of social attitudes. *The Journal of Abnormal and Social Psychology, 26*(3), 249–269.

Thurstone, L. L. (1946). Comment. *American Journal of Sociology, 52*, 39–40.

Tichy, N. M. (1982). Managing change strategically: The technical, political, and cultural keys. *Organizational Dynamics, 11*(2), 59–80.

Trepanier, S. G., Fernet, C., & Austin, S. (2012). Social and motivational antecedents of perceptions of transformational leadership: A self-determination theory perspective. *Canadian Journal of Behavioural Science, 44*, 272–277

Trilling, B., & Fadel, C. (2009). *21st century skills: Learning for life in our times*. New York: Jossey-Bass.

Tschannen-Moran, M., & Hoy, A. W. (2001). Capturing an elusive construct. *Teaching and Teacher Education, 17*, 783–805.

Tyler, R. W. (1973). Assessing educational achievement in the affective domain. *Measurement in Education, 4*(3), 1–8.

Ulrich, D., Halbrook, R., Meder, D., Stuchlik, M., & Thorpe, S. (1991). Employee and customer attachment: Synergies for competitive advantage. *Human Resource Planning, 14*(2), 89–103.

U.S. Department of Education. (2011). *A blueprint for reform: The reauthorization of the elementary and secondary education act*. Retrieved from http://www2.ed.gov/policy/elsec/leg/blueprint/complete-education.pdf.

Valentine, S., Godkin, L., Fleischman, G. M., & Kidwell, R. (2011). Corporate ethical values, group creativity, job satisfaction and turnover intention: The impact of work context on work response. *Journal of Business Ethics, 98*(3), 353–372.
Vijayalakshmi, V. V., & Bhattacharyya, S. (2012). Emotional contagion and its relevance to individual behavior and organizational processes: A position paper. *Journal of Business and Psychology, 27*(3), 363–374.
Vinson, D. E., Munson, J. M., & Nakanishi, M. (1977). An investigation of the Rokeach value survey for consumer research applications. In W. D. Perreault (Ed.), *Advances in consumer research* (Vol. 4, pp. 247–252). Association for Consumer Research.
Wagner, T. (2012). *Creating innovators: The making of young people who will change the world.* New York: Scribner.
Waldron, V. R., & Hunt, M. D. (1992). Hierarchical level, length, and quality of supervisory relationship as predictors of subordinates' use of maintenance tactics. *Communication Reports, 5*, 82–89.
Wang, Y. D., & Hsieh, H. H. (2012). Toward a better understanding of the link between ethical climate and job satisfaction: A multilevel analysis. *Business Ethnics, 105*, 535–545.
Wiener, Y. (1988). Forms of value systems: A focus on organizational effectiveness and cultural change and maintenance. *Academy of Management Review, 13*(4), 534–545.
Wigfield, A., & Cambria, J. (2010). Expectancy-value theory: Retrospective and prospective. In S. Karabenick & T. C. Urdan (Eds.), *Advances in motivation and achievement* (Vol. 16, pp. 35–70). Bingley: Emerald Group Publishing.
Wigfield, A., & Eccles, J. S. (2000). Expectancy-value theory of achievement motivation. *Contemporary Educational Psychology, 25*, 68–81.
Wilkins, A., & Martin, J. (1980). *Organizational legends*. Stanford: School of Business, Stanford University.

Chapter 2
Defining, Measuring, and Scaling Affective Constructs

> The parameter is what we aim to estimate; the corresponding statistic represents our current best estimate of it. Just so, the trait is what we aim to understand, and the corresponding construct represents our current best understanding of it.
>
> Jane Loevinger 1957, p. 642

In Chapter 1, we noted that affective characteristics possess intensity, direction, and a target. We also reviewed several classes of affective characteristics: attitudes, self-efficacy, values, self-concept, and interests.

The remainder of this book focuses on developing self-report affective instruments that can be used in research and evaluation within educational, business, and non-profit organizations. An effective affective instrument produces scores that differentiate people in terms of their level on one or more affective characteristics. This task is challenging because affective characteristics such as self-efficacy, prejudice, anxiety, or attitudes toward school cannot be directly observed. Instead, we must infer people's degree or level of the trait based on a sample of their behaviors. In other words, the person must do something or respond in some overt way for us to make inferences about these internal, latent characteristics.

We have several options for collecting these overt behavioral manifestations of affective characteristics. First, we could collect observational data in a naturalistic setting. Direct observation is a very popular method of data collection in education and the social sciences, and it is the preferred method for collecting certain types of data. However, assessing affective characteristics using direct behavioral observations in naturalistic settings can be problematic. Often, people do not exhibit overt behaviors that can be linked to the affective characteristic of interest. For example, students with and without math anxiety may exhibit the same set of overt behaviors within a math class (or even while taking a math test) even though their internal affective states differ. Or people may exhibit the behavior that links back to the affective characteristic so rarely that it would be nearly impossible to assess a person's level on the trait from a sample of direct behavioral observations. For example, a person who is prejudiced may exhibit overt behaviors that belie his or her attitude; however, those overt behaviors occur relatively infrequently. Therefore, a one-hour direct behavioral observation would probably fail to capture the person engaging in the behavior. In addition, people tend to monitor their behaviors more carefully when they know that they are being observed. Therefore, they may adjust their behaviors in response to the observation process. Thus, although direct observation can be an effective way of collecting certain types of

D. B. McCoach et al., *Instrument Development in the Affective Domain*,
DOI: 10.1007/978-1-4614-7135-6_2, © Springer Science+Business Media New York 2013

information, it is often very difficult to make inferences about people's affective characteristics based solely on observational data. Finally, direct observations are both costly and time consuming, making the method impractical for large-scale data collection.

We have another obvious option for assessing people's levels on an affective characteristic: we can ask them. Self-report instruments require participants to assess their own internal states or traits and provide a self-rating or score. The self-report of the internal characteristic is an overt behavior that we use to infer the person's level on the affective characteristic of interest. Of course, a key question is how well do people's self-reports of their internal states or traits match their actual levels on those states or traits? The stronger the correspondence between people's self-reported responses and their actual level on the affective trait, the better the instrument is at capturing the person's level on the affective trait. However, because we cannot directly observe the affective trait directly, assessing this degree of correspondence is not at all straightforward. This essential problem becomes the focus of much of our instrument development work.

Affective characteristics are *latent constructs*; therefore, their *measurement* relies upon the ability to make inferences from directly observable behaviors (such as responses to items) to the affective characteristic of interest. Because understanding this framework is essential for the successful development of affective instrument, we begin by defining these three critical concepts: latent, construct, and measurement.

Latent Constructs and Measurement

The study of affective characteristics compels researchers to quantify postulated attributes that cannot be observed directly. For example, attitudes, self-efficacy, values, self-concept, and interest are phenomena that are of theoretical interest to social scientists, but which cannot be directly observed or measured. Such variables are often referred to as latent variables, constructs, or factors. A *construct* is a concept, model, or schematic idea (Bollen 2002). The term *latent* means "not directly observable." Thus, *latent constructs* are non-observable concepts. In his review of latent variables, Bollen (2002) identified three non-formal (non-mathematical) definitions of latent variables that psychologists and social scientists routinely adopt when they include these variables in statistical models. He noted that researchers conceive of latent variables as (1) "hypothetical variables" (Harman 1960, p. 12), (2) variables that "cannot be measured" (Joreskog and Sorbom 1979, p. 105), or (3) simply data reduction devices that "attain a parsimonious description of observed data" (Harman 1960, p. 5). In practice, researchers usually adopt all these definitions when working with models that include concepts, constructs, or attributes that cannot be directly observed or measured (MacCallum and Austin 2000).

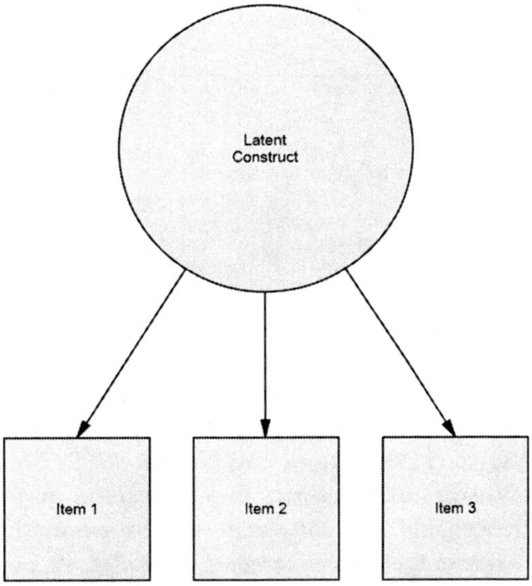

Fig. 2.1 Causal model of responses to survey items

The inability to measure a construct directly represents a measurement challenge: how can researchers capture individual differences in variables that cannot be perceived, but rather can only be inferred? Social scientists have addressed this problem using two critical philosophical assumptions. First, they assume that although systems to measure constructs are completely man-made, the constructs themselves are real and exist apart from the awareness of the researcher and the participant under study (Borsboom 2005; Cook and Campbell 1979; Edwards and Bagozzi 2000; Nunnally and Bernstein 1994). There is certainly a deep and lively debate regarding the level of realism necessary to meet the requirements for measurement (for a detailed treatment, see Borsboom 2003 and 2005); however, the notion that affective latent constructs refer to "real" phenomenon is a common assumption in the social sciences. The second assumption is that although latent constructs are not directly observed, they do have a causal relationship with observed measures. In other words, the latent construct is presumed to "cause" or "determine" the measures, thus such measures represent reflections of construct.[1] Figure 2.1 illustrates this assumption. The affective characteristic—a latent construct—is represented by the circle.

The latent construct is then presumed to cause people's responses to the observed variables, or the indicators. As we shall see, connecting theory to empirical data through causal hypotheses is crucial throughout the validation process.

---

[1] It should also be noted that measures can be viewed as causes of latent constructs (Bagozzi and Fornell 1982; Blalock 1964, 1971; Bollen and Lennox 1991).

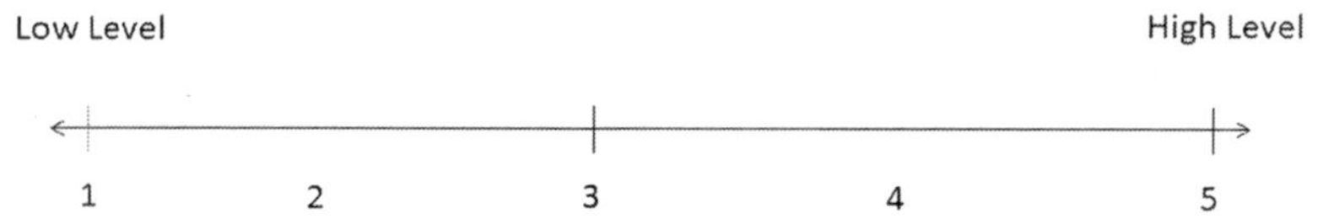

Fig. 2.2 An affective continuum

Measurement

Measurement can be defined as the "assignment of numerals in such a way as to correspond to different degrees of a quality or property of some object or event" (Duncan 1984, p. 176). Measurement consists of rules for numerically representing quantities or degrees of attributes (DeVellis 1991; Duncan 1984; Edwards and Bagozzi 2000; Lord and Novick 1968; Messick 1995; Netemeyer et al. 2003).[2] Wilson (2005) asserts that the central purpose of measurement "is to provide a reasonable and consistent way to summarize the responses that people make to express their achievements, attitudes, or personal points of view through instruments such as scales, achievement tests, questionnaires, surveys, and psychological scales" (Wilson 2005, p. 5). As Wright and Masters (1982) have noted, measurement begins with the concept of a continuum on which people can be located with respect to some trait or construct (Fig. 2.2).

Instruments contain clusters of items. Using the responses on the cluster of items, we generate numbers (item scores) for each person on each of the items. Then we combine the item scores into one overall number, which is often called the *scale score* (or the measure). The scale scores (measures) are the manifest (observed) variables that capture individual differences on the trait(s) of interest. The items themselves are also located on the continuum with respect to their direction and intensity. Variations of judgmental and empirical techniques are used to scale the items. Some scaling procedures calculate numbers called *calibrations*, which indicate the location of an item on the underlying affective continuum. Put more simply, people differ from each other in terms of their level on the latent variable. The measure should capture those differences empirically. The items may also differ from each other in terms of the amount of the latent trait required to endorse an item. For many scaling techniques (i.e., Likert Scaling, Rasch Modeling, and Guttman Scaling), respondents who possess a large amount of the trait in question should generally agree with all questions, whether they are easy or hard to endorse. In contrast, respondents who possess a small amount of the trait may agree with the questions that are easy to endorse but not the questions that are difficult to endorse. Finally, the respondents with the very lowest levels of the trait in question (or perhaps absence of the trait, if that is theoretically possible) should fail to endorse even the easiest questions.

[2] Edwards and Bagozzi (2000, p. 156) stress that a measure refers not to the instrument used to gather data or to the act of collecting data, but to the score generated by these procedures.

During the measurement process, people respond to the series of items that define the construct or trait, and ideally, these items should span a continuum so that some items are easier to endorse and some items are harder to endorse. Then the person's scale score on the trait of interest to be used to make "more or less" comparisons among people. However, the instrument is more than just a series of items: it should provide "a logical argument that the results can be interpreted to help make a decision as the measurer intended them to be" (Wilson 2005, p. 5).

Instantiation and Conceptual Definitions

In affective instrument design, researchers attempt to develop measures of affective characteristics, which are latent constructs. By definition, these abstract concepts lack empirical specificity. As a result, one of the core tasks of instrument designers is to provide concrete "instances" that capture the abstract constructs of interest. The process of specifying concrete instances of abstract concepts is known as instantiation (Jaccard and Jacoby 2010). When instrument designers apply specific meaning to the concepts that prompted their research interest, they have effectively *outlined their constructs* or applied *conceptual definitions* to the constituents of their thoughts (Nunnally and Bernstein 1994). The use of latent variables to provide meaning for unobserved affective concepts requires "simple and precise" theoretical definitions (Bollen 1989, p. 180). Jaccard and Jacoby (2010) provide some practical strategies for developing a conceptual definition of a construct. These include conducting a comprehensive review of the literature, listing key properties of the concept, providing examples of the concept, and enlisting techniques from grounded theory construction (Glaser and Strauss 1967). We return to this issue in Chapter 3.

Operationism or Operationalization

Attributes are the features of a construct that one observes consistently (Pett et al. 2003). Clear definitions of attributes help researchers operationalize and measure the latent constructs of interest. The operational definition describes the procedures we employ to form measures of the latent variable(s) to represent the construct or concept of interest (Bollen 1989). In the social sciences, latent variables are often operationalized through the use of responses to questionnaires or surveys. Then we assign numbers to item responses; these numbers represent categories of observations or responses (Stevens 1946). When this assignment is successful, the properties of number classes (nominal, ordinal, interval, and ratio) become synonymous with the properties of measurement. This "correlation of numbers with entities that are not numbers" is also known more broadly as the representational theory of measurement (Nagel 1931, p. 313).

Wilson (2005) suggests that measurement represents "a reasonable and consistent way to summarize the responses that people make to express their achievements, attitudes, or personal points of view through instruments such as attitude scales, achievement tests, questionnaires, surveys, and psychological scales" (p. 5).

According to fundamental measurement theory, successful measures should:

1. Reduce experiences to *one dimensional* abstraction (i.e., continuum),
2. Provide "*more or less*" a comparison among persons and items,
3. Apply the idea of *linear magnitude* when positioning respondents, and
4. Present a unit determined by a *process* which can be repeated without modification over the range of the variables. (Wright and Masters 1982, p. 3)

The "process which can be repeated without modification" is actually the measurement or *scaling model*. The scaling model describes how people and items interact to produce measures (scores) for people. Several such scaling models have received much attention over the past 80 years. In this chapter, we describe three common models that have been utilized for scaling affective variables: Likert Scaling, Thurstone Scaling, and Rasch Modeling. By far, the most common scaling method for researcher developed instruments is Likert Scaling.

Unidimensionality

Our everyday experience with unobserved affective constructs suggests that they are complex entities. This complexity is magnified by human attempts to define observable indicators of those constructs. Constructing instruments to measure objects—whether those objects are physical or psychological—is difficult because it generally requires the isolation of one aspect or facet for quantification. Bond and Fox (2007) note that "all attempts to make meaningful estimations of the objects under scrutiny focus on only one attribute at a time" (p. 32). This focus on a single attribute or dimension is known as unidimensionality (Bond and Fox 2007).

Instruments may measure multiple facets or dimensions of a complex, multidimensional construct or they may measure multiple simpler, unidimensional constructs. In either case, it is important to develop sets of items that capture each of the dimensions of interest, and those sets of items need to be unidimensional. For example, academic self-concept is generally viewed as a multidimensional construct that has several dimensions (mathematics self-concept, reading self-concept, etc.) (Marsh et al. 1988; Marsh and Shavelson 1985). In the instrument design phase, even though the construct of academic self-concept is multidimensional, it is important to identify all the different dimensions of interest and to develop unidimensional sets of items that capture the essence of each of those dimensions.

More formally, the dimensionality of a set of items equals the number of latent constructs that account for the correlations among the items; this is the number of factors required to reduce the partial correlations among all of the items to 0 (Netemeyer et al. 2003, p. 22). Unidimensionality indicates that the statistical dependence among a set of items can be explained by a single latent trait (Crocker and Algina 2006). In other words, after controlling the latent trait, the partial correlation among each of the pairs of items is 0. Stated differently, after partialling out the effects of the latent variable, there are no correlations among the residuals of the items. If there are no remaining relationships among the items after the latent construct, then the latent construct is able to explain the correlations among the items. Unidimensionality is a critical assumption in the development of affective instruments because it implies that the variance shared by the items is completely accounted for by the latent trait that the scale was designed to measure. Experience with affective characteristics suggests that the standard of strict unidimensionality is often not met in practice. Further, using an exploratory factor analysis (EFA) framework to examine strict unidimensionality is impossible. Instead, unidimensionality within EFA is better understood as the measurement of a "dominant component or factor" (Hambleton et al. 1991, p. 9). However, because the goal is to create scale scores that cleanly and clearly measure constructs of interest, unidimensionality of subconstructs, or dimensions is a critical feature of well-designed instruments.

Measuring Affective Characteristics

Affective measurement is the process of "obtaining a score that represents a person's position on a bipolar evaluative dimension with respect to the attitude [or affect] object" (Fishbein and Ajzen 2010). Table 2.1 highlights some of the most popular adjective pairs that provide endpoints for the affective evaluations of interest to social psychologists.

Affective instruments provide important information about internal traits such as attitudes, values, self-efficacy, etc. Thus, the measurement of affective characteristics may help to predict future behavior (Ajzen 1988; Fishbein and Ajzen 1975, 2010) and to document how individuals change in response to *persuasion* (Cialdini 2001) or other interventions. Behavioral prediction, behavioral change,

Table 2.1 Evaluation Studies Examples (summarized from Fishbein and Ajzen 2010)

Evaluation Task	Reference
Good or bad	Bargh et al. (1992)
Liking or disliking	Murphy and Zajonc (1993)
Desirable or undesirable	Ajzen and Fishbein (1970)
Pleasant or unpleasant	Ajzen and Fishbein (1970)
Favor or oppose	Rosenberg (1956)

and social influence are critical areas of applied psychology that rely heavily on knowledge collected from instruments that measure affective characteristics. Several approaches for affective measurement exist; the instrument developer must select the technique most appropriate for his/her research. In the next section, we discuss common methods for measuring affective characteristics.

Direct Measures of Affective Characteristics

Instrument designers can choose to use either *closed-form* or *open-form* items to serve as indicators of the latent constructs. Open-form questions allow respondents to answer in their own words. This format can be an advantage for researchers who are uncertain about the range or strength of the target population's responses or for researchers who are in the very initial stages of instrument development. Open-form responses typically result in data that are attractive for a wider range of analysts with different research interests (Weisberg et al. 1996). However, practical problems hinder their use within most standard affective instruments. First, respondents approach the items from many different perspectives, making cross-person comparisons an analytical challenge. Open-form items require researchers to develop coding systems so that similar responses can be grouped together for analysis. Given that respondents rarely provide identical answers, qualitative researchers must judge the similarity of the responses to better structure the data. Scaling open-ended data for intensity of responses can be especially problematic. Furthermore, although open-ended questions do permit respondents to provide unanticipated responses, open-ended questions can actually "subtly prevent responses that the investigator considers legitimate" (Schuman and Presser 1996, p. 87). Finally, respondents are far less likely to answer open-ended questions than they are to answer closed-ended questions (Dillman et al. 2009; Schuman and Presser 1996). In our experience, even questions as simple as "age" or "gender" are far more likely to result in missing data when the question is structured as an open-ended response.

Closed-form questions attempt to reduce some of the analytical challenges inherent in open-form questions by providing a set of predetermined response alternatives. In affective instruments, the most common closed-form items provide a statement and then ask respondents to select one response from an ordinal series of response options. By providing the response format, researchers attempt to provide a consistent "frame of reference" for all the respondents (Weisberg et al. 1996, p. 84). However, researchers must exercise great care during the item construction process to leverage the analytical advantages that closed-form questions can provide (Fabrigar et al. 2005). For instance, the response options that are provided with closed-ended questions can have a major impact on how respondents interpret and answer the questions (Dillman et al. 2009).

Single-Item Direct Measures

The use of a single item to measure an affective characteristic is efficient and simple, but the process of deciding on one indicator to represent most affective constructs of research interest is complicated. In cases where researchers are investigating affective constructs with highly restrictive conceptual definitions, single-item measures may be appropriate. An excellent example of an effective, single-item direct measure is the *Wong-Baker FACES Pain Rating Scale* (Hockenberry and Wilson 2009) that is posted on virtually every hospital wall and doctor's office. However, for researchers working with complex psychological constructs, single-item measures are generally inadequate. Human evaluations of psychological objects are not directly observable, making their measurement complicated. Thus, it is unreasonable to expect to be able to measure an affective construct using a single item. Most instrument designers also prefer multiple-item measures given the imperfections associated with item writing. By using multiple-item measures, designers hope to minimize the idiosyncratic features of any single item by including multiple items that measure the same construct. Under this theory, the errors and idiosyncrasies of the items in multiple-item measures "cancel each other out" and provide a score that is more reliable and accurate than any single-item (Fabrigar et al. 2005, p. 27).

Multiple-Item Direct Measures

There are several formal approaches available for researchers who choose to employ multiple-item measures in their instruments. It is very common for social scientists to develop their own instruments in order to best address their specific research needs as well as defray the cost of purchasing commercial tests. Before embarking on an instrument development project, instrument designers should spend time exploring previously published instruments related to their affective domain of interest. Previously developed multiple-item instruments are excellent source for developers to gather ideas about possible indicators and scaling techniques (Robinson et al. 1991). The remainder of this text provides guidance on the development of closed-form multi-item direct measures of affective characteristics.

Scaling Techniques

In this section, we describe three popular scaling techniques, all of which arrive at a single score based upon responses to a set of statements. Theoretically, all of the techniques yield scores that represent the person's location on a continuum with respect to their level on the affective characteristic. Depending on the technique employed, items selected for inclusion in the instrument are based upon different criteria, which results in selecting items with different item-characteristic curves or tracelines. In the following sections, we introduce Thurstone Equal Appealing Intervals, Likert Summated Rating Scales, and Rasch Modeling. We also illustrate the similarities and differences among the three scaling techniques. Many psychological tests and assessments of affective characteristics utilize one of these three traditional approaches to scaling multiple-item measures. Before researchers explore specific applications of these approaches it is important to understand the conceptual foundations of these popular scaling techniques.

Thurstone Equal-Appearing Intervals

Thurstone and Chave (1929) originally developed the *Thurstone technique of equal appearing intervals*.[3] The technique has a long history (Anderson and Bourke 2000; Edwards 1957; Fishbein and Ajzen 1975; Nunnally and Bernstein 1994; Thurstone 1927, 1928, 1931a, b, 1946), and has proven to be an effective method for scaling multi-item direct measures of affective characteristics such as attitudes. The procedure begins by generating a large pool of statements about a specific target psychological object. Through a judgmental procedure, the researchers locate (i.e., calibrate) each of the statements on a favorable/unfavorable evaluative dimension. This results in a scale value for each belief statement.

There two critical phases involved in the development of an affective instrument using Thurstone's Equal-Appearing Interval Technique. The first phase is the item selection process. Instrument designers using this technique start by constructing a large set of items (e.g., 50–100 statements) to operationally define the affective characteristic. Then, to calibrate the items, the instrument developer assembles a large group of judges who are from the target population or who are very similar to the eventual respondents. The judges rate the items with respect to the extent that the items describe the affective characteristic. Historically, Thurstone used an 11 point (0–10) scale to calibrate the items; however, other response scales (1–5, 1–7, 0–100) are equally permissible. The judges are instructed to disregard their personal feelings about the statements and simply decide the degree to which the statement represents a positive or negative reaction to the object being evaluated. It is essential that the judges realize that they are not agreeing or disagreeing with the items. Rather, they are assisting in the quantification of the intensity (i.e., favorable/unfavorable)

[3] Thurstone also developed a technique that used paired comparisons. After the set of items had been scaled by the judges, items were paired with other items with similar scale values; and sets of paired comparisons were developed. In some cases, each item was paired with all other items from other scales on the instrument, and respondents were asked to select the item from the pair that best described the target object. Thus, readers should be aware that some references to Thurstone scaling are actually references to Thurstone's method of paired comparisons.

of the statement. Using the judges' ratings, the instrument developer places the statements on the evaluative continuum, which contains the same number of scale points as the scale that the judges' used. If this process is successful, the ratings of the judges will provide the locations of the items which will span the psychological continuum underlying the affective characteristic.

The distribution of the judges' responses to each item provides important information about the utility of the item. The median (or mean) value represents the location of the item on the psychological continuum. In addition, the interquartile range (or standard deviation) provides an important measure of variability in the judges' opinions. Items with more variable scores are more ambiguous items; judges disagree about whether the item indicates a high or low degree of the trait in question. Using a measure of variability, called the *criterion of ambiguity,* the instrument developer can eliminate items that are rated differently across the judges. Once the scale values are stable across groups of judges, the actual item selection takes place. Ideally, the final set of items should span the item continuum and have low variability. Careful selection of the scale values results in what Thurstone called an *Equal-Appearing-Interval Scale* (Edwards 1957). The instrument developer selects a final pool of items that are equally spaced, unambiguous, and span the entire continuum of intensity. Using the final, scaled version of the instrument, respondents rate the target object with respect to the affective characteristic. To locate a respondent's scale score on the affective continuum using a Thurstone scale, it is necessary to compute the median (or mean) of the scale values for all of the items that the respondent endorsed. This value serves as the scale value for the respondent.

Of course, the calibration of the items should result in scale values that have generality beyond the particular sample of judges used to locate the items on the continuum. According to Thurstone (1928), the validity of the scale depends upon the assumption that the opinions of the judges who helped construct scale do not affect the calibration values of the item stems. He stated "the scaling method must stand such a test before it can be accepted as being more than a description of the people who construct the scale... to the extent that the present method of scale construction is affected by the opinions of the readers who help sort out the original statements into a scale, ... the validity or universality of the scale may be challenged" (Thurstone 1928, pp. 547–548).

The second criterion for selecting items in the Thurstone technique is called the *criterion of irrelevance* (Andersen 1981; Edwards 1957; Fishbein and Ajzen 1975; Thurstone and Chave 1929). The procedure examines the relationship between the judges' ratings of favorable/unfavorable affect in each item and the respondents' scale.

The purpose of the analysis is to identify items that yield responses that appear to represent factors other than the affective characteristic being measured. The criterion of irrelevance assumes that people whose attitudes are located at a particular scale value on the evaluative continuum should select items with scale values near the person's overall attitude score. Item trace lines or item characteristic curves represent the relationship between the probability of endorsing a

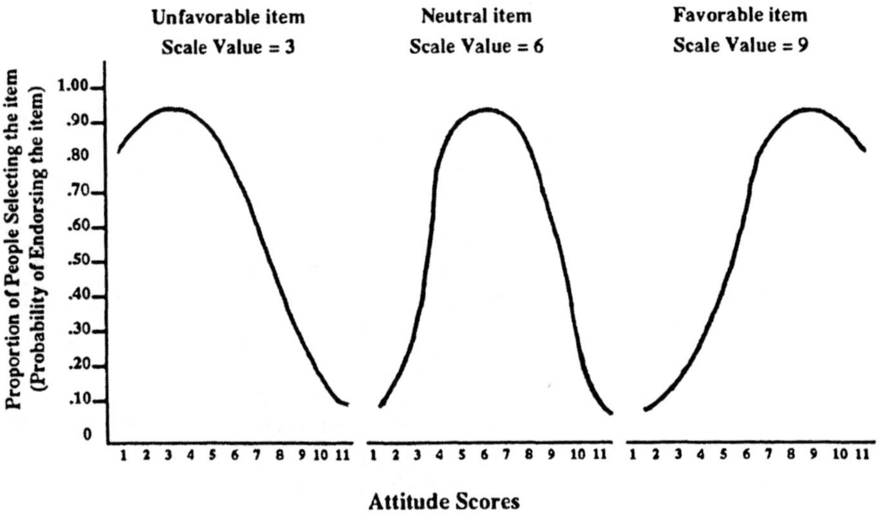

Fig. 2.3 Hypothetical traceline for three Thurstone items with different scale values, adapted from Fishbein and Ajzen (1975)

particular item (or proportion of people endorsing the item) and the item's scale value. Figure 2.3 contains a modified version of Fishbein and Ajzen's (1975, p. 70) trace lines for three items with low, median, and high scale values (i.e., unfavorable, neutral, and favorable items).

The horizontal axis represents the respondents' overall attitude scores, and the vertical axis indicates the proportion of people selecting the item. We generate a trace line for each item on the scale. The peak of the curve for each item should be nearly equal to the scale score for the item. This means that the probability of endorsing the item is highest when a person's scale score is equal to the calibrated item score. Thus, items "passing" the criterion of irrelevance will exhibit unimodal trace lines that peak at the scale-score category containing the item's scale value. When this happens, people whose attitudes are near the scale value on the attitude dimension are most likely to select the item, and the item is retained for the final form of the instrument. If the traceline is uniform, bimodal, or centered at a different scale point, scale irrelevant factors are influencing responses to the item, and the item should be eliminated from the final version of the instrument.

An Example of a Thurstone Scale

Kahn (1974) developed a Thurstone scale to evaluate university-faculty teaching. First, Kahn developed 35 items to describe teaching quality (see Table 2.2). A sample of approximately 300 college students served as the judges. They responded to the form in Table 2.2 by indicating how characteristic the statement was of good quality teaching. Note that the respondents were not asked to rate their particular teacher. Instead, they assisted in scaling the item pool with respect to the degree of teaching quality exhibited in each item. Instead of employing Thurstone's (1931a) 11-point scale, Kahn employed a 4-point scale. There is only one real requirement for the number of scale points during the judgmental phase; the response format must result in adequate variability and reduce the potential for bias that can result from an insufficient number of scale points. Kahn (1974, Unpublished manuscript) sampled several groups of college students and compared the scale values for different subgroups of judges on the basis of gender and level of their program (undergraduate, masters, doctorate). The process of scaling the items continued until stable scale values were found.

Kahn (1974) selected the 20 best items from the pool of items in Table 2.2. Table 2.3 presents the items selected and their scale value weights. (The weights appear in Table 2.3, but they would not appear in the actual instrument.) Using the instructions in Table 2.3, respondents indicated which of the 20 attributes their teacher exhibited. The scale score equals the mean or median of the scale values for the items selected. For example, a respondent checking items 1, 5, 6, 8, and 12 would actually give the instructor a rating of $(3.169 + 3.377 + 3.887 + 3.324 + 3.707)/5 = 3.49$; whereas if items 7, 16, 18, and 19 were checked the rating would be $(1.989 + 2.164 + 1.502 - 0.035)/4 = 1.41$. Clearly, the first rating is higher, indicating better teaching because the student endorsed 4 items that previous judges indicated were characteristic of good teaching.

Final Thoughts About the Thurstone Equal-Appearing Interval Method

Although it is infrequently used, the Thurstone Equal-Appearing Interval method can be an attractive option for researchers interested in the measurement of affective characteristics. One enduring quality of the approach is its superior ability to measure "individuals who hold extreme attitudinal positions" (Roberts et al. 1999, p. 229). A good example of this is the *Punishments for Cheating Scale* developed by Whitley and Kost (1999). Punishment, particularly for students, can be highly variable at the extremes. The developers of the scale found, for example, that the response "expel the student from" represented the most aggressive and "do not punish the student" represented the most passive punishment. These are clearly the most extreme attitudinal possibilities for teachers considering the fate of students caught cheating. Paradoxically, however, teachers or professors who select these extreme statements may, in some instances, appear more moderate in another scaling approach—specifically a Likert scale (Roberts et al. 1999). As a result, researchers who anticipate extreme responses within an affective construct which can be generally well-defined an *unfavorability-favorability* format might well consider Thurstone Equal-Appearing Interval scaling.

Table 2.2 An illustration of the Judges' rating form for the Thurstone technique

"Teaching Quality Survey"

No doubt you have been asked many times to rate your instructor. We are not now asking you to do the same thing, but rather to help define the IMPORTANCE OF VARIOUS TEACHER CHARACTERISTICS. For each of the items, please assign a rating in accordance with your judgement:

(1) Highly uncharacteristic of a good teacher
(2) Usually uncharacteristic of a good teacher
(3) Usually characteristic of a good teacher
(4) Highly characteristic of a good teacher

Rating

1. Gives specific reading assignments
2. Reports test and quiz scores promptly
3. Displays enthusiasm for his subject
4. Relies heavily on class discussion
5. Relies heavily on lecture
6. Defines scope and content of course
7. Displays considerable knowledge of the subject
8. Encourages student initiative
9. Fair to students
10. Relates content of his course to other subject matter
11. Is interested primarily in his subject
12. Is interested primarily in his students
13. Varies level (abstraction) of his presentation
14. Employs humor and anecdotes
15. Makes use of examples and illustrations
16. Responds to individual student needs and problems
17. Meets classes punctually
18. Prepares and organizes his presentations
19. Digresses from topics under discussion
20. Elicits student experiences for illustrative purposes
21. Is available to students outside of classroom
22. Open to suggestions from students for discussion, class, or individual projects
23. Lecture style is difficult to follow
24. Has expectations of students unrelated to course content
25. Lectures complement rather than follow reading assignments
26. Uses pertinent audio/visual presentations
27. Defines expectations for grading purposes
28. Generates enthusiasm in class
29. Evokes student interest in subject
30. Maintains liveliness in discussions and presentations
31. Lectures directly from notes
32. Uses his knowledge of individual students' strengths in developing the course
33. Responds to individual exams and term papers
34. Discusses evaluation of exams and term papers
35. Lectures reflect current developments

Developed by Kahn (1974, unpublished manuscript)

However, there are disadvantages to Thurstone Equal-Appearing Interval scaling. The procedure is time-consuming. Judges may disagree about the scale values for items or different subgroups of judges may produce different scale values for the items. When judges' scores are variable, the calibrated item scores should not be used. Researchers who use the Thurstone technique must ensure the

Table 2.3 An illustration of the respondents' rating form for Thurstone technique

Instructor Evaluation

As a basis for continuing efforts at improvement, your instructor and the department are concerned with gauging the quality and appropriateness of instruction. Your cooperation in furnishing information is essential for this purpose

Please Note:

A. YOUR RESPONSES WILL BE ANONYMOUS AND WILL NOT AFFECT YOUR GRADE IN ANY WAY
B. SOME OF THE ITEMS ARE LESS APPROPRIATE FOR CERTAIN KINDS OF COURSES THAN THEY ARE FOR OTHERS. THEREFORE, CONSIDERING THE TYPE OF COURSE (LECTURE, SEMINAR, PRACTICUM) FILL IN THE RESPONSE POSITION PERTAINING ONLY TO THOSE ITEMS YOU JUDGE TO BE APPROPRIATE DESCRIPTIONS OF YOUR INSTRUCTOR

3.169[a]	1.	Lectures reflect current developments in the field	☐
2.649	2.	Defines expectations for grading purposes	☐
2.404	3.	Meets class punctually	☐
2.112	4.	Uses knowledge of individual student's strengths in developing the course	☐
3.377	5.	Maintains liveliness in discussions and presentations	☐
3.887	6.	Generates enthusiasm in class	☐
1.989	7.	Relies heavily on class discussion	☐
3.324	8.	Responds to individual student needs and problems	☐
3.039	9.	Defines scope and content of course	☐
2.254	10.	Elicits student experiences for illustrative purposes	☐
3.064	11.	Prepares and organizes presentations	☐
3.707	12.	Encourages student initiative	☐
2.999	13.	Responds to individual requests for supplementary materials	☐
2.749	14.	Is interested primarily in students	☐
2.704	15.	Varies level of abstraction of presentation	☐
2.164	16.	Gives specific reading assignments	☐
2.334	17.	Uses pertinent audio/visual presentations	☐
1.502	18.	Digresses from topics under discussion	☐
−0.035	19.	Lectures directly from notes	☐
2.294	20.	Relates content of course to other subject matter	☐

[a] Note that the weights would not appear on the actual form

stability of the scale values using large samples and across subgroups of judges. If scores are not stable, it is necessary to choose another scaling method.

There is typically not a high correlation between the overall attitude score and the selection of items on the Thurstone scale. This is the result of the relationships between item selection and scale values depicted for the three items in Fig. 2.3 are curvilinear in nature. The shape of the trace line differs for items with different scale values. In the Thurstone technique, items are not selected on the basis of the relationship between item endorsement and overall attitude score. This quality of Thurstone Equal-Appearing Interval Scales stands in direct contrast with another scaling option known as the Likert Summated Rating scale, which we consider next.

Likert's Summated Rating Scale Technique

Likert's (1932) method of summated ratings is by far the most popular method for scaling researcher developed measures of affective characteristics. Researchers tend to use Likert response scales because they are relatively easy to construct, produce highly internally consistent data, and can be adapted to measure many types of affective characteristics (Nunnally and Bernstein 1994). Instruments employing Likert's summated rating scale technique contain a set of statements (i.e., items). In addition, developers must choose a "Likert response format" that corresponds with the items. Respondents are then asked to choose a response along the Likert response format that best matches their attitude or feeling. The most common Likert scale is a 5-point agree–disagree scale; however, 7-point scales are rapidly gaining popularity. Tables 2.4a–f contain examples of 5-, 6-, and 7-point response scales that can be used for developing Likert scaled instruments. Using Likert scaling, we sum the responses across the items to compute the scale scores for the affective constructs. Alternatively, we can create a mean score by summing the responses and dividing by the number of items on the scale. This has the advantage of placing the scale score in the same metric as the response scale, which makes interpreting the score much easier.

In contrast with Thurstone scaling, judges are typically not involved in the actual scaling process of Likert items. The evaluation of the favorable/unfavorableness (i.e., positive/negative) of the statement or attribute with respect to the target object is initially determined by the instrument developer and not by an independent set of judges. It is certainly possible (and recommended) that a group of judges could later examine the items and provide insight about the perceived degree of favorableness of the items. However, statements do not receive scale values prior to data collection. When participants respond to the items, they locate themselves on the underlying affective continuum through their intensity and direction ratings. To compute a scale score for a participant, we sum (or take the mean) of their item-level responses across the items defining the characteristic. If you use any negatively worded items or items which are oriented in the opposite direction, it is imperative that you reverse score those items; higher scores on each item and on the scale as a whole indicate a higher degree of the trait or a more positive attitude and lower scores indicate a lower degree of the trait or a more negative attitude.

The development of a Likert scale begins with the selection or development of a large number of items (i.e., statements that represent operational definitions of the affective characteristic). Each construct or dimension needs at least 10–12 items at this stage. After the items are reviewed during the content-validity phase (see Chapter 4 for details regarding content validation), the instrument developer conducts a pilot study. After fairly large, representative sample of people respond to the pilot form of the instrument, we conduct item analysis, factor analysis, and alpha-reliability analyses (which are described in great detail in Chapters 4, 5, and 7).

Table 2.4 Examples of multipoint response scales

7-point	6-point	5-point	4-point	3-point	2-point
(a) *AGREEMENT*					
Strongly agree	Strongly agree	Strongly agree	Strongly agree	Agree	Agree
Agree	Moderately agree	Agree	Agree	Neither agree/disagree	Disagree
Slightly agree	Slightly agree	Neither agree/disagree	Disagree	Disagree	
Neither agree/disagree	Slightly disagree	Disagree	Strongly disagree		*Alternative:*
Slightly disagree	Moderately disagree	Strongly disagree			Yes
Disagree	Strongly disagree				No
Strongly disagree					
Very strongly agree	Very strongly agree	Very strongly agree	Very strongly agree		
Strongly agree	Strongly agree	Agree	Agree		
Agree	Agree	Neither agree/disagree	Disagree		
Neither agree/disagree	Disagree	Disagree	Very strongly disagree		
Disagree	Strongly disagree	Very strongly disagree			
Strongly disagree	Very strongly disagree				
Very strongly disagree					
Completely agree	Completely agree	Completely agree	Completely agree		
Mostly agree	Mostly agree	Agree	Agree		
Moderately agree	Slightly agree	Neither agree/disagree	Disagree		
Neither agree/disagree	Slightly disagree	Disagree	Completely disagree		
Moderately disagree	Mostly disagree	Completely disagree			
Mostly disagree	Completely disagree				
Completely disagree					

(continued)

Table 2.4 (continued)

7-point	6-point	5-point	4-point	3-point	2-point
(b) *FREQUENCY*					
Always	Always	Always	Often	Frequently	Frequently
Frequently	Frequently	Very often	Sometimes	Sometimes	Never
Somewhat frequently	Somewhat frequently	Sometimes	Seldom	Never	
Somewhat infrequently	Somewhat infrequently	Rarely	Never		
Rarely	Rarely	Never			Always
Very rarely	Never				Never
Never					
		Always	Almost always	Always	Often
		Usually	To a considerable degree	Sometimes	Never
		Sometimes	Occasionally	Never	
		Seldom	Seldom		
		Never			
(c) *IMPORTANCE*					
Essential	Essential	Very important	Very important	Very important	Important
Very important	Very important	Important	Important	Moderately important	Unimportant
Important	Important	Moderately important	Of little importance	Unimportant	
Moderately Important	Moderately important	Not very important	Unimportant		
Slightly important	Not very important	Unimportant			
Not very important	Unimportant				
(d) *REFLECT ME*					
Very true of me	Very true of me	True of me	True of me	True of me	True of me
True of me	True of me	Somewhat true of me	Somewhat true of me	Neutral	Untrue of me
Somewhat true of me	Somewhat true of me	Neutral	Somewhat untrue of me	Untrue of me	
Neutral	Somewhat untrue of me	Somewhat untrue of me	Untrue of me		
Somewhat untrue of me	Untrue of me	Untrue of me			
Untrue of me	Completely untrue of me				
Very untrue of me					

(continued)

Table 2.4 (continued)

7-point	6-point	5-point	4-point	3-point	2-point
(e) *QUALITY*					
Outstanding	Outstanding	Very good	Very good	Good	Good
Very good	Very good	Good	Good	Fair	Bad
Above average	Above average	Barely acceptable	Poor	Poor	
Average	Average	Poor	Very poor		Acceptable
Below average	Below average	Very poor			Unacceptable
Poor	Very poor				
Very poor					
Excellent	Excellent	Excellent	Excellent		
Very good	Good	Above average	Good		
Above Average	Above average	Average	Poor		
Average	Average	Below average	Extremely poor		
Below average	Below average	Extremely poor			
Poor	Very poor				
Very poor					
(f) *SATISFACTION*					
Completely satisfied	Completely satisfied	Very satisfied	Very satisfied	Completely satisfied	Satisfied
Mostly Satisfied	Mostly Satisfied	Satisfied, Neither satisfied nor dissatisfied	Satisfied	Somewhat satisfied	Dissatisfied
Moderately satisfied	Moderately satisfied	dissatisfied	Dissatisfied	Dissatisfied	
Neither satisfied nor dissatisfied	Moderately dissatisfied	Very dissatisfied	Very dissatisfied		
Moderately dissatisfied	Mostly Dissatisfied Completely dissatisfied				
Mostly Dissatisfied Completely dissatisfied					

Likert used the *criterion of internal consistency* to select the final set of items. Theoretically, this criterion specifies that people with higher overall attitude scores should tend to agree with favorable or positive items and disagree with unfavorable or negative items. Figure 2.4, adapted from Fishbein and Ajzen (1975), depicts trace lines for two items meeting the criterion of internal consistency. Consider a 10-item attitude scale that employs a 5-point agreement (agree–disagree) response format. The horizontal axis plots the possible range of scores, which in this case is 10–50. The vertical axis plots the probability of endorsing the item or the proportion of people agreeing with the item at various total score intervals. The first traceline in Fig. 2.4 is for a favorable item. Notice that the higher the total score is, the greater the proportion of people who agree with the favorable item. The steeper the slope of this line, the more discriminating the item is. In other words, if the traceline for an item is steep and positive, the total score strongly predicts agreement to a given item. People with high total scores are far more likely to endorse the item than people with low total scores. On the other hand, if the traceline in Fig. 2.4 were flat, that would indicate that the proportion of people who agree with the item is equal across all ranges of the total score. If this were the case, then the item is not related to the total score; therefore, it does not help us to discriminate between high and low scorers on the scale. The tracelines visually depict the correlation of the item score with the total attitude score. Contrary to the Thurstone technique, the trace lines for the favorable and unfavorable items are linear, and the correlation between item endorsement and the attitude score is the criterion used for item selection. Generally speaking, we retain

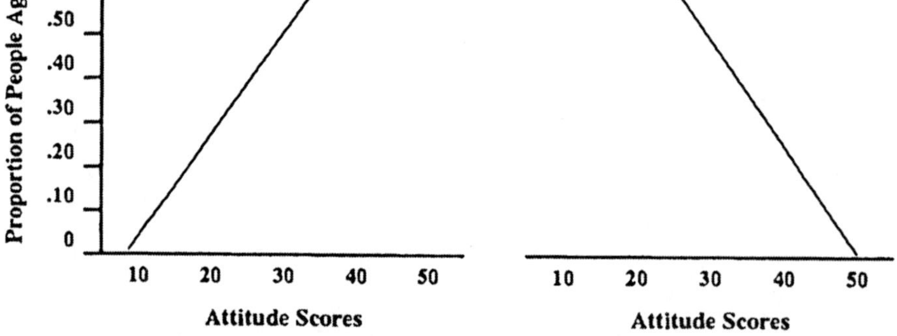

Fig. 2.4 Hypothetical tracelines for two Likert items with internal consistency, adapted from Fishbein and Ajzen (1975)

items that have high item-total correlations, and we eliminate items that have near zero item-total correlations.

The response format for the items should be consistent with the intent of the instrument and must match the content and wording of the items. Several different formats are available; pay careful attention to select the response scale format that matches the item stems. For example, do you want to know if respondents *agree* with the items, or how *frequently* they have experienced the event described by the item? The most common Likert response scales measure agreement (agree–disagree), frequency (always–never), likelihood (unlikely–likely), satisfaction (satisfied–unsatisfied), or quality (good–bad). Tables 2.4a through 2.4e present several popular response formats for the following intensity areas: agreement, frequency, importance, quality, and likelihood. This is in no way an exhaustive list; it is merely a compilation of some of the more popular response formats.

When developing a novel or less popular response format, it is a good idea to conduct a pilot study to validate the ordered nature of the response options. Given that the scaling of people involves assigning ordered numbers to the options, the rank order of the options must be correct. In addition, ideally, the intervals between the options (i.e., steps) should be approximately equal. If there are concerns about the response scale, have a group of about 15 judges independently rank the response options and discuss the intervals between the response options. This group can also provide guidance about the number of scale points that you should use. For example, can they make distinctions between all 7, 9, or 11 of the response scale points that you have generated? Do they think that members of the target population will be able to make distinction between the scale points? Confusion about the response scale can sabotage the entire instrument development and validation process. Poorly conceived response scales compromise the later psychometric assessments of reliability of the data and validity of the inferences from the instrument; therefore, the decision about the response scale is critical.

The Semantic Differential Scale

The semantic differential is a technique that scales people on a set of items called *scales* anchored or bounded on each end with bipolar adjectives.[4] The rated target is called a *concept* and appears at the top of the set of scales. To illustrate, in a study of guidance counselors (Pappalardo 1971) personality traits were assessed by means of the following 7-point evaluative semantic differential scales.

The development of the semantic differential technique is credited to Charles Osgood (1952) and is detailed in the book entitled *The Measurement of Meaning*

---

[4] Up to this point, scale has been used to represent a cluster of items on a particular instrument. For the Semantic Differential technique, Osgood uses the term scale to represent a single item.

(Osgood et al. 1957). Osgood's research focused on the scientific study of language and the meaning of words. Much of our communication takes place through adjectives. For example, teachers are often described in terms of "good" or "bad," "fair" or "unfair," "hard" or "easy," and "effective" or "ineffective". Theoretically, the semantic differential scales bounded by these bipolar adjectives can be represented as a straight-line or geometric *semantic space.* The scales pass through the origin of the semantic space and form a multidimensional geometric space. When individuals rate a concept on a scale, they are effectively differentiating the meaning of the concept. That is, they are expressing the *intensity* and *direction* of affect they feel is associated with the bipolar adjective scale in relation to the targeted concept.

In Osgood et al. (1957) original work 20 different concepts (i.e., target objects) were rated (i.e., differentiated) by 100 people using 50 sets of bipolar adjectives. After collapsing the data across people and concepts, a 50 × 50 matrix of intercorrelations of scales was generated so that a factor analysis could be performed. The purpose of this analysis was to identify the minimum number of orthogonal dimensions necessary to provide a parsimonious description of the relationships among the scales. In other words, the aim was to explore the common meanings of the adjectives across the 20 different concepts (i.e., the measurement of meaning). As a result of these studies, Osgood identified several dimensions of the semantic space. Three consistently identified dimensions were: evaluative, potency, and activity. Examples of the bipolar adjective pairs defining the dimensions are listed in Table 2.5.

Since Osgood's early work in 1957, several researchers have used the semantic differential technique to scale people with respect to affective characteristics. In the fields of psychology and education, most researchers have concentrated on the evaluative dimension as a measure of attitude toward the stated concept. Interested readers are referred to an excellent early volume by Snider and Osgood (1969),

Table 2.5 Typical sematic differential bipolar adjective pairs

Evaluative	Potency	Activity
Good–bad	Large–small	Fast–slow
Beautiful–ugly	Strong–weak	Active–passive
Pleasant–unpleasant	Rugged–delicate	Excitable–calm
Positive–negative	Heavy–light	Busy–lazy
Sweet–sour	Thick–thin	Quick–slow
Valuable–worthless		Hot–cold
Good–bad		
Beautiful–ugly		
Pleasant–unpleasant		
Positive–negative		
Sweet–sour		
Valuable–worthless		
Fair–unfair		

which contains discussions of the theory and development, as well as illustrations of several applications of semantic differentials.

A semantic differential measure typically consists of anywhere between 4 and 10 response scale points. Most often the scales have 7-points for the respondents' ratings. The endpoints denote adjectives with bipolar meaning for evaluation.

In developing a semantic differential, the first step is to identify the concept or target object you want to measure and then review of all possible bipolar adjective pairs that could be used to capture the concept. Osgood et al. (1957) lists the 50 pairs from Osgood's original work (p. 43), as well as several adjective pairs identified through a series of factor analyses carried out in the context of a thesaurus study (pp. 51–61). Additional sources of scales are included Snider and Osgood's book entitled *Semantic Differential Technique* (1969). Next, select appropriate bipolar adjective pairs for differentiating the targeted attitude, self-concept, or value concept. In most applications, the adjectives represent the evaluative dimension.[5] Within the evaluative dimension there may be several sub-dimensions or factors defined by clusters of adjectives. The next step is to select about 10 adjectives that seem logically interrelated. Measuring another evaluative dimension for the same concept would necessitate using another set of about 10 logically interrelated adjectives. The result would be one concept to be rated on 20 bipolar adjective pairs or scales. These scales are then mounted on a single sheet of paper below the concept to be rated. For college students, Osgood suggests the use of a 7-step scale, whereas a 5-step scale may be more appropriate for elementary students (Osgood et al. 1957, p. 85). A set of clear instructions, including examples, is then written and the pilot form of the instrument is completed.

After the semantic differential has been constructed, it is necessary to pilot the form on a representative sample of about 6–10 times the number of people as scales used. The pilot group should be very similar to the group for which the future research is targeted. Clear instructions and clear understanding of the process are necessary to achieve data of good quality.

Given the pilot data, the next step is to conduct a factor analysis as well as item and reliability analyses. The factor analysis will identify the dimensions measured within the set of scales. The item analysis and reliability analyses will further assist in determining which items (i.e., semantic differential scales) best relate to the identified dimensions as well as the alpha reliability of the data from the dimensions. If only a few scales (items) are included and they are not homogeneous in meaning, the resulting factor structure may produce factors defined by too few scales to generate adequate reliability levels. It is important to carefully construct the set of bipolar adjective scales so that the clusters of homogeneous scales result in the desired dimensions in the factor analysis and adequate internal-consistency reliabilities (i.e., Cronbach's alpha reliability).

[5] Some researchers do include a few scales from the potency or activity dimensions to see where these scales load in a factor analysis of the total set of scales. In this situation, the potency and activity scales function as marker scales to facilitate interpretation of the main factor structure.

The semantic-differential technique employs the same *criterion of internal consistency* as the Likert technique for scale selection. To meet the criterion, a scale (i.e., item) must correlate well with the total attitude score. The resulting item characteristic curves or trace lines are linear in nature as illustrated by the Likert technique trace lines presented earlier in Fig. 2.4.

The scoring of semantic differential scales has generated much confusion and resulted in misuse and misinterpretation. Lynch (1973) suggested the following three methods for scoring semantic differentials: by computing mean scores on each scale, by computing mean scores on each dimension, or by computing the *D* statistic. Computing mean scores on each scale may seem intuitive; however, the scales were selected on the basis of their relationship to some larger dimension of meaning. Therefore, interpreting the scales individually ignores the multidimensional nature of the set of adjective pairs as perceived by the respondent. A far better approach is to score the scales in a summative manner by creating means on each dimension identified through the factor analysis.

The final technique involves a form of profile similarity, through the use of the generalized distance formula known as the *D* statistic. Osgood et al. (1957) suggested that this statistic is a multidimensional measure for quantifying similarity in meaning because it allows us to combine ratings across scales and dimensions to form an index of connotative judgment. The formula can be represented as

$$D^2 = \sum_{i=1}^{n} d_i^2$$

where D is the distance between the profile of the two concepts, d_i^2 represents the squared difference in the ratings of the two concepts on the ith bipolar adjective scale. The summation indicates that these squared differences are summed across the number of scales, n, used to rate the two different concepts. Simply, this index represents the sum of the squared distances between two concept profiles and can be readily used as a dependent variable representing profile similarity (i.e., small values mean close profiles). The semantic differential technique continues to be used in studies of attitudes. For example, Conner et al. (2002) assessed attitudes toward eating a healthy diet using 7-point evaluative, bipolar semantic-differential scales: *bad–good*, *harmful–beneficial*, *pleasant–unpleasant*, *unenjoyable–enjoyable*, *wise–foolish*, and *unnecessary–necessary*. The data for these six bipolar adjective scales had an internal-consistency coefficient alpha of 0.84, and an overall attitude score was computed by summing responses to the six scales. In summary, the semantic differential has the potential for being a very valuable technique for scaling people on the evaluative dimension of meaning because the ratings provide a generalized index of attitudes toward selected concept targets. However, instrument developers must select the scales and must be careful to represent the desired evaluative dimensions and use a sensible technique to score the resulting data.

Rasch Model

Rasch models represent a philosophical departure from the scaling approaches described up to this point. Instrument designers that employ Rasch models and scaling techniques are often primarily concerned with the notion of fundamental measurement (Bond and Fox 2007; Wright 1997). "The aim is to provide social scientists with the means to produce genuine interval measures and to monitor the adherence of those scales to scientific measurement principals, so that Rasch estimates of ability, attitude/difficulty become the data for statistical analysis" (Bond and Fox 2007, p. 5).

Rasch models represent a particular solution to the fundamental measurement problem because it is a model-driven scaling approach. In the Rasch model, the probability of a specified response is modeled as a function of person and item parameters. The function, in this approach, is specifically a logistic function of the difference between the "person" parameter and the "item" parameter. In an affective instrument, the parameters in a Rasch model are quantities that represent the level of the characteristic possessed by a person and the level of the characteristic of the item. If a person possesses high level of the characteristic relative to the level of the characteristic measured by the item, then the probability of endorsing the item or responding positively is increased for that item. When a person's location on the latent trait is equal to the level of the item, there is a 0.5 probability of endorsing the item in the Rasch model.

A key feature of Rasch models that makes it different from other scaling approaches is the idea of parameter separation for the "person" and "item" estimates. Parameter separation suggests that parameters for the person level and the item level can be estimated independently of each other. Mathematically, this is accomplished through a procedure known as Conditional Maximum Likelihood estimation. The result of this independent estimation is what psychometricians refer to as "person free measures" and "item free calibrations" (Bond and Fox 2007). This characteristic makes Rasch models unique in their scaling, and it allows users to compare persons and items directly without reference to each other.

For researchers in the domain of affective characteristics, Rasch models can be applied to dichotomous data (i.e., yes/no, agree/disagree), or what is known polytomous data (i.e., Likert scales). What separates adherents to the Rasch model is their commitment to the notion that a logistic function represents the mathematical structure the data must exhibit in order to obtain key parameter measurements from the data. For dichotomous data, the essential parameters are the level of the trait in the individual (B_n) and the difficulty of the item (D_i). The probability of possessing the trait and thus agreeing with the item can be expressed by the equation:

$$P_{ni}(x_{ni} = 1|B_n, D_i) = \frac{e^{(B_n - D_n)}}{1 + e^{(B_n - D_i)}}$$

The dichotomous model can be extended to treat the type of polytomous data that are associated Likert response formats. One Rasch model typically associated with Likert data is the Rating Scale model (RSM). This model has one extra feature over the dichotomous model. In addition to providing person estimates and a threshold estimate for each item, it also provides one set of rating scale thresholds that is common for each item (Andersen 1977; Andrich 1978a, b, c). This suggests that there is a strong conceptual connection between dichotomous and polytomous items in affective instruments that is captured in Rasch models. In a simple agree/ disagree dichotomous item, there is a single threshold that separates agreement from disagreement. In a 5-point, polytomous Likert scale, for example, there are four threshold estimates that separate the five choices (Table 2.6).

The strong assumptions of the Rasch model, however, posit that a single set of threshold values must apply across all the item stems in the scale. In the polytomous model case, each item threshold has its own difficulty estimate (F_n) and represents the 0.5 probability of choosing the disagree response instead of the strongly disagree response.

$$P_{ni1}(x = 1|B_n, D_i, F_1) = \frac{e^{(B_n - D_i - F_1)}}{1 + e^{(B_n - D_i - F_1)}}$$

This approach is different from traditional statistical modeling techniques. Many times, models are chosen based on how well they describe the given data set. As a result, parameters are modified, accepted, or rejected based on their fit of the data. When the Rasch model is applied, researchers aim to identify data that fit the model (Andrich 2004; Wright 1984, 1999). Rasch model proponents refer to this as a fundamental requirement of measurement, and they draw parallels between fundamental measurement in the social sciences and the concept of measurement in the physical sciences. If the data do not fit the model, the measurement provided by the instrument was unsuccessful. Fortunately, for proponents of the Rasch model, many psychological measurements in both the cognitive and affective domains fit the Rasch model. Rasch models have a long history in the area of cognitive and educational test development (Bond and Fox 2007). They are gaining increasing popularity in the area of affective measurement, particularly due to advances in

Table 2.6 5-point agreement scale and 4 thresholds

STRONGLY AGREE
(4th Threshold estimate)
AGREE
(3rd Threshold estimate
NEUTRAL
(2nd Threshold estimate)
DISAGREE
(1st Threshold Estimate)
STRONGLY DISAGREE

computer adaptive testing (CAT). Instrument designers should also be aware that, mathematically, Rasch models are part of a larger set of subset of models described by item response theory (IRT). However, the philosophical insistence of Rasch model proponents on the rigid fit of the data to the limited set of parameters described above, distinguishes Rasch modeling from the rest of the IRT family.

Rasch modeling is often an effective approach for the measurement of affective characteristics. The *Student Feedback about Teaching* (*SFT*) is a Rasch-based Likert response format instrument used in the Australian university system for high-stakes decisions regarding faculty tenure and promotion (Bond 2004). Another instrument, the *Physicians Perceptions Survey* (*PPS*) was developed to test theories of physician perceptions of patient autonomy (Frantom 2001). In both cases, the survey developers employed the Rasch model to assemble "banks" of items that were interchanged across multiple versions of the instrument. It is common for researchers to construct many more items than are necessary for a given survey in the hope that they can develop several equivalent instruments for use over their target population. Survey designers can only do this if the items are determined to be parallel and invariant across subgroups—an explicit feature of instruments that meet Rasch model specifications. Knowledge of the difficulty parameter of each item enables researchers to exchange items (or subsets of items) that measure comparable levels of the affected trait of interest and ensure that every instrument adequately spans the continuum of the domain in the same way.

Instrument developers further capitalize on this invariance property of Rasch scaled items when they administer their surveys in computer adaptive settings (Chae et al. 2000). In Rasch-based CAT, the computer stores and administers items from a relatively large item bank that was developed for a given affective characteristic. A respondent begins the CAT with an initial estimate of the given trait level, which is often times the same for everyone (although it does not have to be if additional information is available to the researcher). The CAT selects items for each respondent based on the scored responses to all previous items. At the initial stages of a CAT, when only a single item or two have been administered, the next item is usually selected by a "step" rule—if the first item was answered correctly, the examinee's original prior $\widehat{\theta}$ is increased by some predetermined amount. If the first item was answered incorrectly, the original estimate of a person's trait level is decreased by the same amount. As the test proceeds and the respondent creates a response pattern of at least one correct and one incorrect response, maximum likelihood estimation (MLE) is used to obtain a new trait level estimate. After each item is administered and scored, the new trait level is used to select the next item. One important characteristic of Rasch-based CAT that separates it from all the previous scaling approaches is that the test termination criterion can be varied for different instrument objectives. Traditionally, CAT tests have been used for selection or classification of individuals. In affective applications, the objective of the instrument may simply be to measure each individual as early as possible. In the context of CAT, these two objectives are operationalized by two different termination rules. For example, in the classification context, an individual's score is compared against some cutoff value. The objective is to make a classification that is as accurate as possible—for example, to classify examinees as "passing" or "failing" for an achievement domain with no more than a strict error rate. When CATs are not used for classification, a different termination rule applies. In this case, the goal is to measure a respondent to a desired level of precision. Instrument designers in this case want scores that are equally accurate across respondents. To accomplish this with Rasch-based CAT applications, researchers can predetermine a standard error of measurement.

Computerized adaptive testing has many benefits for researchers working in the affective domain, but the large number of items and participants needed to create and calibrate the item banks necessary for its implementation are often beyond the scale of most social scientists (Jones and Dages 2003; Meijer and Nering 1999). Even researchers with the means to develop extremely large item pools and gather the requisite number of participants for Rasch-based CAT may not find the investment of time and resources necessary for their larger research goals. There is the possibility that the increasing popularity of CATs for cognitive and achievement testing will likely inspire commercial publishers for development of CATs for applications in the affective domain, making it a more viable option for researchers in the future (Rothstein and Goffin 2006).

Issues to Consider When Developing Multi-Item Measures

Item Wording

One of the most common ways that instrument designers undermine the advantages of closed-form questions is by constructing statements with ambiguous or complex wording in the statement stem. Overly lengthy item stems are generally problematic. Respondents are more likely to misread or misinterpret longer item stems, and longer stems are more likely to contain multidimensional content.

The use of the double-barreled questions/items stems creates ambiguity and confuses respondents. An example of a double barreled item stem is "I do well in classes when I enjoy the content or see the value of what we're learning." Most times, researchers can avoid double-barreled questions by minimizing the use of "and" and "or" in the stem. However, researchers should be aware, that items can present the characteristics of double-barreled questions without using "and" or "or." For example, "We should make our town safer by limiting the amount of low income housing" is also a double-barreled item stem. The instrument designer is introducing two separate issues for consideration by the respondent: the idea of making the town safer and the idea of limiting low-income housing. Some respondents could respond negatively because they do not see the need to make the town safer or because they do not support limiting low-income housing. Double-barreled questions, like the ones in the examples, are implicitly asking more than one question at a time; therefore, respondents are often at a loss for how to answer the item using the response scale provided. The interpretation of the responses to double-barreled item stems is virtually impossible. If a respondent agrees with the item, does that mean that she agreed with one or both portions of the item stem? If the respondent disagrees with the item, does that mean that she disagreed with one or both portions of the item stem? If the respondent provides a neutral response such as "neither agree nor disagree," does that mean that she was truly neutral about all of the content in the question, or did she agree with one portion of the item stem and disagree with the other portion? Given that the researcher cannot determine whether the participant's response addresses the first, second, or both propositions, such questions produce inconsistent and uninterpretable data (Fabrigar et al. 2005; Weisberg et al. 1996).

Instrument designers can also introduce unnecessary complexity by using the word "because" in the item stem. For example, the question "I like school because the cafeteria serves my favorite food" presents two pieces of information for respondents to consider. For a participant to agree, they must agree with both "liking school" and the favorable food situation in the cafeteria. If the respondent only agrees with half of the statement, the participant's response becomes unpredictable and thus unreliable. In general, item stems should avoid using words such as "because." Closed-ended item stems can be quite effective in assessing the degree or level of an affective characteristic. However, they are not particularly effective for determining the reasons why a person feels the way that he does. To obtain answers to "why" questions, survey type items where a respondent can check all applicable responses and open-ended qualitative responses are generally more effective than closed-ended Likert scaled item stems.

Ambiguous items are not always easy to detect because, unlike double-barreled questions, they do not typically present a pattern in their sentence structure. A classic example of an ambiguous item comes from a survey administered by the University of Michigan's Center for Political Studies. One question asked respondents, "How many public officials do you think are a little bit dishonest—most, some, a few, or none?" Weisberg et al. (1996) noted that researchers were surprised to discover that many cynical people were actually answering "none" because they believed that "most public officials are very dishonest and that none are only a little bit dishonest!" (p. 85). Clearly, the ambiguity in the question obscured the interpretation of the survey results.

Multidimensional Items

Designers risk developing problematic items when the item stems they construct tap into more than one dimension. For example, the question, "I get good grades in school," taps into at least two distinct potential constructs: self-concept and motivation. Is the participant's "self-concept" or "motivation" causing the observed response? In reality, it is likely that a combination of the two latent constructs is responsible for the observed response. Therefore, the item is not a clean indicator of either construct. Instead, it is a "muddy" indicator of both constructs. The researcher may have a theory about the exact underlying construct reflecting the item, but the relationship is not clear enough to justify a connection. The proximity of the researcher to the theoretical framework supporting the instrument often makes this type of item multidimensionality difficult to detect. Instrument developers can work to minimize this type of wording problem by presenting potential items to content experts for evaluation.

Acquiescence Bias

Direct, structured measures can also introduce more subtle problems beyond simple wording difficulties. These measures can introduce bias very time the designer makes a word, format, or order choice in the instrument. Acquiescence bias is the "tendency for respondents to agree with attitude statements presented to them" (Schuman and Presser 1996, p. 203). A researcher can introduce *acquiescence bias* into an instrument when he or she constructs questions that promote respondents to agree with a statement regardless of the content (Schuman and Presser 1996; Watson 1992). In a study of this problem, Steenkamp and Baumgartner (1995) demonstrated that in an instrument called the "Change Seeker Index," people's optimum stimulation level can be measured by both the positively worded item "I like to experience novelty and change in my daily routine" and the negatively worded item "I prefer a routine way of life to an unpredictable one full of change." They observed that roughly equal scores on these items indicated that the content of items were being somewhat ignored, allowing the pair to function as an indicator of acquiescent responding. In other cases, respondents may simply agree with a question in order to satisfy the perceived needs of the researcher (Schuman and Presser 1996). Krosnick (1991) also observed that respondents may also exhibit a survey fatigue or apathy that prompts them to simply agree with the item stem.

Persuasive Argument Bias and Nonattention Bias

Another related set of biases common to self-report measures are the *persuasive argument bias* (Fabrigar et al. 2005) and the *nonattention bias* (Barnette 2000; Cronbach 1950). In the persuasive argument bias, the argument articulated in the question works to persuade the respondents in an artificially positive direction. The following question from a Michigan SRC/CPS election study is a good example of this type of bias. The question asks, "Some people feel that the government in Washington should see to it that every person has a job and a good standard of living. Do you have an opinion on this or not?" (Bishop et al. 1982). The authors found that the structure of the question tended to influence responses rather than measure them, thus making this it is biased and problematic question.

Nonattention bias is slightly different from persuasive argument bias in that participants exhibiting this effect tend to use their general feeling toward to subject to govern their response rather than the specific content of the question.[6] This bias is most often observed when groups respond to instruments in close physical proximity or the respondents are highly unmotivated to engage with the instrument. The two cases, while slightly different, do share the important quality that respondents with either of these biases are relying on something other than the item content to generate their responses.

Historically, researchers have tried to combat these effects by recommending the introduction of negatively worded items along with positively worded items in affective instruments (Anastasi 1982; Cronbach 1950; Mehrens and Lehmann 1983; Nunnally and Bernstein 1994; Rossi et al. 1983). However, more recent research cautions against the use of mixed item stems. Although including both positive item stems and negative item stems can potentially mitigate persuasive argument bias and nonattention bias, it routinely introduces psychometric problems for the instrument designer, especially in terms of internal consistency and factor structures (Barnette 1996, 2000; Benson and Hocevar 1985; Eys et al. 2007; Melnick and Gable 1990; Pilotte 1991; Pilotte and Gable 1990; Schriesheim et al. 1991; Wright and Masters 1982). Often, when both positively and negatively worded items are included on the same scale, negatively worded items either break into a separate methodologically based factor (Carleton et al. 2006; DiStefano and Motl 2006; Rodebaugh et al. 2004), or result in a level of multidimensional responding that requires the estimation of a separate negative method factor or correlated errors among negative items (Bollen and Lennox 1991). For example, Kelloway et al. (2002) examined the construct validity of self-reported counterproductive work behaviors (CPBs) and organizational citizenship behaviors (OCBs). Three scales were explored: (1) CPB with only negative items, (2) OCB with only positive items, and (3) the supervision subscale of the Job Descriptive Index (JDI) with both negatively and positively worded items. The results revealed that a four-factor model, specifying three substantive factors (CPBs, OCBs, and supervision satisfaction) and a method factor, produced a significantly better fit and more parsimonious fit to the data than either the one factor, two factor, or three factor models.

The problem can be compounded for children and members of at-risk target groups that are asked to respond to affective instruments. For example, Marsh (1986) observed that the use of negatively worded items (e.g., "I am not smart at mathematics" vs. "I am smart at mathematics") proved to be particularly problematic for younger children and children with poorer reading skills. Since 1990s,

---

[6] Barnette (1999) found that a 5% pattern of nonattention responses can have strong effects on coefficient alpha (usually in the positive direction). This can lead instrument designers to conclude that the data are more internally consistency than they actually are.

the psychometric research has consistently advised against the use of "polar opposite" and "negated polar opposite" items in affective instruments (Chambers and Johnston 2002). Barnette (2000) suggests that if researchers have deep concerns about persuasive argument and nonattention bias in their target group, it is far better to consider reversing the response format order rather than to intersperse negatively worded item stems. This strategy does keep the all the item stems direct and positive; however, it may confuse some respondents. In general, using positively worded items appears to result in more reliable scores and produces cleaner factor structures (Roszkowski and Soven 2010).

Our discussion so far has focused mainly on important psychometric issues associated with mixed item stems. Researchers should be aware that there are theoretical reasons for the problems associated with such mixed items. The psychometric problems resulting from the negation of item stems can best be understood through Pilotte's (1991) discussion of schema theory and linguistics. In reviewing the schema theory research, Pilotte (1991) found that information is processed by matching concepts to prototypes or exemplars of existing knowledge that guide our interpretation and inferences we make from incoming sensory stimuli. The problem develops when we ask respondents (especially young people or poor readers) to process statements in which the exemplars have been implicitly or explicitly negated because we live in the world of "things" rather than "not things" (Pilotte 1991, pp. 2, 6–7). Thus, for both psychometric and theoretical reasons we recommend that instrument developers do not use sets of items written in both positive and negative directions.

Number of Scale Points and Bias

Choosing the number of scale points to use for the response scale is a crucial decision. Oftentimes, instrument developers default to using a 4- or 5-point response scale, without seriously considering the analytic and interpretational ramifications of providing too few scale points. Rating scales with a small number of scale points are less sensitive and less reliable than scales with a larger number of scale points, assuming that respondents can use the larger number of scale points thoughtfully and reliably. Therefore, it is important to give serious consideration to how many scale points the target audience can effectively utilize, and try to provide the maximum number of scale points that are differentiable, given the nature of the construct and the nature of the audience. Bandura (2006) provides concrete advice for those developing self-efficacy scales, and the advice generalizes to the entire affective domain:

> Scales that use only a few scale points should be avoided because they are less sensitive and less reliable. People usually avoid the extreme positions so a scale with only a few steps, may in actual use, shrink to one or two points. Including too few points loses differentiating information because people who use the same category may differ if intermediate steps were included (Bandura 2006, p. 312).

Providing an insufficient list of response choice alternatives in the structured measure can result in *number of scale points bias*. An obvious case of this bias occurs when participants are asked to respond to an item only to discover that the point that best reflects their degree of favorableness is not represented. For example, if respondents are asked to simply either "agree" or "disagree" when in fact that may be "neutral" on the item, they must either (1) choose a response alternative that does not represent their views, or (2) not choose a response alternative, which results in missing data. A more subtle example of number of scale points bias occurs when the points the scale do not contain adequate differentiation. For example, a response format that contains "*seldom*" and "*rarely*" may confuse respondents because *seldom* and *rarely* are virtually synonymous.

The number of scale points matters to respondents. When respondents engage with an item, they are attempting to map the conceptual meaning of their affective characteristic to the scale point it most closely resembles (Ostrom and Gannon 1996). Therefore, the most effective affective instruments have scale points that cover the entire measurement continuum. The meaning of adjacent points should not overlap, nor should there be large gaps between the scale points. In addition, the distance between the response choices should appear to be roughly equally spaced (Aaker et al. 2004, p. 285; Burns and Bush 2000, p. 314; Dillon et al. 1993, p. 276; Hair et al. 2006, pp. 365–366). For instance, compare the following two 6-point frequency scales (Table 2.7).

The first scale spans the entire frequency range from never to always and contains scale points that are differentiated and that "feel" roughly equally spaced. In contrast, the second scale does not span the entire frequency continuum—people who have no option to choose "always" or "never." In addition, the spacing between the scale points does not "feel" equal at all. Instead, rarely and seldom are very similar response choices and often and frequently are very similar response choices. Therefore, those options feel as if they would be close to each other. Furthermore, the gap between seldom and often feels very large. In fact, the gap is so large that it feels as if a necessary scale point (such as "sometimes") is missing. Thus, the first scale meets our criteria of having differentiated scale points that span the intensity continuum and feel roughly equally spaced while the second response scale does not. By spanning the domain of agreement options in the response format, researchers can improve the likelihood that participant responses reflect their true level on the affective characteristic.

The recommendation that the response scale should have differentiated scale points that span the intensity continuum and feel roughly equally spaced is especially crucial when responses are treated as interval level data, which is the case with most traditional forms of analysis. This can be a challenge for instrument designers, and research suggests that the evaluative distances between response

Table 2.7 Comparison of two 6-point Frequency Scales

Never	Rarely	Sometimes	Frequently	Almost always	Always
Almost never	Rarely	Seldom	Often	Frequently	Almost always

points are not always equal (Bendixen and Sandler 1994; Kennedy et al. 1996). With good design, however, the relationship between the idealized and empirical response scale can be very close, which supports the treatment of these scales as equal interval (Kennedy et al. 1996).

The points should also have precise and stable meanings that find agreement among most respondents (Krosnick and Presser 2010). Implied in this last recommendation is the idea that all the scale points should be labeled. Research suggests that respondents have trouble with numerical response scales and rely heavily on verbal cues associated with points to assign meaning to them (Tourangeau et al. 2007). This observation has led researchers to recommend that every scale point receive a label to best help respondents to locate themselves on the response continuum (Krosnick and Fabrigar 1997).[7]

However, instrument developers should not assume that their descriptive choices for each point in the response scale share universal meaning for survey participants. Hardy and Ford (2012) observed that respondents often misapprehend the meaning of words in surveys. Respondents may also attribute different meaning words within the response scales or the item stems. Often the most commonplace words like "many" or "sometimes" cause survey participants the most trouble because they lack specificity. Therefore, when confronted with words that have multiple interpretations, respondents will interpret them in multiple ways. The best approach would be to avoid these words, but given the rich tradition of their use in affective instruments, this not the most easily adopted fix. Potential solutions could include utilizing methodologies such as the Q-sort (Schriesheim et al. 1993) to help measure the differences between individual judges, Anderson and Gerbing's (1991) methods for substantive validity analysis, or cognitive interviewing (Beatty and Willis 2007). None of the solutions offered provide a definitive solution to the problem of lexical misapprehension. As a result, instrument developers are encouraged to explore the approach most suitable for their own research design needs.

Up to this point, most of the discussion of rating scale point bias has centered on the effects of having too few scale points. Bias can also occur with over differentiation of the scale. Research suggests that respondents engage in a complex cognitive process when they attempt to evaluate their affective characteristics through a given item (Strack et al. 1985; Tourangeau and Rasinski 1988). The motivation to perform the cognitive tasks required by the item as designed is what is known as optimizing (Krosnick and Presser 2010). Unfortunately for many

---

[7] This advice is not necessarily consistent when considering items across instruments. Work by Chang (1997), for example, suggests that as long as the number of scale points used in the instrument is consistent, changing the labeling of the anchors in the scale from say 1 = disagree, 2 = somewhat disagree, 3 = somewhat agree, 4 = agree to 1 = strongly disagree, 2 = disagree, 3 = agree, 4 = strongly agree, does not add to the observed variance. One potential implication is that instrument developers need not be "overly concerned" with the practice of using different labels to anchor the Likert response scale for items in different instruments. Still, pilot studies of different formats are always good insurance during the process of instrument development.

instrument designers, the optimization process can be short circuited by what Krosnick (1991) and Simon (1957) call *satisfising*. In this process, Krosnick suggests that respondents "settle for merely satisfactory answers" (Krosnick and Presser 2010, p. 265). Preston and Colman (2000) found that respondents "preferred" instruments with 7-, 9-, and 10-points because they allowed them to express their "feelings adequately" and were also relatively easy to use (p. 12). In their study, respondents indicated that scales with 101-scale points also allowed them to express their feelings; however, the respondents gave the 101-point scales the lowest marks for speed and ease of use. Very large numbers of response options may hinder respondents' ability to interpret and map the scale points.[8]

The issue of satisfising is also a consideration when choosing between offering an odd or even number of scale points. Historically, researchers have expressed concern that respondents with low cognitive skills or low attitude strength are attracted to "middle alternatives"—a form of satisfising; however, little evidence supports these claims (McCoach and Adelson 2010; Kalton et al. 1980; Krosnick 1991; Narayan and Krosnick 1996; Shuman and Presser 1981). O'Muircheartaigh et al. (1999) found that the addition of middle alternatives actually improved the validity and reliability of the ratings. Despite the validity and reliability advantages, however, instrument developers must carefully consider the meaning of the midpoint in the context of the item stem, and they must choose the verbal label for the midpoint response choice very carefully. Generally, it is relatively easy for participants to attribute clear meanings to the "strongly agree" and "strongly disagree" options in the response format. The meaning and appropriate scoring of the "undecided" or "neutral" response categories can be, however, far less obvious. The center point of the response scale could indicate ambivalence (i.e., mixed attitudes toward the target object), indifference (i.e., little concern for the target object), true neutrality, lack of understanding of the item, lack of knowledge (i.e., "Don't Know"), or a form of refusing to answer.

The choice of wording for the midpoint is essential. "Undecided," "Neutral," "Don't Know," and "Neither Agree nor Disagree" have different connotations and cannot be used interchangeably. For example, the "Undecided" category has different characteristics from "Don't Know" category (Harter 1997). Using "Don't Know" for an affective instrument is particularly problematic. "Don't Know" implies that the respondent lacks the knowledge to offer a response. Items on affective instruments measure feelings, not knowledge. When researchers ask questions about affective phenomena, they presume that the respondent is either drawing from previously formed opinions, or that they are drawing on relevant attitudes that allow them to for new, but reasonable evaluations (Zaller and Feldman 1992). Thus, items on affective instruments should be written in such a way that all members of the target population can offer a response. Krosnick (1999)

[8] It should also be noted that extremely long or complex item stems, which we discussed earlier in the chapter, can overburden the cognitive optimizing processes of respondents, causing them to engage in satisfying behavior.

cautions instrument developers not to encourage respondents to supply answers simply to protect themselves from looking uninformed by offering opinions on obscure or fictitious objects.

There is simply no definitive answer to the question of whether to use a mid-point in the response scale. If designers are concerned that respondents may not be responding to the middle category to represent a neutral or mid-range attitude, they are advised to follow the technique described by DuBois and Burns (1975) to examine this issue. The procedure involves plotting respondents' mean scale scores (vertical axis) for each separate response category (horizontal axis; SD, D, U, A, SA) for each of the items. If the middle category is a true neutral response, the plot of means should be in a relatively straight line (upper left to lower right), and the standard deviation (dispersion) of the scores around the means at each response category should be similar. Some researchers may wish to examine this issue empirically during the pilot stages of a new instrument; this could certainly help make an informed decision about how the mid-point is functioning for a particular set of items.

Domain Sampling

Just as the response scale should span the entire continuum of agreement, the collection of items should represent the entire domain of affective characteristic of interest. The measurement of affective constructs must span the domain of content for the affective characteristic and capture the degree to which individuals differ on the trait. As a result, instruments used for measuring differentiation require the construction of a set of items that represents the "expected degree of variation" on the construct (Crocker and Algina 2006, p. 69). In addition to issues of variability, domain sampling also has consequences for the measurement error in the model. When researchers design instruments, they assume that their measures are composed of responses to a representative sample of items from their hypothesized domain of items. The measure is designed to estimate the measurement of the construct we would have been obtained had we administered every item in the domain to the participant (Nunnally and Bernstein 1994). Obviously, it is impossible to administer every item in a content domain; however, that does not imply that the estimation of a respondent's true score is impossible. Domain sampling suggests that we can, in fact, generate reasonable estimates of true scores by sampling items that span the entire construct domain because the process causes random error to "average out" (Nunnally and Bernstein 1994, p. 217). As a result, instrument designers should be careful to ensure, as best they can, that the items they design and select for their surveys span the full domain of content and the full polarity of the construct. We return to the notion of domain sampling in Chapter 3.

How Many Scale Points are Optimal for a Response Scale?

The optimal number of steps to use in the Likert response format continues to be an area of debate. As mentioned earlier, using too few steps may result in failing to illicit the fine grained discriminations, whereas using too many steps can create confusion and frustration, leading to errors of measurement. The optimal number of steps may differ across constructs, contexts, and populations. Over the years, many researchers have examined the issue of the optimal number of rating scale steps. Whereas Cronbach (1950) cautioned that the number of steps issue was also a validity issue, most researchers have focused on differences in score reliability that result from using scales with different numbers of response points. Using simulated data, Bandalos and Enders (1996) found that reliability increased with the level of correlation among the variables and with the number of scale points. However, maximum gains were reached with 5 or 7 scale points, after which reliability values leveled off (across 3, 5, 7, 9, and 11 points). Lozano et al. (2008) examined the effect of the number of response categories on the reliability and validity of data from rating scales. They tested the range of responses from 2 to 9. Results showed that as the number of responses increased, reliability and validity improved. The optimum number of alternatives was between 4 and 7. With fewer than 4 alternatives, the reliability and validity decreased; from seven alternatives and onwards psychometric properties of the scale scarcely increased further. They concluded that the minimum number of response categories for items with Likert-type format should be at least four. Using simulation methods, Cicchetti et al. (1985) investigated the extent to which the number of scale points (2–100) affected reliability. They found that reliability increased steadily up to 7-scale points, and then leveled off, even when the number of scale points was as high as 100.

McDonald (2004) concluded that 5-point scales are best when moderate responses are expected; 7-point scales are better when extreme responses are expected; and 6-point scales should be used when a midpoint is an undesirable response option. Using a sample of middle school students, Pajares et al. (2001) found that a scale with a 0–100 format was psychometrically stronger than a scale with a traditional Likert format when administering writing self-efficacy scales. Weng (2004) examined the impact of the number of response categories and anchor labels on coefficient alpha and test–retest reliability. Categories ranged from 3 to 9. Half of items had all points, and half of items had only end points anchored. His results suggested that either 7- or 6-point scales should be able to provide consistent and reliable participant responses.

The concerns regarding the selection of the number of scale points also extends to the data analysis phase of the instrument development process. Response formats are, regardless of the number of points used, fundamentally categorical entities. Even as designers conceptualize attitudes or affective characteristics as fitting on a continuum, the continuity assumption is violated as soon as researchers apply instruments to measure it (Bollen 1989). The tension between the hypothesized continuous nature of affective characteristics and the categorical indications of them in measurement scales has important analytical consequences. If the constructs in a given study are thought to be at least interval level, but the measurement tools are technically ordinal, how should the analysis of the results proceed? There is no simple answer to this question, but the ability to treat random variables as continuous does allow researchers to leverage all the rich statistical innovations that accompany probability density functions. As a result, it is very common for instrument developers to assume that the random variables in their instrument are continuous in nature. But is this a reasonable assumption? And if so, under what conditions is it reasonable in a given instrument?

Current research suggests that response formats with 5- to 7-points can usually be treated as continuous indicators (Dolan 1994; DiStefano 2002; Rhemtulla et al. 2010). Developers should use extreme caution when trying to use traditionally continuous data analysis techniques with response formats that contain indicators with less than five categories (Beauducel and Herzberg 2006; Johnson and Creech 1983). Estimation techniques for categorical data are becoming more computationally efficient and accessible in software packages for social scientists (e.g., M*plus*; Muthén and Muthén 2012) prompting some to suggest that, if the response format is fundamentally categorical, then it should be treated with categorical data analysis techniques (Wirth and Edwards 2007). This is a philosophical debate that will likely continue into the future even as the current empirical evidence seems to suggest that with enough scale points, instrument response formats can approximate interval level scales.

In conclusion, instrument designers should make the decision about how many scale points to employ on the basis of both practical and empirical considerations. In addition, it is important to consider the context of the items, as well as the training, age, educational level, motivation, and cognitive level of the respondents when selecting the number of steps on the response scale. A greater number of steps in the scale will necessitate a higher level of thought for making fine discriminations between the scale anchor points. If respondents become annoyed or generally confused by the large number of gradations used, they could become careless and provide unreliable data. In general, most current psychological and psychometric findings suggest that seven point scales provide a reasonable compromise between over-simplicity and over complexity. However, instrument designers may find utility in scales that have fewer or more scale points. In general, we recommend that response scales have no fewer than 5 and no more than 11-scale points.

Omitted Important Response Options Bias and Response Distortion Bias

Fabrigar et al. (2005) also point to another potential source of bias in structured items related to the absence of choices in the response format. The authors describe this as *omitted important response options bias*, and it results when the respondent's preferred answer is not listed. An obvious bias problem occurs when elements of a response format are missing, but less obvious problems can result from cases where respondents are forced to make relative rather than absolute judgments of importance. In addition, structured measures can obscure the relative importance of particular response choices unless there is a specific mechanism to do so in the instrument.

Structured items can also be biased by *social desirability* (i.e., giving socially acceptable, usually positive responses) and *faking* (i.e., intentionally untrue responses) (Baron 1996; Hough 1998; Coopersmith 1967, 1989; Martin et al. 2002). Collectively, these practices are often referred to as response distortions (Dilchert et al. 2006; Donovan et al. 2003; McFarland and Ryan 2000). A meta-analysis by Viswesvaran and Ones (1999) concluded that respondents can successfully distort responses. There are individual differences in both the ability and motivation to fake responses (McFarland and Ryan 2000). Attempts by respondents to select socially desirable or even faked responses can appear in any affective instrument, although the concern is often elevated in situations where scores inform high-stakes decisions (Dilchert et al. 2006). A common example of this type of effect is when a personality test is used during the job application process.

Omitted important response and response distortion are two distinct sources of bias that share a common psychometric solution known as ipsative scaling. Instrument designers typically employ normative scales in their response formats. On a normative scale, individuals respond to each item separately; therefore, there is no fixed total score across the scales included in the instrument. Individuals could have all high scores or all low scores across all the subscales; the only score restrictions are the minimum and maximum possible scores associated with the response format. A fundamental difference between normative and ipsative scales is that in an ipsatively scaled item participants are forced into response choices that yield subscale scores that yield a constant sum total (Baron 1996; Hicks 1970). The key feature of ipsative measures is that the sum of each person's scores across all scales is the same as any other person's. The implication of this scaling is that while it is possible to compare scores within an individual, it is difficult, if not impossible, to compare scores across individuals. Normative scales are generally easier to construct and tend to present fewer practical and psychometric problems than ipsative scales. The result of this approach is often referred to additive

Table 2.8 Intercorrelations of subscales on the survey of interpersonal values instrument

	S	C	R	I	B	L
Support		−0.09	0.40	−0.23	−0.12	−0.52
Conformity			−0.38	−0.38	0.39	−0.45
Recognition				−0.30	−0.37	−0.02
Independence					−0.44	0.06
Benevolence						−0.41
Leadership						

ipsative data (AID) (Chan and Bentler 1993). Other ipsatized data approaches include rank ordered or ordinal ipsatized data (OID), and forced-choice ipsatized data (FCID), which results from choices between items that resemble the form "most like me" or "least like me" (Chan and Bentler 1993). In these cases, the instrument can be termed "purely ipsative." Variations on the ipsativity of instruments can result in "partially ipsative" instruments, but this discussion will focus on the consequences of "purely ipsative" measures.

Researchers sometimes employ forced-choice ipsative scales in situations where they suspect that participants may be tempted to distort responses. Research into this approach suggests that forced-choice response scales display less score inflation than more commonly employed normative scales (Bowen et al. 2002; Christiansen et al. 2005). Unfortunately, the reduction of social distortion gained from ipsative scaling may not be worth the deleterious effects the approach has on data reliabilities and the instrument's factor structure (Closs 1996; Meade 2004).

Early work by Clemans (1966) highlighted the core psychometric problems associated with ipsative scaling. His research demonstrated that ipsative scale result in more extreme positive and negative correlations among factors, largely because the column sums of the initial covariance matrix must always equal zero (see Clemans 1966, p. 25). Therefore, examining the interrelationships among the constructs measured by the instrument is no longer straightforward. In an ipsative scale, the correlations partially reflect the nature of the ipsative scoring system rather than the underlying relations between the scales. Consider, for example, Gordon's (1960) early work with the *Survey of Interpersonal Values* (*SIV*), which employs 30 triads to measure the following interpersonal values: Support, conformity, recognition, independence, benevolence, and leadership. Table 2.8 contains the intercorrelations among the six scales on the instrument. The several negative correlations are caused by the interdependence among the scales resulting from the forced-choice format (Gordon 1960, p. 5).

It is inappropriate to use factor analytic techniques to examine the structure of ipsative instruments (Clemans 1966; Guilford 1952). Meade (2004) suggests that it is "impossible" to conduct a legitimate factor analysis with forced-choice ipsative data, because the analysis requires many more parameters to be estimated than are possible in the observed variance–covariance matrix. Because the aim of factor analysis is to generate dimensions or constructs which parsimoniously describe the scale covariations, it is not methodologically sound to factor analyze a matrix whose entries partially reflect negative item dependencies necessitated by ipsative scales rather than the true conceptual interrelationships among the items. A classic study comparing the normative and ipsative form of items designed to measure occupational values provides a compelling illustration of the problems inherent in ipsative scales (McMorris 1971). There were nine items measuring three occupational values areas: Favoritism (FAV), Intellectual Laziness (LAZ), and Greed (GRD). The normative version presented items on a 5-point scale where 1 = "unimportant" and 5 = "very important."

The ipsative scale version was developed using triads; each triad included one item from each of the scales. For example, in the first triad, items 10, 11, and 12 represent the FAV, LAZ, and GRD scales, respectively. Respondents were asked to select a "most" and "least" important statement for each triad. The "most," "blank," and "least" responses were scored 2, 1, and 0, respectively. Consistent with the forced-choice technique, respondents considered all three statements; however, they were only allowed to choose one as the "most" important. They also answered a question designed to ascertain socially desirable responding.

Forty undergraduate education students responded to both forms. Figure 2.5 displays the means, standard deviations, and correlations in a multitrait-multimethod (MTMM) matrix. Although Campbell and Fiske's (1959) original discussion of the MTMM matrix was based upon using different methods of measurement (i.e., paper survey and peer ratings), displaying the correlations in this manner helps highlight the advantage of using ipsative scales with instruments that are susceptible to response distortion and the disadvantage of using ipsative scales to understand relationships among subscales. The MTMM strategy reveals interesting patterns in the correlation matrix. The underlined values in the diagonal represent validity coefficients (homotrait-multimethod or same-trait measured by two methods).[9] The solid triangles in the matrix contain the scale intercorrelations (multitrait-homomethod) for the normative and ipsative forms. For the normative form, it makes sense that those individuals with high scores on Greed tended to also score highly on Favoritism ($r = 0.60$), while the Intellectual Laziness scale was found to have low correlations with Favoritism ($r = 0.17$) and Greed ($r = 0.18$). The correlations resulting from the normative form make conceptual sense; however, the correlations resulting from the ipsative form in the solid triangle are negative and make little, if any, conceptual sense. The bottom row of Table 2.6 presents the correlations between the scale scores and the indication of Social Desirability (SOCD). Indeed, the ipsative version appears to result in scores that are less related to socially desirable responses.

The comparison of normative and ipsative scaling for the same set of items by McMorris illustrates both the positive and negative attributes of ipsative scales. Despite the low validity coefficients due to low reliability levels, the reliabilities of the ipsative and normative scales were generally similar. However, this is not always the case; the reliability of scores from ipsative scales is often problematic (Hicks 1970; Saville and Willson 1991). The interdependence of the scale scores

---

9 Initially, the validity coefficients seem low, but each needs to be considered in light of the alpha reliabilities for the respective scales (in parentheses on the main diagonal). The low number of items used for both the normative and ipsative scales appears to result from low reliability levels, except for the normative GRD scale. The maximum validity coefficient is the square root of the product of the reliabilities of the two scales. For example, while the correlation between IFAV and NFAV was 0.41, the maximum correlation possible was $\sqrt{(0.45)(0.45)}$ or 0.45. The maximum correlation possible between the IGRD and NGRD scales is approximately $\sqrt{(0.75)(0.55)}$ or 0.64 and the correlation reported is only 0.36. For these scales, the normative and ipsative measures using the same items are not highly related. The diagonal validity values are higher than the row and column counterparts in the dashed-line triangles (MTMM). It is difficult to interpret the values in the dashed triangles, since they partially represent the ipsative scales which reflect both the occupational-values content and the ipsative-scale properties.

Means, Standard Deviations, and Correlations
N = 40

	Mean	*SD*	*NFAV*	*NLAZ*	*NGRD*	*IFAV*	*ILAZ*	*IGRD*
NFAV	7.0	2.0	(.45)					
NLAZ	6.8	2.2	.17	(.54)				
NGRD	6.1	2.6	.60	.18	(.75)			
IFAV	3.2	1.3	.41	.01	.05	(.45)		
ILAZ	2.8	1.5	−.33	.35	−.36	−.59	(.59)	
IGRD	3.1	1.3	−.04	−.45	.36	−.32	−.57	(.55)
SOCD	4.2	.8	.32	.18	.31	.06	−.06	.01

Note: Part N (Normative)—3 items/scale, each scored 1–5.
Part I (Ipsative)—3 triads, scored 0–2.

	Item #
FAV–Favoritism	1, 6, 8; 10, 15, 17
LAZ–Intellectual Laziness	2, 4, 9; 11, 13, 18
GRD–Greed (Unethical Remuneration)	3, 5, 7; 12, 14, 16
SOCD–Social Desirability	19

Fig. 2.5 Multi-Trait Multi-Method matrix for three occupational values on normative and ipsative items

resulting from the ipsative technique can seriously limit the alpha internal-consistency reliabilities of the data from the ipsative scales as compared to normative scales (Scott 1968; Tenopyr 1968).

In conclusion, instrument designers should pay close attention to the negative scale intercorrelations resulting from the ipsative scoring system. The correlation matrices generated from ipsative scales present a host of practical and psychometric challenges. Instrument developers attracted to the potential benefits of ipsative scaling may find some techniques that allow for normative scoring from forced-choice data in personality scales (McCloy et al. 2005; Stark et al. 2005, 2006). Dilchert et al. (2006) note that these emerging methods suggest that multidimensional forced-choice format appears resistant to score inflation at the group level, but is not true at the individual level (McCloy et al. 2005). This observation makes the utility of such techniques questionable for use in many affective instrument development projects that are aimed at understanding individual traits. If instrument developers have serious concerns about possible response distortion, there are simpler and potentially more effective approaches available that do not rely on ipsative scaling. One easy method for discouraging response distortion is to include a simple "honesty warning" on the instrument. Honesty warnings encourage participants to answer truthfully on questionnaires and surveys. These warnings oftentimes stress the need for truthful responses while simultaneously guaranteeing the anonymity of the respondent. Dwight and Donovan (2003) observed that these simple instructions have a relatively small but statistically significant effect in reducing mean scores on affective measures ($d = 0.23$). Despite its ease of use, designers should not include these warnings as a matter of routine on every instrument. Some researchers have found that "honesty warnings"—particularly in some high-stakes situations—can have some negative effects on participants. In fact, Vasilopoulos et al. (2005) found that these warnings can threaten the construct validity of affective instruments. Given the potential advantages and disadvantages of this approach, the best advice for designers is to include instructions that encourage truthfulness and requests to avoid carelessness on the instrument.

Instrument designers can also consider making changes to the environment or the testing format. It has long been suggested that efforts to reduce the social interaction during a survey administration could reduce social distortion bias (Martin and Nagao 1989). Unfortunately, a meta-analysis of the effects of paper-and-pencil, face-to-face interactions, and computer-based survey suggests that there are limited difference among administration modes (Richman et al. 1999). This does appear to contradict some of the response distortion effects observed with groups suggesting that the issue of medium effects on instruments is likely complex and idiosyncratic.

Proximity, Primacy, and Recency Effects

Proximity

The order in which questions are asked can have an influence on participants' responses. When participants engaging with an instrument exhibit the tendency to respond in a similar manner to adjacent (i.e., prior) items—this has been called a *proximity effect*. Research by Green and Hershberger (2000) and Green and Yang (2009) supports the observed effect on item order on the factor analyses of affective instruments. The existence of a large proximity effect could result in

Table 2.9 Recommendations for writing item stems

1. Address one dimension within the item stem
2. Response scale should accommodate all possible answers
3. Avoid comparative statements (i.e., I like reading more than I like math)
4. All items should be in the same direction
5. Avoid overly complex and/or "double-barrelled" items
6. Avoid attaching reasons to affect. "I like my school because I have good friends there."
7. Create items that produce variable responses
8. Save demographic items for the end
9. Avoid implying a desired answer within the item stem
10. Use simple and direct wording. Item stems should be several grade levels below the target audience's reading level
11. Do not use slang or jargon
12. Make your response scale as "equal interval" as possible
13. Begin with easy items; Place difficult or sensitive questions toward the end of survey
15. Be sure that the item stem can be answered using the response scale provided
16. When possible, build strength or magnitude into the item stem (Bradburn et al. 2004, p. 124)

contaminated factors during a study of construct validity and in inflated estimates of alpha internal-consistency reliabilities. Melnick (1993) compared two forms of an attitude measure. He administered a form with items grouped by dimension to 350 school administrators; he also administered a version with items randomly placed to 369 administrators. The alpha reliabilities of the dimensions tended to be higher for the form with the grouped items. The interpretation of these observed lower reliabilities has been debated. Veres et al. (1991) assert that the appreciably lower coefficient alphas resulting from the randomly ordered items represent more accurate estimates of reliability. In contrast, Ochieng (2001) maintains that lower coefficient alphas represent an unnecessary reduction in reliability. He suggests that respondents are likely to provide better responses to items when the items are ordered to maximize respondents' understanding of the construct being measured. This appears to be a good point if the respondents are young and/or have lower reading abilities. Despite Ochieng's provocative suggestion for dealing with the proximity effect, the position advocated by Veres et al. (1991) represents the more standard approach in instrument design.[10]

Primacy

Questions that appear early in the instrument can affect how respondents answer subsequent items (Tourangeau and Rasinski 1988). Moore (2002) explored the issue of question order and suggested that groups of items can have specific "additive" or "subtractive" effects. Moore defined additive effects as increases in response means for items when they are grouped with another question or set of questions. To illustrate this point, he provided an example of two questions on racial hostility: one addressing an evaluation of white hostility and the other back hostility. When the questions were presented to respondents individually, or non-comparatively, 41% of respondents indicated that all or most whites disliked blacks, while 46 of respondents indicated that all or most blacks disliked whites. When these same questions were administered on an instrument together, or comparatively, those numbers jumped to 53% and 56%, respectively. For Moore, this typified could be called an additive ordering effect. Moore conducted a similar experiment to demonstrate the possibility of subtractive effects with questions about whether two controversial, but record-setting baseball players, Pete Rose and "Shoeless" Joe Jackson, should be admitted to the Baseball Hall of Fame. In the non-comparative context, 64% indicated that Rose should be admitted, whereas 45% indicated that Jackson should be admitted. In the comparative context, 52% indicated that Rose should be admitted, 33 felt that Jackson should be admitted. It appears that the inclusion of both of these items negatively affected

[10] It should be noted that some recent research suggests there is little or no effect of item ordering on internal consistency of the data. A study by Sparfeldt et al. (2006) found similar factorial structures for groups of high school students presented with items in a blocking order and in a traditional randomized order.

both responses resulting in what he termed a subtractive effect. Moore's research focuses on often highly charged political attitudes over time, and his work suggests that careful thought should be given not only to the ordering but also inclusion of indicators of particularly sensitive affective constructs.

Primacy and recency effects are the results of particular response ordering choices (Krosnick and Alwin 1987; Sudman et al. 1996). A primacy effect occurs when participants are biased toward the closest response they encounter. It has been suggested that unmotivated respondents are most likely to exhibit this type of bias (Fabrigar et al. 2005). The obvious and direct remedies for this problem would include incentives to increase attentiveness and investment in the results. Recency effects occur when respondents are biased toward choosing one of the last options they encounter. This bias is considered to be the result of memory or focus issues in the respondent simply because the last option is the one they are most likely to remember. As general rule, instrument designers can greatly minimize this problem by constructing short, concise item stems, clear response formats, and well-constructed response scales. In addition, given that fatigue plays a role in the manifestation of primacy and recency effects, shorter instruments help to minimize these problems.

Using our collective experience and the literature reviewed in this chapter, we have compiled a list of 16 suggestions for writing self-report items, contained in Table 2.9. Following these guidelines should improve the quality and clarity of the item stems.

Indirect Measures of Affective Characteristics

Direct measures operate on the idea that quantities of affective characteristics in individuals can be measured by explicitly asking them. Currently, they are the most popular approaches in affective measurement, but many researchers have expressed serious concerns with the approach. As noted, participants do distort responses, although many techniques have been developed to mitigate these effects (Paulhus 1991). A more recent concern, however, is how instrument designers can address or measure biases that respondents may not even consciously recognize (Blanton and Jaccard 2006; Greenwald et al. 2003; Wilson et al. 2000). The primary concern is that direct measures are fundamentally flawed in addressing these kinds of implicit or subconscious attitudes or biases. These concerns have prompted the development of indirect measures of affective characteristics. Indirect measures represent measurement outcomes that reflect certain attitudes, cognitions, or feelings in an automatic manner (De Houwer 2006).

The purpose of this book is to aid social scientists in developing direct measures of affective characteristics. In this final section, we address indirect measures and contrast their techniques with direct measures to inform instrument designers of cases where the measurement of their affective constructs may be better served by more indirect approaches. In addition, indirect measures may be useful assessments to gather to establish evidence of construct validity for affective instruments that measure certain types of constructs.

The Lost Letter Technique

Some indirect measures, such as the Lost Letter Technique, use behavioral responses to make inferences about underlying attitudes or affective traits. Stanley Milgram pioneered The Lost Letter Technique in the 1960s to measure attitudes toward controversial political organizations such as the Communist and Nazi parties (Milgram 1969; Milgram et al. 1965). In the lost letter technique, the researcher develops two sets of letters. The first set of letters is addressed to a fictitious organization that clearly supports a somewhat controversial position. The other set of letters is addressed to another fictitious organization that clearly does not support the controversial position or that advocates the polar opposite controversial position. For example, to study people's attitudes about abortion using the lost letter technique, we could create two sets of letters. The first set of letters is addressed to "The Center for the Protection of Abortion Rights;" the second set of letters is addressed to "The Center to Support the Rights of Unborn Children." All the letters share an address accessible to the researcher and contain sufficient postage. The researchers then randomly distribute the letters (usually 200 of each version) throughout the community. People in the community find the letters and conclude that someone "lost" the letter before having a chance to mail it. The design assumes that if the finder agrees with the stance implied by the organization name, he or she is more likely to take steps to mail the letter. Evaluations of the affective characteristic can then be calculated by counting the number of letters returned for each group.

Similar versions of the Lost Letter Technique have been modified to reflect more modern communication media. In an experiment designed at measuring attitudes about the one-time presidential candidate Ross Perot, Stern and Faber created "lost emails" about fundraising for Perot and sent them to email addresses randomly selected from a "white pages" on the world-wide-web. Since the techniques cannot account for a myriad of factors besides attitude that would prevent the forwarding of lost communications, the technique gives only a rough estimate of general attitudes on subjects (Fabrigar et al. 2005). It is generally impossible to identify individuals that choose to mail or not mail letters, and this prevents the collection of additional data on participants. Even more importantly, it prevents the use of this technique to measure a particular individual's attitudes. The technique could, however, find some novel applications as social media increases the ability to document communication among people.

Response Latency Tests

A rapidly emerging area of indirect measurement uses response latencies to assess affective characteristics. The most popular of these measures is known as *Implicit Association Test* (*IAT*—Greenwald et al. 1998). The central premise of these implicit measures is that affective characteristics can be engaged automatically without conscious interference by the respondent. Response latency tasks require participants to respond quickly to words that are associated with various levels of the affective characteristic. Target words first appear as affective objects, and then they are valenced by additional words that reflect positive or negative concepts. In a simple example of an attempt to measure implicit attitudes of children toward adults, the attitude object may be represented by "teacher" and valenced by the words "good" or "bad." The measurement of these attitudes is a function of speed with which participants make particular sets of associations and the contrasts in the response speed across different types of associations.

Cunningham et al. (2001) explored the consistency, stability, and convergent validity of implicit measures of racism. In their study, they administered three relatively implicit measures of racism (IAT, response-window evaluative priming,[11] and the response window IAT[12]) and one direct measure of racism (Modern Racism Scale, McConahay 1986). The results suggested that implicit measures are relatively stable over time; however, the degree of measurement error is high.[13] In addition, the authors reported that the direct measure of racism was moderately correlated with all three implicit measures, contradicting the idea that there is a complete dissociation between direct and indirect measures.[14]

Relative to other direct and indirect measures of affective characteristics, response latency tests are still in their infancy, and researchers are still exploring the psychometric properties of such tasks. The technique does appear to show promise in some areas of stereotype and self-esteem research; however, the response mechanisms underlying measures such as the implicit association test are not fully understood (Fazio and Olson 2003).[15]

---

[11] The response-window evaluative priming instrument participants respond to words that have a negative or positive evaluative meaning by pressing one key for good words and another key for bad words. Immediately preceding each word, a white or black face appeared for 200 ms and participants were required to respond within 200–600 ms (Draine and Greenwald 1998).

[12] The response-window IAT is identical to the IAT except that it requires participants to respond within 225–675 ms of the stimulus presentation.

[13] Cunningham et al. (2001) report that estimates of Cronbach's alpha indicated that more than 30% of the observed variance in the measures was due to random error.

[14] Cunningham et al. (2001) also note that "although multiple measures of implicit and explicit attitudes are robustly correlated, the two kinds of attitude measures tap unique sources of variances (Cunningham et al. 2001, p. 170); a single-factor [confirmatory factor analysis] solution does not fit the data".

[15] A recent meta-analysis of IAT studies examining six criterion categories (interpersonal behavior, person perception, policy preferences, microbehaviors, reaction times, and brain

Sequential Evaluative Priming

Another judgmental bias measure is known as the *sequential evaluative priming* procedure or the *bona fide pipeline technique* (Fazio et al. 1995). The *sequential evaluative priming* technique assumes that when participants are presented with visual examples of a psychological object (e.g., a teacher or textbook), a spontaneous affective evaluation occurs in the mind of the participant. This mechanism requires respondents to engage in a dual judgment task where psychological objects are presented first as primes. The primes are then followed by positive and negative target words, and then participants are prompted to judge the valence of each word as quickly as possible. Similar to other response latency measures like the IAT, relative judgment times in sequential evaluative priming provide evaluation evidence for the attitude toward the psychological objects under study (Fazio et al. 1986).

Information Error Technique

The *information error technique* is one of the oldest indirect measurement technique based on judgmental biases (Hammond 1948). The technique requires the researcher to construct a comprehensive list of knowledge questions about a topic surrounding the affective characteristic of interest. The questions must be at a level of sophistication so that respondents are not completely certain of the answers. The designer then supplies responses that represent both positive and negative evaluation of the affective characteristic. In one variation of the technique, both answer choices are wrong, but they are wrong in different directions (i.e., one is an overestimate and the other is an underestimate of the correct response).

The primary assumption is that when respondents do not know answers to questions, they will guess, and those guesses are not random. Instead of guessing, respondents respond in a pattern that is consistent with their underlying affective orientation or beliefs. The scale is bipolar with gradations of responses placed along the response format (Antonak and Livneh 1995). It is common for designers

(Footnote 15 continued)
activity) for two versions of the IAT (stereotype and attitude IATs), three strategies for measuring explicit bias (feeling thermometers, multi-item explicit measures such as the Modern Racism Scale, and ad hoc measures of intergroup attitudes and stereotypes), and four criterion-scoring methods (computed majority-minority difference scores, relative majority-minority ratings, minority-only ratings and majority-only ratings) suggested that IATs were poor predictors of every criterion category. The only exception to these finding were in brain activity. Ultimately, the researchers found that the IATs performed no better than simple explicit measures for these same criteria (Oswald, F. L., Mitchell, G., Blanton, H., Jaccard, J., & Tetlock, P. E. (in press). Predicting ethnic and racial discrimination: A meta-analysis of IAT criterion studies. *Journal of Personality and Social Psychology*).

to mix unrelated items into the instrument in order to minimize satisfising behavior. Given the complexity of the item stems and response format, this is often a difficult instrument to construct. In addition, because the instrument is deliberately designed to prevent respondents from engaging with the indicator content, it can be hard for researchers to distinguish between response bias and true indirect affective evaluations.

Physiological Measures

A final category of indirect measurement relies on signals from a variety of physiological responses. In the past, many of these approaches have presented significant interpretive problems for researchers. Measures like the galvanic skin response (GSR) have proven to be resource-intensive and largely disappointing (Kidder and Campbell 1970). Many newer techniques, such as event-brain potentials, do appear to hold promise and appear to be making important contributions to research within the affective domain. Advances in temporal resolution, lower costs, and sensitivity to cognitive processing fuel the continued exploration of this emerging area (Fabiani et al. 2000). These physiological techniques, as well as most indirect affective characteristic measures, require development approaches that are radically different from more accessible direct measures. Even so, researchers should be aware of the advantages and disadvantages of these indirect approaches, especially as opportunities to integrate them into traditional approaches increases.

Summary

The measurement of affective characteristics is a challenging task for researchers. Affective characteristics are unobservable and complex. They require that instrument designers carefully define psychological constructs, develop plausible indicators of those constructs, develop interpretable response scales, apply scaling techniques, and weave the items together in a coherent way to obtain estimates of the affective constructs of interest. There is no one to answer the question of how best to measure affective characteristics. The only certainty is that the instrument development process requires a great deal of time and knowledge of both the content area of the survey and the psychometric techniques necessary to develop an instrument. The measurement and scaling information in this chapter provides an introduction to many of the complex issues faced by instrument developers as they set out to measure an affective construct. We hope that the guidance in this chapter helps instrument developers to make informed decisions during the initial phases of the instrument design process.

In the following four chapters, we introduce the concept of validity and present the validation process as a method to develop an argument that supports the validity of the inferences you would like to make using your instrument.

References

Aaker, D. A., Kumar, V., & Day, G. S. (2004). *Marketing research*. New York: Wiley.

Ajzen, I. (1988). *Attitudes, personality, and behavior*. Chicago: Dorsey Press.

Ajzen, I., & Fishbein, M. (1970). The prediction of behavior from attitudinal and normative variables. *Journal of Experimental Social Psychology, 6*, 466–487.

Anastasi, A. (1982). *Psychological testing* (5th ed.). New York: Macmillan.

Andersen, E. B. (1977). Sufficient statistics and latent trait models. *Psychometrika, 42*, 69–81.

Andersen, L. W. (1981). *Assessing affective characteristics in the schools*. Boston: Allyn and Bacon.

Anderson, L. W., & Bourke, S. F. (2000). *Assessing affective characteristics in the schools* (2nd ed.). Mahwah: Erlbaum.

Anderson, J. C., & Gerbing, D. W. (1991). Predicting the performance of measures in a confirmatory factor analysis with a pretest assessment of their substantive validities. *Journal of Applied Psychology, 76*, 732–740.

Andrich, D. (1978a). Application of a psychometric model to ordered categories which are scored with successive integers. *Applied Psychological Measurement, 21*, 581–594.

Andrich, D. (1978b). Rating formulation for ordered response categories. *Psychometrika, 43*, 561–573.

Andrich, D. (1978c). Scaling attitude items constructed and scored in the Likert tradition. *Educational and Psychological Measurement, 38*, 665–680.

Andrich, D. (2004). Controversy and the Rasch model: A characteristic of incompatible paradigms? *Medical Care, 42*, 1–16.

Antonak, R. F., & Livneh, H. (1995). Development, psychometric analysis, and validation of an error-choice test to measure attitude towards persons with epilepsy. *Rehabilitation Psychology, 40*(1), 25–38.

Bagozzi, R. P., & Fornell, C. (1982). Theoretical concepts, measurements, and meaning. In C. Fornell (Ed.), *A second generation of multivariate analysis* (Vol. 1, pp. 24–38)., Praeger NY: New York.

Bandalos, D. L., & Enders, C. K. (1996). The effects of nonnormality and number of response categories on reliability. *Applied Measurement in Education, 9*(2), 151–160.

Bandura, A. (2006). Guide for constructing self-efficacy scales. *Self-Efficacy Beliefs of Adolescents, 5*, 307–337.

Bargh, J. A., Chaiken, S., Govender, R., & Pratto, F. (1992). The generality of the automatic attitude activation effect. *Journal of Personality and Social Psychology, 62*(6), 893–912.

Barnette, J. J. (1996). Responses that may indicate nonattending behaviors in three self-administered educational attitude surveys. *Research in the Schools, 3*(2), 49–59.

Barnette, J. J. (1999). Nonattending respondent effects on internal consistency of self-administered surveys: A Monte Carlo simulation study. *Educational and Psychological Measurement, 59*, 38–46.

Barnette, J. J. (2000). Effects of stem and Likert response option reversals on survey internal consistency: If you feel the need, there is a better alternative to using those negatively worded stems. *Educational and Psychological Measurement, 60*, 361–370.

Baron, H. (1996). Strengths and limitations of ipsative measurement. *Journal of Occupational and Organizational Psychology, 69*, 49–56.

Beatty, P. C., & Willis, G. B. (2007). Research synthesis: The practice of cognitive interviewing. *Public Opinion Quarterly, 71*, 287–311.

Beauducel, A., & Herzberg, P. Y. (2006). On the performance of maximum likelihood versus means and variance adjusted least squares estimation in CFA. *Structural Equation Modeling: A Multidisciplinary Journal, 13*(2), 186–203.

Bendixen, M., & Sandler, M. (1994). *Converting verbal scales to interval scales using correspondence analysis*. Johannesburg: University of Witwatersrand.

Benson, J., & Hocevar, D. (1985). The impact of item phrasing on the validity of attitude scales for elementary school children. *Journal of Educational Measurement, 22*, 231–240.

Bishop, G. F., Oldendick, R. W., & Tuchfarber, A. J. (1982). Political information processing: Question order and context effects. *Political Behavior, 4*(2), 177–200.

Blalock, H. M. (1964). *Causal inferences in nonexperimental research*. Chapel Hill: University of North Carolina Press.

Blanton, H., & Jaccard, J. (2006). Arbitrary metrics in psychology. *American Psychologist, 6*(1), 27–41.

Blalock, H.M. (Ed.) (1971). Causal Models in the Social Sciences. Chicago:Aldine.

Bollen, K. A. (1989). *Structural equation models with latent variables*. New York: Wiley.

Bollen, K. A. (2002). Latent variables in psychology and the social sciences. *Annual Review of Psychology, 53*, 605–634.

Bollen, K. A., & Lennox, R. (1991). Conventional wisdom on measurement: A structural equation perspective. *Psychological Bulletin, 101*(2), 305–314.

Bond, T. G. (2004). Validity and assessment: A Rasch measurement perspective. *Metodologia de las Ciencias del Comportamiento, 5*(2), 179–194.

Bond, T. G., & Fox, C. M. (2007). *Applying the rasch model: Fundamental measurement in the human sciences* (2nd ed.). Mahwah: Lawrence Erlbaum.

Borsboom, D. (2003). The theoretical status of latent variables. *Psychological Review, 110*, 203–219.

Borsboom, D. (2005). *Measuring the mind: Conceptual issues in contemporary psychometrics*. Cambridge: Cambridge University Press.

Bowen, C. C., Martin, B. A., & Hunt, S. T. (2002). A comparison of ipsative and normative approaches for ability to control faking in personality questionnaires. *International Journal of Organizational Analysis, 10*, 240–259.

Bradburn, N., Sudman, S., & Wansink, B. (2004). Asking questions: the definitive guide to questionnaire design. San Francisco: Jossey-Bass.

Burns, A. C., & Bush, R. F. (2000). *Marketing research*. Upper Saddle River: Prentice Hall.

Campbell, D. T., & Fiske, D. W. (1959). Convergent and discriminant validation by multitrait-multimethod matrix. *Psychological Bulletin, 56*, 81–105.

Carleton, R. N., McCreary, D., Norton, P. J., & Asmundson, G. J. G. (2006). The brief fear of negative evaluation scale, revised. *Depression and Anxiety, 23*, 297–303.

Chae, S., Kang, U., Jeon, E., & Linacre, J. M. (2000). *Development of computerized middle school achievement test [in Korean]*. Seoul: Komesa Press.

Chambers, C. T., & Johnston, C. (2002). Developmental differences in children's use of rating scales. *Journal of Pediatric Psychology, 27*(1), 27–36.

Chan, W., & Bentler, P. M. (1993). The covariance structure analysis of ipsative data. *Sociological Methods and Research, 22*, 214–247.

Chang, L. (1997). Dependability of anchoring labels of Likert-type scales. *Educational and Psychological Measurement, 57*(5), 800–807.

Christiansen, N. D., Burns, G. N., & Montgomery, G. E. (2005). Reconsidering forced-choice item formats for applicant personality assessment. *Human Performance, 18*, 267–307.

Cialdini, R. B. (2001). *Influence: Science and practice* (4th ed.). Boston: Allyn & Bacon.

Cicchetti, D. V., Shoinralter, D., & Tyrer, P. J. (1985). The effect of number of rating scale categories on levels of interrater reliability: A Monte Carlo investigation. *Applied Psychological Measurement, 9*(1), 31–36.

Clemans, W. V. (1966). *An analytical and empirical examination of some properties of ipsative measures, Psychometric Monographs, 14*. Princeton: Psychometric Corporation.
Closs, S. J. (1996). On the factoring and interpretation of ipsative data. *Journal of Occupational & Organizational Psychology, 69*, 41–47.
Conner, M., Norman, P., & Bell, R. (2002). The theory of planned behavior and healthy eating. *Health Psychology, 21*, 194–201.
Cook, T. D., & Campbell, D. T. (1979). *Quasi-experimental design: Design and analysis issues for field settings*. Chicago: Rand-McNally.
Coopersmith, S. (1967, 1989). *The antecedents of self-esteem*. San Francisco: Freeman.
Crocker, L., & Algina, J. (2006). *Introduction to classical and modern test theory*. Pacific Grove: Wadsworth.
Cronbach, L. J. (1950). Further evidence on response sets and test design. *Educational and Psychological Measurement, 10*, 30–31.
Cunningham, W. A., Preacher, K. J., & Banaji, M. R. (2001). Implicit attitude measures: Consistency, stability, and convergent validity. *Psychological Science, 12*(2), 163–170.
De Houwer, J. (2006). What are implicit measures and why are we using them. In R. W. Wiers & A. W. Stacy (Eds.), *The handbook of implicit cognition and addiction* (pp. 11–28). Thousand Oaks: Sage Publishers.
DeVellis, R. F. (1991). *Scale development: Theory and application. Applied Social Research Methods Series*, 40, Newbury Park: Sage.
Dilchert, S., Ones, D. S., Viswesvaran, C., & Deller, J. (2006). Response distortion in personality measurement: Born to deceive, yet capable of providing valid self-assessments? *Psychology Science, 48*, 209–225.
Dillman, D. A., Smyth, J. D., & Christain, L. M. (2009). *Internet, mail, and mixed-mode surveys: The tailored design method* (3rd ed.). Hoboken: Wiley.
Dillon, W. R., Madden, T. J., & Firtle, N. H. (1993). *Essentials of marketing research*. Homewood: Irwin.
DiStefano, C. (2002). The impact of categorization with confirmatory factor analysis. *Structural Equation Modeling: A Multidisciplinary Journal, 9*(3), 327–346.
DiStefano, C., & Motl, R. W. (2006). Further investigating method effects associated with negatively worded items on self-report surveys. *Structural Equation Modeling: A Multidisciplinary Journal, 13*, 440–464.
Dolan, C. V. (1994). Factor analysis of variables with 2, 3, 5 and 7 response categories: A comparison of categorical variable estimators using simulated data. *British Journal of Mathematical and Statistical Psychology, 47*, 309–326.
Donovan, J. J., Dwight, S. A., & Hurtz, G. M. (2003). An assessment of the prevalence, severity, and verifiability of entry-level applicant faking using the randomized response technique. *Human Performance, 16*, 81–106.
Draine, S. C., & Greenwald, A. G. (1998). Replicable unconscious semantic priming. *Journal of Experimental Psychology: General, 127*, 286–303.
DuBois, B., & Burns, J. A. (1975). An analysis of the meaning of the question mark response category in attitude scales. *Educational and Psychological Measurement, 35*, 869–884.
Duncan, O. D. (1984). *Notes on social measurement: Historical and critical*. New York: Russell Sage Foundation.
Dwight, S. A., & Donovan, J. J. (2003). Do warnings not to fake reduce faking? *Human Performance, 16*(1), 1–23.
Edwards, A. L. (1957). *Techniques of attitude scale construction*. New York: Appleton-Century-Crofts.
Edwards, J. R., & Bagozzi, R. P. (2000). On the nature and direction of the relationship between constructs and measures. *Psychological Methods, 5*, 155–174.
Eys, M. A., Carron, A. V., Bray, S. R., & Brawley, L. R. (2007). Item wording and internal consistency of a measure of cohesion: The group environment questionnaire. *Journal of Sport & Exercise Psychology, 29*, 395–402.

Fabiani, M., Gratton, G., & Coles, M. G. H. (2000). Event-related brain potentials: Methods, theory, and applications. In J. T. Cacioppo, L. Tassinary, & G. Berntson (Eds.), *Handbook of psychophysiology* (2nd ed., pp. 53–84). New York: Cambridge University Press.

Fabrigar, L., McDougall, B. L., & Krosnick, J. A. (2005). Attitude measurement: Techniques for measuring the unobservable. In T. C. Brock & M. C. Green (Eds.), *Persuasion: Psychological insights and perspectives* (2nd ed.). Thousand Oaks: Sage.

Fazio, R. H., & Olson, M. A. (2003). Implicit measures in social cognition research: Their meaning and use. *Annual Review of Psychology, 54*, 297–327.

Fazio, R. H., Sanbonmatsu, D. M., Powell, M. C., & Kardes, F. R. (1986). On the automatic activation of attitudes. *Journal of Personality and Social Psychology, 50*, 229–238.

Fazio, R. H., Jackson, J. R., Dunton, B. C., & Williams, C. J. (1995). Variability in automatic activation as an unobtrusive measure of racial stereotypes: A bona fide pipeline? *Journal of Personality and Social Psychology, 69*, 1013–1027.

Fishbein, M., & Ajzen, I. (1975). *Belief, attitude, intention, and behavior: An introduction to theory and research*. Reading: Addison-Wesley.

Fishbein, M., & Ajzen, I. (2010). *Predicting and changing behavior: The reasoned action approach*. New York: Taylor and Francis Group.

Frantom, C. G. (2001). *Paternalism and the myth of perfection: Test and measurement of a theory underlying physicians' perceptions of patient autonomy*. Unpublished doctoral dissertation, Denver: University of Denver.

Glaser, B. G., & Strauss, A. L. (1967). *The discovery of grounded theory: Strategies for qualitative research*. Chicago: Aldine.

Gordon, L. V. (1960). *SRA manual for survey of interpersonal values*. Chicago: Science Research Associates.

Green, S. B., & Hershberger, S. L. (2000). Correlated errors in true score models and their effect on coefficient alpha. *Structural Equation Modeling, 7*(2), 251–270.

Green, S. B., & Yang, Y. (2009). Commentary on coefficient alpha: A cautionary tale. *Psychometrika, 74*(1), 121–135.

Greenwald, A. G., McGhee, D. E., & Schwartz, J. L. K. (1998). Measuring individual differences in implicit cognition: The implicit association task. *Journal of Personality and Social Psychology, 74*, 1464–1480.

Greenwald, A. G., Nosek, B. A., & Banji, M. R. (2003). Understanding and using the Implicit Association Test: An improved scoring algorithm. *Journal of Personality and Social Psychology, 85*, 197–216.

Guilford, J. P. (1952). When not to factor analyze. *Psychological Bulletin, 49*, 31.

Hair, J. F., Bush, R. P., & Ortinau, D. J. (2006). *Marketing research*. Boston: McGraw Hill.

Hambleton, R. K., Swaminathan, H., & Rogers, H. J. (1991). *Fundamentals of item response theory*. Newbury Park: Sage Publications.

Hammond, K. R. (1948). Measuring attitudes by error-choice: An indirect method. *Journal of Abnormal Psychology, 43*(1), 38–48.

Hardy, B. & Ford, L. (2012). When often becomes always, and sometimes becomes never: miscomprehension in surveys. In: Academy of Management Annual Meeting 2012, 3-7th August 2012, Boston, MA.

Harman, H. H. (1960). *Modern factor analysis*. Chicago: University Chicago Press.

Harter, J. K. (1997). The psychometric utility of the midpoint on a Likert scale. *Dissertation Abstracts International, 58*, 1198.

Hicks, L. E. (1970). Some properties of ipsative, normative, and forced-choice normative measures. *Psychological Bulletin, 74*(3), 167–184.

Hockenberry, M. J., & Wilson, D. (2009). *Wong's essentials of pediatric nursing* (8th ed.). St. Louis: Mosby.

Hough, L. M. (1998). The effects of intentional distortion in personality measurement and evaluation of suggested palliatives. *Human Performance, 11*, 209–244.

Jaccard, J., & Jacoby, J. (2010). *Theory construction and model-building skills: A practical guide for social scientists*. New York: Guilford Press.

Johnson, D. R., & Creech, J. C. (1983). Ordinal measures in multiple indicator models: A simulation study of categorization error. *American Sociological Review, 48*, 398–407.

Jones, J. W., & Dages, K. D. (2003). Technology trends in staffing and assessment: A practice note. *International Journal of Selection and Assessment, 11*, 247–252.

Joreskog, K. G., & Sorbom, D. (1979). *Advances in factor analysis and structural equation models*. Cambridge: Abt Books.

Kalton, G., Roberts, J., & Holt, D. (1980). The effects of offering a middle response option with opinion questions. *The Statistician, 29*, 11–24.

Kahn (1974) Instructor evaluation using the Thurstone technique. University of Connecticut, Storrs, CT, Unpublished manuscript.

Kelloway, E. K., Loughlin, C., Barling, J., & Nault, A. (2002). Self-reported counterproductive behaviors and organizational citizenship behaviors: Separate but related constructs. *International Journal of Selection and Assessment, 10*, 143–151.

Kennedy, R., Riquier, C., & Sharp, B. (1996). Practical applications of correspondence analysis to categorical data in market research. *Journal of Targeting, Measurement and Analysis for Marketing, 5*, 56–70.

Kidder, L. H., & Campbell, D. T. (1970). The indirect testing of social attitudes. In G. F. Summers (Ed.), *Attitude measurement* (pp. 333–385). Chicago: Rand McNally.

Krosnick, J. A. (1991). Response strategies for coping with the cognitive demands of attitude measures in surveys. *Applied Cognitive Psychology, 5*, 213–236.

Krosnick, J. A. (1999). Survey Methodology. *Annual Review of Psychology, 50*, 537–567.

Krosnick, J. A., & Alwin, D. F. (1987). An evaluation of a cognitive theory of response-order effects in survey measurement. *Public Opinion Quarterly, 51*(2), 201–219.

Krosnick, J. A., & Fabrigar, L. R. (1997). *Designing rating scaling for effective measurement in surveys. Survey measurement and process quality*. New York: Wiley.

Krosnick, J. A., & Presser, S. (2010). Question and questionnaire design. In James. D. Wright & Peter. V. Marsden (Eds.), *Handbook of survey research* (2nd ed., pp. 263–313). Emerald Group: West Yorkshire.

Likert, R. (1932). A technique for the measurement of attitudes. *Archives of Psychology, 140*, 152.

Loevinger, J. (1957). Objective tests as instruments of psychological theory. *Psychological Reports, 3*, 635–694.

Lord, F. M., & Novick, M. R. (1968). *Statistical theories of mental test scores*. Reading: Addison-Wesley.

Lozano, L. M., García-Cueto, M., & Muñiz, J. (2008). Effect of the number of response categories on the reliability and validity of rating scales. *Methodology, 4*, 73–79.

Lynch (1973) Multidimensional measurement with the D statistic and semantic differential. Northeastern University, Boston, Unpublished manuscript

MacCallum, R. C., & Austin, J. T. (2000). Applications of structural equation modeling in psychological research. *Annual Review of Psychology, 51*, 201–226.

Marsh, H. W. (1986). Negative item bias in rating scales for preadolescent children: A cognitive-developmental phenomenon. *Developmental Psychology, 22*, 37–49.

Marsh, H. W., & Shavelson, R. J. (1985). Self-concept: Its multifaceted, hierarchical structure. *Educational Psychologist, 20*(3), 107–123.

Marsh, H. W., Byrne, B. M., & Shavelson, R. J. (1988). A multifaceted academic self-concept: Its hierarchical structure and its relation to academic achievement. *Journal of Educational Psychology, 80*(3), 366–380.

Martin, C. L., & Nagao, D. H. (1989). Some effects of computerized interviewing on job applicant responses. *Journal of Applied Psychology, 74*, 72–80.

Martin, B. A., Bowen, C. C., & Hunt, S. T. (2002). How effective are people at faking personality questionnaires? *Personality and Individual Differences, 32*, 247–256.

McCloy, R. A., Heggestad, E. D., & Reeve, C. L. (2005). A silk purse from the sow's ear: Retrieving normative information from multidimensional forced-choice items. *Organizationa Research Methods, 8*, 222–248.

McCoach, D. B., & Adelson, J. (2010). Dealing with dependence (Part I): Understanding the effects of clustered data. *Gifted Child Quarterly, 54*, 152–155.

McConahay, J. B. (1986). Modern racism, ambivalence, and the modern racism scale. In J. F. Dovidio & S. L. Gaertner (Eds.), *Prejudice, discrimination and racism* (pp. 91–125). FL, Orlando: Academic Press.

McDonald, J. L. (2004). The optimal number of categories for numerical rating scales. *Dissertation Abstracts International, 65,* 5A. (UMI No. 3134422).

McFarland, L. A., & Ryan, A. M. (2000). Variance in faking across noncognitive measures. *Journal of Applied Psychology, 85*, 812–821.

McMorris, R. (1971). *Paper presented at the annual meeting of the Northeastern Educational Research Association*. Ellenville: Normative and ipsative measures of occupational values.

Meade, A. W. (2004). Psychometric problems and issues involved with creating and using ipsative measures for selection. *Journal of Occupational and Organizational Psychology, 77*, 531–552.

Mehrens, W., & Lehmann, I. (1983). *Measurement and evaluation in education and psychology* (3rd ed.). New York: Holt, Rinehart & Winston.

Meijer, R. R., & Nering, M. L. (1999). Computerized adaptive testing: Overview and introduction. *Applied Psychological Measurement, 23*, 187–194.

Melnick, S. A. (1993). The effects of item grouping on the reliability and scale scores of an affective measure. *Educational and Psychological Measurement, 3*(1), 211–216.

Melnick, S. A., & Gable, R. K. (1990). The use of negative item stems: A cautionary note. *Educational Research Quarterly, 14*(3), 31–36.

Messick, S. (1995). Validity of psychological assessment: Validation of inferences from persons' responses and performances as scientific inquiry into score meaning. *American Psychologist, 50*(9), 741–749.

Milgram, S. (1969). Comment on a failure to validate the lost letter technique. *Public Opinion Quarterly, 33*, 263–264.

Milgram, S., Mann, L., & Harters, S. (1965). The lost-letter technique. *Public Opinion Quarterly, 29*, 437–438.

Moore, D. W. (2002). Measuring new types of question-order effects: Additive and subtractive. *Public Opinion Quarterly, 66*, 80–91.

Murphy, S. T., & Zajonc, R. B. (1993). Affect, cognition, and awareness: Affective priming with optimal and suboptimal stimulus exposures. *Journal of Personality and Social Psychology, 64*, 723–739.

Muthén, L. K., & Muthén, B. O. (2012). *Mplus user's guide* (7th ed.). Los Angeles: Muthén & Muthén.

Nagel, E. (1931). Measurement. *Erkenntnis, 2*(1), 313–335.

Narayan, S., & Krosnick, J. A. (1996). Education Moderates Some Response Effects in Attitude Measurement. *Public Opinion Quarterly, 60*, 58–88.

Netemeyer, R. G., Bearden, W. O., & Sharma, S. (2003). *Scaling procedures: Issues and applications*. Thousand Oaks: Sage Publications.

Nunnally, J. C., & Bernstein, I. H. (1994). *Psychometric theory* (3rd ed.). New York: McGraw-Hill.

O'Muircheartaigh C. A., Krosnick J. A., & Helic A. (1999). *Middle alternatives, acquiescence, and the quality of questionnaire data*. Presented at Annual Meeting American Association of Public Opinion Research, Fort Lauderdale.

Ochieng, C. O. (2001). *Implications of Using Likert Data in Multiple Regression Analysis*. Unpublished Doctoral Dissertation, University of British Columbia.

Osgood, C. E. (1952). The nature and measurement of meaning. *Psychological Bulletin, 49*, 197–237.

Osgood, C. E., Suci, C. J., & Tannenbaum, P. H. (1957). *The measurement of meaning*. Urbana: University of Illinois Press.

Ostrom, T. M., & Gannon, K. M. (1996). Exemplar generation: Assessing how respondents give meaning to rating scales. In N. Schwarz & S. Sudman (Eds.), *Answering questions* (pp. 293–318). San Francisco: Jossey-Bass.

Pajares, F., Hartley, J., & Valiante, G. (2001). Response format in writing self-efficacy assessment: Greater discrimination increases prediction. *Measurement and Evaluation in Counseling and Development, 33*, 214–221.

Pappalardo, S. J. (1971). *An investigation of the efficacy of "in-basket" and "role-playing" variations of simulation technique for use in counselor education*. Unpublished doctoral dissertation, Albany: State University of New York.

Paulhus, D. L. (1991). Measurement and control of response bias. In J. P. Robinson, P. R. Shaver, & L. S. Wrightsman (Eds.), *Measures of personality and social psychological attitudes* (pp. 17–59). San Francisco: Academic Press.

Pett, M. A., Lackey, N. R., & Sullivan, J. J. (2003). *Making sense of factor analysis: The use of factor analysis for instrument development in health care research*. Thousand Oaks: Sage.

Pilotte W. J, (1991). The impact of mixed item stems on the responses of high school students to a computer anxiety scale (Doctoral Dissertation, University of Connecticut, Storrs).

Pilotte, W. J., & Gable, R. K. (1990). The impact of positive and negative item stems on the validity of a computer anxiety scale. *Educational and Psychological Measurement, 50*, 603–610.

Preston, C. C., & Colman, A. M. (2000). Optimal number of response categories in rating scales: Reliability, validity, discriminating power, and respondent preferences. *Acta Psychologica, 104*, 1–15.

Rhemtulla, M., Brosseau-Liard, P., & Savalei, V. (2010). How many categories is enough to treat data as continuous? A comparison of robust continuous and categorical SEM estimation methods under a range of non-ideal situations. Retrieved from http://www2.psych.ubc.ca/~mijke/files/HowManyCategories.pdf.

Richman, W., Kiesler, S., Weisband, S., & Drasgow, F. (1999). A meta-analytic study of social desirability distortion in computer-administered questionnaires, traditional questionnaires, and interviews. *Journal of Applied Psychology, 84*, 754–775.

Roberts, J. S., Laughlin, J. E., & Wedell, D. H. (1999). Validity issues in the Likert and Thurstone approaches to attitude measurement. *Educational and Psychological Measurement, 59*(2), 211–233.

Robinson, J. P., Shaver, P. R., & Wrightsman, L. S. (1991). *Measures of personality and social psychological attitudes*. San Diego: Academic Press.

Rodebaugh, T. L., Woods, C. M., Thissen, D., Heimberg, R. G., Chambless, D. L., & Rapee, R. M. (2004). More information from fewer questions: The factor structure and item properties of the original and brief fear of negative evaluation scales. *Psychological Assessment, 16*, 169–181.

Rosenberg, M. J. (1956). Cognitive structure and attitudinal affect. *The Journal of Abnormal and Social Psychology, 53*, 367–372.

Rossi, P. H., Wright, J. D., & Anderson, A. B. (1983). *Handbook of survey research*. New York: Academic Press.

Roszkowski, M., & Soven, M. (2010). Shifting gears: Consequences of including two negatively worded items in the middle of a positively worded questionnaire. *Assessment & Evaluation in Higher Education, 35*(1), 117–134.

Rothstein, M. G., & Goffin, R. D. (2006). The use of personality measures in personnel selection: What does current research support? *Human Resource Management Review, 16*, 155–180.

Saville, P., & Willson, E. (1991). The reliability and validity of normative and ispative approaches in the measurement of personality. *Journal of Occupational Psychology, 64*, 219–238.

Schriesheim, C. A., Eisenbach, R. J., & Hill, K. D. (1991). The effect of negation and polar opposite item reversals on questionnaire reliability and validity: An experimental investigation. *Educational and Psychological Measurement, 51*, 67–78.

Schriesheim, C. A., Powers, K. J., Scandura, T. A., Gardiner, C. C., & Lankau, M. J. (1993). Improving construct measurement in management research: Comments and a quantitative approach for assessing the theoretical content adequacy of paper-and-paper survey-type instruments. *Journal of Management, 19*, 385–417.

Schuman, H., & Presser, S. (1996). *Questions and answers in attitude surveys: Experiments on question form, wording, and context*. Thousand Oaks: Sage.

Scott, W. A. (1968). Comparative validities of forced-choice and single-stimulus tests. *Psychological Bulletin, 70*(4), 231–244.

Simon, H. A. (1957). *Models of man: Social and rational*. New York: John Wiley and Sons.

Snider, J. G., & Osgood, C. E. (1969). *Semantic differential technique: A sourcebook*. Chicago: Aldine.

Sparfeldt, J. R., Schilling, S. R., Rost, D. H., Thiel, A. (2006). Blocked versus randomized format of questionnaires: A confirmatory multigroup analysis. *Educational and Psychological Measurement, 66*(6), 961–974.

Stark, S., Chernyshenko, O. S., & Drasgow, F. (2005). An IRT approach to constructing and scoring pairwise preference items involving stimuli on different dimensions: The multiunidimensional pairwise-preference model. *Applied Psychological Measurement, 29*, 184–203.

Stark, S., Chernyshenko, O. S., Drasgow, F., & Williams, B. A. (2006). Examining assumptions about item responding in personality assessment: Should ideal point methods be considered for scale development and scoring? *Journal of Applied Psychology, 91*, 25–39.

Steenkamp, J. E. M., & Baumgartner, H. (1995). Development and cross-national validation of a short-form of CSI as a measure of optimum stimulation level. *International Journal of Research in Marketing, 12*, 97–104.

Stevens, S. S. (1946). On the theory of scales and measurement. *Science, 103*, 667–680.

Strack, F., Schwarz, N., & Gschneidinger, E. (1985). Happiness and reminiscing: The role of time perspective, affect, and mode of thinking. *Journal of Personality and Social Psychology, 49*, 1460–1469.

Sudman, S., Bradburn, N. M., & Schwarz, N. (1996). *Thinking about answers: The application of cognitive processes to survey methodology*. San Francisco: Jossey-Bass.

Tenopyr, M. L. (1968). *Internal consistency of ipsative scores: The "one reliable scale" phenomenon*. Paper presented at the 76th annual convention of the American Psychological Association, San Francisco.

Thurstone, L. L. (1927). The method of paired comparisons for social values. *Journal of Abnormal and Social Psychology, 21*, 384–400.

Thurstone, L. L. (1928). Attitudes can be measured. *American Journal of Sociology, 33*, 529–554.

Thurstone, L. L. (1931a). The measurement of attitudes. *Journal of Abnormal and Social Psychology, 26*, 249–269.

Thurstone, L. L. (1931b). The measurement of change in social attitudes. *Journal of Social Psychology, 2*, 230–235.

Thurstone, L. L. (1946). Comment. *American Journal of Sociology, 52*, 39–50.

Thurstone, L. L., & Chave, E. (1929). *The Measurement of Attitude*. Chicago: University of Chicago Press.

Tourangeau, R., & Rasinski, K. A. (1988). Cognitive processes underlying context effects in attitude measurement. *Psychological Bulletin, 103*, 299–314.

Tourangeau, R., Couper, M. P., & Conrad, F. (2007). Colors, labels, and interpretive heuristics for response scales. *Public Opinion Quarterly, 71*(1), 91–112.

Vasilopoulos, N. L., Cucina, J. M., & McElreath, J. M. (2005). Do warnings of response verification moderate the relationship between personality and cognitive ability? *Journal of Applied Psychology, 90*, 306–322.

Veres, J. G., Sims, R. R., & Locklear, T. S. (1991). Improving the reliability of Kolb's revised LSI. *Educational and Psychological Measurement, 51*, 143–150.

Viswesvaran, C., & Ones, D. S. (1999). Meta-analyses of fakability estimates: Implications for personality measurement. *Educational and Psychological Measurement, 59*(2), 197–210.

Watson, D. (1992). Correcting for acquiescent response bias in the absence of a balanced scale: An application to class consciousness. *Sociological Methods & Research, 21*, 52–88.
Weisberg, H. F., Krosnick, J. A., & Bowen, B. D. (1996). *An introduction to survey research, polling, and data analysis* (3rd ed.). Newbury Park: Sage.
Weng, L. J. (2004). Impact of the number of response categories and anchor labels on coefficient alpha and test-retest reliability. *Educational and Psychological Measurement, 64*, 956–972.
Whitley, B. E., & Kost, C. R. (1999). College students' perceptions of peers who cheat. *Journal of Applied Social Psychology, 29*, 1732–1760.
Wilson, M. (2005). *Constructing measures: An item response modeling approach*. Mahwah: Erlbaum.
Wilson, T. D., Lindsey, S., & Schooler, T. Y. (2000). A model of dual attitudes. *Psychological Review, 107*, 101–126.
Wirth, R. J., & Edwards, M. C. (2007). Item factor analysis: Current approaches and future directions. *Psychological Methods, 12*, 58–79.
Wright, B. D. (1984). Despair and hope for educational measurement. *Contemporary Education Review, 3*(1), 281–288.
Wright, B. D. (1997). A history of social science measurement. *Educational Measurement: Issues and Practice, 16*(4), 33–45.
Wright, B. D. (1999). Fundamental measurement for psychology. In S. E. Embretson & S. L. Hershberger (Eds.), *The new rules of measurement: What every educator and psychologist should know* (pp. 65–104). Hillsdale: Lawrence Erlbaum Associates.
Wright, B. D., & Masters, G. N. (1982). *Rating scale analysis*. Chicago: MESA Press.
Zaller, J. R., & Feldman, S. (1992). A simple theory of the survey response: Answering questions versus revealing preferences. *American Journal of Political Science, 36*, 579–616.

Chapter 3
Evidence Based on Test Content

"Validity is simple; Validation can be difficult"
M. Kane 2009, p. 49

Defining Validity

The investigation of the validity of the interpretations of data from and affective instrument assesses the degree to which inferences about the constructs of interest are plausible and supported by appropriate evidence (Kane 1992). Contrary to popular belief, an instrument or assessment is not, nor can it be "valid." Even though we commonly speak of instrument validation, it is not the instrument itself that is validated, but rather the inferences and interpretations of the obtained scores (Messick 1989, 1995).[1] The investigation of validity is an ongoing process of accumulating various sources of evidence in support of our test score interpretations (Kane 1992). The process continually addresses the appropriateness of the inferences to be made from scores obtained from the instrument. Thus, validity focuses on the interpretations one wishes to make for a test score in a particular situation. As stated in the *Standards for Educational and Psychological Tests*:

> Validity refers to the degree to which evidence and theory support the interpretation of test scores entailed by proposed uses of tests. Validity is, therefore, the most fundamental consideration in developing and evaluating tests. The process of validation involves accumulating evidence to provide a sound scientific basis for proposed score interpretations. It is the interpretations of tests scores required by proposed uses that are evaluated, not the test itself. (American educational research association [AERA], American Psychological Association [APA], & National Council on Measurement in Education [NCME] 1999, p. 9)

Messick (1995) defines validity broadly as "an evaluative summary of both the evidence for and the actual—as well as potential—consequences of score interpretation and use (i.e., construct validity conceived comprehensively)"

[1] It should be noted that there is a re-emerging school of thought that suggests that validity is in fact a property of instruments (Borsboom et al. 2003, 2004). Proponents of this approach to validity argue that there is a "scientific realism" to the unobserved latent constructs that affective instruments are designed to measure (Hood 2009). In contrast, supporters of the "inferential" approach to validity advocated by Messick (1989) make no strong assumptions on the psychological reality of the constructs under investigation.

D. B. McCoach et al., *Instrument Development in the Affective Domain*,
DOI: 10.1007/978-1-4614-7135-6_3,

(Messick 1995, p. 742). In the not so distant past, it was common for measurement students to learn about three major types of validity: content validity, criterion-related validity, and construct validity. This often led to the mistaken notion that there were various distinct types of validity. We wish to unequivocally dispel the myth of the triumvirate of validities. Instead, "the construct validity of score interpretation comes to undergird all score-based inferences—not just those related to interpretive meaningfulness but also the content- and criterion-related inferences specific to applied decisions and actions based on test scores" (Messick 1995, p. 744). This unitary and "comprehensive view of validity integrates considerations of content, criteria, and consequences into a construct framework for empirically testing rational hypotheses about score meaning and utility" (Messick 1995, p. 742). Thus, "Construct validity is based on an integration of any evidence that bears on the interpretation or meaning of the test scores—including content- and criterion-related evidence—which are thus subsumed as part of construct validity" (Messick 1995, p. 742). This idea is not new. In fact, Over 55 years ago, Loevinger (1957) stated that "Evidence for construct validity can be broken down into evidence that the test measures something systematic and evidence for the particular interpretation of what it measures. The degree of internal structure of the items and the magnitude of external correlations are the former, or psychometric, evidence; the nature of the structure, content of the items and nature of the external relations are the latter, or psychological, evidence" (p. 687).

In this context, instrument validation is an ongoing empirical evaluation of the meaning and consequences of the measures we have created. Therefore, "validation combines scientific inquiry with rational argument to justify (or nullify) score interpretation and use" (Messick 1995, p. 742). Although validity can never be definitely established, it requires evidence that

1. The instrument measures what it claims to measure,
2. The scores on the instrument demonstrate adequate reliability for the intended purpose, and
3. The scores derived from the instrument relate to other key variables or measures in a way that supports the hypothesized relations among the variables (Sireci 2009).

At the heart of all validity studies is the deceptively simple notion: are we measuring what we claim to be measuring?

The idea of building a validity argument has become common parlance in measurement and assessment circles. This view of validity underscores the importance of accumulating and arsenal of evidence and coherently synthesizing that evidence to support claims about the ability to make specific inferences from an assessment. The essence of the validity argument is that the goal of the validation process is to build an argument that supports using the instrument for a particular purpose (Sireci 2009). Kane (1992) describes the argument-based approach to validity as a process whereby one chooses the interpretation, specifies the interpretive argument associated with the interpretation, identifies competing interpretations, and develops evidence to support the intended interpretation and to refute the competing interpretations. The amount of evidence and the types of evidence needed in a particular case depend on the inferences and assumptions in the interpretive argument (Kane 1992, p. 534).

In other words, the validator must (1) determine the inferences to be made from the scores on the instrument, (2) develop hypotheses and decide sources of evidence that would support or refute those inferences, (3) gather the data necessary to evaluate the hypotheses, and (4) weigh the evidence for or against the argument, based on the analyses of the collected data (Sireci 2009). In contrast to the notion that test developers validate instruments and test users choose validated assessments to use, the recent focus on validity as an interpretation has led to a more distributed view of instrument validation in which "validation is the joint responsibility of the test developer and the test user" (AERA, APA, and NCME 1999, p. 11). However, the idea that the test consumer shares some responsibility in the validation process dates back to Cronbach and Meehl (1955), who stated "a consumer of the test who rejects the authors' theory cannot accept the author's validation. He must validate the test for himself if he wishes to show that it represents the construct as he defines it" (Cronbach and Meehl 1955, p. 291). The instrument developer and the instrument consumer share equally in ensuring that the instrument is used appropriately, in ways that provide appropriate inferences. "The test developer is responsible for furnishing relevant evidence and a rationale in support of the intended test use. The test user is ultimately responsible for evaluating the evidence in the particular setting in which the test is to be used" (AERA, APA, and NCME 1999, p. 11). Test developers create assessments for a given purpose. However, it is fairly common for test consumers to use assessments for a purpose other than the one that the developer intended. "When the use of the test differs from that supported by the test developer, the test user bears special responsibility for validation" (AERA, APA, and NCME 1999, p. 11).

Messick (1995) argues that there are two major threats to construct validity: *construct underrepresentation* and *construct irrelevant variance*. In the case of construct underrepresentation, "the assessment is too narrow and fails to include important dimensions or facets of the construct" (Messick 1995, p. 742). In the case of *construct-irrelevant variance*, "the assessment is too broad, containing excess reliable variance associated with other distinct constructs as well as method variance such as response sets or guessing propensities that affects responses in a manner irrelevant to the interpreted construct" (Messick 1995, p. 742). Messick asserts that both threats are salient for all assessments. Therefore, he argues that a primary validation concern is "the extent to which the same assessment might underrepresent the focal construct while simultaneously contaminating the scores with construct-irrelevant variance" (Messick 1995, p. 742). In essence, Messick reminds us that constructs that are defined too narrowly may fail to fully capture the construct of interest, whereas constructs that are defined too loosely or broadly may fail to capture the construct clearly and sharply. Thus, we must find a way to fully capture the construct without bringing extraneous constructs into the operationalization. This is truly a challenge.

Validity Evidence

Arguments for validity are based upon two basic types of evidence: judgmental and empirical, or the combination of both types. The judgmental evidence is generally gathered prior to the actual administration of the items to the target group and consists mainly of methods for examining the adequacy of the operational definition of the affective characteristics in light of their conceptual definitions. Empirical evidence involves examining relationships among items within the instrument, as well as relationships of the instrument to other instruments measuring similar or different constructs. Clearly, the context of the theory underlying the variables measured and the probable uses of the instrument figure prominently when evaluating these relationships. In this chapter, we describe validity evidence based on instrument (i.e., test) content. We describe several techniques for gathering appropriate judgmental and empirical evidence for validity evidence for affective/attitude instruments. In Chapters 4 and 5, we provide an overview of techniques for gathering validity evidence based on the internal structure of the instrument. In Chapter 6, we present techniques for gathering validity evidence based on relationships to external measures.

Evidence Based on Instrument Content

Definition

The validity of test score interpretations depends on the definition of the domain of content and the relationship between the domain content and the content of the instrument (Kane 2009). Validity evidence based on instrument content should receive the highest priority during the early stages of the instrument development process. Unfortunately, some developers rush through the item development and content validation process with little appreciation for its enormous importance, only to find that their instrument "does not work" (i.e., lack of construct validity for score interpretations or internal consistency reliability for the data) after obtaining the response data. The importance of the analysis of instrument content is evident when one considers the conceptual and operational definitions of the affective characteristics.

Over 40 years ago, Cronbach (1971) described the validity evidence of test content (formerly referred to as "content validity") as the answer to the question: *To what extent do the items on the test (instrument) adequately sample from the intended universe of content*? Underlying any affective characteristic, a theoretical rationale and conceptual definition must describe the universe of possible items or content areas to be included in the instrument. Given the conceptual definitions for the constructs of interest, the developer must then generate the operational definitions—the sets of items. The responses obtained from administration of the instrument then reflect these operational definitions and are used to make inferences back to the conceptual definitions underlying the affective characteristics. Therefore, the congruence between the conceptual definitions and the operational definitions is critically important. If the operational definition fails to adequately capture the conceptual definition, then the instrument cannot capture the construct that it was designed to measure and the rest of the validation process is built on a flawed foundation. Thus, unless the instrument developer carefully addresses the process of obtaining validity evidence based on content, interpretation of the resulting data will most likely be meaningless (i.e., lack valid scores interpretations).

Gathering evidence of content validity involves measuring "the degree to which elements of an assessment instrument are relevant to and representative of the targeted construct for a particular assessment purpose" (Haynes et al. 1995, p. 238). It is also important to remember that "content validity is a dynamic aspect of an instrument. As constructs are refined over time, the content validity of instruments intended to assess them will necessarily decline" (Haynes et al. 1995; Vogt et al. 2004, p. 231). Therefore, it may be necessary to revisit the conceptual and operational definitions of a construct, as well as the evidence of the content validity of the instrument, even after the initial validation of the instrument has been completed.

Gathering Evidence of the Validity of Content

Validity evidence based on content is primarily *judgmental* in nature and is mostly gathered prior to the actual administration of the instrument. Two primary sources become the focus of the validity evidence: the conceptual and the operational definitions of the affective characteristics. The conceptual definition of a construct is the abstract verbal description of the construct, which includes its attributes and defining features. The operational definition of the construct is the way that the construct is actually measured in practice (i.e., the measure scale, item(s), etc.).

There are two critical junctures in the measurement of abstract constructs. First, the conceptual definition for the construct must capture the essence of the construct in question. When a construct is defined precisely and that definition has achieved near universal acceptance, then the development of the conceptual definition is a fairly straightforward task. However, for constructs that have inconsistent definitions or fuzzy boundaries, this task can be far more challenging (Haynes et al. 1995). Second, it is essential that the operational definition capture the conceptual definition as completely and accurately as possible. Operational representations of abstract constructs will never fully and completely capture the construct. However, it is important that the operational definition capture the essence of the construct. Inadequate sampling necessarily leads to invalid inferences regarding test score interpretations. Put simply, correspondence between the operational and conceptual definitions is essential for evidence based on test content.

The Relationship of the Conceptual Definition and the Operational Definition

To illustrate the sampling of content from the domain of the construct, we have created three figures. Figure 3.1 demonstrates the process of sampling from a domain of content to develop adequate operational definitions of the constructs of interest. There is a domain or universe of content from which we wish to sample. This universe or domain is represented by the large circle. Within that domain or universe of content, there may be multiple dimensions, facets, or factors, which are represented by the clouds. The X's represent hypothetical items, which are drawn from each of the dimensions. It is important to ensure that we adequately sample from each of the dimensions. Therefore, we would like the items to be a representative sample from across the entire area of the dimension.

In contrast, Fig. 3.2 illustrates the concept of construct underrepresentation visually. Notice that all of the items are drawn from a small section of the construct. Using the set of items from Fig. 3.2 would not adequately capture the full domain of content and would therefore result in construct underrepresentation. In such a situation, the operational definition (the scale or the set of items) does a poor job capturing the full domain of content from the original construct.

Figure 3.3 illustrates the concept of construct irrelevant variance. Notice that some of the items measure the dimension of interest and some of the items measure content that is outside the dimension of interest. Alternatively, a single question could simultaneously measure two or more dimensions or constructs, which would also result in construct irrelevant variance. For example, math word problems simultaneously assess both math ability and reading ability. The co-mingling of reading ability within the math assessment introduces construct irrelevant variance into the measure of math ability. Affective measures that contain item stems that are difficult to read may introduce construct irrelevant variance for the same reason.

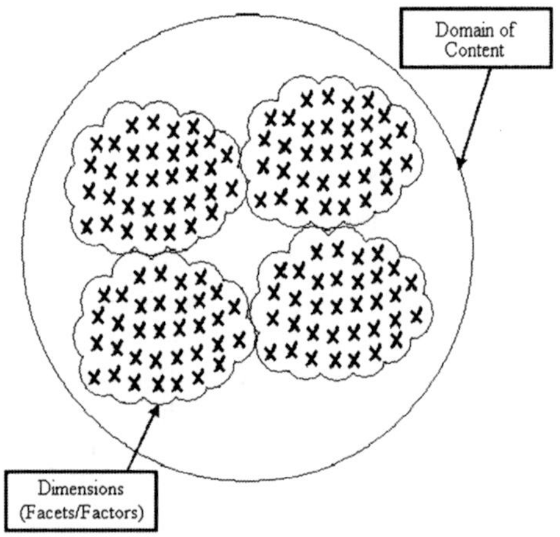

Fig. 3.1 Dimensions within a content domain

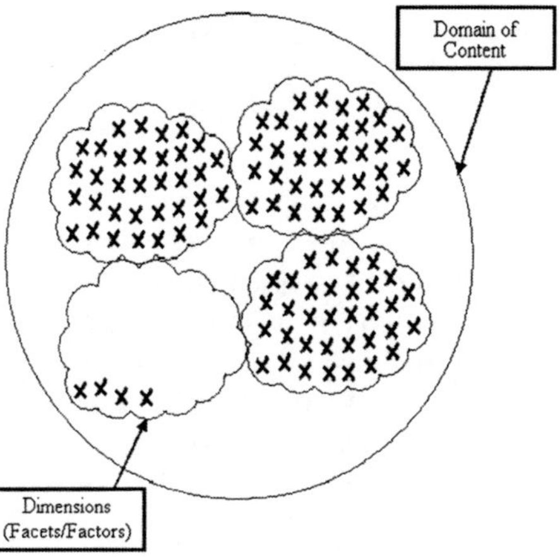

Fig. 3.2 Under-represented construct within a content domain

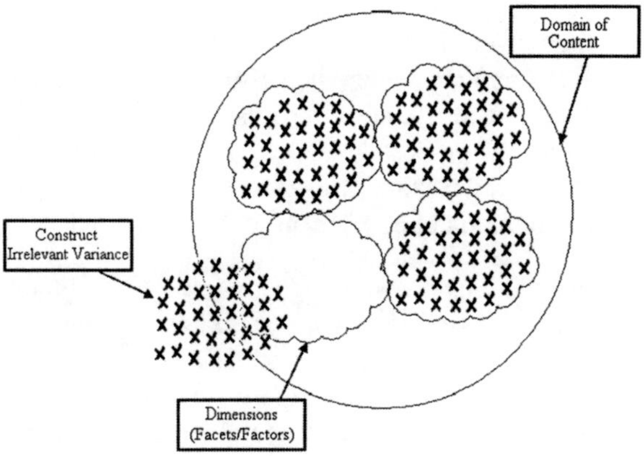

Fig. 3.3 Construct irrelevant variance

How many constructs are represented in Fig. 3.1? We could describe Fig. 3.1 as 4 smaller, unidimensional constructs that are strongly related to each other. Alternatively, we could describe Fig. 3.1 as one larger, more diffuse multidimensional construct that comprises four dimensions or facets. In some sense, during the item writing and content validation phase, the decision about whether to view the construct as a single, larger, higher order, multidimensional construct with four dimensions or four strongly related but more constrained lower order constructs is not a critical one. The universe of content and the sampling from that universe should be similar under either conception. (During the analytic phase, this is a critical distinction: the model for a single higher order factor would be more constrained than the model for four-related unidimensional factors.)

Conceptual Definitions

The theoretical basis for the conceptual definitions is developed through a comprehensive review of appropriate literature. Instrument developers must specify and summarize their literature base when describing the instrument. Understanding the theoretical lens and empirical research from which the developer formulated the instrument is essential. The evidence for the validity of the content revolves around judgments regarding the universe of content from which the instrument developers have sampled in developing the instrument.

Clark and Watson (1995) asserted that the importance of the literature review "cannot be overstated" (p. 311). They provided three reasons that the literature review is essential in the initial phases of instrument development:

1. The literature review clarifies the nature and the range of the content of the target construct and/or dimensions.
2. The literature review may uncover problems with existing measures of the constructs, providing the developer with helpful hints about pitfalls to avoid in the new scale.
3. The literature review helps to evaluate whether the proposed scale is actually needed at all. "Unless the prospective test developer can clearly articulate ways in which the proposed scale will represent either a theoretical or empirical improvement over existing measures, it is preferable to avoid contributing to the needless proliferation of assessment instruments" (Clark and Watson 1995, p. 311).

In addition to a thorough review of the literature, consultation with content experts can also aid in the development of the conceptual definitions. One structured way to gather such feedback is to establish a panel consisting of content experts with professional expertise in the area of the affective characteristic under consideration. It is essential that the content experts be thoroughly grounded in the literature representing the affective characteristic. We recommend providing the panel of experts with a bibliography and summary of the literature used as a definition of the universe of content. Individually or as a group, the experts can then review the materials and comment on the adequacy of the conceptual definition of the affective characteristic as it relates to the proposed use of the instrument. They can also provide guidance about whether all important literature related to the construct of interest has been reviewed and included. Simple rating sheets can be developed for this task so that the experts can rate and comment on such areas as comprehensiveness of theory and adequacy of sampling from the content universe. Following this review of the theoretical base, the development of the operational definitions can begin.

Operational Definitions

The operational definitions are the vehicles by which the developer samples from the universe of content specified by the conceptual definition. The items must reflect the conceptual definitions that were developed and reviewed. The items must span the entire domain of content within the dimensions being assessed. In addition, the development of the items should be linked to the results of the literature review and the expert feedback provided during the development of the conceptual definition. Finally, the representation of the content should be approximately proportional to the importance of that content for the scale (Clark and Watson 1995; Loevinger 1957). It may also be helpful to consult members of the target population when developing items to ensure that the items capture the affective characteristics that they were designed to measure and to confirm that they can be clearly understood and answered by members of the target population (Vogt et al. 2004).

After developing the items, it is essential that the operational definitions be reviewed by the same content experts who aided in the development of the conceptual definitions. In addition, we recommend including supplementary content experts who were not part of the development of the conceptual definition to aid in the evaluation of the operational definitions. The content experts should review the items for content coverage. The items within a dimension should represent the scope of the dimension or construct being measured, and the relevance of the items to that construct or dimension should be unambiguous (Haynes et al. 1995).

The solicitation of expert feedback on the instrument can be either qualitative or quantitative in nature. We recommend collecting both qualitative and quantitative information from the expert judges. McKenzie et al. (1999) recommend collecting qualitative feedback from the expert jurors first, incorporating their changes into the instrument, and then soliciting quantitative feedback from the jurors. If this is not possible, then collect qualitative and quantitative feedback about the instrument simultaneously.

Table 3.1 contains a generic list of potential questions designed to solicit qualitative feedback from content experts. This is in no way meant to be a comprehensive list of content validation questions. Instead, it provides a sample of the types of questions that are frequently used to solicit feedback during the content validity phase.

To gather quantitative evidence of content adequacy, we recommend creating a content validity form that systematically collects information about whether the expert can match each item to its intended domain or dimension of content as well as his or her opinion about well the item captures the essence of that domain.[2]

To collect quantitative evidence, raters complete a rating form that asks them to evaluate each of the item stems. The form should name and briefly describe each

[2] An example of a content validation form from Baslanti and McCoach's work on the CSAS appears in Appendix A.

Table 3.1 Sample questions to solicit feedback from content experts

• Do you have any suggestions regarding the definitions of the constructs?
• Do the items appear to cover the full range of content within each construct? Do you have any suggestions for improving content coverage?
• Are the instrument items clearly worded and unambiguous? Are they appropriate for secondary school and university students? Do you have any suggestions for improving the item stems (feel free to provide comments directly on the item stems regarding rewording and/or eliminating)?
• Do you have any suggestions for items that you would add?
• Please feel free to add any additional thoughts or comments below.

dimension measured by the instrument. A sample content validity sheet, similar to the ones that we routinely employ is included in Table 3.2. The form begins with instructions regarding the rating task and then lists the definitions of the categories. The judges are then asked to (1) assign each item to the category it best fits; (2) to indicate how certain they feel about their assignment of the item to the category; and (3) indicate how relevant or essential they feel that the item is for the construct.

For each item, the rater must select which domain the item measures, and this task is completed independently. This provides an objective assessment how well the content experts felt that the item matched the domain. It is important that the experts be blind to the intentions of the instrument developer during this task. Experts may agree that an item measures a given construct or dimension when they are told what domain the item is designed to measure, but they may be unable to match the item to the correct dimension when given the choice of several similar domains/dimensions. In addition, we always provide a "none of the above" option. That way, if the rater feels that the item does not measure any of the domains/dimensions described on the sheet, he/she does need to try to guess which of the described dimensions the author intended to measure. Without such an option, the content validator may randomly select the correct category for the item, artificially inflating the percentage of correct classifications for that item. The rating about the certainty with which the item belongs on a given domain/dimension provides the rater with the opportunity to indicate any doubts or uncertainty that he or she may have with regards to the item placement. Finally, the rater's perception of the appropriateness or relevance of the item for that dimension provides an opportunity for the rater to assess the centrality, relevance, or importance of the item to the domain in question.

Waltz et al. (1991) suggest that the accuracy of each content expert can be checked by placing a certain number of non-representative or incongruent items on the instrument. The instrument developer can then check to see how many of these irrelevant items each content expert detected. If a content expert fails to detect these aberrant items, the ratings of that judge should not be used.

After the raters complete the content validity forms, we tally the responses to the content validity ratings and establish criteria for evaluating the questions. Generally, questions should be placed in the correct content category by most or

Table 3.2 Example form for expert content validation

Item	Category						Certainty				Relevance		
1. Getting A's is very difficult for me	I	II	III	IV	V	VI	1	2	3	4	1	2	3
2. I feel alienated at school	I	II	III	IV	V	VI	1	2	3	4	1	2	3
3. I am not motivated to study for exams	I	II	III	IV	V	VI	1	2	3	4	1	2	3
4. I dislike my courses	I	II	III	IV	V	VI	1	2	3	4	1	2	3
5. School is of no value to me	I	II	III	IV	V	VI	1	2	3	4	1	2	3
6. I wish that I went to a different school	I	II	III	IV	V	VI	1	2	3	4	1	2	3
7. I feel socially isolated at school	I	II	III	IV	V	VI	1	2	3	4	1	2	3
8. I put forth minimal effort on my schoolwork	I	II	III	IV	V	VI	1	2	3	4	1	2	3
9. Most teachers here are poor teachers	I	II	III	IV	V	VI	1	2	3	4	1	2	3
10. I do not feel like I belong at this school	I	II	III	IV	V	VI	1	2	3	4	1	2	3
11. I have trouble keeping track of my assignments	I	II	III	IV	V	VI	1	2	3	4	1	2	3
12. I hate school	I	II	III	IV	V	VI	1	2	3	4	1	2	3
13. I feel powerless at school	I	II	III	IV	V	VI	1	2	3	4	1	2	3
14. I have trouble keeping track of my school supplies	I	II	III	IV	V	VI	1	2	3	4	1	2	3
15. People say that I am a lazy student	I	II	III	IV	V	VI	1	2	3	4	1	2	3
16. Nobody at this school cares about me	I	II	III	IV	V	VI	1	2	3	4	1	2	3
17. I feel depressed when I am at school	I	II	III	IV	V	VI	1	2	3	4	1	2	3
18. I withdraw at school	I	II	III	IV	V	VI	1	2	3	4	1	2	3
19. People think that I am smarter than I actually am	I	II	III	IV	V	VI	1	2	3	4	1	2	3
20. I have trouble concentrating on my schoolwork	I	II	III	IV	V	VI	1	2	3	4	1	2	3
21. My teachers have negative attitudes toward me	I	II	III	IV	V	VI	1	2	3	4	1	2	3
22. I have no plans for the future	I	II	III	IV	V	VI	1	2	3	4	1	2	3
23. I am unable to do well in school	I	II	III	IV	V	VI	1	2	3	4	1	2	3
24. I feel alone at school	I	II	III	IV	V	VI	1	2	3	4	1	2	3
...	I	II	III	IV	V	VI	1	2	3	4	1	2	3

all of the judges, and the judges should be certain about their placement. In addition, most or all of the judges should feel that the item is highly relevant to the construct. When computing the certainty and relevance ratings, it is important to exclude from the computations any raters who misplaced the item into the incorrect category. After all, we do not care how certain a rater feels that the item belongs in the "wrong" content category! Occasionally, the majority of raters place an item in a category other than the one that the developer had intended. Careful consideration should be given to such items. Were they unclear? Was the developer's original conception of the item's placement flawed? Usually, such items are removed from the survey. However, occasionally, the instrument developer may recognize a flaw in his or her original thinking and move the item to the other domain/dimension.

After compiling the judges' scores, we typically compute the percentage of judges that rate the item in the top "certainty" and "relevance" categories as well as the mean certainty and relevance for each of the items. Once we tabulate the responses and triangulate the quantitative and qualitative data, we can use the information to make decisions as to which items should be retained for the pilot instrument, which items need to be modified, and which items should be eliminated. Table 3.3 provides an example of how the quantitative information from the content validity form can be tabulated and used to make decisions about the disposition of items.

In addition, it is possible to calculate an average congruency percentage to estimate the content validity of an instrument (Popham 1978). Content experts read the domain specifications for an instrument and then decide the congruence of each item with the specifications. The proportion of items rated congruent is calculated for each rater and then converted into a percentage. Next, the researcher

Table 3.3 Example of a table for item structure and content validation results

	Item no.	Subscale	Agreement (%)	Certainty	Relevance
I feel alienated at school	2	1	100.0	4.0	3.0
I feel socially isolated at school	7	1	100.0	3.8	2.9
I do not feel like I belong at this school	10	1	100.0	3.8	2.9
I withdraw at school	18	1	100.0	3.6	2.9
I feel alone at school	24	1	100.0	4.0	3.0
I feel powerless at school	13	1	38.0	2.0	1.9
Getting A's is very difficult for me	1	2	100.0	3.8	2.9
People think that I am smarter than I actually am	19	2	100.0	4.0	2.9
I am unable to do well in school	23	2	88.0	4.0	2.7
I wish that I went to a different school	6	3	63.0	2.9	2.3
I hate school	12	3	75.0	3.1	2.6
I dislike my courses	4	3	100.0	3.9	2.9
My teachers have negative attitudes toward me	21	3	75.0	3.4	2.4
Most teachers here are poor teachers	9	3	100.0	3.8	2.7
Nobody at this school cares about me	16	3	88.0	3.6	2.7
I feel depressed when I am at school	17	3	88.0	3.3	2.8
I am not motivated to study for exams	3	4	100.0	3.8	2.7
I put forth minimal effort on my schoolwork	8	4	88.0	3.3	2.8
I have trouble keeping track of my assignments	11	4	100.0	3.8	2.6
I have trouble keeping track of my school supplies	14	4	88.0	3.4	2.8
People say that I am a lazy student	15	4	88.0	3.1	2.7
I have problems in concentrating on my schoolwork	21	4	100.0	3.6	3.0
I have trouble concentrating on my schoolwork	20	4	100.0	3.6	2.7
I have no plans for the future	22	5	75.0	3.3	2.3
School is of no value to me	5	5	88.0	3.7	2.8
…					

calculates the mean percentage for all the experts participating in the assessment of the instrument's content validity to determine the average congruency percentage. Waltz et al. (1991) suggest that an acceptable average congruency—percentage is 90% or higher (Beck and Gable 2001).

Additionally, several content validity indices to evaluate item appropriateness exist (e.g., McKenzie et al. 1999). The index of content validity (CVI) provides one method to quantify an instrument's content validity. The CVI summarizes the content experts' ratings of the content relevance of the items on an instrument. Normally, the CVI uses a 4-point Likert scale, where 1 equals *not relevant* to 4, *very relevant*. The CVI represents the proportion of items on an instrument that achieved a rating of 3 or 4 by the content experts (Beck and Gable 2001).

The instrument developer establishes the criteria for reviewing the feedback from content experts. Examples of such criteria can be an average congruency percentage of at least 90% or a CVI of at least 0.80. Then, based on these criteria, the researcher makes decisions about retaining, rewording, or removing items. Because the content validity experts are expected to have extensive knowledge in the construct being measured, low percentages of agreement about the placement or relevance of an item should raise a red flag. If only one of the judges has rated the items differently than the remaining judges, it may be the lack of knowledge or misinterpretation of the judge that is to blame. However, when multiple judges have indicate that there is an issue with the item, then the instrument designer should take this feedback very seriously (Beck and Gable 2001).

After incorporating the revisions from the content experts, it can be helpful conduct focus groups with small groups of members of the target population to gauge their understanding of and reactions to the instrument. Also, target group members may be able to aid in wording the items in ways that are clear to the target population (Vogt et al. 2004). The importance of establishing the correspondence between the conceptual and operational definitions associated with the affective instrument cannot be overstated. It is essential to gather information to defend the argument that the items developed adequately sample from the intended universe of content being assessed. Generally, the validity argument regarding content is mostly based upon judgmental data. Given that arguments for the validity of the content are convincing and that appropriate revisions in the instrument have been made, after this stage, the basis of the argument switches from judgmental to mostly empirical data. Chapters 4–6 discuss methods to assess the other sources of evidence necessary to support meaningful score interpretations. "Content related validity evidence is essential for almost all interpretations, but it is, in itself, not enough for most interpretations" (Kane 2009, p. 61).

Evidence Based on Test Content Example

Beck and Gable (2000, 2002) utilized a variety of qualitative and quantitative techniques to provide evidence of the validity of test content when they developed the *Postpartum Depression Screening Scale* (*PDSS*). This 35 item Likert-type self-report instrument assesses seven dimensions of a mother's postpartum depression. Beck and Gable (2001) illustrated the important role qualitative research can play to establishing validity evidence based on instrument content. They discuss the content domain, conceptual and operational definitions, item generation, and judgmental evidence of content validity. Beck and Gable (2001) describe how the sequence of qualitative research studies conducted by Beck (1992, 1993, 1996) formed both the basis for developing the conceptual definitions and item generation, which in turn provided strong support for validity evidence based on content of the PDSS:

> Two of the studies (Beck 1992, 1996) were phenomenological studies and one study (Beck 1993) was a ground theory study. No one qualitative approach is better than another for specifying the content domain. For this program of research on postpartum depression, phenomenology was used in conjunction with grounded theory to provide a more complete and holistic description of this mood disorder. Wilson and Hutchinson (1991) claim that the triangulation of two qualitative approaches allows illumination of clinical realities that escape alternative approaches. By means of a phenomenological study, Beck (1992) first examined the experience of postpartum depression. Seven mothers were interviewed regarding their subjective experiences. Colaizzi's (1978) method of phenomenological analysis was used to analyze the verbatim transcripts. In this method, all significant statements that pertain directly to the phenomenon of study are extracted from the interview transcripts. Next, the meaning of each significant statement is spelled out in what is called a formulated meaning. All the formulated meanings are organized into clusters of themes and then combined into an exhaustive description of the phenomenon. The researcher may return to the study participants and ask them to review this description to determine if it compares with their own experience of the phenomenon under study. Any new, relevant data shared by the participants are then incorporated into the final description of the essence of the phenomenon. Forty-five significant statements were extracted from the interview transcripts and clustered into 11 themes which described the essence of this experience (p. 203).
>
> In her second qualitative study using grounded theory, Beck (1993) developed a substantive theory of postpartum depression entitled "Teetering on the Edge". Loss of control emerged as the basic social psychological problem, that is, the main concern the mothers had to contend with while they were suffering with postpartum depression. Women attempted to cope with this loss of control in all aspects of their lives, emotions, and thought processes, through the following four-stage process:
>
> 1. Encountering Terror,
> 2. Dying of the Self,
> 3. Struggling to Survive, and
> 4. Regaining Control.
>
> In the first stage of Encountering Terror women were suddenly hit with the symptoms of postpartum depression such as horrifying anxiety attacks, relentless obsessive thinking, and enveloping fogginess. The second stage, called Dying of Self, consisted of the mothers isolating themselves, feeling unreal, and for some women, actually contemplating and attempting ending their lives. In Struggling to Survive the women used strategies such as prayer, joining a support group, and battling the health care system. In the fourth and final stage of "Teetering on the Edge," mothers regained control of their lives. This grounded theory study confirmed and extended Beck's (1992) earlier findings. The first two stages of "Teetering on the Edge" confirmed the first nine themes from the phenomenological

> study. Loss of control, identified in Themes 10 and 11, was not only confirmed in "Teetering on the Edge," but emerged as the basic social psychological problem in postpartum depression. The grounded theory method enhanced the completeness of the knowledge concerning postpartum depression by focusing on process. In the last two steps of "Teetering on the Edge," the strategies women used to regain control of their lives and their consequences emerged. The third qualitative study in Beck's (1996) research program was a phenomenological study which specifically investigated the meaning of postpartum depressed mothers' experiences interacting with their infants and older children. Mothers were overwhelmed by the responsibilities of caring for their children. Guilt, irrational thinking, feelings of loss, and anger filled mothers' daily interactions with their children. While caring for their infants, mothers just went through, the motions, acting like robots. In order to survive, women erected a wall to separate themselves emotionally from their infants and older children and consequently failed to respond to their infants' cues. Detrimental relationships with a mother's older children materialized as her depression deepened (pp. 203–205).

These extensive qualitative studies by Beck (1992, 1993, 1996) resulted in the conceptual definitions and the later operational definitions (i.e., item statements). Given the extensive qualitative work that preceded the development of the instrument, the operationalization of the construct more realistically reflected the mothers' experiences with the phenomenon (i.e., postpartum depression) being assessed. In fact, many of the final items employed in the *PDSS* were essentially edited quotes from the mothers who had participated in the qualitative studies. Beck and Gable (2001) emphasized the importance of developing appropriate conceptual definitions prior to operationalizing the constructs and designing the instrument.

Summary

In this chapter, we have examined the issue of the validity in the framework of accumulating theory and judgmental/empirical evidence to support meaningful interpretations of scores obtained from affective instruments. The instrument developer must ensure that the relevant content is assessed and reflected in the items written for the instrument. As part of this process external experts evaluate the alignment of the operational definitions (item stems) and the conceptual (construct) definitions underlying the instrument. The validity of content is and should be primarily a judgmental process; however, it is possible to use optional simple empirical procedures for an a posteriori examination of validation of instrument. We also presented sample rating forms that can be used to gather quantitative data regarding the content experts' opinions.

References

American Educational Research Association (AERA), American Psychological Association (APA) and National Council on Measurement in Education (NCME). (1999). *The standards for educational and psychological testing*. Washington, DC: American Educational Research Association.

Beck, C. T., & Gable, R. K. (2001). Ensuring content validity: An illustration of the process. *Journal of Nursing Measurement, 9*(2), 201–215.

Beck, C. T. (1992). The lived experience of postpartum depression: A phenomenological study. *Nursing Research, 41*, 166–170.

Beck, C. T. (1993). Teetering on the edge: A substantive theory of postpartum depression. *Nursing Research, 42*, 42–48.

Beck, C. T. (1996). Postpartum depressed mothers' experiences interacting with their children. *Nursing Research, 45*, 98–104.

Beck, C. T., & Gable, R. K. (2000). Postpartum depression screening scale: Development and psychometric testing. *Nursing Research, 49*, 272–282.

Beck, C. H., & Gable, R. K. (2002). *Postpartum depression screening scale*. Los Angeles: Western Psychological Services.

Borsboom, D., Mellenbergh, G. J., & Van Heerden, J. (2003). Validity and truth. In H. Yanai, A. Okada, K. Shingemasu, Y. Kano, & J. J. Meulman (Eds.), *New developments in psychometrics: Proceedings of the international psychometrics society 2001* (pp. 321–328). Tokyo: Springer.

Borsboom, D., Mellenbergh, G. J., & Van Heerden, J. (2004). The concept of validity. *Psychological Review, 111*, 1061–1071.

Clark, L. A., & Watson, D. (1995). Constructing validity: Basic issues in objective scale development. *Psychological Assessment, 7*(3), 309–319.

Colaizzi, P. (1978). Psychological research as the phenomenologist views it. In R. Valle & M. King (Eds.), *Existential phenomenological alternative for psychology* (pp. 48–71). New York: Oxford University Press.

Cronbach, L. J. (1971). Test validation. In R. L. Thomdike (Ed.), *Educational measurement* (2nd ed., pp. 443–507). Washington, DC: American Council on Education.

Cronbach, L. J., & Meehl, P. E. (1955). Construct validity in psychological tests. *Psychological Bulletin, 52*(4), 281–302.

Haynes, S. N., Richard, D. C., & Kubany, E. S. (1995). Content validity in psychological assessment: A functional approach to concepts and methods. *Psychological Assessment, 7*(3), 238–247.

Hood, S. B. (2009). Validity in psychological testing and scientific realism. *Theory and Psychology, 19*(4), 451–473.

Kane, M. T. (1992). An argument-based approach to validity. *Psychological Bulletin, 112*(3), 527–535.

Kane, M. T. (2009). Validating the interpretations and uses of test scores. In R. W. Lissitz (Ed.), *The concept of validity: Revisions, new directions, and applications* (pp. 39–64). Charlotte: Information Age Publishing.

Loevinger, J. (1957). Objective tests as instruments of psychological theory. *Psychological Reports, 3*, 635–694.

McKenzie, J. F., Wood, M. L., Kotecki, J. E., Clark, J. K., & Brey, R. A. (1999). Establishing content validity: Using qualitative and quantitative steps. *American Journal of Health Behavior, 23*, 311–318.

Messick, S. (1989). Meaning and values in test validation: The science and ethics of assessment. *Educational Researcher, 18*(2), 5–11.

Messick, S. (1995). Validity of psychological assessment: Validation of inferences as scientific inquiry into score meaning. *American Psychologist, 50*, 741–749.

Popham, W. J. (1978). *Criterion-reference measurement*. Englewood Cliffs: Prentice Hall.

Sireci, S. G. (2009). Packing and unpacking sources of validity evidence: History repeats itself again. In R. W. Lissitz (Ed.), *The concept of validity: Revisions, new directions, and applications* (pp. 19–37). Charlotte: Information Age Publishing.

Vogt, D. S., King, D. W., & King, L. A. (2004). Focus groups in psychological assessment: Enhancing content validity by consulting members of the target population. *Psychological Assessment, 16*(3), 231–243.

Waltz, C., Strickland, O., & Lenz, E. (1991). *Measurement in nursing research* (2nd ed.). Philadelphia: F. A. Davis.

Wilson, H. S., & Hutchinson, S. A. (1991). Triangulation of qualitative methods: Heideggerian hermeneutics and grounded theory. *Qualitative Health Research, 1*(2), 263–276.

Chapter 4
Evidence Based on the Internal Structure of the Instrument: Factor Analysis

> Measurement is the first step that leads to control and eventually to improvement. If you can't measure something, you can't understand it. If you can't understand it, you can't control it. If you can't control it, you can't improve it.
>
> H. James Harrington.

We now turn to evidence based on the internal structure of the instrument. "Analyses of the internal structure of a test can indicate the degree to which the relationships among test items and test components conform to the construct on which the proposed test score interpretations are based" (AERA, APA, and NCME 1999, p. 13). The most common analytic technique for examining the internal structure of an instrument is factor analysis (both exploratory—EFA and confirmatory—CFA). In this chapter, we briefly describe exploratory factor analysis (EFA) and confirmatory factor analysis (CFA), provide recommendations for using the techniques to establish the internal structure of the instrument, and illustrate their uses in the context of instrument development. Entire books have been written about each of these topics (i.e., Brown 2006; Fabrigar and Wegener 2012; Loehlin 2004; Pett et al. 2003; Thompson 2004), and this chapter cannot possibly address all of the conceptual, statistical, and analytic details of each of the techniques. Therefore, we encourage instrument developers to extend their reading on each of these topics.

Factor Analysis

"Factor analysis refers to a set of statistical procedures designed to determine the number of distinct constructs needed to account for the pattern of correlations among a set of measures" (Fabrigar and Wegener 2012, p. 3). Factor analysis addresses the question: To what extent do certain latent explanatory concepts (constructs) explain the pattern of correlations in the responses to the instrument items? Are the clusters of items that are designed to measure a single construct unidimensional? How many dimensions (or constructs) are present in the items based on the current set of responses? If the structure of the covariation among items is consistent with the factor structure that the researcher has posited, then the internal structure of the instrument is consistent with the hypothesized constructs, which provides some (albeit limited) evidence that "supports the intended interpretation of test scores for the proposed purpose" (AERA, APA, and NCME 1999, p. 11).

D. B. McCoach et al., *Instrument Development in the Affective Domain*,
DOI: 10.1007/978-1-4614-7135-6_4, © Springer Science+Business Media New York 2013

Consider the set of items displayed in Table 4.1, which are adapted from the McAnallen Anxiety in Math Teaching Survey (MAMTS). (See McAnallen 2010 for the full and final version of the instrument). The adapted attitude instrument contains 18 items, which are designed to measure two constructs: general mathematics comfort/anxiety and math teaching comfort/anxiety. Also, note that some items are written in a negative direction (where agreeing to the item would be indicative of a more negative trait-*anxiety*) and some are written in a positive direction (where agreeing with the item is indicative of a more positive trait-*comfort*). For ease of interpretation, the negatively worded items were reverse-scored prior to running the factor analyses, computing reliability coefficients, and creating subscale scores. A great deal of recent research suggests that all items within a scale should be written in one direction—either positive or negative (See Chapter 2, Direct Measures of Affective Characteristics). Generally, negatively worded items demonstrate a method effect of sorts when combined with positively worded items, which results in a certain degree of multidimensionality. In this particular instrument, the use of positively and negatively worded items within the same construct appeared to work surprisingly well during the initial exploratory factor analysis, and so, after reverse scoring the negative items, they provided a

Table 4.1 McAnallen anxiety in math teaching survey: items and factors

Item	Factor
1. I was one of the best math students when I was in school	I
2. Having to work with fractions causes me discomfort	I
3. I feel confident in my ability to teach mathematics to students in the grade I currently teach	II
4. I am confident that I can learn advanced math concepts	I
5. When teaching mathematics, I welcome student questions	II
6. I have trouble finding alternative methods for teaching a mathematical concept when a student is confused	II
7. I find it difficult to teach mathematical concepts to students	II
8. I feel confident using sources other than the mathematics textbook when I teach	II
9. I don't have the math skills to differentiate instruction for the most talented students in my classes	II
10. I dislike having to teach math every day	II
11. I avoided taking nonrequired math courses in college	I
12. I have a lot of self-confidence when it comes to mathematics	I
13. I am confident that I can solve math problems on my own	I
14. I become anxious when I have to compute percentages	I
15. I have math anxiety	I
16. It makes me nervous to think about having to do any math problem	I
17. I am comfortable working on a problem that involves algebra	I
18. I have strong aptitude when it comes to math	I

Note The McAnallen *Anxiety in Math Teaching Survey* was adapted to yield the 18-item scale above. Factor I items measure General Math Anxiety/Comfort, whereas Factor II items measure Math Teaching Anxiety/Comfort. For the full and final version of the MAMTS see McAnallen (2010)

meaningful and interpretable solution. However, we caution readers yet again to be careful about mixing positive and negative item stems within a factor; generally, the results are not as pleasing as they appear in this particular example. Further, when we apply CFA techniques to this example later in the chapter, we see evidence of these negative method effects, which we did not observe during the EFA.

The ultimate goal for conducting the factor analysis (and the entire instrument development process) is to create a subscale that measures the construct of interest. Rather than analyzing data one question at a time, we want to create a subscale that captures the essence of our latent construct and allows us to have an observable measure of that construct. Imagine analyzing these data at the item level! First, no one item fully or adequately captures the essence of the construct. Second, in terms of reporting data to users, listing and describing each of the items one at a time would be a very cumbersome and inefficient manner for describing the concepts measured by the instrument. Moreover, some of the items are fairly strongly correlated with each other, suggesting that respondents who endorse one of those items are more likely to endorse other similar items. On the other hand, some of the items from different subscales do not correlate strongly with each other. Any item level analyses would fail to take these patterns of correlations into account.

As described in Chapter 3, the first step in the instrument validation process is to establish evidence based on test content through multiple processes (reviewing the literature, conducting qualitative and quantitative content validation procedures, etc.). After the completion of the item writing and the gathering of some preliminary content validity evidence, the next step in the sequence is to determine whether the internal structure of the instrument appears to be consistent with the hypothesized structure of the instrument.

We should note, though, that the factor analysis only assists in identifying clusters of variables (e.g., items) that share variation. Once the factors are named, it is essential to further examine the relationships between the derived factors and other variables (see Chapter 6) and to buttress an arsenal of validity evidence that "supports the intended interpretation of test scores for the proposed purpose" (AERA, APA, and NCME 1999, p. 11). As such, the factor analysis serves as a prelude to more extensive examinations of the existence of meaningful constructs (AERA, APA, and NCME 1999; Nunnally and Bernstein 1994). Thus, strong factorial evidence is necessary, but not sufficient, for establishing evidence of the validity of a given instrument for an intended purpose.

Exploratory and Confirmatory Analyses

EFA is a statistical method used to explore the dimensionality of an instrument by finding the smallest number of interpretable factors needed to explain the correlations among set of items. The method is exploratory because it imposes no a priori structure on the linear relationships between the items and the factors. In this way, EFA reduces data into a "smaller set of k latent factors to represent the larger set of j variables" (Henson and Roberts 2006, p. 395). Thus, factor analysis provides a method of identifying, within a given set of items, subsets of those items that are clustered together by shared variation to form constructs or factors.

In a purely exploratory analysis, we enter the items into the analysis without specifying any a priori factor structure; therefore in the initial (pilot) phase of instrument development, the results of EFA provide an initial exploration of the relationships between the judgmentally developed content categories (see Chapter 3, Evidence based on test content) and the empirically derived constructs. As such, we are actually testing hypotheses regarding the interrelationships among the items. We then examine these derived constructs in light of theoretical predictions that follow from the literature review and of operational definitions of the targeted categories specified during the content validity process. In one sense, we can consider any factor analysis executed for the purpose of supporting construct validity interpretations to be either supportive of our initial hypotheses about the structure of the items or not. Methodological differences among various types of factor analysis, however, provide bases for determining whether we describe the analysis as "exploratory" or "confirmatory."

One of the major methodological differences between EFA and CFA is the amount of information that is initially specified by the researcher, rather than generated by the analysis. In *CFA*, the researcher postulates a specific model a priori and then tests whether the data fit the model. Thus, a CFA model explicates the entire factor structure a priori: CFA specifies the number of factors as well as which factor each item is hypothesized to measure. In this way, CFA provides information about how well a hypothesized factor model fits a new sample from a target population. When researchers are interested in comparing the fit of a new sample from the same population, the goal of the CFA can be viewed as a pure confirmatory analysis of the proposed factor structure. In contrast, if the researcher analyzes the fit of a factor model fit in two samples from different populations, then CFA provides a test of measurement invariance for the hypothesized model. In both cases, the CFA places restrictions on factor loadings, variances, covariances, and residual variances. In *EFA*, the number of factors and the relationship of items to factors are generally determined through the analysis process rather than by the instrument developer's theoretical predictions. Although some researchers specify a priori the number of factors they wish to obtain in their EFA-based solely on their theoretical expectations, we do not support this approach. After deriving the factors from the EFA, the developer must determine whether the empirical evidence based on the internal structure of the instrument is sufficiently similar to the judgmentally developed content categories to buttress the budding validity argument.

There are several areas in which CFA provides information superior to that resulting from EFA. These areas include: (1) the ability to yield unique factorial solutions; (2) the definition of a testable model; (3) assessments of the extent to which a hypothesized model fits the data; (4) specific data on individual model parameters to aid in improvement of the model; (5) the ability to adequately test factorial invariance across groups (Marsh 1987); and (6) the ability to compare and evaluate competing theoretical models empirically.

In spite of the obvious advantages of CFA, the choice between the two types of factor analysis often boils down to the researcher's degree of certainty about the factor structure of the instrument. The very first pilot of a new instrument should utilize EFA techniques, which allow for the greatest flexibility of potential solutions. Once preliminary evidence of the factor structure has been established using EFA, modify the instrument as needed (based on the results of the EFA and preliminary reliability analyses), and then subject the modified instrument to a more rigorous test of the factor structure using CFA techniques *with a separate sample*. In other words, as a general rule, establishing the internal structure of an instrument requires the collection of *at least* two samples: a preliminary pilot sample of the original instrument using EFA and a second pilot sample of the revised instrument using CFA.

Factor analysis is a complex, but essential technique in instrument development, whichever method is chosen. Unfortunately, factor analysis is often employed but not always well understood (Conway and Huffcutt 2003; Fabrigar et al. 1999; Ford et al. 1986; Henson and Roberts 2006). For this reason, we place considerable emphasis on factor analysis as a technique for examining the validity of construct interpretations. Thus, we spend considerable time discussing its purpose and general strategy and illustrate its use in instrument development. We emphasize the decisions that analysts need to make prior to conducting factor analyses as well as the interpretation of the factor analysis output. The context for this analytic work, examining the existence of hypothesized constructs and developing a new instrument to measure those constructs, drives the recommendations that we make regarding the use of factor analytic techniques throughout this chapter.

Relationships of Constructs to Content Categories

The constructs that empirically are either identified by the EFA or supported by the CFA, based on the analysis of actual response data, should correspond to the judgmentally specified item clusters or categories examined during the evidence based on test content stage of instrument development described in Chapter 3. Simply put, the EFA factors are creations based on the patterns of covariation among the items. Ideally, these factors should reflect the judgmental categories from which the conceptual and operational definitions of the affective characteristic were developed. In the case of CFA, the model representing these constructs should fit the data adequately. For either type of factor analysis, if the theoretical constructs and the empirically derived factors do not correspond, it calls into question the construct interpretations and the researcher's ability to make meaningful inferences. For the EFA, two types of problems could occur. First, the factor analysis could fail to generate any conceptually meaningful factors. Second, the factor analysis could produce what appear to be meaningful factors; however, they may not correspond to the originally conceived judgmental categories. In the first situation, the developer has a very serious problem. The analysis of actual responses to the items describes what the instrument really measures. Given no clear factors, the developer must solve the problem solved through the three *R's*: re-think, rewrite, and re-administer. This requires reexamination of the conceptual and operational definitions, as well as reassessment of the content by expert judges. Following these revisions, new response data should be gathered for another factor analysis. In the second situation, the developer has an instrument that may measure some meaningful constructs, albeit not the ones that he or she had originally intended to measure. Although this is certainly a better situation, the lack of correspondence of the constructs to the judgmental categories deserves careful examination. Why did the responses cluster together in the way that they did, rather than in the way that the researcher hypothesized? Often, the answer becomes obvious to the researcher after viewing the results of the EFA. However, in such a scenario, it is also wise to share the results of the factor analysis with the expert judges who helped with the content validation to make sense of the unexpected results and to strategize about revisions to the instrument and/or construct definitions.

For the CFA, unsatisfactory results would include some topics we discuss later: low measurement weights (factor loadings), high modification indices, high standardized residuals, and low values on fit statistics, indicating a poor fit of the data to the model representing the hypothesized factor structure. These issues could signal a lack of correspondence between the theoretical framework and the response patterns. In extreme situations, it is possible that a poorly specified CFA model may fail to converge, because the model specified by the researcher is so discrepant from the actual structure of the data. (This is one of the reasons that we recommend using EFA with the first pilot sample for a newly developed instrument.) Again, unsatisfactory CFA results suggest that the researcher needs to reexamine the content and structure of the instrument.

Of course, the ideal situation is to find a clear correspondence between the earlier evidence based on instrument content and the empirical support for the internal structure of the instrument. Falling short of this goal is a signal for problems in the future use of the instrument. We now turn our attention to more detailed descriptions of the EFA and CFA processes, beginning with EFA. We outline a general strategy for conducting EFA in a defensible manner. This process has been improved through years of instrument development work and is based on recommendations within the field of factor analysis.

Exploratory Factor Analysis

Purpose and Strategy

The purpose of factor analysis within the instrument design process is to empirically examine the interrelationships among the items and identify clusters of items that share sufficient covariation to justify their existence as a factor or construct measured by the instrument. The factor analysis solution provides information about which items are most related to a given factor, as well as how these items relate to the other factors in the solution (Gorsuch 1997). The goal of any factor analysis is to reduce the number of elements from a larger number of items (or measures) to a smaller number of broader, more generalizable latent constructs. Thus, we seek to identify the smallest number of factors needed to reproduce the original data (Gorsuch 1997). The aim of factor analysis, then, is to seek parsimony in the description of the instrument (i.e., to employ a minimum amount of information to describe the maximum amount of variation shared among the items). Mathematically, EFA "seeks the set of equations that maximize the multiple correlations of the factors to the items" (Gorsuch 1997, p. 533). Factor analysis uses the item-level intercorrelation matrix. In fact, factor analyses can be conducted with a correlation matrix; it is not necessary to conduct this analysis with raw data.

Using mathematical procedures beyond the scope of this book, the EFA procedure "decomposes" the correlation matrix into a set of roots (eigenvalues) and vectors (eigenvectors). These roots and vectors are then appropriately scaled (multiplied together) to generate a matrix, the (unrotated) factor matrix. Whereas the correlation matrix has the same number of rows and columns as items contained in the instrument, the factor matrix contains the same number of rows as there are items and the same number of columns as there are factors derived in the solution. Rotating the factor matrix helps make the solution more interpretable. The rotated factor matrix is often referred to as a *pattern matrix*, and its elements are called *pattern coefficients*. (Sometimes people refer to these pattern coefficients as "factor loadings"; however, loading is a vague term, because it could apply to either pattern coefficients or structure coefficients when using an oblique rotation). The entries in the pattern matrix are akin to standardized regression coefficients. They provide a measure of the relationship between each item and the derived factor after controlling for all the other factors in the model.

After examining the results of the EFA, the instrument developer examines the empirically derived factors. It is useful to list the items defining each factor and determine whether items that are clustered together seem to be indicators of the construct of interest. If the items clearly share some conceptual meaning, this concept is named, described, and referred to as the construct measured by the instrument.

Steps in Conducting an Exploratory Factor Analysis for Instrument Development

We recommend using the following six-step procedure to conduct an EFA within the instrument development process:

1. Determine how many factors to extract, using extraction criteria outlined in this chapter. Make this decision *after* conducting a preliminary EFA to obtain the

results of the parallel analysis, minimum average partial procedure, and the scree plot.
2. Decide on an extraction technique.
3. Decide on a rotation technique.
4. Rerun the factor analysis, using the extraction and rotation criteria that you determined in steps 1–3.
5. Examine the output to determine the number of "robust" factors. Determine which items correlate with which derived factors and which items do not, and the degree of relationship between the items and the factors.
6. Name the factors, define them, describe them, and determine what it means to be high or low on each of the derived factors.

Sample Size Requirements

What is the sample size needed to conduct an EFA? Generally, sample size requirements are framed in terms of the number of respondents needed in relation to the number of variables (items) to be factored. Recommendations regarding the *N*:p ratio [i.e., number of observations for each variable (*N*) versus the number of variables (p)] vary. For example, Nunnally (1978) suggested an *N*:p of 10:1, whereas Cattell (1978) used 6:1, and Everitt (1975) suggested 5:1. Arrindell and van der Ende (1985), Velicer and Fava (1998) have provided reviews of this topic, and MacCallum et al. (1999) conducted a series of simulation studies to examine the optimal sample size for EFA. Although an *N*:p ratio of 10:1 has been touted as the general rule of thumb, such high *N*:p ratios are not necessary to produce stable factor solutions under certain conditions. Instead, MacCallum et al. (1999) found that the sample size necessary to conduct an EFA was dependent on several factors, including the communalities of the items and the degree of overdetermination of the factor solution. The communality of an item is the proportion of variance in the item that is accounted for by the extracted factors. For example, if the communality of an item is 0.49, that means that 49% of the item's variance is explained by the extracted factors and 51% is unique variance, in that it is not explained by the factors. *Overdetermination* refers to "the degree to which each factor is clearly represented by a sufficient number of variables" (MacCallum et al. 1999, p. 89). Overdetermined solutions exhibit high loadings on at least three or four (or more) variables as well as clear simple structure. Simple structure refers to a solution in which each item has a large factor loading on one primary factor and near zero loadings on all other factors. Thus, in an overdetermined solution, each factor contains at least three or four (or more) items with high loadings on one factor and near zero loadings on all other factors. MacCallum et al.'s (1999) study demonstrated that:

- Larger sample size, higher communalities and high overdetermination increase the chances of adequately reproducing the population factor pattern.

- With a high degree of overdetermination and high communalities (>0.6), it is possible to achieve stable factor solutions, even with *N* below 100. With moderate communalities (about 0.5) and a high degree of overdetermination, between 100 and 200 subjects are required to adequately recover the population factors.
- With low communalities and only 3–4 high loadings on each factor, over 300 subjects may be required to adequately reproduce the population factor structure.
- In the worst case scenario, with low communalities and poorly determined factors, very large samples (500 or more) are required to recover the population factors.

Although the results above may appear to be good news for those wanting to conduct factor analyses on pilot data from very small samples, we actually see this as providing important cautions for instrument developers. MacCallum (MacCallum et al. 1999) found that small sample sizes work well *only* when the factor structure is very clear, the number of items per factor is large, and the communalities are high. These are qualities that mature, previously validated instruments may possess; however, they are not qualities that are typical for newly created, never-before-piloted instruments. In addition, small *N*:p ratios are dangerous because small and *ill-conceived samples of respondents that do not provide inter-item correlations similar to the target population could result in erroneous conclusions about factor structure*. Therefore, we recommend gathering a sample of *at least* 200 people that represent the target population and trying to adhere to the 10:1 *N*:p ratio as closely as possible. In this way, you will be reasonably well assured of being able to produce a stable factor solution, even in the worst case scenario.

In addition to the sample size, the *representativeness* of the sample is also critical. Although it is generally impossible to obtain a random sample of your population of interest for the pilot sample, it is critical to amass as representative a sample as possible. The sample should "represent" the target population both conceptually and statistically. In particular, the pilot participants should have the same expected level (mean) and the same degree of variability (variance) as the target population. For example, if a researcher wanted to validate an attitude toward school instrument, he or she would not want to administer the pilot version to 200 students who are in detention for bad behavior. Similarly, he or she would not want to administer the survey to 200 honors students. Instead, the researcher needs to sample 200 students from a cross-section of the school population so that honors students, detention students, and average students are all included in the sample. Having a diverse and representative sample is very important during the pilot process.

Three Critical Decisions in Exploratory Factor Analysis

There are three critical decisions that an analyst must make when conducting an EFA: (1) What extraction criteria to use; (2) How many factors to extract; and (3) What type of rotation method to use.

Extraction Criteria

Extraction refers to the analytic process by which we estimate the parameters of the factor solution (the factor pattern matrix, the structure coefficients, and the interfactor correlations. The factor extraction process removes the maximum amount of variance common to sets of variables from the original correlation matrix. After this common variance (i.e., first factor) has been extracted, the remaining residual correlation matrix contains the remaining unexplained variability. Then, the second factor, which is unrelated to the first factor, extracts as much of the remaining variance among the variables as possible (Henson and Roberts 2006). The process continues until some extraction criterion has been reached. Beyond this point, additional factors should explain only relatively trivial amounts of variance.

There are a variety of ways to extract factors. Two of the most common factor extraction methods are principal component analysis (PCA) and principal axis factoring (PAF). (Technically, PCA is not actually a factor analysis technique; it is a data reduction technique; however, given that it is generally discussed in the context of EFA, we continue the tradition here.) Analytically, principal components analysis attempts to explain all of the variance in the set of items, while common factor analysis models only common variance. PCA and PAF differ in terms of the initial communalities that they use to derive the factor solution. The initial communalities are the numbers that are placed in the diagonal of the correlation matrix at the outset of the EFA. Thus, in essence, through the selection of a particular extraction criterion, the researcher has a choice of what values to insert in the diagonal of the correlation matrix prior to the factoring. The choice made reflects how the researcher wishes to deal with the variances of the items. The total variance (V_x) of an item theoretically consists of common (V_c) and unique (V_u) variance, such that $V_x = V_c + V_u$. Common variance is that portion of the total variance that is shared with the other items; unique variance is that portion that is uncorrelated or not shared with the other variables. The values selected for the diagonal of R (i.e., the correlation matrix) are estimates of the amount of variance shared by the particular item and all the other items (i.e., the initial communality estimates). Because PCA attempts to model all of the variance in all of the original variables, the initial communality estimates, which are placed in the diagonal of the correlation matrix, are all 1's. Operationally, the l's represent the total amount of variance for each variable which has been entered into the factor analysis. The use of l's in the diagonal indicates that all of the variance (i.e., common and unique) for each variable has been entered into the analysis. No distinction is made between common and unique variance: they are operationally merged together.

A second approach, PAF, consists of inserting squared multiple correlations (SMCs) into the diagonal of the correlation matrix prior to the factoring procedure. These SMCs represent an estimate of how much of the variance of each item is shared with the set of remaining items, which provides an estimate of the common variance. The SMCs are good initial estimates of the common variance in each item. Because this procedure attempts to distinguish between common and unique variance, it is called a *common factor analysis*. Most psychometrically inclined researchers favor this approach since they feel that much of the error variance (noise) in the analysis has been removed. Operationally, the resulting factor structures from the principal component and principal axis factor solutions are often quite similar, although the factor loadings produced by principal components analysis are generally larger than factor loadings produced by PAF.

Some analysts, especially statisticians, tend to prefer *principal components analysis* (PCA). PCA is computationally simpler than factor analysis, and PCA is less prone to nonconvergence issues than common factor analysis. Other analysts, especially those trained in the psychometric tradition; tend to prefer *PAF*. The common factor model is more aligned with the measurement of latent constructs. Further, the common factor model specifies certain hypotheses about the data; therefore, it is a testable model. PCA is not (Fabrigar et al. 1999).

Ultimately, whether to use PCA or PAF is more of a theoretical and substantive question than a statistical one. The decision depends upon the reason for conducting the analysis. Common factor analysis (PAF) seeks to explain the patterns of correlations among measured variables, whereas PCA seeks to account for variance in the measured variables by determining linear combinations that retain as much information as possible from the original observed variables (Fabrigar et al. 1999). If the purpose of the analysis is to reduce many variables into a smaller set of variables for further analysis, then principal components analysis is a very reasonable choice. However, if you have a theoretical rationale for believing that a small number of latent constructs or factors explain the patterns of correlations among your observed variables, then you should analyze your data using PAF (Bandalos and Finney 2010).

In reality, if you have a large number of observed variables and the communalities for your observed variables are relatively high, you should get similar results whether you use PCA or PAF (Thompson 1992). However, factor loadings (the elements of the pattern or structure matrices) are higher when you conduct a principal components analysis. Therefore, retaining variables that have loadings above a certain criterion may lead you to retain items in a PCA that you would have eliminated with PAF. For example, many people retain items that have a pattern coefficient (factor loading) of at least 0.40 on a factor. More items will have loadings of 0.40 using PCA than will using PAF. Moreover, some evidence suggests that the PCA loadings are upwardly biased and that the coefficients produced by common factor analyses using PAF are more accurate (Costello and Osborne 2005).

In our experience, when the factor solution is stable, both PCA and PAF produce similar results (although the factor loadings for the PCA are generally slightly higher than those for the PAF solution). Thus, running the EFA using both the PCA and PAF extraction techniques can provide an informal diagnostic check on the stability of the model. (We would be worried if things actually looked substantively different across the two solutions!). However, given our focus on the development of instruments to measure latent variables, the use of common factor analytic approaches seems far more defensible than does the use of PCA.

Common factor analysis is a broader term for a family of exploratory factor analyses that attempt to identify underlying factors from the data and separate common and unique variance. PAF is one of the most popular methods of conducting common factor analysis, but it is certainly not the only method. In addition to PAF, maximum likelihood (ML) methods exist for conducting EFA, and they have been gaining popularity in recent years. ML methods have several potential advantages over PAF. First, ML produces a likelihood ratio, which can be used to generate measures of model fit and compare the fit of competing models to each other. Although this would, at first blush, appear to be a great advantage to ML, using the likelihood ratio test to evaluate model fit in EFA appears to have serious limitations (Fabrigar and Wegener 2012). Using measures of model fit such as the CFI, the TLI, or the RMSEA to evaluate the fit of an EFA using ML seems to be more advisable (Fabrigar and Wegener 2012). In addition, "ML estimates vary less widely around the actual parameter values than do estimates obtained by other methods, assuming the model is correct and the distributional assumptions hold" (Briggs and MacCallum 2003, p. 28). "However, if the sample is small or the data are not normal, the advantage of ML over other methods may not hold" (Briggs and MacCallum 2003, p. 28). In fact, Briggs and MacCallum (2003) found that, when the factors were not equally strong, ML methods had trouble recovering weaker factors. In addition, ML exhibited more problems recovering the correct factor structure when there were errors in the data (minor second factors, nonlinear relations between observed variables and factors, etc.) or when sample sizes were small. They concluded:

> Our findings clearly show that OLS performs better than ML in recovering weak common factors when moderate error in the data is present, regardless of the source of the error. Given these findings, we recommend use of OLS in EFA in practice to increase the likelihood that all major common factors are recovered. At a minimum, we would urge researchers using EFA and favoring ML estimation to also apply OLS estimation and to compare solutions. From our perspective, a finding of substantial differences between such solutions should probably lead the investigator to favor OLS (Briggs and MacCallum 2003, p. 54).

For this reason, when forced to choose a sole extraction technique, we tend to favor the use of PAF over ML. When we estimate ML EFA solutions, we always estimate a PAF solution, as well, and compare the results. Again, in our experience, stable solutions with strong simple structure and overdetermined factors with high loadings and high communalities will look quite similar, regardless of the extraction technique employed. However, less stable solutions or solutions with weaker factors may look somewhat different. Thus, using the multiple extraction techniques can serve an informal diagnostic function: "good" solutions reveal themselves in their consistency across extraction techniques, and less stable solutions become apparent when examined through a variety of extraction techniques. However, when reporting the results of factor analyses, we tend to report the results of the PAF, for the reasons outlined above.

How Many Factors to Extract?

The second major decision pertains to the number of factors to be extracted from the solution. It is important to try to extract the correct number of factors before interpreting the results of the factor analysis. Both *underextraction* (extracting too few factors) and *overextraction* (extracting too many factors) are problematic, albeit for different reasons. Underextraction compresses the items into too small a factor space. This is analogous to trying to fit into a pair of jeans that is far too tight! Forcing items into too small of a factor space results in a loss of information, the fusing of two or more factors, distortions in the factor solution, and/or an increases in error in the loadings (O'Connor 2000; Zwick and Velicer 1986). However, overextraction can also be problematic. Overextraction diffuses variables across a large factor space. It can lead to "factor-splitting," too many factors with very few or no high loadings, trivial factors, or "bloated specifics". (Bloated specifics are "factors" where there is only one item with a high loading on the factor). Generally, underextraction is considered the more grave error than overextraction. "Extracting too few factors can radically change one or more factors while extracting an additional factor when 'in the right range' leaves the earlier ones unchanged" (Gorsuch 1997, p. 546). One pragmatic advantage of erring on the side of overextracting factors is that an overextracted solution is usually fairly obvious: there are factors that contain very few or no high loadings. In contrast, an underextracted solution is not as obvious to the "naked eye," and therefore, is more likely to be accepted as the correct solution.

There are several criteria that can be used to determine the number of factors to extract: (1) Kaiser's criterion; (2) the scree plot; (3) parallel analysis; and (4) the minimum average partial procedure. We provide explanations of each of the criteria, followed by suggestions for combining the criteria to make an ultimate decision about the number of factors to extract.

1. *Kaiser's criterion*: *Eigenvalues > 1 rule*

"Kaiser's criterion", a procedure developed by Guttman (1953) and popularized by Kaiser (1958), is by far the most frequently used method of determining the number of factors to extract and the default extraction criterion in many statistical software packages, including SPSS. Kaiser's criterion was originally developed for PCA. Recall that in PCA, initial communalities for all items are (1) Thus, Kaiser's criterion suggests retaining all factors with eigenvalues (roots) greater than or equal to 1.0 (i.e., the unity criterion) (Comrey and Lee 1992; Kaiser 1960; Rummell 1970). The rationale for this criterion is that the contribution of each item to the total variance in the solution is 1 (i.e., its value in the diagonal of *R*); therefore, the unity criterion specifies retaining only factors accounting for as much variance as a single item (Comrey 1988; Comrey and Lee 1992). There is an alternate version of Kaiser's criterion for PAF extraction (i.e., when SMCs have been inserted into the diagonal of *R*). This criterion suggests extracting factors with roots greater than or equal to zero. Comrey (1988) notes that a common factor analysis with a zero-root criterion will lead to more factors retained than a PCA employing the unity criterion. In practice, the PCA version of Kaiser's criterion is more frequently applied, given that this is the version that is implemented in SPSS. However, parallel analysis methods (discussed shortly) provide the option of using either the PCA roots (which tend to have a mid-range of 1) or the PAF roots (which tend to have a mid-range of 0).

Although Kaiser's criterion (using the eigenvalues > 1 from PCA) is the most commonly used method for determining the number of factors to extract, it tends to overestimate the number of factors needed (although under certain conditions it can also underestimate the number of factors) (O'Connor 2000; Zwick and Velicer 1986). Further, an eigenvalue above 1.0 represents a very different proportion of the total variance depending on the number of items in a scale. For example, if there are 5 items on a scale, then an eigenvalue of 1 represents 20% of the total variance. In contrast, if there are 50 items on a scale, an eigenvalue of 1 represents 2% of the total variance. Thus, in our experience, the eigenvalue > 1 rule is more likely to suggest overextraction as the number of items on the instrument increases.

2. *The Scree Test*

A second option available for determining the number of factors is called the *scree test*. The scree test is a visual analysis of the eigenvalues. This procedure, suggested by Cattell (1966), involves plotting the eigenvalues or latent roots (y axis) against the factor number (x axis) and examining the shape of the resulting curve. The point (factor number) at which the curve stops decreasing and straightens indicates the maximum number of factors to be extracted in the solution. A visual analysis of the scree plot reveals the point at which the slope flattens to near zero. Cattell (1966) suggests that factors beyond this point represent "factorial litter" or *scree*. "Scree" actually refers to the rock rubble near the side wall in the bottom of a quarry. Thus, we are looking for the point at which the eigenvalues appear to dissolve into rubble (figuratively, of course.). The point just prior to the start of the scree indicates the number of factors to extract. A well-defined scree plot often contains an elbow, and the number of factors to extract is the number of factors that occur just before the elbow. The scree plot provides a nice visual depiction of the eigenvalues and does help to make salient where large drops in eigenvalues occur. However, the scree test is not without its problems.

Sometimes there are no clear elbows, or there are multiple elbows. In such scenarios, it is difficult to determine exactly where the scree begins. Thus, the interrater agreement of screeplot interpretations is actually quite low. Streiner (1998) found "Novices were slightly more reliable than experts; and both were more reliable with artificial data (intraclass correlations of 0.33 and 0.33, respectively) than with real data (intraclass correlations of 0.05 and 0.00)" (p. 687). Given the unreliability of the scree plot, it can be used as one possible indicator but should never used as the sole criterion for determining the number of factors to extract.

3. *Parallel Analysis*

Parallel analysis involves the calculation of eigenvalues from random data and comparison of those average eigenvalues to the eigenvalues obtained from a sample dataset. The number of eigenvalues from the real data that have values that are larger than the eigenvalues from the random data provides an estimate of the number of factors to extract (Fabrigar and Wegener 2012). The intuition behind parallel analysis is simple. Imagine a dataset in which all of the variables were generated randomly. In this scenario, the correlations between any two variables would be very small and would be a result of "noise" in the dataset. If we were to factor analyze such data using PCA, the first eigenvalue would be the largest, the second eigenvalue would be the next largest, etc. However, the eigenvalues for such a dataset would gently decline, given that there are no real factors or components within the data.

We can simulate multiple "no factor" datasets of this sort, average the eigenvalues of the "no factor" datasets, and compare the magnitude of the no-factor eigenvalues to the eigenvalues from our actual data. In comparing our sample results to no factor results, if our sample eigenvalues are larger than eigenvalues from random data, then we conclude we may have a real factor. On the other hand, if our eigenvalues are smaller than those generated from the "no-factor" data, the factor in question has an eigenvalue smaller than that expected from random numbers and is almost certainly not a true factor. Under certain conditions, parallel analysis tends to overfactor. From a conceptual standpoint, just because a factor has an eigenvalue that is larger than the average eigenvalue produced by randomly generated data does not necessarily mean that the factor is real or interpretable. "Indeed one might argue that the parallel analysis criterion that a factor must simply outperform what would be expected from a random factor is a comparatively lenient standard by which to judge what constitutes a major common factor" (Fabrigar and Wegener 2012, p. 60). For that reason, some researchers choose to extract only as many factors as have eigenvalues greater than the eigenvalues at the 95th percentile for randomly generated data. Generally, using means or 95th percentiles will result in the same conclusions; however, when the solutions diverge, the 95th percentile criterion always suggests fewer factors than the mean criterion. Thus, it is a bit more conservative. Also, because parallel analysis involves simulations of randomly generated data, it is possible to get slight differences in results, depending on the computer program used, the seed value, and the number of randomly generated datasets. Given the speed of current computers, we recommend generating at least 1,000 random datasets.

A recent study by Slocum-Gori and Zumbo (2011) indicated that parallel analysis was the most accurate single criterion for determining the optimal number of factors to extract. Unfortunately, parallel analysis is not currently built into the SPSS factor analysis routine. However, O'Connor (2000) has created macros in SPSS and SAS to conduct parallel analyses. These are available at https://people.ok.ubc.ca/brioconn/nfactors/nfactors. O'Connor's macro can perform the parallel analysis procedure using either PAF or PCA. In addition, Patil et al. (2007) have created a web-based parallel analysis workbook (http://ires.ku.edu/~smishra/parallelengine.htm) that will compute the eigenvalues for randomly generated datasets of a given magnitude, using O'Connor's macro in SAS. These results can be used with any statistical software program.

Even though we advocate using PAF to conduct the factor analysis, the recommendations about whether to apply parallel analysis using PCA or parallel analysis using PAF are inconclusive. Conceptually, given that there are not any factors underlying the data, trying to explain the total variance in the randomly generated dataset might seem more sensible than trying to explain only the common variance, which is sure to be quite small. In one of the more recent research studies on the topic, Crawford et al. (2010) compared the PA–PAF and PA–PCA techniques using the mean eigenvalue rule and the 95th percentile eigenvalue rule. They found that PA-PCA was "more negatively affected be the presence of one or more strong general factors" (p. 897) and that in those situations, PA–PCA was more likely to underfactor. However, in cases with one factor or multiple uncorrelated factors, PA–PCA generally "performed as well as or better than PA-PAF" (p. 897). This simulation also revealed some inconsistency in the decision to use the 95th percentile rule or the mean rule, although the researchers appeared to favor the use of the mean criterion over the 95th percentile criterion under the majority of situations.

Given the lack of consensus about which form of parallel analysis to use (PCA or PAF), we recommend that researchers conduct the parallel analysis using both the PCA and PAF extractions and compare the results. The PAF extraction of the parallel analysis routine generally (but not always) produces more factors than the PCA extraction. The PA–PCA extraction is more likely to underfactor, whereas the PA–PAF extraction may overfactor. We also recommend that researchers examine the results for the mean eigenvalue of the randomly generated data, as well as the 95th percentile of the eigenvalues for the randomly generated data. When these four parallel analysis criteria agree (PA–PCA mean, PA–PAF mean, PA–PCA 95th percentile, and PA–PAF 95th percentile), the decision about how many factors to extract is an easy one. When the four criteria disagree, then closer examination of the results of the parallel analysis, in conjunction with the MAP procedure (see below), the scree plot, and the pattern matrix should help determine how many factors to extract.

4. *Minimum Average Partial Procedure (MAP)*

The *minimum average partial procedure* (Velicer 1976) involves conducting a full PCA and computing the average squared partial correlation between each pair of items after each component is extracted. The number of factors that produces the smallest average squared partial correlation is considered to be the optimal number of factors. Ideally, if the extracted factors explain the pattern of covariation in the original correlation matrix, then the partial correlations between all pairs of variables should be near 0. However, some partial correlations could be negative and other partial correlations could be positive. Therefore, the partial correlations are squared, and the average squared partial correlation is used as an indication of the fit of the factor solution to the correlation matrix. The MAP procedure is relatively simple: after extracting the first component, the average squared partial correlation is computed using the residual matrix. Then, the second component is extracted and the average squared partial correlation is computed using the new residual matrix. At a certain point, this average squared correlation actually begins to rise. Thus, the graph that is produced by plotting the average squared correlations is U-shaped. The MAP procedure favors the number of factors that produces the smallest squared partial correlations.

The revised MAP procedure (Velicer et al. 2000) works in the exact same way; however, instead of using average squared partial correlations, it utilizes the average partial correlation raised to the 4th power. Frequently, the MAP and the revised MAP suggest the same number of factors. However, there is some evidence to suggest that the revised MAP test performs a bit better than the original MAP test (Velicer et al. 2000). The MAP procedure was developed for use with PCA. Therefore, its use in common factor analysis is somewhat controversial.

Unfortunately, the MAP procedure is not currently built into the SPSS factor analysis routine. However, O'Connor (2000) has created macros in SPSS and SAS to conduct both the MAP and the revised MAP tests simultaneously. These are available at https://people.ok.ubc.ca/brioconn/nfactors/nfactors.

Given the plethora of methods to determine the number of factors to extract, how do we make a reasonable and definitive decision? Recent work in the area of EFA has proposed innovative methods for combining decision rules systematically (Slocum-Gori and Zumbo 2011) or multistep procedures, such as the hull method (Lorenzo-Seva et al. 2011), to determine the optimal number of factors to extract. We favor a holistic and judgmental approach whereby the researcher simultaneously examines the following criteria:

1. The scree plot and the magnitudes of the eigenvalues, as well as the proportion of variance explained by each additional factor.
2. The parallel analysis, using both PCA and PAF extractions, and examining both the mean and 95th percentile criteria.
3. The minimum average partial test, both in its original and revised formats.
4. The elements of the pattern matrix, keeping in mind that factors containing one or fewer loadings above 0.40 may be indicative of overextraction and items

with many double loadings or seemingly nonsensical groupings of disparate items may be indicative of underextraction.

5. The residuals of the EFA solution. The residuals are the differences between the actual correlations and the correlations that are implied by the factor analysis model being fit. Studying the residual matrix can provide clues as to where the factor solution is doing a good job reproducing the sample correlations, and can also help isolate the correlations between pairs of variables that are not being well reproduced by the factor analysis model. Studying the patterns of residuals can sometimes provide insight into potential sources of misfit in the EFA solution.

It is often helpful to make a summary table that contains the results of the criteria above. Ultimately, the researcher must make an educated decision, based on his or her knowledge of the subject area and the results of these analyses, choosing the number of factors to extract. Once that decision has been made, we recommend forcing the factor solution to the chosen number of factors. Then examine, interpret, and report the results of that analysis. Finally, when reporting the results of the EFA, it is essential to explain the decision-making criteria and the decision-making reasoning employed when deciding how many factors to extract and how many factors to retain (Henson and Roberts 2006), so that readers can decide for themselves the defensibility and sensibility of the approach.

What Type of Rotation Technique to Use?

The final decision pertains to the choice of rotation procedures. *Factor rotation* involves rotating the reference axes of the extracted factors around their origin to a solution that exhibits simple structure (Lackey et al. 2003) (Rotation of the factor matrix will become clearer when the illustration is presented in a later section). The underlying factor structure that provides the parsimonious description of the correlation matrix exists in a geometric space. Each item is a point in a geometric space: factors are geometric clusters of items. However, we must find a solution (i.e., a reference system) that allows us to view the clusters in a clear and theoretically meaningful manner. The factors in the initial factor matrix are actually axis systems (x and y axes) in the geometric sense, and they can be rotated to obtain a clearer picture of the clusters of items (i.e., points in space) within the geometric space. The closer we can get a cluster of items to a particular axis, the more the cluster will contribute to the naming of the factor. To understand this point, imagine we are standing in the corner of a room. The three-dimensional room actually has an *x*, *y*, and *z* axis. Pretend there is a cluster of about 10 pingpong balls (items) hanging from the ceiling forming the shape of a large ellipse. To name the cluster, we need to assign it in the simplest two-dimensional case to the right wall (*y* axis) or the floor (*x* axis). Since the ellipse is not really near the wall or floor, we envision rotating the room, so that the ellipse gets closer to the wall and farther away from the floor. Note that we kept the wall and floor at right angles (This is the essence of orthogonal rotation techniques.). In another situation, we might have two ellipses, neither of which is really near the wall nor floor. The optimal way to get the floor and wall nearer to the two ellipses may be to allow the wall and floor to have less than a right angle (i.e., an oblique angle).

When we rotate a factor matrix in an attempt to locate clusters of items nearer to an axis and keep the axes at right angles, we have performed an *orthogonal rotation* called a *varimax rotation* (Kaiser 1958). Using this procedure, the axes (factors) are independent or not related. An *oblique rotation* allows the axes to collapse, so that the derived factors are correlated to some extent. The smaller the angle in an oblique rotation, the more strongly the factors correlate with each other. The principal of rotating the factor matrix will become clearer when actual data are used to illustrate the technique in the next section.

A final comment regarding varimax and oblique rotations is in order. Some researchers have become confused after running a varimax rotation—they operationally state that their derived factors are now uncorrelated. It is the axis system that remains uncorrelated. When, in order to name a factor, one selects those items correlating above, say, 0.50 with the factor, the resulting scale scores formed by summing responses to the selected items are not orthogonal; they usually have moderate correlations. Thus, the derived factors are orthogonal, but the scale scores used to describe the factors (or the factor scores) are not orthogonal.

So, should you use a varimax rotation or an oblique rotation? If you believe that your factors are correlated, then we favor using an oblique rotation. The advantages of the varimax rotation, in terms of its mathematical elegance and simplicity, are no longer compelling reasons for favoring a varimax rotation in the era of high-speed computers. (Admittedly, if you had to find the solution by hand, you might choose a varimax rotation!)

Another term that confuses many applied researchers is *factor scores*. In most cases, developers select items that have high "loadings" (pattern coefficients) on the factor and average individuals' responses to the items to generate "scores on the factor." It is an error to report these scores as factor scores; these scores should always be referred to as subscale scores, mean scores, or "scores on the items defining the factor (Glass and MacGuire 1966)." True factor scores are formed by combining information from the factor-loading matrix with other matrices we are not discussing to yield a new matrix with the same number of rows as individuals and columns as factors. The factor score matrix is like the original raw data matrix, which had the same number of rows as individuals and columns as items, except that the columns no longer reflect the number of items, because a data reduction technique (factor analysis) has been carried out. Thus, each person has a new score on each factor, and these data could be entered into a new analysis, such as regression, where the factor scores would be predictors. Simply put, when computing the mean of all items defining a factor, do not call the result a factor score: it is a scale score, a subscale score, or a mean score. For those interested in learning more about factor scores, DiStefano et al. (2009) provide an excellent introduction to the topic and explicate the advantages and disadvantages of the various methods for deriving factor scores.

Computer Output: Exploratory Factor Analysis

The 18 items presented in Table 4.1 are excerpted from the *McAllen Anxiety in Mathematics Teaching Survey* (McAnallen 2010), which was administered to a sample of 691 teachers from eight states. We use these data and analyses to illustrate how EFA can be used to examine the internal structure of an instrument. These 18 attitude items were rated on a 5-point Likert scale (*strongly disagree*, 1; *disagree*, 2; *uncertain*, 3; *agree*, 4; *strongly agree*, 5). The underlined item numbers indicate negative item stems which were reverse scored (i.e., 5 = 1; 4 = 2; 2 = 4; 1 = 5) prior to the analysis, so that high scores would reflect more positive attitudes toward math (i.e., less math anxiety; greater math comfort) and low scores reflect more negative attitudes toward mathematics (i.e., greater math anxiety). We note again that developers should generally *not use mixed item stems*, so reverse scoring is generally not needed. Tables 4.2, 4.3, 4.4, 4.5, 4.6, and 4.7 contain the EFA output. For instructional purposes, we highlight various aspects of the SPSS output to illustrate how the EFA information can be used to examine evidence of the internal structure of an affective instrument.

We generally recommend that choosing one preferred method of extraction and a preferred method of rotation prior to conducting the analysis and use any supplementary runs purely for diagnostic purposes (to examine the stability of the solution and to provide additional clues as to the likely sources for model misfit). Thus, we present the full results of the current analysis using PAF and oblimin rotation, which is our preferred method of analyzing EFA data. However, we also briefly discuss the results of PCA and varimax rotation for pedagogical purposes. In practice, it is uncommon for the results of several different EFA analyses to be reported simultaneously, and we discourage this practice.

Means and Standard Deviations

The item means (after reverse scoring of negative item stems) and standard deviations in Table 4.2 seem typical for such attitude items, and sufficient variability in responses appears to be present. Generally, standard deviations near 1 are typical for 5-point response scales and standard deviations of 1 or higher are typical for 7-point response scales. If the means were near either extreme on the response scale and the standard deviations were low, the resulting correlations between items would tend to be low, and this would adversely affect the factor analysis results. It is also helpful to look at the frequency distributions for each of the items prior to conducting a factor analysis. Using standard EFA procedures, we make the assumption that our data are at least interval level and multivariately normally distributed. Therefore, ideally, we would like the items to follow an approximately normal distribution. Moderate departures from normality are generally not problematic; however, extremely skewed and/or kurtotic responses can

Table 4.2 McAnallen anxiety in math teaching survey: item descriptive statistics

Descriptive statistics

	Mean	Standard deviation	Analysis N
1. I was one of the best math students when I was in school	2.84	1.204	593
2. Having to work with fractions causes me discomfort	3.61	1.112	593
3. I feel confident in my ability to teach mathematics to students in the grade I currently teach	4.32	0.827	593
4. I am confident that I can learn advanced math concepts	3.81	1.012	593
5. When teaching mathematics, I welcome student questions	4.46	0.706	593
6. I have trouble finding alternative methods for teaching a mathematical concept when a student is confused	3.52	1.065	593
7. I find it difficult to teach mathematical concepts to students	4.07	0.874	593
8. I feel confident using sources other than the mathematics textbook when I teach	4.15	0.892	593
9. I don't have the math skills to differentiate instruction for the most talented students in my classes	3.81	1.006	593
10. I dislike having to teach math every day	4.38	0.788	593
11. I avoided taking non-required math courses in college	3.00	1.323	593
12. I have a lot of self-confidence when it comes to mathematics	3.39	1.054	593
13. I am confident that I can solve math problems on my own	3.85	0.850	593
14. I become anxious when I have to compute percentages	3.60	1.167	593
15. I have math anxiety	3.76	1.137	593
16. It makes me nervous to think about having to do any math problem	4.00	0.872	593
17. I am comfortable working on a problem that involves algebra	3.54	1.087	593
18. I have strong aptitude when it comes to math	3.32	1.028	593

be. In Chapter 2 (Direct Measures of Affective Characteristics), we reviewed research on the optimal number of scale points for affective instruments. We concluded that using conventional analytic techniques (which assume an interval level of measurement) is most defensible when there are a moderately large number of response options (at least five, although seven is probably better still). However, from an analytic standpoint, it is not the number of scale points provided in the instrument, but rather the number of scale points that the respondents actually use that determines the appropriateness of conventional analytic techniques. As an example, imagine that you asked a question on a 1–7 response scale but respondents only used two response points (6 and 7). Even though you designed the question to use a 7-point scale, your data are actually dichotomous. Thus, conventional factor analysis techniques would be inappropriate for such an item. This is one of the many reasons that it is crucial to examine frequencies and descriptive statistics for each item prior to conducting a factor analysis.

Table 4.3 McAnallen anxiety in math teaching survey: interitem correlations

	1.	2.	3.	4.	5.	6.	7.	8.	9.	10.	11.	12.	13.	14.	15.	16.	17.	18.
1. I was one of the best math students when I was in school	1.00																	
2. Having to work with fractions causes me discomfort	0.44	1.00																
3. I feel confident in my ability to teach mathematics to students in the grade I currently teach	0.19	0.20	1.00															
4. I am confident that I can learn advanced math concepts	0.44	0.37	0.40	1.00														
5. When teaching mathematics, I welcome student questions	0.20	0.21	0.55	0.41	1.00													
6. I have trouble finding alternative methods for teaching a mathematical concept when a student is confused	0.07	0.20	0.35	0.21	0.29	1.00												
7. I find it difficult to teach mathematical concepts to students	0.17	0.30	0.45	0.34	0.32	0.49	1.00											
8. I feel confident using sources other than the mathematics textbook when I teach	0.10	0.16	0.30	0.27	0.36	0.25	0.34	1.00										
9. I don't have the math skills to differentiate instruction for the most talented students in my classes	0.14	0.19	0.40	0.30	0.30	0.47	0.46	0.27	1.00									
10. I dislike having to teach math every day	0.24	0.30	0.43	0.33	0.34	0.29	0.42	0.25	0.38	1.00								
11. I avoided taking non-required math courses in college	0.45	0.32	0.20	0.47	0.20	0.18	0.26	0.17	0.26	0.34	1.00							
12. I have a lot of self-confidence when it comes to mathematics	0.56	0.49	0.37	0.61	0.36	0.27	0.37	0.28	0.36	0.45	0.57	1.00						
13. I am confident that I can solve math problems on my own	0.46	0.42	0.34	0.58	0.33	0.30	0.39	0.30	0.36	0.38	0.50	0.72	1.00					

(continued)

Table 4.3 (continued)

	1.	2.	3.	4.	5.	6.	7.	8.	9.	10.	11.	12.	13.	14.	15.	16.	17.	18.
14. I become anxious when I have to compute percentages	0.36	0.54	0.21	0.40	0.25	0.25	0.34	0.15	0.26	0.32	0.36	0.48	0.46	1.00				
15. I have math anxiety	0.50	0.52	0.27	0.47	0.26	0.23	0.36	0.22	0.25	0.42	0.46	0.62	0.54	0.64	1.00			
16. It makes me nervous to think about having to do any math problem	0.46	0.51	0.30	0.49	0.30	0.30	0.40	0.23	0.36	0.44	0.46	0.64	0.60	0.55	0.69	1.00		
17. I am comfortable working on a problem that involves algebra	0.40	0.38	0.24	0.49	0.27	0.21	0.25	0.19	0.28	0.33	0.45	0.57	0.57	0.40	0.45	0.534	1.00	
18. I have strong aptitude when it comes to math	0.58	0.47	0.29	0.59	0.28	0.22	0.30	0.23	0.33	0.36	0.51	0.75	0.66	0.47	0.60	0.63	0.59	1.00

Table 4.4 McAnallen anxiety in math teaching survey EFA: eigenvalues and variance explained

Total variance explained

Factor	Initial eigenvalues			Extraction sums of squared Loadings			Rotation Sums of Squared Loadings[a]
	Total	% of Variance	Cumulative %	Total	% of Variance	Cumulative %	Total
1	7.579	42.106	42.106	7.095	39.417	39.417	6.668
2	1.931	10.726	52.832	1.360	7.554	46.971	4.666
3	1.064	5.912	58.743				
4	0.879	4.883	63.627				
5	0.774	4.301	67.928				
6	0.695	3.861	71.788				
7	0.613	3.403	75.192				
8	0.558	3.101	78.292				
9	0.522	2.901	81.194				
10	0.514	2.854	84.048				
11	0.494	2.746	86.793				
12	0.430	2.389	89.183				
13	0.398	2.210	91.393				
14	0.385	2.139	93.532				
15	0.378	2.101	95.634				
16	0.306	1.702	97.336				
17	0.258	1.432	98.768				
18	0.222	1.232	100.000				

Extraction Method: Principal Axis Factoring

[a] When factors are correlated, sums of squared loadings cannot be added to obtain a total variance

Interitem Correlations

Examining the interitem correlations (Table 4.3), it is difficult to identify clusters of items that relate to each other without relating to other items that are not in the cluster. Clearly, such an eyeball approach (inter-ocular procedure) to factor analysis would be difficult, especially with a large number of items. Still, truly problematic items may be detectable through examination of the correlation matrix. For example, if an item is essentially uncorrelated with all of the other items in the matrix, it will not fare well in the factor analysis, and could be removed prior to the procedure. Conversely, if two items are extremely highly correlated with each other ($r = 0.85$ or above), this suggests a level of redundancy between the 2 items that is problematic both conceptually and statistically (you are essentially asking the exact same question twice!). In this case, it is advisable to remove one of the two redundant prior to conducting the factor analysis.

Table 4.5 McAnallen anxiety in math teaching survey EFA: initial and final communalities

Item	Initial	Extraction
1. I was one of the best math students when I was in school	0.442	0.459
2. Having to work with fractions causes me discomfort	0.412	0.373
3. I feel confident in my ability to teach mathematics to students in the grade I currently teach	0.447	0.477
4. I am confident that I can learn advanced math concepts	0.502	0.481
5. When teaching mathematics, I welcome student questions	0.390	0.351
6. I have trouble finding alternative methods for teaching a mathematical concept when a student is confused	0.343	0.357
7. I find it difficult to teach mathematical concepts to students	0.433	0.481
8. I feel confident using sources other than the mathematics textbook when I teach	0.213	0.220
9. I don't have the math skills to differentiate instruction for the most talented students in my classes	0.373	0.399
10. I dislike having to teach math every day	0.364	0.365
11. I avoided taking nonrequired math courses in college	0.403	0.396
12. I have a lot of self-confidence when it comes to mathematics	0.711	0.732
13. I am confident that I can solve math problems on my own	0.605	0.607
14. I become anxious when I have to compute percentages	0.499	0.410
15. I have math anxiety	0.632	0.595
16. It makes me nervous to think about having to do any math problem	0.614	0.617
17. I am comfortable working on a problem that involves algebra	0.447	0.444
18. I have strong aptitude when it comes to math	0.671	0.691

Extraction Method: Principal Axis Factoring

Kaiser–Meyer–Olkin and Measures of Sampling Adequacy

Additional EFA output is available in most computer programs and merits some discussion. The *Kaiser–Meyer–Olkin test* (KMO) and measures of sampling adequacy for individual items (MSA) assess the appropriateness of the correlation matrix for factor analysis. As such, the KMO and MSA are computed on the raw correlation matrix prior to conducting any factor analyses. The KMO is an index for comparing magnitudes of the observed correlation coefficients to magnitudes of partial correlation coefficients, after controlling for all of the other variables included in the correlation matrix. If the items share common factors, the partial correlations between all pairs of items should be small when the correlation between those items and all the other items have been removed (Lackey et al. 2003). The KMO ranges from 0 to 1. If the sum of the partial correlations is large relative to the sum of the correlations, KMO is small, and EFA may be inappropriate. If the sum of the partial correlations is small relative to the sum of the correlations, KMO is large, and EFA may be appropriate. The anti-image correlation matrix contains the partial correlations between items after controlling for all other items on the off-diagonal and measures of sampling adequacy (MSA) for each of the items on the diagonal (Lackey et al. 2003). Ideally, correlation matrices with one or more large general factors should exhibit relatively large MSAs on the

Table 4.6 McAnallen anxiety in math teaching survey EFA: unrotated factor matrix

Factor matrix[a]

	Factor	
	1	2
12. I have a lot of self-confidence when it comes to mathematics	0.842	−0.153
18. I have strong aptitude when it comes to math	0.792	−0.254
16. It makes me nervous to think about having to do any math problem	0.776	−0.123
13. I am confident that I can solve math problems on my own	0.775	
15. I have math anxiety	0.743	−0.206
4. I am confident that I can learn advanced math concepts	0.693	
17. I am comfortable working on a problem that involves algebra	0.648	−0.155
14. I become anxious when I have to compute percentages	0.627	−0.130
11. I avoided taking nonrequired math courses in college	0.608	−0.165
1. I was one of the best math students when I was in school	0.586	−0.339
2. Having to work with fractions causes me discomfort	0.586	−0.172
10. I dislike having to teach math every day	0.561	0.222
7. I find it difficult to teach mathematical concepts to students	0.551	0.422
3. I feel confident in my ability to teach mathematics to students in the grade I currently teach	0.506	0.470
9. I don't have the math skills to differentiate instruction for the most talented students in my classes	0.495	0.393
5. When teaching mathematics, I welcome student questions	0.477	0.351
8. I feel confident using sources other than the mathematics textbook when I teach	0.368	0.291
6. I have trouble finding alternative methods for teaching a mathematical concept when a student is confused	0.417	0.429

Extraction Method: Principal Axis Factoring

[a] 2 factors extracted. 5 iterations required

diagonal of the anti-image correlation matrix and relatively small off-diagonal elements. Lackey et al. (2003) provide a lucid and detailed description of the KMO and MSA, and we encourage interested readers to consult Chapter 3 of their textbook on factor analysis for further details. The KMO for the current example is 0.94 and all of the individual MSAs are above 0.895, indicating the appropriateness of this correlation matrix for factor analysis.

Eigenvalues and Proportion of Variance Explained

Table 4.4 lists the eigenvalues and the percent of variance accounted for by each derived factor in the EFA solution. The eigenvalues or lambdas represent the roots we described earlier. The size of the root is directly related to the importance of the derived factor, and the sum of the roots will equal the total amount of variance entered into the factor analysis. This variance is actually the sum of the diagonal entries in the correlation matrix that was factored. Recall that PCA uses 1's in the

Table 4.7 McAnallen anxiety in math teaching survey EFA: pattern matrix

Pattern matrix[a]

	Factor	
	1	2
18. I have strong aptitude when it comes to math	0.850	
12. I have a lot of self-confidence when it comes to mathematics	0.796	
15. I have math anxiety	0.768	
1. I was one of the best math students when I was in school	0.767	−0.200
16. It makes me nervous to think about having to do any math problem	0.718	0.112
13. I am confident that I can solve math problems on my own	0.676	0.164
17. I am comfortable working on a problem that involves algebra	0.647	
11. I avoided taking nonrequired math courses in college	0.625	
2. Having to work with fractions causes me discomfort	0.615	
14. I become anxious when I have to compute percentages	0.608	
4. I am confident that I can learn advanced math concepts	0.570	0.191
3. I feel confident in my ability to teach mathematics to students in the grade I currently teach		0.709
7. I find it difficult to teach mathematical concepts to students		0.667
6. I have trouble finding alternative methods for teaching a mathematical concept when a student is confused		0.631
9. I don't have the math skills to differentiate instruction for the most talented students in my classes		0.615
5. When teaching mathematics, I welcome student questions		0.562
8. I feel confident using sources other than the mathematics textbook when I teach		0.456
10. I dislike having to teach math every day	0.236	0.441

Extraction Method: Principal Axis Factoring
Rotation Method: Oblimin with Kaiser Normalization
[a] Rotation converged in four iterations

diagonal of the original correlation matrix. These l's represent the amount of variance for each item that is entered into the analysis. Thus, the sum of the diagonal entries in the correlation matrix, R (i.e., the trace of R), equals 18 (the number of items) and represents the total variance in the solution. Theoretically, in a common factor analysis, SMCs are inserted into the diagonal of R, so that the trace of R is less than the number of items. However, SPSS always reports initial eigenvalues that correspond to a PCA extraction, even when running analyses using PAF extractions. Because the sum of the roots equals the sum of the items, the amount of variance accounted for by each factor prior to rotation is obtained by dividing the root by the number of items. Thus, in our example, $7.579/18 = 0.4210$, indicating that Factor I accounts for 42.1% of the total variance in the items prior to rotation. Also, note that the output indicates the two-factor solution has accounted for 52.8% of the total variance.

Number of Factors

Using the standard defaults in SPSS, the number of factors extracted will be equal to the number of factors associated with eigenvalues or roots greater than 1.00, using the initial eigenvalues from the PCA solution. Although the default option in most computer programs will use the unity root criterion, it is generally considered one of the weakest methods for determining the number of factors to extract.

Instead, we recommend that researchers specify the number of factors to be extracted based on the results of parallel analysis, which is considered to be the single best indicator of the true number of factors, in combination with the results of the MAP, the scree plot, etc. that we described earlier. Forcing the number of extracted factors to the number of hypothesized factors a priori is unacceptable (unless supported by the results of the parallel analysis and/or other extraction decision criteria). Given the potential inaccuracy of the factor extraction criteria and the fact that different criteria often suggest extracting different numbers of factors, you may choose to run two or three different EFAs, extracting a different number of factors each time, and compare the results of the analyses to make a final decision about how many factors to extract. Ultimately though, you must decide upon one EFA solution, and this is the solution that you report and interpret.

In this example, we ran the parallel analysis using PCA, the parallel analysis using PAF, the MAP, and the revised MAP. As is often the case, these tests gave conflicting advice. The parallel analysis using PCA suggested extraction of two factors with both the mean and 95th percentile criteria. The parallel analysis using PAF suggested extracting four factors with both the mean and 95th percentile criteria. The original MAP suggested extracting two factors; the revised MAP suggested three factors. Figure 4.1 illustrates the scree plot based on the PCA components, as it is reported in SPSS. Examination of this scree plot clearly suggested extracting two factors. The eigenvalue above 1 rule suggested extracting three factors. Our experience has been that the parallel analysis using PAF sometimes tends toward overextraction. (The Chi-square goodness of fit test, available using the ML extraction in SPSS, also has a strong tendency to over-factor. In this case, it suggested extracting seven factors!) After examining these criteria, we concluded that the most likely solution was probably a two-factor solution; however, we also examined the pattern matrix of the three-factor solution. The third factor in the three-factor solution had only one pattern coefficient above 0.40, and that coefficient was 0.433. Thus, it seemed as if extracting two factors was the most reasonable decision. Therefore, we ran our EFA with two factors, and those are the results that we report and interpret.

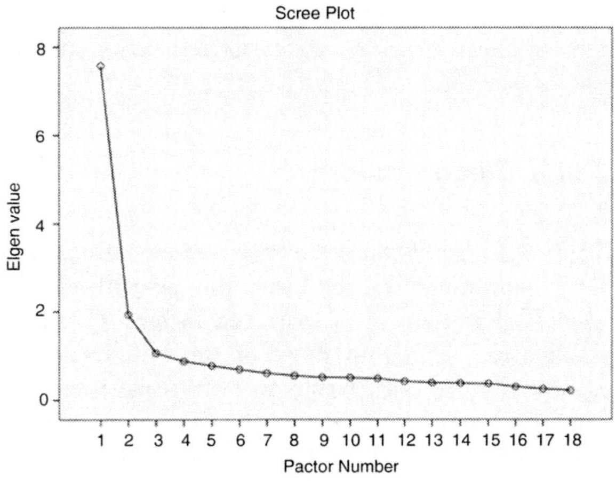

Fig. 4.1 Selecting a number of items to extract: a sample scree plot

Initial Communalities

Table 4.5 contains a listing of estimated communalities. Communalities represent the amount of variance in each item accounted for by the solution. The initial communality estimates are computed prior to the analysis and represent the diagonal entries in *R* or the total amount of variance entered into the solution for each variable. In PAF, the initial communality of an item is the multiple R-squared (SMCs) of that item with all of the other items on the scale. In other words, imagine building a multiple regression equation where item 1 is the dependent variable and items 2–18 were the 17 independent variables used to predict item 1. The initial communality is the R^2 for that regression equation. Obviously, if the initial communality is low, the variable does not share much variance with any of the other variables in the instrument, which would be a problem. Ideally, we would like to see communalities that are high, or at least moderate (0.40 and above). If communalities are near 0 (less than 0.10 or 0.20), we recommend returning to the inter-item correlation matrix to examine the pattern of correlations between that item and the other items on the scale. If the item is essentially unrelated to all of the other items on the scale, it may be advisable to remove that item prior to conducting the factor analysis, as the item is essentially “all noise“. In a PCA, the initial communalities are always equal to 1 because the researcher is trying to explain all of the variance in every item.

Unrotated Factor Matrix

The next matrix (Table 4.6) represents the derived factor-loading matrix prior to rotation. This matrix has the same number of rows as items and columns as the number of derived factors. The entries represent correlations between each item and the derived factor prior to rotation. By design, the first factor contains most of the variance; therefore, the unrotated factor solution is not easily interpretable.

Final Communalities

Table 4.5 also contains the final communalities resulting from the solution. These final communalities represent the proportion of variance in the item that is explained by the set of extracted factors. Often, the values of the final communalities are similar to those of the initial communalities; however, that is not necessarily the case. Using an orthogonal rotation, the sum of the squared factor loadings for the item is equal to the communality of the item. Using an oblique rotation technique, which allows the factors to be intercorrelated, the sum of the squared loadings from the unrotated factor matrix reproduces the extraction communalities. For example, for item 1, the loadings are 0.586 and −0.339. Thus, the sum of the squared loadings is $0.586^2 + -0.339^2$, which equals 0.459.

Rotation

Recall that the unrotated factor matrix in Table 4.6 contained many high entries in Factor I and that the other factors contained few large entries. The unrotated matrix will always lead to one overall factor determined by most of the items and some other generally uninterpretable factors. Thus, we rotate the factors (in a geometric sense) to attempt to see a clearer factor structure. To understand the rotation concept, note that two factors at a time can be plotted in a geometric space as is illustrated in Fig. 4.2. We have plotted all items on both the unrotated and orthogonally rotated matrices in Fig. 4.2. In a varimax rotation, the axis system remains at right angles (90°); this implies that the factors are orthogonal or independent. The correlations listed under Factors I and II in the factor matrix are then the coordinates to be plotted. For example, in the varimax rotated matrix, item 1 has coordinates of 0.68 "over" and 0.04 "up," with axes I and II, respectively. When we observe the factor structure exhibited in the unrotated and rotated matrices, it is obvious why the unrotated matrix is of little value to the instrument developers: all of the items cluster near Factor I. When the correlations are plotted for the varimax rotated matrix, it is clear that items 12, 18, 16, and 15 contribute most to the name of Factor I, and items 3, 6, 7, and 9 contribute most to the naming of Factor II. There are two clear clusters, and once the solution is rotated, the clusters sit much more closely to the separate axes. The actual naming of the factors will be discussed in a later section. Clearly, the rotation process has distributed the total amount of variance accounted for by the two factor solution across the factors.

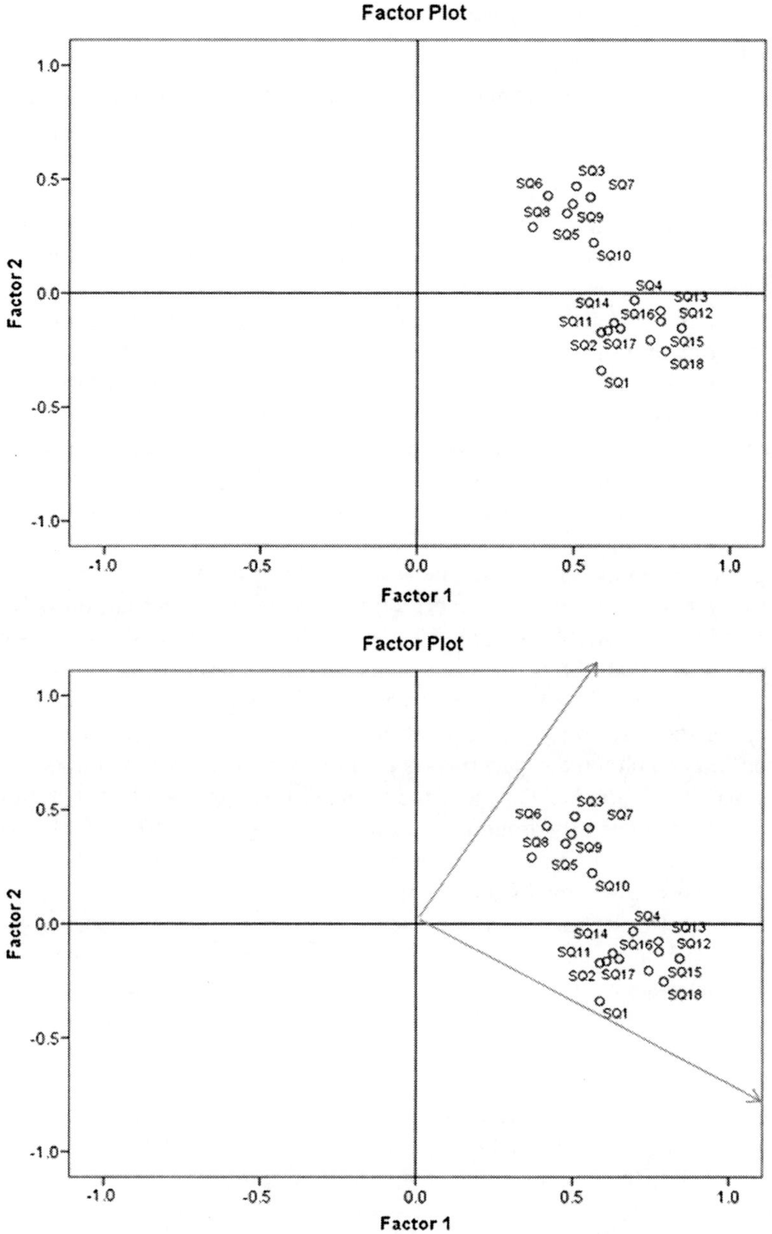

Fig. 4.2 Unrotated and rotated axes and their relationship to items graphed onto a factor plot

Oblique Rotation

Having briefly discussed varimax rotation techniques, we now turn our attention to the oblique rotation of the factor matrix. We recommend using oblique rotation techniques whenever you expect the factors to be correlated (which is almost always!). In a varimax rotation, the axis system is maintained at 90°. The axis system is simply rotated in all possible directions, so that the x (Factor I) and y (Factor II) axes each are as close as possible to a distinct cluster of items. Therefore, the entries listed under Factor I in the factor-loading matrix will have high loadings on Factor I and low loadings on Factor II; for Factor II the reverse is true. Refer again to Fig. 4.2, which contains the plot for Factors I and II resulting from the varimax rotation. Notice that, if we envisioned an ellipse around the cluster of primary items defining each factor, we would see that the ellipses are not located directly next to either axis system. That is, the ideal axis system for describing the relationship between Factors I and II appears to be one with less than a 90° angle. In other words, although the axis system representing the factors is orthogonal, the clusters of items actually used to define the factor are not orthogonal. Given that most constructs we seek to measure are likely to be related, we recommend examining and interpreting a factor solution that allows the axis system to be less than 90°, the oblique rotation. In this rotation, the axis system can collapse to less than 90° so that each axis becomes closer to the cluster of items defining the factor. The smaller the angle (i.e., the greater the reduction in the angle), the more strongly the two factors are correlated.[1] Figure 4.3 repeats the varimax-rotated plot and superimposes the plot of a corresponding oblique rotation for the data (see footnote 1). Using the axes produced by the oblique rotation, the items cluster very clearly around one of the two axes, suggesting simple structure. Figure 4.3 clearly illustrates the advantages of the oblique rotation over the varimax rotation in terms of producing simple structure.

The entries in the rotated factor matrix with an oblique rotation are generally referred to as pattern coefficients. They are like partial standardized regression weights that capture the relationship between the item and the factor after controlling for the effects of the other factor(s). As mentioned earlier, it is no longer appropriate to calculate sums of squares of the row or column entries, since the entries are partial regression coefficients. If, for some reason, you wanted to calculate the percent of variance accounted for by the oblique factors after rotation, you would have to refer back to the varimax rotation, identify the comparable factor, calculate the column sums of squares in the varimax matrix, and divide by the total sum of the roots (or the number of items for PCA). The variance

[1] The correlations represent the cosine of the angle between the two factors. Noting that the cosine curve can be used to calculate angles for various correlations, readers may wish to estimate the actual angle between axes. For example, when the correlation is zero, the angle is 90° (varimax).

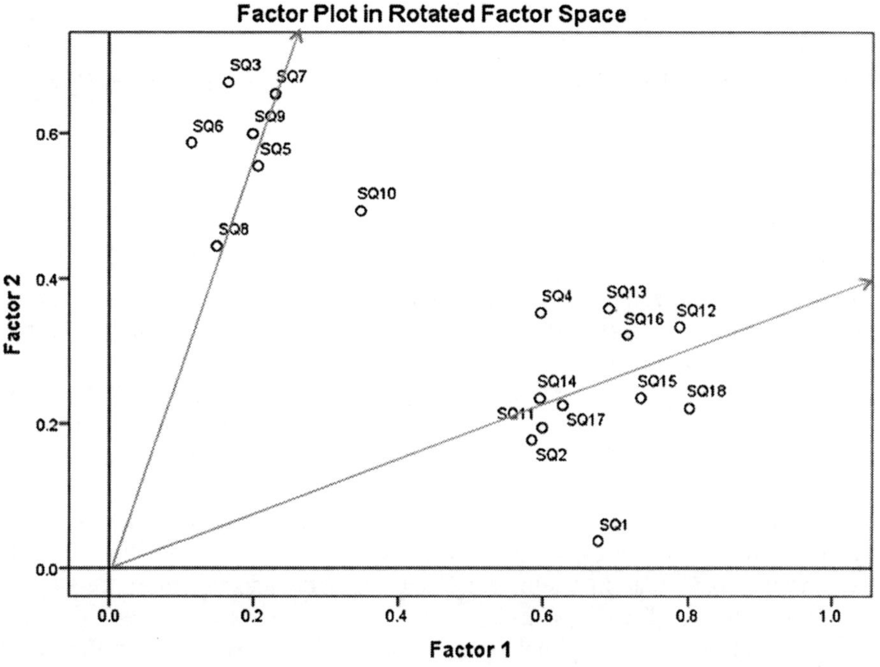

Fig. 4.3 An example of oblique (nonorthogonal) axis rotation to items on a factor plot

accounted for after rotation will be the same for each factor for both the oblique and varimax solutions.

Factor Correlations

The factor correlation matrix contains correlations between the derived factors. No such matrix is generated when using a varimax rotation because the off-diagonal entries are always zero. The factor correlations indicate the extent to which the derived factors or axes are related to each other. For example, Factors I and II are correlated at 0.55. This indicates that the factors are not independent constructs; they are moderately strongly positively correlated. We perceive this as evidence that we were well advised to use an oblique rotation.

Why do people tend to run varimax rotations when the oblique rotation tells us if the factors are related and provides the equivalent of a varimax solution if the factor correlations are near zero? The reason for the popularity of the varimax rotation is historical; varimax rotation first appeared in 1958 when Kaiser reported its use and reliable oblique rotation programs were not readily available in most canned computer programs until the 1970s. You may wish to analyze your data using both an orthogonal and an oblique rotation technique for pedagogical reasons when you are learning factor analysis. However, there is really no reason to ever favor an orthogonal rotation over an oblique rotation when designing affective instruments, so we recommend that you run and report the results using an oblique rotation technique.

Structure Matrix

Analyses that allow the factors to be correlated actually generate two "factor loading" matrices: the pattern matrix, which represents the partial standardized regression weights for the direct effect of the factor on the item after controlling for the other factors, and the structure matrix, in which the "factor loadings" represent the simple bivariate correlations between the items and the factors. The existence of two separate "factor loading" matrices in oblique rotations is the reason that the term "factor loading" has fallen out of favor. A "factor loading" could be a pattern coefficient or a structure coefficient. Therefore, when describing the results of your analyses, you should always refer to "factor loadings" from the pattern matrix as "pattern coefficients" and "factor loadings" from the structure matrix as "structure" coefficients.

If the factors were completely uncorrelated, then the elements in the pattern matrix and the elements in the structure matrix would be completely identical. The more correlated the factors are, the more the pattern matrix and the structure matrix diverge. When factors are highly correlated, the pattern matrix may appear to have very clean "simple structure" (i.e., each item has high loadings on only one factor and near zero loadings on all the other factors); however, the elements of the structure matrix may appear more muddled where an item may have structure coefficients that are fairly large on two or more factors. Why does this happen? Remember, the structure coefficient is the simple bivariate correlation between the item and the factor. To obtain the structure matrix, the pattern matrix is multiplied by the factor correlation matrix. (In an orthogonal rotation, the pattern matrix and the structure matrix are the same because the correlation between the factors is 0; therefore, the pattern matrix is multiplied by an identity matrix, which produces the same (pattern) matrix (Henson and Roberts 2006).

A simple example illustrates this process. Imagine you have two correlated factors, and an item has a pattern coefficient of 0.70 on Factor 1 and a pattern coefficient of 0.10 on Factor 2, and the two factors are correlated at 0.50. We can use the tracing rule (Loehlin 2004) to estimate the model-predicted correlation between that item and Factor 2. The model-predicted correlation is the sum of the product of the compound paths, being sure to only trace through one correlational path per trace. In this example, we multiply 0.70 * 0.50, which gives us 0.35 and add it to the direct path (0.10). Thus, the model-implied correlation between item 1 and Factor 2 is 0.45, even though the direct effect of Factor 2 on item 1 after controlling for Factor 1 (the pattern coefficient) is only 0.10. Now imagine if the correlation between the two factors were 0.80. Then the model-implied correlation between Factor 2 and item 1 would be 0.70 * 0.80 + 0.10 or 0.66. Thus, the higher the interfactor correlations are, the larger the structure coefficients of the non-primary factors will look when compared to the pattern coefficients. If you only look at the pattern matrix and your items exhibit simple structure, you could forget what the strong correlation between factors indicates in terms of the actual bivariate correlations between items and factors. This is the reason that some journals (such as *Educational and Psychological Measurement*) require the reporting of structure coefficients. To determine the structure of the instrument (i.e., which items belong with which factors), you should generally interpret the pattern matrix. However, you should always examine the structure matrix and use it as a "reality check" on the true simple bivariate correlational structure between the items and the factors.

Factor Interpretation

Now that we have reviewed the computer output, we are ready to interpret the factor structure. To understand the nature of the factors, we examine the factor pattern matrix. Ideally, we would like all of our items to have high pattern coefficients on one primary factor and near zero pattern coefficients on all other factors. For ease of interpretation, we display only those loadings above 0.10, as illustrated in Table 4.7. It is helpful to circle or highlight all of the pattern coefficients above 0.40 (minimally) or above 0.50 (ideally) to identify the items that contribute most to naming the factor. If an item has a loading above 0.40 on more than one factor, that item is multidimensional and should be eliminated from the item pool. In fact, we recommend eliminating any item that has a loading of 0.30 or higher on more than one factor. That secondary loading of 0.30 (after controlling for the effects of the primary factor) indicates that the item response is driven by both latent constructs. Thus, the item is not a clean and simple indicator of either one of the constructs.

To avoid confusion in interpreting the factors, we recommend coding the response format, so that high scores are associated with positive attitudes, positive item stems, and positive coefficients in the pattern and structure matrix. For example, for a Likert 5-point agreement scale, code a 5 for "strongly agree" to an item such as "I have strong aptitude when it comes to math." Then, examine the signs of the pattern matrix to see if the positive item stem is associated with a positive pattern coefficient. If *all* items on a factor are coded in the sample direction, then all of the pattern coefficients should have the same sign (either positive or negative). If *all* of the positive item stems defining the factor (loadings above 0.40) have negative loadings, you can simply reflect the factor (reverse all of the + and − signs for that factor). This merely locates the factor in a different quadrant geometrically; it does not change the magnitude of the relationships among items or factors. (Think about it this way: 90° backward and 270° forward are actually the same.) Reflecting a factor in the oblique factor pattern matrix also necessitates reversing all of the signs in the factor's row and column in the factor correlation matrix. Because the factor is now located in a different quadrant, the direction of the relationships of the factor with other factors has also changed. In most cases, reflecting all appropriate factors will result in all positive relationships in the factor correlation matrix. If there are a few negative loadings (i.e., a bipolar factor) within a particular factor, look at the item stems to see if the content is stated in a negative direction (e.g., I do not have the math skills to differentiate instruction for the most talented students in my classes.). If you did not yet reverse score the negative item stems, the negative loading merely reflects the negative relationship of the negative item with the positive factor and it can simply be ignored (However, do not forget to reverse code any negatively loading items prior to the reliability analysis). If you already reverse scored every negative item stem prior to the factor analysis, you have a problem. That is, the hypothesized direction of response does not agree with the response direction of the item as perceived by the respondent. A review of the item stem is in order. Why would responses to the item in question be negatively related to responses to the other items on the factor?

After identifying the items that have pattern coefficients of 0.40 (or 0.50) or greater on one primary factor and have pattern coefficients below 0.30 on all other secondary factors, it is often helpful to create tables for the pattern matrix and the structure matrix, listing the item numbers, item stems, and ranked loadings for each factor. You are now ready to interpret the factors. The items with the highest pattern coefficients are best explained by or share the most variance with the factor. Your job is to determine what concepts define the factor, and whether the empirically derived factors correspond to the theoretical constructs that you operationalized during the "content validity" phase. Review the item content to identify the underlying theme shared by the items. Respondents tended to rate these items in a consistent manner on the basis of some cognitive conceptual framework, and this consistency is what created the intercorrelations among the items and contributed to the development of the factor. What were the respondents perceiving when they read the items?

Describing the Factor

Careful consideration of the item content should have facilitated naming the factors. In Table 4.7, we named the two factors–Factor I, General Math Anxiety/Comfort; Factor II, Math Teaching Anxiety/Comfort. After naming the factor, you are ready to write the factor description. Three components are crucial for a proper factor description. First, state the name you have given to the factor. Second, justify the name by merging some actual item and/or construct content into your description. Third, describe the perceptions or attributes of a person with a high score on the factor and a person with a low score on the factor. For Factor I, the description could be:

> Factor I was named General Math Anxiety/comfort, because items defining the factor described the teacher's general comfort or anxiety level with general math content. Given that all negative items were recoded, teachers with high scores on the factor would exhibit comfort and confidence with general math content, whereas teachers with low scores on the factor would experience general math anxiety.

When describing the factors, it is also helpful to describe the intercorrelations among the factors. General Math Anxiety and Math Teaching Anxiety are fairly strongly positively correlated, which makes sense. Teachers who tend to be fearful and anxious about math also tend to be fearful and anxious about teaching math. Conversely, teachers who are comfortable and confident with math tend to report more comfort teaching math concepts.

Given the exploratory nature of EFA and the difficulties inherent in creating psychometrically strong, conceptually meaningful subscales, the next stage in providing evidence of the internal structure of the instrument requires revising the instrument based on the results of the factor analysis, collecting a new sample of participants, and subjecting the item responses to a CFA.

Confirmatory Factor Analysis

In CFA, the instrument developer specifies a priori which items will load on each factor according to prior research.[2] The results of CFA indicate how well the empirical data actually conform to the CFA model. CFA provides a more stringent test of whether the pattern of relationships among the items could be explained by the hypothesized factor structure. CFA provides several advantages over EFA. First, in EFA, the analyst has no direct control over the linkages between indicators and factors; however, in CFA, the researcher can clearly specify a priori the linkage between factors and indicators (Kline 2010). Also, in EFA, the researcher cannot constrain an item to be an indicator of only one factor (Kline 2010, p. 58). In addition, because CFA permits the comparison of several rival nested models, it allows researchers to reject specified models, and compare several competing models empirically. Thus, CFA respects the role of falsification within scientific inquiry (Thompson 1997). Finally, the CFA model can reward parsimony (Thompson 1997). By convention, if there are no statistically significant differences among the hypothesized models, researchers using CFA favor the most parsimonious of the competing models.

---

[2] Much of the discussion of model fit in confirmatory factor analysis models has been adapted from McCoach (2003). SEM isn't just the School wide Enrichment Model anymore: Structural Equation Modeling (SEM) in gifted education. *Journal for the Education of the Gifted, 27,* 36–61.

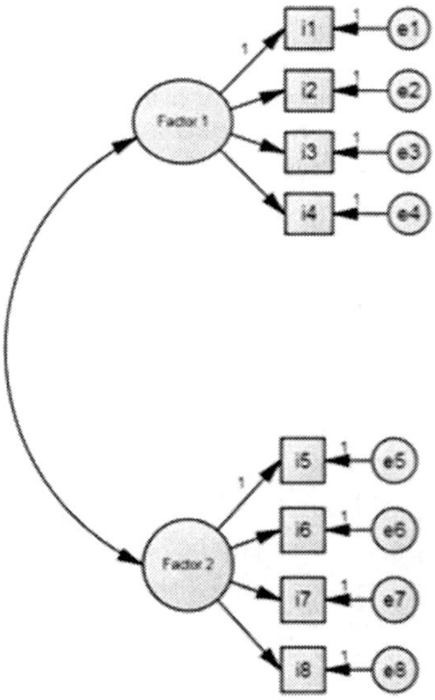

Fig. 4.4 Path diagram of a simple CFA model

CFA models are often depicted graphically, and a graphical representation of the model is one of the easiest ways to understand the CFA model. Thus, Fig. 4.4 shows a simple CFA model, as drawn in AMOS 20.

In a standard CFA model, each item is represented as having two sources of influence—a single factor that the indicator is supposed to measure and all other unique sources of variance, which are represented by measurement error term (e). Conceptually, this is similar to the EFA model. A person's response to an item is determined partially as a function of his or her standing on the factor and partially as a function of error, noise, or other unmeasured variables. In a standard CFA model, each item loads on only one factor (there is only one direct path from a factor to a given item). Of course, an item could be predicted by two or more factors. However, this is indicative of multidimensionality. If the item is an indicator of two factors, where will you place the item when it is time to create scale scores?

In a standard CFA model, the measurement error terms (e's) are independent of each other and of the factors. This assumption can be relaxed and tested by allowing errors to correlate with each other. However, if the errors of 2 items do correlate with each other, that means the 2 items share something in common that is not explained by the factor. Technically, a correlated error indicates that the residuals of the 2 items (the unexplained variance in the items) are related. This is indicative of unmodeled multidimensionality, which is quite problematic from an instrument design perspective, because each item on the final instrument should be a clean, clear indicator of the construct that it is designed to measure. However, it is not uncommon for items to share correlated residuals when:

1. The 2 items are negative. Often, negatively worded items share residual variance. This is yet another reason that we recommend avoiding the use of a combination of positively and negatively worded items on the same scale (under most normal circumstances).
2. The 2 items use the same word or words, especially if the words are uncommon. Using the same phrase or even the same sentence structure may have the same effect, especially if the phrase you are using is unusual.
3. The 2 items are overly redundant—they have such similar content that they are essentially repetitions of each other. This may signal the need to eliminate one of the 2 items from the final survey to avoid redundancy and shorten the length of the survey. For example, "School is hard" and "School is difficult" are so similar in content that only one of those 2 items may be needed for the final version of the instrument.

CFA belongs to a family of techniques known as structural equation modeling. Several excellent introductory books on CFA (Brown 2006) and structural equation modeling (Byrne 2010; Kline 2010) exist, and our descriptions of CFA, multiple groups CFA (in Chapter 5) and SEM (in Chapter 6) are not meant as complete overviews of the topics. Instead, they are conceptual introductions to the techniques, with a focus on their utility within the instrument design process. Still, we must explain a few technical details about CFA model identification and specification.

Conducting a CFA first requires specifying an a priori model. In AMOS, this is most easily accomplished by drawing a path diagram, such as the one in Fig. 4.4. It is also important to determine whether the model is identified. A model is said to be identified if it is theoretically possible to calculate a unique estimate of every one of its parameters (Kline 2010). In general, for a CFA model to be identified, there must be at least as many elements in the variance/covariance matrix as there are parameters to be estimated within the model. A parameter is an unknown characteristic of the population that we are trying the estimate in the specified SEM model: these are the *unknowns*. The elements of the variance/covariance matrix represent the pieces of information that we have: these are the *knowns*. Thus, to be identified, there must be at least as many knowns (pieces of information) as there are unknowns (parameters to be estimated). If we try to estimate more unknowns than knowns, the model is underidentified, and no solution is possible. If we estimate exactly as many knowns as we have unknowns, the model is said to be "just identified." In such a scenario, there are unique estimates for all of our parameters; however, we cannot test the fit of the model. If we have more knowns than unknowns, the model is overidentified, and there are multiple potential solutions. In such a scenario, we favor the solution that maximizes the likelihood of observing the parameter estimates given the data. Measures of model fit (such as Chi-square) are available for overidentified models; thus, it is possible to evaluate the fit of an overidentified model. In SEM, model fit really evaluates the degree to which the variance/covariance matrix that is implied by the model matches the population covariance matrix implied/estimated by the data.

In addition, in a CFA model, we estimate a latent variable (the factor), which has no inherent scale, because it is not actually measured or observed. Thus, we need a way of scaling the latent variable. There are two options for doing this: fixing the variance of each latent variable in the model to 1 or fixing one unstandardized pattern coefficient for each factor to be 1. The variable whose unstandardized regression coefficient is fixed to 1 becomes the "marker variable" for the factor, and the factor's variance is scaled in the same metric as the marker variable. Although both scaling methods are acceptable for single group models, the more common method for scaling the latent variable is the marker variable strategy, so that is the method that we illustrate.

What are the parameters that we estimate in a CFA model? In a CFA model, if we use the marker variable strategy described above, we estimate an unstandardized path coefficient for F-1 items per factor, where F is the number of items in the factor. This is because 1 item per factor serves as the marker variable, and its regression coefficient is constrained to 1. In addition, we estimate a factor variance for each of our latent variables and an error variance for each of our items. Generally, standard CFA models allow all factors to be intercorrelated; therefore, we estimate interfactor correlations for all of the factors in the model. If we allow any errors to be correlated, then we must count those correlations as parameters to be estimated as well. Thus, in our simple example, we are estimating 17 parameters: 6 paths (3 paths on factor 1, 3 paths on factor 2; two paths are constrained to be 1 for the marker variables), 2 factor variances, 8 error variances, and 1 correlation between the factors. How many knowns do we have? The number of knowns is equal to the number of unique elements in the variance/covariance matrix, and this can be calculated using the following formula: $V(V + 1)/2$, where V is the number of observed variables, which in this case are our items. There are 8 items. Therefore there are $8*9/2$, or 36 unique elements in the variance/covariance matrix. The degrees of freedom for the model = the number of knowns minus the number of unknowns. In this example, we have 36 knowns and 17 unknowns, thus the degrees of freedom for the model are 19(36–17). This means that we are making 17 more constraints than there are pieces of information provided.

Model Fit in Confirmatory Factor Analysis

How do we know if the data "fits" the CFA model that we have specified? Hypothesis testing in CFA departs from traditional tests of significance. Usually, when we conduct statistical tests, the null hypothesis is that there is no relationship among a set of variables or that there are no statistically significant differences among a set of variables. In such cases, if we reject the null hypothesis, we conclude that there are statistically significant relationships or differences, which is often what we hope to show. In CFA, the traditional logic of model fit is reversed. Instead, the null hypothesis is that the population covariance of observed variables equals the covariance matrix implied by a particular model. Under certain distributional assumptions (normality, etc.), we can use a test statistic with a Chi-squared (χ^2) distribution to test the null hypothesis that the specified model exactly reproduces the population covariance matrix of observed variables (Bollen and Long 1993). Therefore, in CFA, we evaluate exact model fit by comparing the χ^2 of the specified model to the critical value for χ^2 with degrees of freedom equal to the *df* we calculated above. However, χ^2 is notoriously sensitive to sample size; therefore, almost any model with a very large sample size has a statistically significant χ^2, even if there is a trivial amount of data misfit. Furthermore, ML estimation techniques require large sample sizes. Thus, in this scenario, because we want to fail to reject the null hypothesis, having large sample sizes works against us when we are examining the fit of our model. In addition, knowing that the model-implied covariance matrix does not exactly fit the population covariance matrix does not tell us about the degree to which the model does or does not fit the data. (It also does not tell us anything about where the misfit is occurring.) Generally, our statistical models are simplifications of reality. We try to capture the essence of a very complex system without completely recreating it. Therefore, it is not surprising that the model-implied covariance matrix fails to exactly reproduce the population covariance matrix (McCoach 2003).

To quantify the degree of model data misfit, SEM researchers have developed a plethora of fit indices (i.e., CFI, TLI, RMSEA, SRMR, etc.). These fit indices attempt to correct the problems that result from judging the fit of a model solely by examining the model χ^2. Ideally, the values of most fit indices should not be influenced by sample size. Most SEM programs provide multiple fit indices in the output. Fit indices fall into three general categories: absolute fit indices, incremental fit indices, and information criteria. Absolute fit indices evaluate the degree to which the specified model reproduces the sample data. Some of the more commonly used absolute fit indices include the root-mean-square error of approximation (RMSEA) and the standardized root-mean-square residual (SRMR). The RMSEA has become one of the most popular fit indices, perhaps because confidence intervals can be computed around the point estimate of the RMSEA. RMSEA is a function of the degrees of freedom in the model, the χ^2 of the model, and the sample size. Although RMSEA is considered one of the best fit measures, it may not perform well in models with very small *df* (e.g., $df = 1$) (Kenny et al. 2011). The SRMR represents a standardized summary measure of the model-implied covariance residuals, which are the differences between the observed covariances and the model-implied covariances (Kline 2010). "As the average discrepancy between the observed and the predicted covariances increases, so does the value of the SRMR" (Kline 2010, p. 129). Both the RMSEA and the SRMR approach 0 as the fit of the model nears perfection. Hu and Bentler (1999) suggest that SRMR values of approximately 0.08 or below and values of approximately 0.06 or below for the RMSEA indicate acceptable fit of the model to the data (McCoach 2003).

Incremental fit indices measure the proportionate amount of improvement in fit when the specified model is compared with a nested baseline model, which is generally a "worst case scenario" or independence model (Hu and Bentler 1998). Some of the most commonly used incremental fit indices include the nonnormed fit index (NNFI), also known as the Tucker–Lewis Index (TLI) and the comparative fit index (CFI). These three indices approach 1.00 as the model fit improves, and the TLI can actually be greater than 1.00 when the fit of the data to the model is close to perfect. Generally speaking, TLI and CFI values at or above 0.95 indicate an acceptable level of fit (Hu and Bentler 1995, 1999). TLI and CFI values below 0.90 generally indicate that the fit of the model to the data is less than satisfactory (McCoach 2003).

Information criteria, such as the Akaike Information Criterion (AIC) and the Bayesian Information Criterion (BIC) can also be used to select among models, and are often used to compare nonnested models. These criteria are a function of the number of parameters and the negative 2 log-likelihood (−2LL), which is influenced by sample size. Unlike the fit indices described above, there is no way to interpret AIC or BIC values in isolation. They are only meaningful when they are used to compare competing models. Information criteria are gaining popularity in the SEM literature, and they do exhibit some nice features. However, Preacher and Merkle (2012) caution that AIC, BIC, and rankings based on BIC can be highly variable, even at large sample sizes.

Many factors such as sample size, model complexity, and the number of indicators, can affect fit indices differentially (Gribbons and Hocevar 1998); therefore, a researcher should examine more than one measure of fit when evaluating a SEM model. Given the vast array of fit indices, most researchers focus on and report about three. Currently, three of the most popular fit indices at seem to be the RMSEA, SRMR, and CFI. Because they are computed using very different methods, using these three indices in combination should result in a reasonably well-rounded view of model fit with relatively few indices.

The Chi-square Difference Test for Nested Models

Two models are said to be nested "if one is a proper subset of the other" (Kline 2010, p. 214). In other words, if model B is a simplification of model A in that it constrains certain parameters from model A to be 0, then those two models are nested. If model C adds free parameters to model B, then models B and C are nested. However, if a model simultaneously constrains certain parameters to be 0 and adds parameters to be freely estimated, that model will not be nested within the original model. If a path is removed or added between two variables, the two models are nested models. However, if a *variable* is added or removed, the models are not nested models. We can use the Chi-squared difference test to compare two nested models. It is inappropriate to use the χ^2 difference test to compare nonnested models (McCoach 2003). Additionally, the two nested models need to be based on the same sample and have the sample size.

To compute the χ^2 difference test, we subtract χ^2 of the less-parsimonious (more parameterized) model (${\chi^2}_2$) from the χ^2 of the more-parsimonious (less parameterized) model ($\chi^2{}_1$). The model that estimates the larger number of free parameters always has the lower χ^2. We then subtract the degrees of freedom of the less-parsimonious model (df_2) from the degrees of freedom for the more-parsimonious model (df_1). The model that estimates the larger number of free parameters will also always have the lower degrees of freedom. Then we compare this χ^2 difference ($\chi^2{}_1 - \chi^2{}_2$) to the critical value of χ^2 with $df_1 - df_2$ degrees of freedom. If this value is greater than the critical value of χ^2 with df_1–df_2 degrees of freedom, we conclude that deleting the paths and simplifying the model have significantly worsened the fit of the model. If the value of $\chi^2{}_2 - \chi^2{}_1$ is less than the critical value of χ^2 with $df_1 - df_2$ degrees of freedom, then we conclude that the model simplification has not significantly worsened the fit of the model. When the Chi-square test is nonsignificant, we choose the more-parsimonious model (the one that has more degrees of freedom) as the better model. When the χ^2 is statistically significant, then we favor the more-parameterized, more-complex model (the model with fewer df). A word of caution is in order: because χ^2 is affected by sample size, the χ^2 difference test will also be affected by sample size. Therefore, it is much easier to find a significant χ^2 difference between two nested models with a large sample than it is with a small sample. Therefore, any results should be viewed as a function of the power of the test, as well as a test of the competing models (McCoach 2003).

Respecification

What happens if the specified CFA model exhibits poor fit? When a CFA model does not fit well, you may wish to change certain aspects of the model and fit a modified or revised model. In SEM, this process is called *respecification*. In contrast to traditional statistical techniques, in CFA and SEM, it is common to specify, estimate, and evaluate several competing models before adopting a final model. Prior attempting to respecify the CFA model, you should examine the CFA output to understand your present model and to formulate ideas about possible improvements. One caveat: extensive respecifications of a CFA model render the analyses exploratory and may necessitate the collection of an additional pilot sample to provide additional evidence of the stability of the posited factor structure.

What Should Researchers Examine in the Confirmatory Factor Analysis Output?

First, examine the magnitude of the path coefficients. All of the path coefficients should be statistically significant. As in multiple regression, divide each unstandardized path coefficient by its standard error to compute a critical ratio. If this ratio is greater than or equal to $|1.96|$, the path is considered statistically significant. If the ratio of the unstandardized path coefficient to its standard error is less than $|1.96|$, the path is considered nonstatistically significant (McCoach 2003). It is rare for an item to have a nonstatistically significant path from its hypothesized factor. However, if this occurs, it means that the factor and the item are essentially unrelated. Therefore, that item should be eliminated from the survey or it belongs on a different factor. In reality, the statistical significance of the path coefficient is a very low threshold. Ideally, the standardized path coefficients should be at least 0.40 or 0.50 for all items, and path coefficients of that magnitude will be statistically significant unless the sample size is very small (too small to have any confidence in the results of the factor analysis!). Items with very low path coefficients (0.10 or 0.20) are not good indicators of that factor, and they may need to be eliminated or respecified to be indicators of another factor. If an item has a very low standardized path coefficient on all potential factors, it may ultimately need to be removed from the final version of the instrument. Be careful though—if you remove one or more items from a CFA, the models are not nested, and you cannot compare competing models using a Chi-square difference test.

Also, check the statistical significance of the error variances. This suggestion may seem odd; however, there should be at least some unique variance in each item that is *not* explained by the factor. Otherwise, the item and the factor are completely redundant, because the lack of error variance suggests that the factor completely explains the item variance. Furthermore, sometimes, CFA analyses produce Heywood cases, which are inadmissible solutions in which one of the error variances is negative and/or one of the correlations is above 1.0. (Variances can never be negative, so never trust a solution with negative variances!) When you obtain an admissible solution or notice an out-of-bounds estimate, it is critical to carefully examine the model to determine the source of the problem. Never report or interpret inadmissible solutions.

Additionally, look at the correlations among the factors on the instrument. Ideally, these correlations should be less than 0.85. Correlations that are too close to 1.0 are indicative of discriminant validity problems. If two factors are correlated above 0.85, the two factors may actually be measuring the same underlying construct. Therefore, the items may be better modeled with a single-factor solution. In general, we recommend that when two factors are correlated at/above 0.85, you should collapse the items into a single factor; then test the fit of the single-factor model against the fit of the two-factor model. Because these two models are nested, use the Chi-squared test (described below) to test the fit of the competing models.

Finally, if the model fit is less than stellar, be sure to examine the residual matrix and the standardized residual matrix. These matrices can provide insight into possible sources of model misfit. The residuals are the differences between the model-implied covariance matrix and the covariance matrix. Because covariances are unstandardized, it is virtually impossible to compare the magnitudes of unstandardized residuals. The standardized residuals provide a method of comparing the residuals across pairs of variables. Where there are large standardized residuals, the model is doing a poor job reproducing that covariance. Sometimes this occurs because the 2 items are more correlated with each other than the model allows. Sometimes the items are less correlated with each other than the model suggests. Often, the same variable is a source of misfit with several other variables. Studying the residual and standardized residual matrices often provide insights into possible reasons for poor model fit.

Modification Indices

In addition, examining modification indices (sometimes called Lagrange Multiplier tests) may also provide clues about potential sources of model misfit. Any model that has positive degrees of freedom estimates fewer parameters than there are knowns (elements of the variance/covariance matrix). Thus, models with positive *df* contain model constraints or simplifications. The modification indices indicate how much the χ^2 of the model would decrease if you added a particular parameter to the model (i.e., freed the parameter). Thus, they provide insight into which parameters could be added to improve model fit. It is tempting to use these modification indices to make changes to improve the fit of the model. Proceed very cautiously! Sometimes the modifications suggested by the SEM program are illogical and indefensible. For example, in AMOS, the modification indices for a CFA include suggestions to add paths from one item to another item and to add correlations from an error to a factor. These are things that we would *never* do in a CFA framework. We recommend going through the modification index output and crossing out the nonsensical suggestions before you begin looking at the tables. Also, the modification indices are univariate procedures. Therefore, based on the modification indices, you should only make one change at a time to your model, because each change will change the values of the modification indices for the remaining constrained parameters.

Respecification of CFA models should be guided by theory, not simply by a desire to improve measures of model fit. Models that are driven by respecifications based on modification indices are far less likely to be replicable. In addition, once you start tinkering with the model using the modification indices, you are no longer engaged in a purely "confirmatory" analysis. It is better to specify competing models a priori and to test those competing models than to tinker endlessly with your model, using the modification indices. Having said that, if you are trying to create a new instrument, the modification indices (in conjunction with the residuals, path coefficients, etc.) can provide you with insights about which items are problematic as well as why/how they are problematic. These insights may help you to realize that an item needs to be reworded, revised, or removed from the final version of a survey. Finally, remember, every time you modify a survey by removing items or revising items, you should collect a new pilot sample and

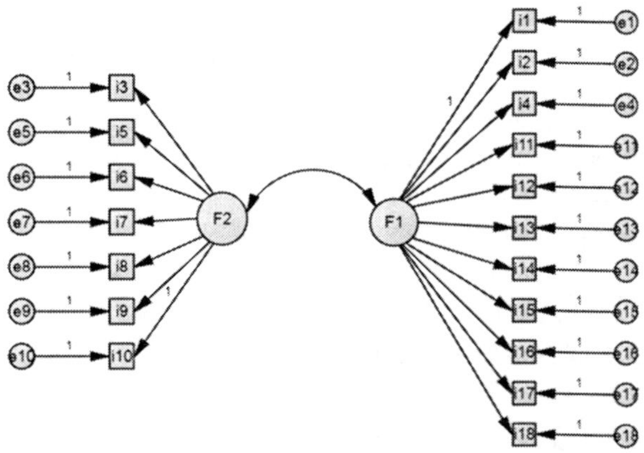

Fig. 4.5 Path diagram of the CFA model for the McAnallen anxiety in math teaching survey instrument

reanalyze the data using CFA to ensure that the model is behaving consistently with your hypothesized factor structure!

A good analyst uses modification indices very cautiously. Because CFA and SEM models are so open to modification and manipulation, they allow for a great deal of artistic license on the part of the analyst. Factor analysis is half art, half science. It is this freedom that makes CFA so powerful and so appealing, but also so prone to misuse.

Confirmatory Factor Analysis Example: McAnallen Anxiety in Math Teaching Survey[3]

To demonstrate the use of CFA, we subjected the McAnallen Anxiety in Math Teaching Survey (McAnallen 2010) to a CFA. Figure 4.5 displays the graphical input file. For pedagogical reasons, we use the same dataset to illustrate the differences in the EFA and CFA procedures. (In reality, the dataset that we are using is not the initial pilot dataset for this instrument; it is the dataset collected on the revised version of the instrument.) However, when validating a new instrument, it is imperative to collect a new dataset prior to conducting a CFA. Further, you cannot publish results that report the results of an EFA and a CFA on the same dataset. Appendix B contains the AMOS results from the CFA analyses.

The initial CFA model does not exhibit good fit. The χ^2 is 635.48 with 134 degrees of freedom. The CFI (0.91), RMSEA (0.07), and SRMR (0.05) indicate marginal fit. The standardized measurement weights are all above 0.45. In fact, all but one of the standardized measurement weights are above 0.55. The correlation between Factor I, General Math Anxiety/Comfort and Factor II, Math Teaching Anxiety/Comfort is 0.64, which is fairly high; however, it not surprising given the

[3] The full CFA output for this example is contained in Appendix B.

theoretical relationship between the two constructs. All of the error variances are statistically significant. The SMCs represent the proportion of the variance in an item that is explained by the factors. If an item is specified to be an indicator of only one factor (which is normally the case in standard CFA models), then the squared multiple correlation is simply the square of the standardized path coefficient. The standardized residual covariance matrix in AMOS is reported in a z-score like metric (this is not the case for most other SEM programs!), so values greater than |2| indicate that the model-implied variance/covariance matrix is doing a relatively poor job of reproducing that particular element of the variance/covariance matrix. In this example, there are several pairs of high standardized residual covariances: SQ15 and SQ16; SQ6 and SQ18; SQ10 and SQ2, SQ11, SQ12, SQ15, SQ16; SQ14 and SQ 7, SQ15; SQ2 and SQ3, SQ10; SQ 1 and SQ3, SQ6, SQ 7, SQ8, and SQ9; SQ3 and SQ5. This may indicate some potential problems with items 1 and 10, which exhibit several sets of large standardized residuals.

Next, examination of the modification indices (MI) reveals some very large MIs. Again, this means that if we were to freely estimate the parameter associated with the large MI, we could expect our model χ^2 to decrease by approximately that amount. In this case, the modification indices help us to understand many of the large standardized residuals. The largest modification indices for correlated errors occur between e14 and e15 (69.0), e2 and e14 (52.6), e3 and e5 (47.8), and e15 and e16 (44.7). In addition, there was a large modification index that suggested correlating the error from item 1 "I was one of the best math students when I was in school" with the math teaching comfort/anxiety factor. Although we would never correlate an error from an item with a factor, we could estimate a path from the math teaching comfort/anxiety factor to item 1. By adding a second path, we are saying that item 1 is an indicator of both general math anxiety and math teaching anxiety. Examining the content of the questions, correlating one pair of errors made conceptual sense. Item 2 "Having to work with fractions causes me discomfort" and item 14 "I become anxious when I have to compute percentages" share similar mathematical content, as well as a focus on anxiety. We suspected that the other three large modification indices were due, in part, to using a combination of positive and negative items in the instrument, as these three sets of items seemed to share the same valence, but not necessarily the same content.

For purposes of comparison, we sequentially added the four correlated errors (e14 and e15, e2 and e14, e3 and e5, and e15 and e16) and an additional path from math teaching comfort/anxiety to item 1. (We do this for pedagogical reasons and for comparative purposes, and we caution the reader NOT to blindly make model modifications that are suggested by the MI unless they also seem to be theoretically defensible). After adding these five parameters, the fit of the CFA model improved dramatically. The χ^2 was 372.92 with 129 degrees of freedom. The CFI was 0.96, the RMSEA was 0.05, and the SRMR was 0.04. The measurement weights and the factor correlations were very similar across both solutions. Interestingly, the path from the math teaching comfort/anxiety factor to item 1 was −0.32. This means that after controlling for a teacher's general math anxiety, the

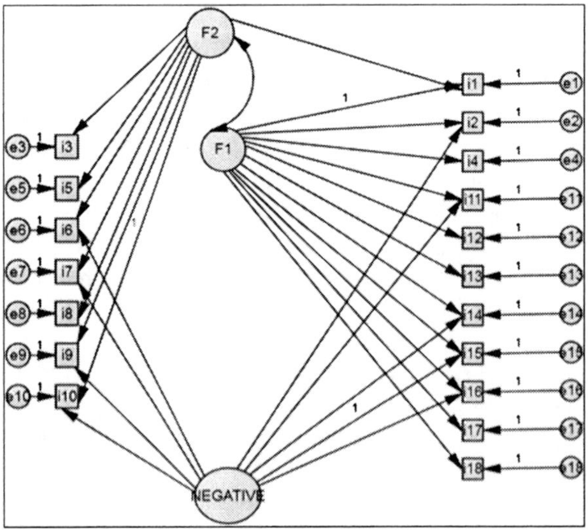

Fig. 4.6 CFA with negative method factor

partial correlation between the math teaching comfort/anxiety factor and item 1 ("I was one of the best math students when I was in school") was negative. In other words, holding constant general math comfort/anxiety level, teachers who had higher levels of math teaching comfort actually responded more negatively to that item; conversely, teachers who had lower math teaching comfort actually responded more positively to that item. This is a somewhat surprising result. Although the model fit dramatically improved with the addition of these five parameters and the standardized residual matrix looked much better, these changes were troubling from a theoretical standpoint. They made little substantive sense and were not theoretically justified.

Therefore, our next model attempted to deal directly with the issue of having both positive and negative items on the same factor. Often, when half of the items are positive and half are negative, there is a method effect (See Chapter 2 for a review of this literature). There are many ways to model this method effect; however, one of the most common ways is to create a method factor, which we called "negative," depicted in Fig. 4.6. This negative method factor contains direct paths to every negative item. Conceptually, this method factor should be uncorrelated with the two substantive factors. We fit the model with the negative method factor and the double loading on item 1, but without any of the four correlated errors estimated above. The fit of the method effect solution was comparable to the fit of the model with the four correlated errors. We could not compute a Chi-square difference test for these two models because they are not nested. However, the χ^2 for the method effect model was 354.79 with 124 degrees of freedom. The CFI was 0.96, the RMSEA was 0.05, and SRMR was 0.04. The measurement weights for the negative method factor ranged from a low of 0.04 for item 11 to a high of 0.53 for item 14. The measurement weights on the substantive factors remained high, even though the negative items also had double loadings from the negative method effect factor. Although the model with the four correlated errors and the model with the negative method factor appear to exhibit comparable fit, the model with the negative method factor is more theoretically defensible than the model with the four correlated errors.

We could, of course, continue to tinker with the CFA results to try to improve fit further; however, we caution readers not to obsess about fit indices and not to make changes that are not theoretically meaningful or justified.

Our next step is to decide what the CFA results suggest from an instrument design and development perspective. Although the CFA with the negative method factor fits well and is a reasonable model from a statistical point of view, it is problematic in terms of what it tells us about the structure of the instrument. These results suggest that there is multidimensionality present in all of the negatively worded items. The degree of that multidimensionality varies from item to item, and the standardized measurement weights for the negative method factor tell us about the degree to which that multidimensionality is present in each of the items. Given that we want each of our items to be a clean, unidimensional indicator of just one factor, the presence of the method effect is troubling. What should we do next? We need to consider eliminating or rewording item 1, which loads on both of our substantive factors, albeit in a very strange manner. We should also consider rewriting all of the items on the instrument so that they are either positive or negative, which was one of our recommendations in Chapter 2 (Direct Measures of Affective Characteristics). Of course, if we make further revisions to the instrument, we need to collect an additional pilot sample and reanalyze the data using CFA.

We hope that this short introduction to CFA has provided the reader with insight into how CFA can be used to provide information about the internal structure of the instrument.

Treating Item Responses as Ordinal: Exploratory and Confirmatory Factor Analyses

The prior example of EFA employed items that were rated on a 5-point Likert scale. Generally, with at least five scale points, analysts treat data as continuous for the purposes of their analyses and use traditional factor analytic methods (although it would certainly be more technically correct to model the data as ordinal.) However, there are research projects that make use of a 2-point response format (e.g., *yes/no*). Under such circumstances, it is inappropriate to use standard ordinary least squares or ML techniques to analyze binary response data (Wirth and Edwards 2007). In fact, we recommend using techniques that treat response data as ordinal with four or fewer scale points. With five or six scale points, it is still a good idea to treat data as ordinal, although the consequences for not doing so are likely far less severe, and may in fact be negligible, depending on the structure of the data. With seven or more scale points (and if the data are reasonably nonkurtotic and nonskewed), treating data as interval-level continuous data is usually relatively safe (DiStefano 2002; Dolan 1994; Rhemtulla et al. 2012).

The CFA model for categorical indicators differs from a standard CFA model for normally distributed indicators in two critical ways: the model that is assumed and the estimation method that is utilized. First, in categorical CFA, although the observed indicators, y_i, are dichotomous or ordinal variables with a limited number of response categories, we assume that there are i underlying latent response variables, y_i^*, which are continuous in nature. Thus, categorical CFA models a linear relationship between the underlying latent response variables, y_i^*, and the factor (Finney and DiStefano 2006; Long 1997). The scores on the observed variables, y_i, are a function of the level of the underlying latent response variable, y_i^*. For a dichotomous model, $y_i = 1$ if $y_i^* > \tau$ and $y_i = 0$ if $y_i^* \leq \tau$ (Long 1997). τ is the threshold or the cut point on the latent response variable. It can be thought of as the quantity of the latent response variable that it takes to observe a change in category on the observed ordinal (or dichotomous) variable. There are always $k - 1$ thresholds, where k = the number of response categories.

To appropriately model binary or ordered indicators, it is important that the analysis technique utilizes correlations (or covariances) among the underlying response variables, rather than correlations among the observed response variables (Finney and DiStefano 2006.) Polychoric or tetrachoric correlation matrices are more appropriate than Pearson's correlation coefficients when data are binary or ordinal. In addition, the analysis must employ an appropriate estimator. For models with dichotomous indicators, rather than utilizing standard ML estimation, Mplus uses "weighted least square parameter estimates using a diagonal weight matrix with standard errors and means and variance adjusted Chi-squared statistics that use a full weight matrix" (Muthen and Muthen 2007, p. 484) (WLSMV). This is the recommended approach for estimating models with categorical dependent variables (Finney and DiStefano 2006). Using the MPLUS software program, it is easy to estimate both EFA and CFA models, treating the response scales as ordinal. Now that it is becoming easier to estimate such models using relatively common software packages, more applied researchers are treating Likert scale data as ordinal. We see this as a very positive trend.

Conclusion

In this chapter, we have presented EFA and CFA and demonstrated their utility in determining the internal structure of affective instruments. In Chapter 5, we present additional techniques that can be used to examine the internal structure of affective instruments.

References

American Educational Research Association (AERA), American Psychological Association (APA) & National Council on Measurement in Education (NCME). (1999). *The standards for educational and psychological testing*. Washington: American Educational Research Association.

Arrindell, W. A., & Van der Ende, J. (1985). An empirical test of the utility of the observations-to-variables ratio in factor and components analysis. *Applied Psychological Measurement, 9*(2), 165–178.

Bandalos, D. L., & Finney, S. J. (2010). Factor analysis: Exploratory and confirmatory. In G. R. Hancock & R. O. Mueller (Eds.), *The reviewer's guide to quantitative methods in the social sciences* (pp. 125–155). Florence: Routledge Education.

Bollen, K. A., & Long, J. S. (1993). *Testing structural equation models*. Newbury Park: Sage.

Briggs, N. E., & MacCallum, R. C. (2003). Recovery of weak common factors by maximum likelihood and ordinary least squares estimation. *Multivariate Behavioral Research, 38*(1), 25–56.

Brown, T. A. (2006). *Confirmatory factor analysis for applied research*. New York: The Guilford Press.

Byrne, B. M. (2010). *Structural equation modeling with AMOS: Basic concepts, applications and programming* (2nd ed.). New York: Taylor and Francis Group.

Cattell, R. B. (1966). *Handbook of multivariate experimental psychology*. Chicago: Rand-McNally.

Cattell, R. B. (1978). *The scientific use of factor analysis*. New York: Plenum Press.

Coletta, A. J., & Gable, R. K. (1975). The content and construct validity of the Barth scale: Assumptions of open education 1. *Educational and Psychological Measurement, 35*(2), 415–425.

Comrey, A. L. (1988). Factor-analytic methods of scale development in personality and clinical psychology. *Journal of Consulting and Clinical Psychology, 56*(5), 754–761.

Comrey, A. L., & Lee, H. B. (1992). *A first course in factor analysis* (2nd ed.). Hillsdale: Lawrence Erlbaum Associates.

Conway, J. M., & Huffcutt, A. I. (2003). A review and evaluation of exploratory factor analysis practices in organizational research. *Organizational Research Methods, 6*(2), 147–168.

Costello, A. B., & Osborne, J. W. (2005). Best practices in exploratory factor analysis: Four recommendations for getting the most from your analysis. *Practical Assessment Research and Evaluation, 10*(7), 1–9.

Crawford, A. V., Green, S. B., Levy, R., Lo, W., Scott, L., Svetina, D., et al. (2010). Evaluation of parallel analysis methods for determining the number of factors. *Educational and Psychological Measurement, 70*(6), 885–901.

DiStefano, C. (2002). The impact of categorization with confirmatory factor analysis. *Structural Equation Modeling, 9*, 327–346.

DiStefano, Christine, Zhu, Min, & Mîndrilă, Diana (2009). Understanding and using factor scores: Considerations for the applied researcher. *Practical Assessment, Research and Evaluation, 14* (20), 1–11.

Dolan, C. V. (1994). Factor analysis of variables with 2, 3, 5, and 7 response categories: A comparison of categorical variable estimators using simulated data. *British Journal of Mathematical and Statistical Psychology, 47*, 309–326.

Everitt, B. S. (1975). Multivariate analysis: The need for data, and other problems. *British Journal of Psychiatry, 126*, 237–240.

Fabrigar, L. R., & Wegener, D. T. (2012). *Exploratory factor analysis*. New York: Oxford University Press.

Fabrigar, L. R., Wegener, D. T., MacCallum, R. C., & Strahan, E. J. (1999). Evaluating the use of exploratory factor analysis in psychological research. *Psychological Methods, 4*(1), 272–299.

Finney, S. J., & DiStefano, C. (2006). Non-normal and categorical data in structural equation modeling. In G. R. Hancock & R. O. Mueller (Eds.), *Structural equation modeling: A second course*. Greenwich: Information Age Publishing.
Ford, J., MacCallum, R., & Tate, M. (1986). The application of factor analysis in psychology: A critical review and analysis. *Personal Psychology, 39*, 291–314.
Glass, G. V., & Maguire, T. O. (1966). Abuses of factor scores. *American Educational Research Journal, 3*, 297–304.
Gorsuch, R. L. (1997). Exploratory factor analysis: Its role in item analysis. *Journal of Personality Assessment, 68*(3), 532–560.
Gribbons, B. C., & Hocevar, D. (1998). Levels of aggregation in higher level confirmatory factor analysis. *Structural Equation Modeling, 5*(4), 377–390.
Guttman, L. (1953). Image theory for the structure of quantitative variates. *Psychometrika, 18*, 277–296.
Henson, R. K., & Roberts, J. K. (2006). Use of exploratory factor analysis in published research: Common errors and some comment on improved practice. *Educational and Psychological Measurement, 66*(3), 393–416.
Hu, L. T., & Bentler, P. M. (1995). Evaluating model fit. In R. Hoyle (Ed.), *Structural equation modeling: Concepts, issues and applications* (pp. 76–99). Thousand Oaks: Sage.
Hu, L., & Bentler, P. M. (1998). Fit indices in covariance structure modeling: Sensitivity to underparameterized model misspecification. *Psychological Methods, 3*(4), 424–453.
Hu, L., & Bentler, P. M. (1999). Cutoff criteria for fit indexes in covariance structure analysis: Conventional criteria versus new alternatives. *Structural Equation Modeling, 6*(1), 1–55.
Kaiser, H. F. (1958). The varimax criterion for analytic rotation in factor analysis. *Psychometrika, 23*, 187–200.
Kaiser, H. F. (1960). Varimax solution for primary mental abilities. *Psychometrika, 25*, 153–158.
Kenny, D. A., Kaniskan, B., McCoach, D. B. (2011). *The performance of RMSEA in models with small degrees of freedom*. Unpublished paper, University of Connecticut.
Kline, R. B. (2010). *Principles and practice of structural equation modeling* (3rd ed.). New York: Guilford.
Lackey, N. R., Sullivan, J. J., & Pett, M. A. (2003). *Making sense of factor analysis: The use of factor analysis for instrument development in health care research*. Thousand Oaks: Sage.
Loehlin, J. C. (2004). *Latent variable models: An introduction to factor, path, and structural analysis* (4th ed.). Hillsdale: Erlbaum.
Long, J. S. (1997). *Regression models for categorical and limited dependent variables: Advanced quantitative techniques in the social sciences*. Thousand Oaks: Sage.
Lorenzo-Seva, U., Timmerman, M. E., & Kiers, H. L. (2011). The Hull method for selecting the number of common factors. *Multivariate Behavioral Research, 46*(2), 340–364.
MacCallum, R. C., Widaman, K. F., Zhang, S., & Hong, S. (1999). Sample size in factor analysis. *Psychological Methods, 4*(1), 84–99.
Marsh, H. W. (1987). Application of confirmatory factor analysis to the study of self-concept: First- and higher-order factor models and their invariance across groups. *Psychological Bulletin, 97*, 562–582.
McAnallen, R. R. (2010). *Examining mathematics anxiety in elementary classroom teachers*. (Doctoral Dissertation). Retrieved from DigitalCommons@UConn. (AAI3464333).
McCoach, D. B. (2003). SEM isn't just the Schoolwide Enrichment Model anymore: Structural Equation Modeling (SEM) in gifted education. *Journal for the Education of the Gifted, 27*, 36–61.
Muthen, L. K., & Muthen, B. O. (2007). *Mplus: The comprehensive modeling program for applied researchers* (5th ed.). Los Angeles: Muthen & Muthen.
Nunnally, J. C. (1978). *Psychometric theory* (2nd ed.). New York: McGraw-Hill.
Nunnally, J. C., Bernstein, I. H. (1994). *Psychometric Theory* (3rd ed.). New York: McGraw-Hill.
O'Connor, B. P. (2000). SPSS and SAS programs for determining the number of components using parallel analysis and Velicer's MAP test. *Behavior Research Methods, Instruments, and Computers, 32*(3), 396–402.

Patil, V. H., Singh, S. N., Mishra, S., Donavan, D. T. (2007). Parallel analysis engine to aid determining number of factors to retain [Software]. Retrieved from http://ires.ku.edu/~smishra/parallelengine.htm. University of Kansas.

Pett, M. A., Lackey, N. R., & Sullivan, J. J. (2003). *Making sense of factor analysis: The use of factor analysis for instrument development in health care research*. Thousand Oaks: Sage.

Preacher, K. J., & Merkle, E. C. (2012). The problem of model selection uncertainty in structural equation modeling. *Psychological Methods, 17*(1), 1–14.

Rhemtulla, M., Brosseau-Liard, P. E., & Savalei, V. (2012). When can categorical variables be treated as continuous? A comparison of robust continuous and categorical SEM estimation methods under suboptimal conditions. *Psychological Methods, 17*(3), 354–373.

Rummell, R. J. (1970). *Applied factor analysis*. Evanston: Northwestern University Press.

Slocum-Gori, S. L., & Zumbo, B. D. (2011). Assessing the unidimensionality of psychological scales: Using multiple criteria from factor analysis. *Social Indicators Research, 102*(3), 443–461.

Streiner, D. L. (1998). Factors affecting reliability of interpretations of scree plots. *Psychological Reports, 83*, 687–694.

Thompson, B. (1992). A partial test distribution for cosines among factors across samples. In B. Thompson (Ed.), *Advances in social science methodology* (Vol. 2, pp. 81–97). Greenwich: JAI.

Thompson, B. (1997). The importance of structure coefficients in structural equation modeling confirmatory factor analysis. *Educational and Psychological Measurement, 57*(1), 5–19.

Thompson, B. (2004). *Exploratory and confirmatory factor analysis: Understanding concepts and applications*. Washington: American Psychological Association.

Velicer, W. F. (1976). Determining the number of components from the matrix of partial correlations. *Psychometrika, 41*(3), 321–327.

Velicer, W. F., Eaton, C. A., & Fava, J. L. (2000). Construct explication through factor or component analysis: A review and evaluation of alternative procedures for determining the number of factors or components. In R. D. Goffin & E. Helmes (Eds.), *Problems and solutions in human assessment: Honoring Douglas Jackson at seventy* (pp. 41–71). Boston: Kluwer.

Velicer, W. F., & Fava, J. L. (1998). The effects of variable and subject sampling on factor pattern recovery. *Psychological Methods, 3*, 231–251.

Wirth, R. J., & Edwards, M. C. (2007). Item factor analysis: Current approaches and future directions. *Psychological Methods, 12*, 58–79.

Zwick, W. R., & Velicer, W. F. (1986). Factor influencing five rules for determining the number of components to retain. *Psychological Bulletin, 99*, 432–442.

Chapter 5
Additional Evidence Based on the Internal Structure of the Instrument

We continue our overview of techniques that provide validity evidence based on the internal structure of the instrument (American Educational Research Association 1999). Although the most common analytic technique for examining the internal structure of an instrument is factor analysis (FA) (both exploratory and confirmatory), the use of latent class analysis (LCA) and item response theory (IRT) or Rasch modeling can also aid in the development of affective instruments. In this chapter, we also discuss the issue of measurement invariance, both from a multiple group CFA perspective and from a Rasch modeling perspective. Our presentation introduces these techniques, provides recommendations for using the techniques to establish the internal structure of the instrument, and illustrates their use in the context of instrument development. Again, this chapter cannot possibly do justice to all of the conceptual, statistical, and analytic details of each of the techniques; however, we hope that this introduction may also serve as jumping off point for those who are interested in further exploring these topics.

Latent Class Analysis

In traditional FA, the latent variable or factor is assumed to be normally distributed and measured on a continuous scale. In other words, we assume that people can be spread along a continuum with regard to their level of the construct. Thus, people are "more" or "less" self-efficacious, motivated, or self-regulated, and they have more positive or more negative attitudes toward school. However, latent constructs do not need to be continuous in nature. Instead, the latent construct might be a dichotomy, categorization, or ordination of some sort. For example, whereas intelligence is generally assumed to be a continuous latent trait, a learning disability is usually viewed as a categorical latent variable: a person either has a disability or he/she does not.

LCA is "a qualitative analog to FA," (McCutcheon 1987) in which the latent construct is assumed to be categorical in nature. Using multivariate observed data, the procedure is used to identify unobserved *categorical* variables that account for

D. B. McCoach et al., *Instrument Development in the Affective Domain*,
DOI: 10.1007/978-1-4614-7135-6_5,

the covariance between two or more observed variables (McCutcheon 1987). These unobserved categorical variables represent a typology for the subgroups within the sample, referred to as latent classes (Hadzi-Pavlovic 2009). In a two-class LCA model, the latent trait is assumed to be dichotomous. It is also possible to estimate latent class models for traits that have more than two classes. For example, one could imagine three latent classes of drug abusers: a normative class (i.e., does not abuse drugs), a recreational class (i.e., uses drugs occasionally), and an addicted class (i.e., exhibits a dependence on drugs). These latent classes can be ordinal in nature, such as non-drug users, recreational (light) drug users, and heavy drug users. Alternatively, the classes can represent unordered categories such as popular kids, geeks, and "normal" kids. The classes are 'latent' because class membership cannot be directly observed. These latent variables are categorical because each subject is either a member or non-member of a given latent class. Within each latent class, measured variables are assumed to be statistically independent of one another. Therefore, the entire set of relationships among these measured variables can be explained by a person's class membership; they are completely explained by the classification scheme resulting from the categorical latent variable. Thus, members of the same latent class have similar response patterns on the measured variables. "The overall objective of performing a LCA on a set of variables is to arrive at an array of latent classes that represents the response patterns in the data, and to provide a sense of the prevalence of each latent class and the amount of error associated with each variable in measuring these latent classes" (Collins and Lanza 2010, p. 27).

It is also possible to specify more than one latent variable, each of which has two or more latent classes. For example, the first latent categorical variable could be gifted or not gifted, the second latent categorical variable could be learning disabled or not, and a given person would be cross-classified on both latent constructs, resulting in four possible outcomes: gifted without a learning disability, gifted with a learning disability, non-gifted without a learning disability, or not gifted with a learning disability. (Alternatively, such a model could be expressed as a single latent construct with four classes. The assumptions about the model and the constraints that are placed on the model are different across those two scenarios.)

Given that indicators (items) can be either continuous or categorical and latent constructs can be either continuous or categorical, we can classify the analytic techniques that we describe in Chapters. 4 and 5 using these distinctions. Figure 5.1 contains a decision tree for determining the appropriate analytic model given the assumptions about the nature of the latent variable (categorical or continuous) and the assumptions about the observed indicators (categorical/ordinal or interval.) (Collins and Lanza 2010).

LCA and FA share some important similarities and some striking differences. Both FA and LCA are data reduction techniques. Both latent classes and factors are unobserved constructs. However, though both techniques are focused on the data structure, FA is based on the structure of the variables, and LCA is based on the structure of the cases. Therefore, LCA is sometimes referred to as a person-centered analysis.

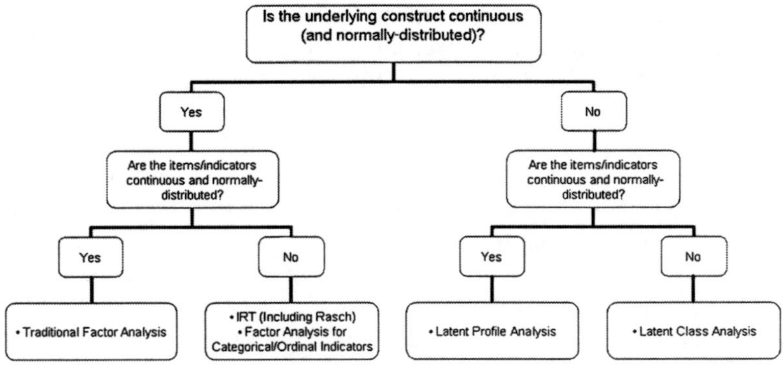

Fig. 5.1 Decision tree for selecting the most appropriate modeling method

Magidson and Vermunt (2004) outline four limitations of exploratory factor analysis (EFA) that are addressed by LCA. First, traditional factor analysis assumes all variables are *continuous* in nature. Second, FA assumes *multivariate normality* to justify the linear model underpinning the analyses. Third, FA assumes that the underlying constructs (latent variables) can be measured on an *interval* or *ratio* scale. Fourth, the results from an EFA are *not truly unique* in that different rotations provide somewhat different results (Magidson and Vermunt 2004). In addition, these traditional data reduction methods (such as cluster analysis and EFA) do not allow for the simultaneous inclusion of covariates.

LCA is analogous to cluster analysis. Like cluster analysis, LCA is used to uncover groups based on observed data, as well as to assign cases to groups. However, while traditional cluster analysis and FA techniques require variables to be linear and to have a similar variation and scale, LCA explicitly relaxes these assumptions. Instrument designers routinely deal with psychological variables that do not meet the assumptions demanded by traditional cluster analysis. LCA provides an opportunity to provide validity evidence in research designs that require categorical data analysis with discrete latent variables.

Strengths of LCA

LCA has several analytical strengths. First, LCA is both model based and probabilistic. In other words, latent class analyses utilize a statistical model which is postulated for the population from which the sample is drawn (Vermunt and Magidson 2002). Because LCA is model based, researchers can use statistical analyses to compare the fit of competing models. LCA techniques assume that the observed data "is generated by a mixture of underlying probability distributions" (Vermunt and Magidson 2002, p. 2). Thus, LCA utilizes a probabilistic approach to clustering. As a result, "although each object is assumed to belong to one class or cluster, it is taken into account that there is uncertainty about an object's class membership" (Vermunt and Magidson 2002, p. 2).

Latent class analyses produce two essential parameters: latent class probabilities and conditional probabilities. Latent class probabilities describe the distribution of classes or levels of the latent variable within which the observed measures are locally independent of one another (McCutcheon 1987). The latent class probability indicates the number and relative size of classes or types that exist in the data. The relative size of the latent class probabilities can be compared to determine if the latent classes are evenly distributed across the population or if one or more of the latent classes represents a significantly larger portion of the population. The conditional probabilities represent the chance probability that an individual in a particular class provides a particular response to an observed item (McCutcheon 1987). For example, for a dichotomous item, if the conditional probability for that item is 0.60 for latent class 1, this means that people in latent class 1 have a 60% chance of endorsing item 1.

Additionally, the output includes statistical fit indices that can be used to assess model fit and help decide on the number of classes. Moreover, this implies that the model can be replicated with an independent sample (Muthén and Muthén 2000a, b).

Assumptions of Latent Class Analysis

LCA requires several assumptions. First, we assume that we have a *correctly specified model*. In other words, the model *correctly captures the number* of latent classes. Second, we assume that each observation belongs to *only one* latent class. Finally, we assume that respondents within each of the latent classes are *homogeneous*. More formally, we make the assumption of local independence, which states that within any given class, there is no association between observations. In other words, after accounting for class membership, people's responses to items are independent of each other (Hadzi-Pavlovic 2009). Although more modern analytic methods allow researchers to model dependencies among residuals in an LCA framework, this is generally not done. Further, from an instrument design perspective, correlating residuals in a LCA is analogous to correlating residuals in a FA, and this practice would generally be frowned upon. Instead, our goal is to identify latent categorical constructs that completely explain the pattern of relationships among the items on a subscale.

Identification

In LCA, identification is somewhat complex, largely because it depends on the number of *items*, the number of *classes*, the number of *latent constructs*, and the number of *response categories* within each item. Although it is difficult to provide simple and general rules for the identification of latent class models, Vermunt and Magidson (2004) provide some concrete guidance in this area: "For an unrestricted LC analysis, one needs at least three indicators, but if these are dichotomous, no more than two latent classes can be identified" (p. 549). In the case of four dichotomous variables, "the unrestricted three-class model is not identified, even though it has a positive number of degrees of freedom. With five dichotomous indicators, however, even a five-class model is identified" (p. 549). It is fairly common for latent class models with positive degrees of freedom to be underidentified, and identification problems tend to increase as the number of latent classes and/or the number of parameters being estimated increases (Collins and Lanza 2010).

Number of Classes Versus Number of Factors

As a very loose rule of thumb, a dataset that is analyzed using both FA and LCA will often produce one more latent class than the number of factors that are extracted (Nylund et al. 2007). In addition, it is important to consider the theoretical and conceptual meaning and implications of increasing the number of latent classes within one categorical latent variable versus increasing the number of categorical latent variables.

Exploratory Versus Confirmatory Latent Class Analysis

Although LCA is generally regarded as an exploratory technique, it can be conducted in a manner that is more exploratory or one that is more confirmatory in nature. Conducting *Confirmatory LCA* (CLCA) involves the placement of constraints on model parameters to reflect the researchers' substantive hypotheses (Finch and Bronk 2011). "Unlike exploratory LCA, which does not incorporate a priori substantive hypotheses about latent groups in the population, CLCA allows the researcher to specify response patterns in the observed variables that correspond to what would be expected by underlying groups given a specific hypothesis. These specifications take the form of restrictions on the conditional probabilities for item endorsement for different latent classes" (Finch and Bronk 2011, p. 147). Our example will demonstrate the use of LCA within an exploratory framework. Interested readers should consult Finch and Bronk (2011) for an excellent tutorial on conducting latent class analyses within a confirmatory framework using M*plus*.

Evaluation of Model Fit

Model selection in LCA can be quite challenging. Generally, the most central decision is how many classes to specify (Collins and Lanza 2010). As in FA and other types of modeling techniques, we generally favor more parsimonious models, as long as they provide adequate model fit. Evaluating the fit of a latent class model is a judgment call and is "half art/half science". Model selection and model evaluation decisions should consider statistical criteria such as fit measures, the parsimony of the model, and the interpretability of the solution (Collins and Lanza 2010).

Multiple statistics are used for the evaluation of model fit in LCA. The overall fit of the model to the data is assessed using the likelihood ratio Chi-squared statistic, conventionally noted as G^2. The likelihood ratio Chi-squared statistic is similar to the Pearson χ^2 statistic in that it represents differences based on observed and expected frequencies, but the G^2 is based on the logarithm of the ratio of observed and expected frequencies. Models with values for (G^2, *df*) that exceed the critical value are considered not to fit the data; otherwise the model is considered plausible.

In addition to assessing the absolute fit of a specific model to the data, it is often necessary to compare alternate models. For most model-based estimation techniques, the first step is to calculate the Chi-square difference test. These comparisons are based on nested models, in which the second model is a restricted version of the first. Most typically, the Chi-square difference represents the difference between the G^2 and degrees of freedom for the competing models. This difference is used to evaluate whether the more complex model provides a significantly better fit to the data. If the difference in the G^2 for two models is larger than the critical value of Chi-square with degrees of freedom equal to the difference in the number of the degrees of freedom, then we determine that there is a statistically significant difference between the two models. A statistically significant difference implies that the more parameterized (less parsimonious) model fits better than the more constrained (more parsimonious) model. Non-statistical significance suggests no meaningful difference between the two models. In such cases, we always favor the more parsimonious (more constrained) model. For LCA, there are technical issues regarding the use of the Chi-square difference test, and models that differ in terms of the number of latent classes may or may not be nested, depending on the circumstances (Collins and Lanza 2010). Most importantly, the Chi-square (likelihood ratio) difference test is not appropriate for the comparison of models that differ with respect to the number of latent classes (Collins and Lanza 2010; Lin and Dayton 1997). As such, it is important to use various other measures to evaluate model fit.

Latent class analyses offer multiple measures of model fit, all of which should be evaluated in the context of substantive theory. Lo et al. (2001) proposed an approximation of the Chi-square (likelihood ratio) difference test for the comparison of latent class models based on the work of Vuong (1989). The *Vuong-Lo-Mendell-Rubin likelihood ratio test* compares the fit of neighboring class models. In essence, Vuong-Lo-Mendell-Rubin likelihood ratio test compares the fit of the specified model to the fit of a model generated by the elimination the first class in the user-specified model. A statistically significant p value indicates a statistically significant improvement in fit for the estimated model as compared to a model with one fewer class. When the Vuong-Lo-Mendell-Rubin test is not statistically significant, we favor the model with fewer classes (Muthen and Muthen 2010). Another summary of model fit is *entropy*, which represents the degree to which the classes are partitioned from one and other (Dias and Vermunt 2006). Higher entropy values represent well-partitioned classes. Latent class analyses also produce *information criterion measures*, including Akaike's Information Criterion (AIC; Akaike 1987) and Bayesian Information Criterion (BIC; Schwartz 1978), and the sample size adjusted Bayesian Information Criterion (SABIC; Sclove 1987). In general, lower values on these information criteria are indicative of better fit. One critical difference between the AIC and the BIC and SABIC is that the BIC and SABIC take sample size into account in their computations whereas the AIC does not.

Unfortunately, little consensus exists on the most appropriate statistic to determine the correct number of classes for a given set of data. Therefore, it is important to examine multiple measures of fit, and to couple that information with theoretical expectations and common sense. Moreover, it is possible for the information criteria to differ in from each other in terms of which model they favor. The differences across the measures of information criteria tend to be more pronounced when the sample size is larger. In such scenarios, the BIC tends to favor more parsimonious models and the AIC tends to favor less parsimonious models, especially with large sample sizes. Thus, the AIC tends to direct the researcher to more complex models while the BIC tends to select simpler models (Bozdogan 1987). Several suggest that the BIC tends to be superior to the other information criterion in identifying the model with the correct number of classes (Hagenaars and McCutcheon 2002; Magidson and Vermunt 2004; Nylund et al. 2007). Henson et al. (2007) used simulated data to characterize the accuracy of the various relative model fit statistics using latent variable mixture modeling across variable sample sizes and sample characteristics. Their analyses identified the sample size adjusted BIC (SABIC) as the most accurate indicator of correct classification, particularly for small sample sizes. They found the AIC was comparable to the Vuong-Lo-Mendell-Rubin likelihood ratio test: both were less accurate than the BIC. Additionally, they found entropy was highly inaccurate for small samples and unbalanced mixture proportions. Similarly, Nylund et al. (2007) suggest using a combination of the BIC and p values from the Vuong-Lo-Mendell-Rubin likelihood ratio test in initial latent class analyses.

Classification

Classification statistics help bring meaning to the latent classes. Latent class probabilities describe the distribution of classes within which the observed measures are locally independent of one other (McCutcheon 1987). The latent class probability indicates the relative size of classes that exist in the data, which in turn represent the distribution of the classes across the population. Be cautious when using very small latent classes: such classes may represent either a substantial classification of the data or a statistical artifact of the analyses not related to theory. Therefore, measures of model fit must be considered in the context of classification statistics as well as the interpretability of the final solution. After examining the relative size of the latent classes, it is important to review the latent conditional probabilities.

For each case in the analysis, there is a set of latent class probabilities defined based on the vector of responses or data for that case. These probabilities are a function of the model parameters. If, for example, three classes are defined, each case has three latent class probabilities, which represent the probability of classifying the given case in class 1, 2, or 3. All cases are assigned to the class for which it has the highest probability of membership. Latent conditional probabilities are analogous to factor loadings, and they represent the association between the observed variables and each of the latent classes (McCutcheon 1987). Careful study of the conditional probabilities helps to reveal the nature of the identified classes as well as the functioning of the instrument. Ideally, conditional probabilities should be homogeneous within classes and exhibit a high degree of separation. "When a set of item-response probabilities is characterized by good latent class separation, the pattern of item response probabilities across indicator variables clearly differentiates among the latent classes" (Collins and Lanza 2010, p. 57). Reliable classifications require very high posterior probabilities for membership in one class and very low posterior probabilities for membership in all other classes. To evaluate the overall reliability of the classification scheme, we examine the *average posterior probabilities* (Boscardin 2012). Ideally, the average posterior probabilities should be very high for the classes into which the observations are placed and the average posterior probabilities should be very low for the other classes. In addition, entropy can provide information about the reliability of classification. Entropy ranges from 0 to 1, and an entropy value of 1 signifies perfect classification (Boscardin et al. 2008; Muthén and Muthén 2000).

Latent Class Analysis Example[1]

To illustrate, consider the LCA used to examine the construct validity of the data from the *Survey of Knowledge of Internet Risk and Internet Behavior* administered to 1,366 grade 6–8 students from three middle schools (Gable et al. 2011; Kite et al. 2010a, b). This instrument contains 26 statements constructed to describe students' knowledge of Internet risks and Internet behaviors. Students are asked to

---

[1] Material from Gable et al. (2011) included with permission from Sage Publications.

"Agree" or "Disagree" with each statement. Responses were coded "1" or "0" to reflect a high level of the attribute measured by the scale.

The *Internet Knowledge Scale* was composed of seven items describing knowledge of appropriate behavior on social networks and potential risk of Internet predators (Franek 2005, 2006; McKenna 2007). Data analyses indicated that the seven knowledge items spanned a unidimensional, hierarchically ordered continuum consistent with the Rasch measurement model so that support was present for construct validity of the Knowledge Scale interpretations (Gable et al. 2011). In contrast, the remaining 19 items on the instrument were designed to identify whether or not students had experienced (e.g., Bully Victim) or exhibited specified behavioral attributes (e.g., Bully Behavior). These dimensions were categorical, where the data indicated that the students either did or did not endorse the experience or exhibit the behavior. For this illustration, we focus solely on the LCA of the Bully Behavior and Bully Victim scales.

The Bully Victim dimension consisted of three items probing students' self-report of having been bullied through electronic means. Bullying Behavior contained seven items that directly queried the students on their bullying behaviors on both *MySpace* and instant messenger sites. The study examined the relationship between cyber bullying and cyber victimization, as well as the proportions of students who would be classified as cyber bullies, cyber victims, both, or neither.

In the hypothesized model, students could fall into one of four categories: victims, bullies, both victims and bullies, or neither victims nor bullies. There are two ways to approach such a LCA. The first option is to model one latent variable with four classes. The second option is to model two categorical latent variables, each with two categories. This model hypothesized two categorical latent variables: bully and victim, each of which contained two classes: behavior present or behavior absent. The two categorical latent variable by two latent class model for the Bully Behavior and Bully Victim scales produced a posterior probability for the most likely class membership for each of the latent class analyses for each person within each class. Ideally, the probability of membership for the most likely class should be much higher than the probability of class membership for the next most likely class, which would be considered support for the internal structure of the instrument.

The LCA procedure provided empirical support for the 2 categorical latent variable by 2 latent class model for the Bully Behavior and Bully Victim dimensions. This model contained two latent variables, each with two classes. The first latent variable was the Bully Behavior variable, and the two latent classes modeled were "bully" and "non-bully." The second latent variable was the Bully Victim variable, and it also contained two latent classes: "victim" and "non-victim." Each student in the sample was then categorized into one of the two latent classes for each of these two latent variables in a 2×2 cell matrix, based on their probability of membership in each of the classes. Thus, a student was either a bully or a non-bully and a victim or a non-victim. Because the two classes of these two latent variables were crossed, a student was categorized into one of the four cells: "pure" bully but not victim (i.e., latent class pattern 1, 1), "pure" victim but not

Table 5.1 Classification of students as bullies, victims, both, or neither based on their most likely latent class pattern

Latent class pattern	Classification	Class count	Proportion
1, 1	"Pure" bully	82	0.06
1, 2	"Mixed"—both bully and victim	223	0.15
2, 1	Normative: neither bully nor victim	1,012	0.74
2, 2	"Pure" victim	69	0.05

Table 5.2 Average latent class probabilities for most likely latent class pattern by latent class membership

Latent class pattern	Latent class membership			
	Bully	Mixed	Normative	Victim
Probability of being classified as a:				
Bully	*0.804*	0.082	0.113	0.001
"Mixed"—both bully and victim	0.074	*0.862*	0.024	0.040
Normative: neither bully nor victim	0.019	0.008	*0.948*	0.025
Victim	0.000	0.129	0.048	*0.822*

bully, both bully and victim (mixed), or neither bully nor victim (normative class). Table 5.1 contains the class counts and the percent of students who fall into each of the 4 latent class pattern classifications. Approximately 74% of the sample was neither bullies nor victims, 5% of the sample was pure victims, 6% of the sample was pure bullies, and 15% of the sample were both bullies and victims.

Entropy is a measure of the certainty or accuracy of classification. As we noted earlier, the entropy of a model can range from 0 to 1. Values near "1" indicate a high degree of certainty of classification, whereas values near 0 indicate a great degree of uncertainty of classification. The entropy value for the 2 $\times$ 2 model was 0.84, which indicated an adequate classification rate.

The likelihood ratio Chi-square test was not statistically significant ($\chi^2(990) = 843.01$), which indicated non-rejection of the null hypothesis that the model fit the data. In other words, there was not statistically significant model-data misfit, indicating that the 2 $\times$ 2 model fit the data reasonably well. Table 5.2 contains the average latent class probabilities for the most likely latent class combination. Overall, the predicted probabilities (diagonal values) were quite high for the most likely class combination, and quite low for the other class combinations. The normative class was the easiest class to classify: the average latent class probability for the normative class was 0.95.

Further analyses examined if students classified into the four respective groups endorsed the items as predicted. Table 5.3 contains the model results for the 2 $\times$ 2 LCA of the Bully Victim and Bully Behavior items. The table contains threshold values and probabilities of endorsement for each of the items on the Bully Victim and Bully Behavior dimensions for each of the four groups (bully, victim, mixed, and neither). The threshold values are similar to a mean or intercept for each group,

Table 5.3 Model results for the latent class analysis of the Bully Victim and Bully Behavior items

Items[a]	Threshold value	Standard error	Probability of endorsement	Standard error
Latent class pattern 1, 1: bully group				
V1b	3.71	0.28	0.03	0.01
V18b	3.62	0.30	0.03	0.01
V35b	2.51	0.15	0.08	0.01
V5b	0.18	0.14	0.46	0.04
V11b	−0.17	0.18	0.52	0.05
V17b	1.45	0.17	0.19	0.03
V23b	−0.13	0.21	0.53	0.05
V27b	0.32	0.18	0.42	0.04
V30b	0.19	0.14	0.45	0.03
V38b	−0.14	0.14	0.53	0.04
Latent class pattern 1, 2: mixed				
V1b	−0.22	0.17	0.56	0.04
V18b	−0.87	0.21	0.71	0.04
V35b	−0.67	0.17	0.66	0.04
V5b	0.18	0.14	0.46	0.04
V11b	−0.07	0.18	0.52	0.05
V17b	1.45	0.17	0.19	0.03
V23b	−0.13	0.21	0.53	0.05
V27b	0.32	0.18	0.42	0.04
V30b	0.19	0.14	0.45	0.03
V38b	−0.14	0.14	0.53	0.04
Latent class pattern 2, 1: normative				
V1b	3.71	0.28	0.03	0.01
V18b	3.62	0.30	0.03	0.01
V35b	2.51	0.15	0.08	0.01
V5b	3.49	0.32	0.03	0.01
V11b	3.76	0.27	0.02	0.01
V17b	4.71	0.44	0.01	0.00
V23b	4.88	0.54	0.01	0.00
V27b	3.99	0.30	0.02	0.01
V30b	2.64	0.17	0.07	0.01
V38b	2.57	0.18	0.07	0.01
Latent class pattern 2, 2: victim				
V1b	−0.22	0.17	0.56	0.04
V18b	−0.87	0.21	0.71	0.04
V35b	−0.67	0.17	0.66	0.04
V5b	3.49	0.32	0.03	0.01
V11b	3.76	0.27	0.02	0.01
V17b	4.71	0.44	0.01	0.00
V23b	4.88	0.54	0.01	0.00
V27b	3.99	0.30	0.02	0.01
V30b	2.64	0.17	0.07	0.01
V38b	2.57	0.18	0.07	0.01

[a] Bully Victim items: V1b, V18b and V35b; Bully Behavior items: V5b–V38b

reported in logit units. Thus, a high threshold value indicates that a given item was rarely endorsed (or difficult to agree with) for members of that group. In contrast, a large negative threshold value indicates that a given item was frequently endorsed (or very easy to agree with) for members of that group. Table 5.3 also reports the probability of endorsement, which is a transformation of the threshold in a logit metric to a simple probability scale. The probability of endorsement indicates model predicted probability of endorsing an item, conditional on group membership for each of the four groups. For example, students in the bully and normative groups had a threshold value of 3.71 on item v1b (I have been bullied by another student while online), corresponding to a probability of 0.03 of endorsing that item. In contrast, victims and mixed profile students (who are both bullies and victims) have a threshold value of −0.22, which indicates an expected probability of endorsement of 0.56. In other words, non-victims have only a 3% chance of agreeing with that item, while victims have a 56% chance of agreeing with that item.

Examination of Table 5.3 reveals that the Bully Behavior questions were far more likely to be endorsed by bullies and mixed (bully/victim) students, whereas the Bully Victim questions were far more likely to be endorsed by the victim and mixed (bully/victim) students. The normative group had high thresholds and low probability values for all items, indicating that the students in the normative group were highly unlikely to endorse any of the 10 items. These findings are consistent with theoretical expectations and thus provide evidence supportive of the hypothesized structure for the Bully Victim and Bully Behavior dimensions.

Thus, students fell into one of four mutually exclusive groups: those who were solely bullies ($n = 82$, 6% of the sample), those who were solely victims ($n = 69$, 5% of the sample), those who were both cyber bullies and cyber victims ($n = 203$, 15% of the sample), and those who were neither bullies nor victims ($n = 1{,}012$, 74% of the sample). Table 5.4 contains the mean scores for each of the four groups on each of the dimensions. Because the items were dichotomous, a student-level mean of "0" occurs when a student did not endorse any of the items in that dimension, whereas a mean of "1" indicates that the student endorsed all of the items for that dimension. Thus, the group-level mean scores in Table 5.4 represent the proportion of the items on the scale endorsed by the students in each of the four groups.

As would be expected, the normative group (those who were neither victims nor bullies, $n = 1{,}012$) had very low mean scores for both the Bully Victim ($M = 0.05$, $SD = 0.11$) and the Bully Behavior dimensions ($M = 0.03$, $SD = 0.07$). Those in the bully group ($n = 82$) had high means on the Bully Behavior dimension ($M = 0.42$, $SD = 0.13$) and low means on the Victim dimension ($M = 0.00$, $SD = 0.00$). Those in the victim group ($n = 69$) had high means on the Victim dimension ($M = 0.80$, SD $= 0.16$) and low means on the Bully Behavior dimension ($M = 0.05$, $SD = 0.07$). Finally, those in the combined bully/victim group ($n = 203$) had elevated scores on both the Bully Behavior dimension ($M = 0.48$, $SD = 0.23$) and the Bully Victim dimension ($M = 0.64$, $SD = 0.27$).

Follow-up analyses examined whether there were differences among the classes of students on external variables, which would provide additional evidence about construct interpretations (Chapter 6 provides additional information about using

Table 5.4 Scale means categorized by Bully/Victim status: proportion of items endorsed by category

Dimension	Category							
	Bully only		Both victim and bully		Neither victim nor bully		Victim	
	6%, $n = 82$		15%, $n = 203$		74%, $n = 1{,}012$		5%, $n = 69$	
	Mean	SD	Mean	SD	Mean	SD	Mean	SD
Bully Victim score (1 = endorses all)	0.00	0.00	0.64	0.27	0.05	0.11	0.80	0.16
Bully behavior score (1 = endorses all)	0.42	0.13	0.48	0.23	0.03	0.07	0.05	0.07
Parent involvement (1 = highest involvement)	0.12	0.24	0.23	0.32	0.28	0.35	0.30	0.36
Internet behavior (1 = highest usage)	0.73	0.36	0.78	0.32	0.43	0.41	0.70	0.36
Adult notification (1 = highest notification)	0.29	0.34	0.34	0.37	0.59	0.40	0.62	0.39
Knowledge (1 = highest knowledge)	0.43	0.23	0.50	0.25	0.47	0.28	0.51	0.25

relations to external variables to provide evidence about the supporting the interpretation of the constructs). Bullies and bully/victims were less likely to report that they would notify adults about Internet bullying ($p < 0.001$), and the Cohen's d effect size for the difference between the respective means (0.66) indicated a moderately large effect. In addition, bullies and bully/victims reported less Parental Involvement than the other two groups ($p < 0.001$) although the Cohen's d for this effect (0.25) was more modest. The students who were either victims, bullies, or both reported using the Internet more frequently than those who were neither bullies nor victims, and size of this effect was also large ($d = 0.84$). Finally, a series of Chi-square contingency table analyses run using the demographic variables revealed that the two bully groups were more likely to report getting in trouble in school (69 vs. 31%; χ^2 (1) = 67.0; $p < 0.001$; phi = −0.22; Cramer's $V = 0.22$) and less likely to report getting good grades (73.7 vs. 86.4%; χ^2 (1) = 26.2; $p < 0.001$; phi = −0.14; Cramer's $V = 0.14$) than the two non-bully groups (Table 5.5).

In summary, this section has illustrated how the LCA procedure utilized categorical data to examine support for the construct validity of score interpretations. Successful classification of students into predicted groups, especially for the Bully Behavior and Bully Victim dimensions, provided support for meaningful score interpretations (i.e., construct validity).

Table 5.5 Scale means categorized by adult notification and parental involvement status: proportion of items endorsed by category

Dimension	Parent notification/involvement category							
	Would tell/ parents check		Would tell/ parents don't check		Wouldn't tell/ parents check		Wouldn't tell/ parents don't check	
	37%, $n = 500$		20%, $n = 274$		2%, $n = 22$		42%, $n = 568$	
	Mean	SD	Mean	SD	Mean	SD	Mean	SD
Bully victim score (1 = endorses all)	0.14	0.28	0.15	0.28	0.29	0.35	0.19	0.31
Bully behavior score (1 = endorses all)	0.07	0.17	0.09	0.16	0.26	0.26	0.18	0.24
Parent involvement (1 = highest involvement)	0.63	0.27	0.00	0.00	0.70	0.10	0.06	0.13
Internet behavior (1 = highest usage)	0.39	0.40	0.51	0.40	0.69	0.39	0.61	0.41
Adult notification (1 = highest notification)	0.86	0.20	0.83	0.17	0.00	0.00	0.12	0.16
Knowledge (1 = 100% correct)	0.54	0.28	0.50	0.28	0.49	0.30	0.40	0.25

Item Response Theory and Rasch Models

Rasch and IRT techniques have been used extensively to develop most state-wide cognitive achievement tests (see, for example, Wright and Stone 1979), and less commonly, affective instruments (Wright and Masters 1982). Although IRT and Rasch models appear to be quite distinct from factor analytic models, in reality, the linkages between FA with dichotomous or ordinal items and the two parameter IRT model have been well-established. However, the focus of attention and the measurement and analytic traditions of FA and IRT are quite different. Because of these differences in emphasis and technique, lessons in the IRT and Rasch traditions may prove quite useful to affective instrument developers as they construct and validate their scales. What are the advantages of using Rasch Modeling and IRT approaches in affective instrument design? First, Rasch/IRT models estimate item difficulties and person abilities and locate them on the same scale of measurement. In addition, there is a rich tradition of examining person and item misfit in IRT, and techniques have developed to assess person and item misfit. Further, some IRT models cannot be easily re-parameterized as factor analytic models. Finally, a tremendous amount of psychometric and measurement work has been done within the framework of Rasch modeling and IRT. For these reasons, using Rasch and IRT techniques can be beneficial for obtaining empirical support for valid interpretations of instrument scores (Beck and Gable 2001).

The choice of an item factor analysis (IFA) model and estimation method often depend on whether the research focuses more on the item level or the scale level and whether the it focuses more on individual or group characteristics (Wirth and Edwards 2007). For instance, IRT-based IFA lends itself to examining individual item characteristics or obtaining scores for individual participants. "The IRT literature offers numerous models with parameters that apply directly to the items and are intended to explain the interaction between people and items. The history of IRT has largely been focused on these item-level properties and has seen extensive research on scale development, scoring, and other aspects of assessment" (Wirth and Edwards 2007, p. 70). In contrast, SEM-based IFA provides a powerful and flexible method for examining the structural makeup of a scale (e.g., number of factors, cross-loadings, correlated errors, higher order factors). "The SEM literature offers the CCFA [categorical CFA] model with parameters that are intended to explain the relationship between constructs (or factors) and latent response distributions. The history of SEM has largely been focused on the latent factors and has seen extensive research on multiple factor analysis, higher order FA, and measurement models within larger structural models such as latent growth models" (Wirth and Edwards 2007, p. 70).

We begin with a brief explanation of IRT, then we provide a brief explanation of Rasch modeling as a special case of IRT with especially appealing measurement characteristics, and we explain the utility of the Rasch model within the instrument design process. We end with a short illustration of a Rasch analysis of an affective instrument.

Item Response Theory and the Rasch Model

IRT comprises a family of mathematical models which are useful in the design and analysis of a variety of psychological and educational measuring instruments (Weiss and Yoes 1991). Like classical test theory (CTT), IRT provides a method to estimate both *difficulty* parameters for each item and *ability estimates* for each examinee. However, IRT offers several important advantages over CTT. CTT represents item parameters as means and person parameters as true scores. However, in CTT, these item and person parameters are sample dependent. Unlike CTT, IRT allows for the separation of the *person* and *item* parameters. In IRT, the ability estimate of an examinee is not dependent on the sample of items, and the difficulty estimate of an item is not dependent upon the ability levels of the sample of examinees (Hambleton et al. 1991, p. 19).

When the IRT model fits the data, the same *item characteristic curve* (ICC) is obtained for the test item regardless of the distribution of ability in the group of examinees used to estimate the item parameters. Hence the ICC is invariant across the two populations. The *invariance property* of the item difficulty and person ability parameters is one of the most attractive features of IRT.

In the simplest IRT model, the ICC represents the relationship between the probability of success (i.e., correct response) on an item and the ability measured by the item (Hambleton et al. 1991). In Fig. 5.2, the horizontal axis represents the ability level (usually called *theta* in IRT) of the examinee, the vertical axis represents an examinee's probability of responding positively to the question. The more difficult question, or a question with a higher *b* value, is located further to the right on the diagram. In Fig. 5.2, an examinee of a given ability level is more likely to give a correct response to question 1 than to question 2. The one parameter IRT model contains separate estimates of the difficulty parameters, called *b*, for each of the questions. Implicit in this model is the restrictive assumption that all items are equally discriminating (Hambleton et al. 1991).

In a two-parameter IRT model, both item discrimination, designated as *a*, and item difficulty or *b* may vary for each question on the test. An ICC with a steeper slope represents a more discriminating item. In Fig. 5.3, curve 1 represents an easier, but more discriminating item than curve 2. Note that the ICC for these two items are disordinal: they cross. Therefore, even though item 1 is easier to agree with in general, respondents with lower ability levels are more likely to endorse item 2 because it does not discriminate as well as item 1.

Item response models contain several very attractive features. First, in CTT, item difficulty estimates are sample dependent and person ability estimates are item dependent. Therefore, one cannot separate the ability and the item parameters. The property of invariance of item and ability parameters in IRT represents an improvement over CTT. The property of invariance "implies that the parameters that characterize an item do not depend on the ability distribution of the examinees and the parameter that characterizes an examinee does not depend on the set of test items (Hambleton et al. 1991, p. 18). Therefore, knowing the ability level of an examinee allows us to determine the probability that the examinee will successfully answer any of the calibrated questions, whether or not the questions were administered to the examinee (Embretson 1999). This property is essential to many IRT applications such as equating, adaptive testing, and examining differential item functioning (DIF). By extension, it is possible to obtain unbiased estimates of item properties from unrepresentative samples. In contrast to CTT, "IRT item parameters are not biased by the population ability distribution" (Embretson 1999, p. 2).

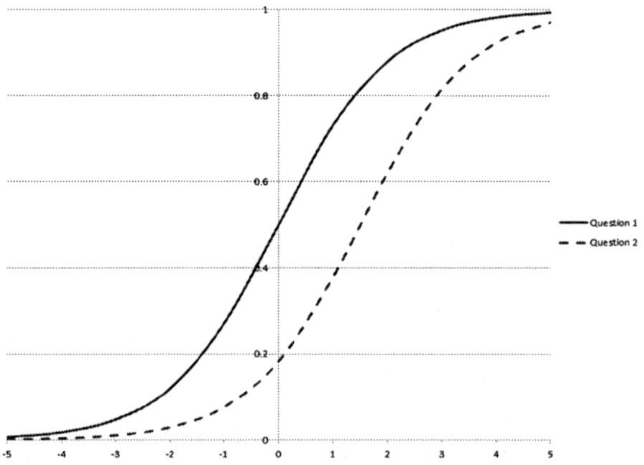

Fig. 5.2 One-parameter item characteristic curves for dichotomous items

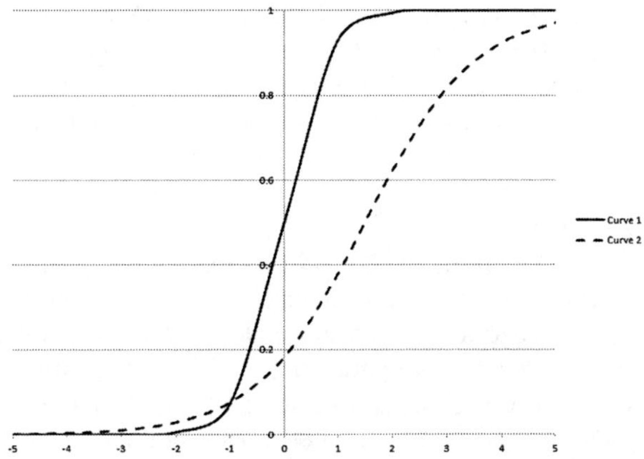

Fig. 5.3 Two-parameter item characteristic curves for dichotomous items

When IRT models are implemented, "(a) person trait level estimates are controlled for the properties of items that are administered, and (b) item difficulty estimates are controlled for the trait levels of the particular persons in the calibration sample. In this sense, item-free person estimates and population-free item estimates are obtained" (Embretson 1999, p. 8).

Another advantage of IRT is that test makers can assess the precision or reliability of each item in isolation. In IRT, analysis occurs at the item level. In CTT, the contribution of an item to the overall reliability of the test depends in large part on the covariance between the item and other items on the test. Therefore, in CTT isolating the contribution of a single item to the overall reliability and the standard error of measurement (SEM) of the test is impossible. By contrast, in IRT, the selection of items is based on the total amount of information that each item contributes to the test (Hambleton et al. 1991). Therefore, test makers can choose items "to produce a test that has the desired precision of measurement at any ability level, for example, at a cut-off score" (Hambleton et al. 1991, p. 100).

IRT techniques allow test developers to explore whether an item functions the same way in different groups. DIF occurs when examinees of the same ability level who belong to different reference groups exhibit different probabilities of success on an item (Hattie et al. 1999). Examining the DIF allows test developers to identify questions that may be biased against particular subgroups of examinees. In addition, IRT provides a statistic indicating the precision of a person's ability estimate. This statistic is similar to the SEM in CTT; however, in IRT this estimate can vary for each examinee. Measures of ability are generally more precise when the examinee's score in the average range of ability on the test, and less precise at either extreme of ability.

The IRT model explicitly handles the dichotomous nature of certain response data, the difficulty of items, and the effects of guessing, all of which are ignored in CTT. Furthermore, IRT allows test constructors to create shorter, adaptive tests that can be as reliable as longer tests created using CTT techniques (Embretson 1999). Also, IRT allows for comparison of test scores across multiple forms when test difficulty levels vary across persons (Embretson 1999). In addition, IRT allows researchers to examine person fit statistics in a more sophisticated fashion than is possible in CTT. The analysis of person fit statistics allows test developers to categorize the kinds of errors that test takers make. Finally, IRT handles missing data quite easily. Using IRT, tests can measure and compare the ability levels of a diverse pool of test takers without administering the same questions to each examinee.

The emphasis in IRT is in estimating the "difficulty" of each item statement as well as each person's "ability" level, which in attitude measures, assesses their proclivity to agree with or "endorse" the item statements on the scale. In fact, in Rasch models (one-parameter IRT models), difficulty is the only parameter estimated; Rasch models assume that all items are equally discriminating. Of course, factor analyses of the items can provide insight into the tenability of that assumption. If items are equally discriminating, they should have very similar factor loadings.

How to Choose Between Rasch and IRT Models

A Rasch model is for all practical purposes virtually identical to a one-parameter IRT model (Rasch 1966). When items are equally discriminating, and items have parallel ICC, then the measurement properties of a scale that fits the Rasch model have some attractive features. "The advantage of the Rasch measurement model is that the ICC is defined by the logistic distribution, and this distribution has the same form for all items; only the location (difficulty) on the item calibration scale—and of course the observed probabilities—change item by item. Thus, the decision, when the data fit the model, is based on the same theoretical frame for all items. The fitting values for items are calculated person by person and item by item, and unexpected answers increase misfit. This is a very accurate and objective way to calculate problems for a single item" (Tormakangas 2011, p. 319). If data fit a Rasch model, then items can be located on an item map (i.e., a Wright map), and the meaning of this location or distance "is the same no matter where you are on the map" (Wilson 2005, p. 118). To use an interpretation tool like the Wright map, the set of items need to conform to a Rasch model. If the order of item difficulty depends on the location of the scale (which is the case for 2 parameter IRT models), then the Wright map no longer holds (Wilson 2005, p. 120). "The order (on the map) of the item responses must remain the same for all respondents, and the order of respondents (on the map) must remain the same for all item responses" (Wilson 2005, p. 118).

Although Rasch models are most commonly applied to dichotomous items, there are extensions to the Rasch model that are applicable to other response formats. The Rasch model can be used for Likert-type, successive-integer response formats to quantify both the affective nature of a *statement*, and the attitude of the *person* responding. This technique has direct consequences for both *statements* and *persons,* given that parameter estimates are estimated for both statements and people. Wright and Masters' book *Rating Scale Analysis* (1982) presents the rating-scale model described by Andrich (1978a, b, c) and Masters (1980) in the context of scaling (i.e., calibrating) items and measuring people's affective characteristics with items employing Likert-response formats. Johnson et al. (1991), and Masters and Hyde (1984) illustrate the use of the Rasch latent trait model for Likert scaling.

Rasch Models

Rasch models are well suited to examine the following issues:

1. *Item calibration*: Where is each statement (item) is located on the affective continuum?
2. *Measuring people*: Where is each person located on the affective continuum?
3. *Item Fit.* How well do the statements (items) fit the model?
4. *Person Fit.* How well do the people fit the model?

Calibrating Items for Measuring People

The typical 5-point agree Likert response format consists of ordered response alternatives such as:

Strongly Disagree	DisAgree	Neutral	Agree	Strongly Agree
1	2	3	4	5

According to Wright and Masters (1982, p. 48), "completing the kth step" represents the selection of the kth step over the $(K - 1)$th step on the response continuum. (Note that a 5-point response format has four steps or thresholds, such as $1 - 2 = 1$ step, $2 - 3 = 1$ step, etc.). Given this format, a person selecting the "agree" option has chosen "disagree" over "strongly disagree" and "neutral" over "disagree," but has not chosen "strongly agree" over "agree." These ordered steps in the response format represent the relative difficulties in responding to the item and are assumed to be constant across all of the items.

Given this assumption, the person and item parameters are estimated simultaneously. To be more specific, the procedure estimates a position for each person on the affective-variable continuum being measured (i.e., person parameter), a scale value for each item (i.e., item parameter), and m (e.g., 4) response thresholds for the $m + 1$ (e.g., 4 for a 5-point Likert agreement scale) response categories employed. Figure 5.4 contains these values for the ICC, which are called *ogives,* for a hypothetical attitude item. For ease of illustration, only the "strongly disagree" and "disagree" curves are included for the 5-point scale. (Remember that for the Rasch Dichotomous Model employed in achievement tests only one such curve exists per item.) The curve illustrates the estimated probability of person *n* responding "strongly disagree" (i.e., 1) rather than "disagree" (i.e., 2) on this item as a function of the person's affective characteristic parameter *A*, and an item scale value parameter *SV*, which dictates the transition from responding "strongly disagree" to responding "disagree" on the item (see Wright and Masters 1982, pp. 55, 128, 130). The values marked off on the horizontal axis represent units called *logits* from the logistic scale, varying from −3 to +3 (Ludlow and Haley 1995). (The logistic scale can be converted to the normal curve using a conversion factor.) High logit values are associated with items with which it is easy to agree (i.e., low difficulty and a high attitude score); low logit values are associated with items with which it is easy to disagree (i.e., high difficulty and low attitude score). Once the ICC for an item have been centered on their scale value, it is possible to estimate the probability of any person selecting any one of the response alternatives. To do this, we locate the person's attitude estimate in logits on the horizontal axis and project a vertical line to the height of one of the curves, then read off the probability value from the vertical axis. For example, in Fig. 5.4, a person with an attitude estimate of −1 logits has a 0.35 probability of disagreeing and a 0.65 probability of strongly disagreeing with this item. Further, the average scale value in logits for a set of items will always equal zero. After calculating the standard deviations (*S*) of the scale values in logits, we can determine the probabilities of selecting each response option for people with attitude raw score levels of $X + S$, $X + 2S$, $X - S$, and $X - 2S$.

The rating-scale model attempts to locate the items on the affective continuum and estimates scale values on the basis of peoples' responses to the items. We can also test whether each item fits the rating-scale model, which reflects the extent to which the responses support the existence of continuum underlying the affective characteristic. Generally, instrument developers discard items not fitting the model from the item set. Thus, the item fit statistic is extremely important in instrument development as an item-analysis procedure.

The item-fit statistic can also be used to generate empirical evidence for the question of including the "neutral" response option on a Likert scale. Masters and Hyde (1984) examined the response options for a set of attitudes toward school

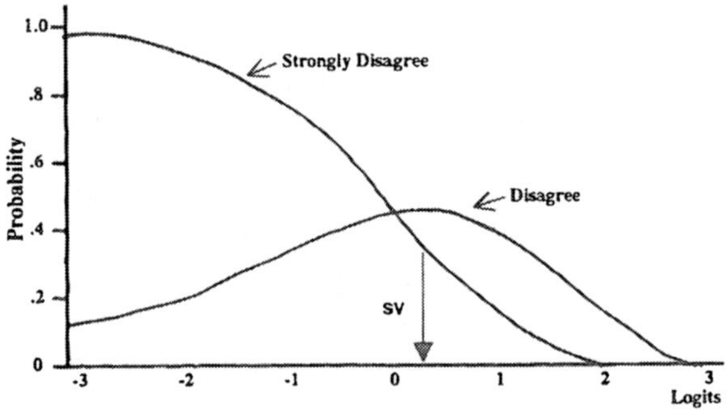

Fig. 5.4 Item characteristic curves for two response choices of an affective likert-scale item

items. For an item that showed poor fit to the Rasch model, Masters and Hyde (1984) created four attitude groups representing low to high attitudes and calculated the proportions of students in each group responding "disagree," "undecided," and "agree" to the item. They then plotted the proportions along with the Rasch model probability of selecting each option to study the nature of an item's misfit with the model. For one of the misfitting items, more students than expected (based on the model) selected the "neutral" option. Thus, the misfit of this item could be attributed to a use of the "neutral" response, suggesting that it is not another point on an ordered continuum.

These analyses also provide information regarding the extent to which people fit the hypothesized model. People whose responses are inconsistent with the statement difficulty ordering can be easily identified for follow-up study of their response frequencies, as well as other cognitive and affective characteristics. Wright and Masters (1982) also illustrate how the analysis of *person fit* can be used to examine the *response styles*, or sets, which result when not all people use the response options in the same way. That is, some people may tend to select extreme responses, "agree" responses, or the "true" option for various rating scales. Wright and Masters (1982, Chapter 6) provide an interesting illustration of how the rating-scale model analysis of "person fit" can be used to ascertain if the positive and negative items really measure the same affective characteristics. Ten positive and 10 negative "attitude toward drugs" items were compared for 75 students. The person-fit analysis indicated that the positive and negative item stems did not provide consistent information regarding a person's attitude. Therefore, it would be inadvisable to create a 20-item scale by simply reverse scoring 10 of the items. Because the goal was to locate each person on the affective continuum, differences in response styles would present a problem for the combined 20 items.

Example of a Rasch Analysis Employed in Instrument Design

This section illustrates how the FA and Rasch procedures can complement each other and contribute valuable information to the instrument development process. Gable et al. (1990) compared the utility of the information yielded by the classical FA and Rasch models to examine the psychometric qualities of the *School Situation Survey* (*SSS*) (Helms and Gable 1989), a 34-item attitude instrument that assesses seven variables—four Sources and three Manifestations of school-related stress for grades 3–12 students. The classical techniques employed to develop the *SSS* included (a) the specification and review of items for defining the targeted variables, as well as support for validity evidence based on instrument content, (b) Likert's summated rating technique, utilizing the "criterion of internal consistency," (c) correlational (e.g., path analysis) and FA results that supported the existence of empirically derived clusters of items that were conceptually meaningful and corresponded to the content domains targeted by the developers, and (d) in light of Nunnally's domain sampling model, a review of the reliability indices that lent further support to the adequacy of item sampling. However, these classical procedures did not clearly isolate a problem with the validity of the construct interpretation for one targeted variable.

Gable et al. (1990) analyzed data from 1,958 grade 6–8 students under the assumption that the data fit a Rasch rating scale model (Andrich 1978a; Wright and Masters 1982). These Rasch analyses demonstrated:

1. a lack of adequate variable (i.e., construct) definition, and
2. the use of item-and person-fit statistics to reveal item content ambiguity.

Inadequate Definition of a Variable

Analyses of the data indicated that most of the *SSS* items fit a Rasch rating scale model. Student responses spanned the Likert response continuum. Further, the "ability" estimates were spread across much of the continua for each of the targeted scales. It was thus possible to describe high- and low-scoring students on each of the scales. However, the Rasch latent trait technique did uncover a problem with one of the *SSS* Source of Stress scales: Academic Stress. Figure 5.5 presents the variable map for students completing the three items: 21, *I worry about not doing well in school*; 28, *I am afraid of getting poor grades*; and 34, *I worry about taking tests.* The **x** under the People column indicates the positions of the 1,829 students and three items on the Academic-Stress scale. Of particular importance are the positions of the three items on the continuum that facilitate the definition of the variable. The three item difficulty estimates (i.e., positioned at the "always" response to the items) were clustered near the center of the continuum, with item calibration values between 0.06 and −0.05 logits.

Although the response-frequency data indicated that the ratings were distributed across most of the score range, the item difficulties suggested that there was a "weakness in variable definition." The lack of differentiation (i.e., lack of spread across the variable map) among items is a construct validity issue, as it results in little meaningful information about the Academic-Stress construct. The items do not adequately span the difficulty continuum for the construct, which hinders the scale's ability to differentiate between high and low scoring students. Thus, the Rasch latent trait model identified the restricted nature of the item definition of the targeted variable. Clearly, the Academic Stress subscale requires a few new items that assess different locations on the underlying continuum to be developed (In general, it is difficult to adequately assess affective constructs with only 3 items).

In contrast, the item difficulties of the six items ($N = 1{,}958$) on the Behavioral Manifestation of Stress scale in Fig. 5.6 indicate a higher degree of differentiation of the construct for the following items: (a) 29, *I try to get attention by action silly in class*; (b) 27, *I talk back to my teacher*; (c) 4, *I get into fights*; (d) 25, *I yell at my*

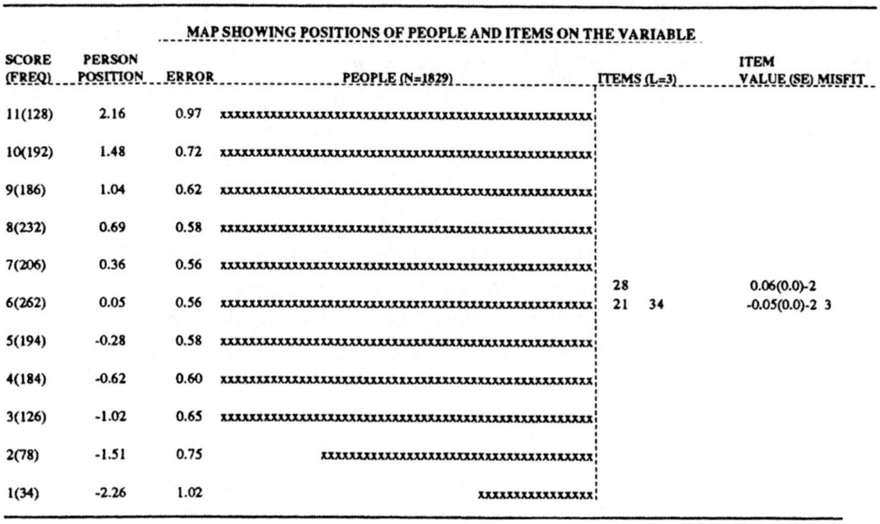

Fig. 5.5 Item-person map for the academic stress scale on the sources of stress scales instrument

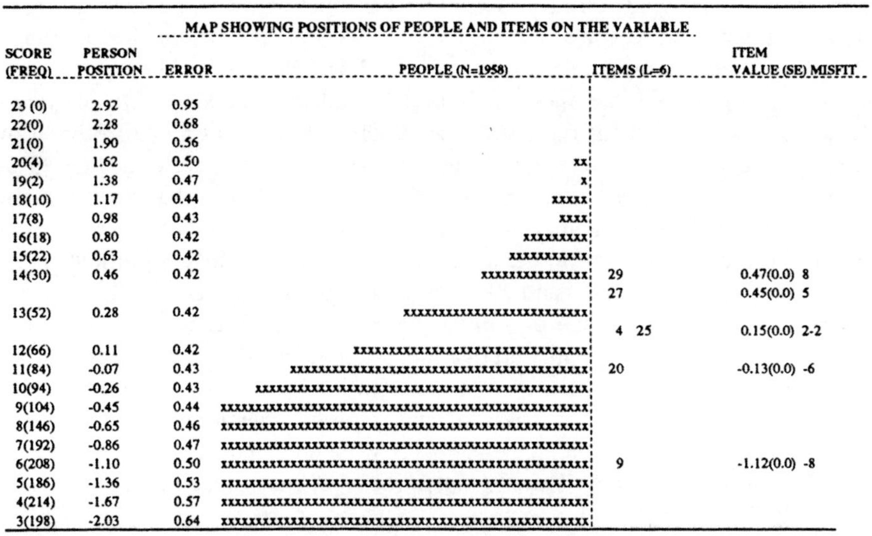

Fig. 5.6 Item-person map for the behavioral manifestation of stress scale on the sources of stress scales instrument

classmates; (e) 20, *I pick on other students*; and (f) 9, *I talk in class when I should be quiet*.

The item positions on Fig. 5.6 demonstrate that these items are spread out in their calibrations. Hence, a more complete score interpretation is possible for both low- and high-scoring people. At the upper end of the continuum, the hardest items to agree with (i.e., Items 29, 27, 4, and 25) define an "aggressive behavioral act" depicted by *action sill, talk back, get into fights, and yell at classmates.* On the other hand, the item located at the bottom of the map (item 9—*talk in class*) is the easiest to agree with. Thus, the continuum of responses for the Behavioral Manifestation of Stress scale seemed reasonable and consistent with the original conception of the scale or construct.

Rasch analysis provides an elegant method for examining item difficulty. However, even if a researcher does not conduct a Rasch or IRT analysis, it is always a good idea to look at the means for the items on each of the subscales. Ideally, some items should be harder to agree with than others. If all of the items on a subscale have similar means, then the items from that subscale are probably not spanning the full difficulty continuum, and it may be difficult distinguish high and low scorers than it would be if the item means spanned a wider band on the continuum.

Item Fit

Returning to our example from the *School Situation Survey*, examining item and person fit also provides further insight into the functioning of the instrument. The item-fit-statistic information for the $N = 1{,}598$ students responding to the six Behavioral scale items indicated that items 27 and 29, with calibration values of 0.45 and 0.47, were the most difficult for students to respond to at *always*. However, these two items did not fit the Rasch measurement model. Why? Low-scoring students who were not expected to respond *always*, were, in fact, giving such a response. These were students who, in general, felt that they exhibited relatively few of the behaviors targeted by the remaining four items on the scale, but unexpectedly said that they *always* exhibited the behaviors identified in items 27 ("talk back to teachers") and 29 ("try to get attention by acting silly in class"). To clarify this situation, we examined the response frequencies for each of the items. Relatively few students said that they "talk in class" (Item 9), yet relatively few also said that they always "try to get attention by acting silly in class" (Item 29) or always "talk back to teachers" (Item 27). A consideration of the structure of Item 29 suggests that competing behaviors may be involved. A student may tend to feel that he or she "always" wants "attention" but may, nonetheless, not tend to "act silly."

Person Fit

To evaluate person fit, we now examine of the response patterns for those students with large positive-fit statistics (i.e., $t > 2.00$). Numerous students scored higher than expected (i.e., responding *always*) on Items 27 and 29. To illustrate this

Person-Measurement Roster										
Estimation					*Responses, expected responses and standardized residuals for misfitting people. Items listed in serial order, misfit |T| = 2.00*					
Seq Num	*Score*	*Measure*	*Error*	*Misfit*						
39	8	−0.65	0.46	3.03	1	1	0	2	0	4
					1	3	1	1	1	1
					0	−1	−1	0	−1	3
196	16	0.80	0.42	4.51	4	0	4	4	0	4
					2	4	3	2	2	2
					1	−5	1	1	−2	2
201	5	−1.36	0.53	2.44	0	0	1	1	0	3
					1	2	1	1	1	1
					−1	−1	0	0	0	3
171	14	0.46	0.42	3.02	1	4	1	0	4	4
					2	3	2	2	2	2
					−1	0	−1	−2	2	2
86	6	−1.10	0.50	2.24	1	0	1	1	0	3
					1	2	1	1	1	1
					0	−2	0	0	−1	3

Fig. 5.7 A selection of individual response sets to items on the School Situation Survey instrument that display unexpected results

finding, we selected a few of the students who exhibited unexpected response patterns.

The six right-most columns in Fig. 5.7 contain the three rows of information for each of the five misfitting people. The first row provides the actual responses to the six items; the second row contains his or her responses expected under the model; and the third row provides the standardized residuals for that individual (Wright and Masters 1982). In the survey, the actual rating options were 1 = *never* to 5 = *always*; however, these were transformed to 0–4 for the analyses. Therefore, a score of 4 on the first row on the right hand side of the table indicates a response of "always". For example, Person 39 (far-left column) has responded "4" to item 29 (far-right column), while, given that person's total score, the model expects a response of "1," a response more consistent with the person's responses to the remaining five items. The discrepancy between the actual and expected response results is a standardized residual value of 3. Person 171 exceeded his or her expected response for items 9, 27, and 29. Person 196 exhibited an interesting but extreme pattern, using the extremes of the response scale. With only six items, one large unexpected response can inflate the fit statistic for a given person.

In summary, the use of such techniques as FA, correlations, and alpha reliability are crucial in the instrument development process; however, the use of Rasch modeling techniques can provide additional insight into the functioning of the items, as well as the response patterns within the sample. When the targeted variables are conceptually identified and then operationally defined through the item-writing process, instrument developers need to place greater emphasis on spanning the underlying psychological continuum for a targeted variable. Systematic expert judgments need to be gathered, using appropriate rating procedures, to examine the estimated item placement along the underlying psychological continuum prior to gathering actual respondent data. Rasch analysis can supplement more traditional analyses to test the developer's original conception of the variable for consistency with respondent score patterns.

Understanding Rasch-Model Residuals Through Analysis of Person Characteristics and Item Structure

In the previous section, we examined item and person fit statistics to reveal potential item-content ambiguity. Unexpected patterns of standardized residuals for persons not fitting the Rasch model provide important information about the characteristics of the persons and of the structure of the items (see Gable et al. 1990, 2011). Given adequate information about the people and a clear understanding of item content, these essentially descriptive and graphic analyses can contribute greatly to a better understanding of the data. Such insights aid in making more informed instrument revisions, which should ultimately lead to more meaningful (i.e., valid) inferences from test scores. Using one of the misfitting *School Situation Survey* items described in the earlier section (Item 29: *I try to get attention by acting silly in class)*, we conducted an analysis of the standardized residuals for 1,039 students in grades 5, 7, and 9.

The residual analyses are useful because they can reveal unexpected person-by-item response interactions. The overall fit statistic for the item (3.96) indicated that there were unexpected responses made by numerous students. As is often the case with a misfitting item, it was unclear whether the misfit was due to certain systematic characteristics of the students or the item structure. The next section explores these two areas.

Person Characteristics

Plotting the standardized residuals (on the *x*-axis) against the person estimates (on the *y*-axis) provides important information about whether unexpected responses were coming from high-scoring or low-scoring students. Figure 5.8 provides the plot of standardized residuals for item 29 against person estimates (i.e., logits). Section A of the plot contains 43 people whose standardized residuals are greater than +2.0. Therefore, they were more likely to agree with item 29 than would be expected given their responses to the other 5 items. Section B contains the

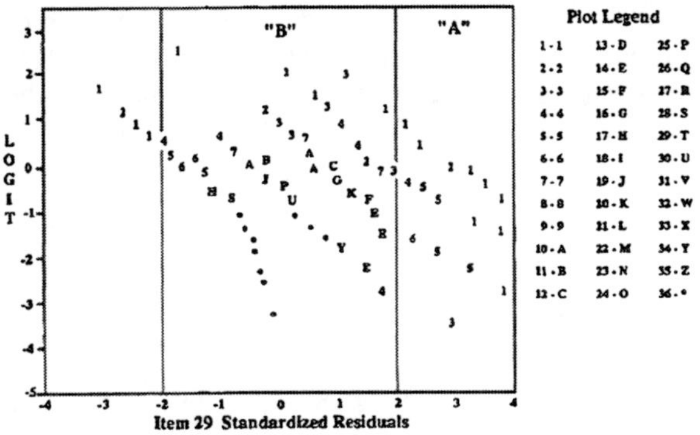

Fig. 5.8 Standardized residuals plotted against person estimates for item 29 of the School Situation Survey

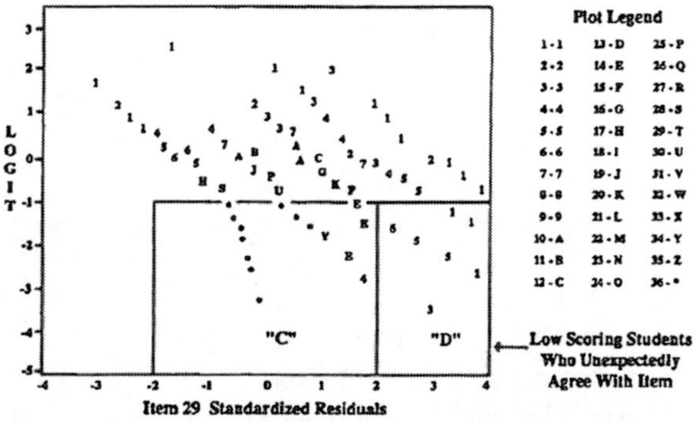

Fig. 5.9 Standardized residuals plotted against person estimates for item 29 of the School Situation Survey, focusing on individuals with unexpected responses

standardized residuals for people with more typical response patterns ($n = 875$). In Fig. 5.9, we further disaggregated the data. Section C and Section D contain people with low overall scores (logit $= -1$) on the trait. In Fig. 5.9, Section D identifies the 22 low-scoring (i.e., less frequent self-perceived behavioral displays) students who unexpectedly agreed with item 29. In contrast, Section C represents students who have low overall scores on the trait but whose actual responses to item 29 were more consistent with their expected responses to item 29, given their responses to the other 5 items on the scale.

We conducted exploratory descriptive and inferential tests to determine if any individual characteristics (i.e., general anxiety, stress due to teacher interactions, grade level, gender, number of siblings, reading level, and math level) related to the response patterns for the targeted item. Two discriminant-function analyses of the (a) atypical versus typical and (b) low-stress atypical versus low-stress typical groups failed separate the groups, given the small samples in the atypical group.

However, there were some interesting non-significant trends in the data for item 29: *I try to get attention by acting silly in class.* The group of students who gave low ratings to the other items on the Behavioral Manifestations of Stress scale. That is, they perceived that they do not tend to manifest such behaviors as "getting into fights," "talking in class when they should be quiet," "picking on other students," "yelling at classmates," and "talking back to teachers." However, they did indicate that they "get attention by acting silly in class." As compared to the students whose responses are more typical for the Behavioral Manifestations of Stress items, members of this group tended to be lower achievers in math and reading and to perceive higher levels of source-related stress based on their views of how teachers feel and act toward them.

Item Structure

At this point, the investigation turned to the structure of the item. Given that only a few students were found to be in the low-stress/unexpected agreement ($n = 22$) and high-stress/unexpected disagreement ($n = 9$) groups, we know that the item-fit statistic (3.96) was created by additional factors. The factor-analysis results for the total group of 1,038 students indicated that item 29 always exhibited the lowest correlation with the derived factor (Helms and Gable 1989). The structure of the item is problematic because there are two separate components within the question, "trying to get attention" and "acting silly". Some students may "try to get attention in class by acting silly." Clearly, such students should endorse the item. However, other students may try to get attention in ways other than acting silly. How should these students respond to the question? Should they endorse the item because they agree with the first part or not endorse the item because they disagree with the second part of the item? Similarly, students could act silly in class for reasons other than attention seeking. Finally, it is unclear whose attention the silly behavior is designed to capture: The teacher's? The other students'? It appears that the potential double-barreled nature of the item has contributed to the lower correlations with the remaining five items defining the scale, and may contribute to the unexpected person-by-item response interactions for a subset of students. The follow-up analyses suggest that this may be especially true for the students in the low-stress atypical group who tended to have lower reading scores. Perhaps some of these atypical students, who had lower reading scores, only attended to the first part of the question, "I try to get attention in class," perceived the question as a pro-social behavior, and agreed with the item.

In summary, this section has illustrated the use of descriptive/graphic and inferential techniques to analyze residual patterns (i.e., difference between observed and expected responses) generated under the Rasch rating scale model. The use of exploratory techniques to analyze person characteristics and item structure can provide a better understanding of unexpected person-by-item response patterns. Such explorations are important for instrument development and analysis activities because they assist in better understanding of the structure and functioning of the instrument. Ultimately, such analyses provide greater insight into the item and scale functioning, which ultimately provides greater evidence of the construct validity of score interpretations.

Construct Invariance

Multiple Group Confirmatory Factor Analysis

To make meaningful inferences about between group differences in responses, it is essential to examine empirical support for the *invariance* of the internal structure across the subgroups being studied. Often, researchers compare scale- or dimension-level means across various demographic groups without any evidence that the theoretical interpretation and inferences from the factor analytic derived constructs are the same across groups. If the measurement instrument functions differently across different subpopulations, then the scores are not equivalent across the groups: the scores mean different things in different groups. It is easy to see how such an issue threatens the researcher's ability to draw reasonable inferences about the constructs of interest. A measurement invariance study examines the extent that the derived constructs have the same meaning across demographic characteristics of various targeted reporting groups. Measurement invariance studies determine whether the values of model parameters (the measurement weights, etc.) vary across groups. In other words, does group membership moderate the relations specified in the model?

Several measurement strategies can be used to examine measurement invariance. Here we discuss two commonly employed analyses within the instrument design literature: multiple group confirmatory factor analysis (MG-CFA) and Rasch modeling. First, we turn our attention to MG-CFA. Our discussion of MG-CFA is conceptual and lacks the detail found in books such as Brown (2006), an invaluable source book for conducting CFA and MG-CFA. Afterward, we briefly consider Rasch approaches to measurement invariance, again, staying very conceptual in our approach.

There are many recent examples of measurement invariance studies using MG-CFA. Tovar and Simon (2010) employed MG-CFA to examine the factorial structure of the *Sense of Belonging Scales* for a diverse sample of college students. Their analyses across groups suggested a different factor structure than the one reported by the instrument developers. Sass (2011) employed the MG-CFA approach for examining data from 491 elementary and middle school teachers regarding behavior and instructional management dimensions. Although some between group differences were noted, they did not affect the interpretation of calculated mean differences. Sass (2011) also discusses possible causes of invariant items, measurement bias, and item invariance, and suggestions for addressing the lack of construct invariance. Researchers wishing to use the MG-CFA approach may also wish to examine the article by Dimitrov (2010), which describes the logic and procedures for testing factorial invariance and includes M*plus* computer codes for MG-CFA analyses.

In a multiple group CFA (MG-CFA), we estimate the same model in 2 or more samples and compare the unstandardized solutions across the groups. In particular, we are most interested in comparing the values of the unstandardized measurement weights (pattern coefficients) and the item intercepts across the two groups. Let's talk conceptually about what differences on those parameters mean, starting with the item intercepts. The item intercept is the mean or expected value of the item, after controlling for the factor. Thus, if an item has an invariant intercept, individuals with the same mean score on the latent variable would be expected to get the same score on the item, regardless of their group membership. On the other hand, if an item has an intercept that varies across two subpopulations (a non-invariant intercept), then people who have the same level on the construct would be expected to differ in terms of their mean score on the item. For example, in one study of kindergarteners' vocabulary knowledge, we discovered that there were gender differences for the word "slumber." What does it mean if there are gender differences on the item intercepts for "slumber"? Girls had higher intercepts than boys. In other words, after controlling for overall vocabulary knowledge, girls were more likely know the word slumber than boys were. Why? Young girls were familiar with the concept of a "slumber party" (young boys were not!) They could leverage that information to answer the slumber question correctly. Thus slumber is not a good vocabulary word to use when assessing overall vocabulary knowledge because girls are advantaged and will generally do better on that item than boys with similar levels of vocabulary knowledge.

What does it mean if the measurement weights (pattern coefficients, or in common parlance, factor loadings) differ across two groups? Remember that the measurement weights are akin to partial standardized regression coefficients from multiple linear regression, and they capture the "direct effect" of the factor on the item, which is like a partial correlation between the factor and the item after controlling for any other (correlated) factors that also contain paths to the item. Again, thinking in terms of a regression framework, the measurement weight essentially tells us how much we would expect the item score to increase for a one unit increase in the factor. Thus, the higher this value is, the greater is the influence the factor on the item. Imagine an extreme scenario where the measurement weight is near zero. That means that a person's level on the construct does not predict their score on the item. When the coefficient is very high, the person's level on the construct is very predictive of their response to the item. Therefore, these measurement weights can be thought of as "discrimination" parameters in that items with low measurement weights do not discriminate between those who are high and low on the construct, whereas items with high measurement weights are "very discriminating:" people who are high and low on the construct would respond quite differently to that item. Let's return to our example from above, slumber. Slumber did not discriminate equally well across the two genders either. Slumber was much more discriminating (had a higher measurement weight) for boys than girls. In other words, overall vocabulary knowledge predicted boys' knowledge of the word slumber much better than it predicted girls' knowledge of the word slumber. This makes sense: both high and low scoring girls knew what a slumber party was, so knowledge of the word slumber was not a good indicator of overall vocabulary knowledge for girls. However, for boys, slumber was "just another word," so it was a reasonably good indicator of overall vocabulary knowledge for boys.

If the instrument exhibits measurement invariance, then these parameters (the measurement weights and the item intercepts) should have the same unstandardized values across the two groups. We can statistically test whether there are differences in the parameter estimates across the two groups, and we can isolate which parameters vary across the two groups. When an item functions differently across two known subgroups, this is often referred to as differential item functioning (DIF).

Generally, MG-CFA involves systematically placing a series of cross-group equality constraints on the parameters in the CFA model. These cross-group equality constraints force the unstandardized estimates of that parameter to be equal across all samples. Then we compare the fit of the constrained model to the unrestricted model using Chi-square difference test. If the fit of the constrained model is statistically significantly worse than that of the unconstrained model, we conclude that the parameters are unlikely to be equal in the populations from which the samples were drawn (Brown 2006).

There are many taxonomies for the order in which parameter constraints should be applied in multiple groups CFA. We recommend placing cross-group equality constraints in the following order. (This taxonomy is adapted slightly from Brown 2006).

1. Unconstrained Common Model (Configural Model).
2. Constrain measurement weights (factor loadings).
3. Constrain factor intercepts.
4. Constrain measurement errors and covariances among measurement errors (optional).
5. Constrain structural paths to be equal.
6. Constrain structural means and intercepts to be equal.
7. Constrain structural variances, covariances, and disturbances to be equal (optional).

For the purposes of establishing the measurement equivalence of an instrument, we are really only interested in the measurement model, thus, we only need to concern ourselves with steps 1–4. Further, step 4 is quite stringent, and not completely necessary for establishing reasonable levels of measurement invariance for affective instruments (although it is commonly applied in the development of large scale cognitive and achievement assessments). Therefore, we recommend following a simple three step procedure, which we outline in more detail below.

Step 1: Unconstrained common model (configural model)

First, run the completely unconstrained multiple groups CFA model. This serves as the baseline model. The Chi-square and *df* for this completely unconstrained model are equal to the sum of the Chi-squares and *df* for the models run separately for each subgroup in a single group CFA and then added together. Therefore, running an unconstrained CFA in a multiple groups framework is equivalent to running multiple single group CFAs simultaneously. Although we are providing a conceptual overview to this process, a couple of technical suggestions merit explanation.

Identification of Multiple Groups CFA Models

First, recall that we used a marker variable strategy to scale the latent variable. Conducting a multiple group CFA necessitates the use of a marker variable strategy. Never use a fixed factor variance strategy: fixing the factor variances to be equal across the groups is something that should be empirically tested, not assumed. It is relatively common for subgroups to have different variances on a variable. Fixing those variances to be equal when they are not would adversely impact the results. (Note: technically, you could fix the factor variance in one of the two groups to be 1 and constrain the unstandardized path coefficient for one item to be equal across the groups; however, this is rarely if ever done in practice.) Now the choice of marker variable is essential. The measurement weight (factor loading) for the marker variable is constrained to be 1 across both groups; therefore, the direct effect of the factor on that item is constrained to be the same across groups. Thus, it is essential to pick an item that is most likely to be invariant across the two groups (Going back to our prior example, slumber would NOT be a good marker variable!)

Second, we have not yet discussed identification for mean structures because our initial discussion of CFA did not include means and intercepts at all. The mean structure must also be identified in an SEM model, and the identification of the mean structure must be considered separately from the identification of the measurement model (In other words, it is not possible to "buy" degrees of freedom from a measurement model and apply them to the mean structure if the mean structure is underidentified). The number of "knowns" is the number of observed means, which in a CFA is equal to the number of items on the instrument. For a CFA model with latent means, each latent variable also has a mean. Therefore, identifying a CFA model that includes means and intercepts requires adopting a strategy that is analogous to the marker variable strategy for the intercepts. In a single group framework, it is necessary to constrain the intercept of one item per factor to be equal to 0, which results in a just-identified structural model. This variable should be the same marker variable that was used for the measurement weights. The latent mean is scaled in the metric of the marker variable. In a multiple group CFA, the intercept of the marker variable is constrained to be 0 across all of the groups. Again, to use this strategy in a multiple groups framework requires carefully considering which variable to make the marker variable because the intercept of this variable needs to be invariant across groups. One other possibility exists for scaling the latent means in a MG-CFA framework. Instead of fixing one intercept per factor to be zero, we can instead fix the mean of each latent factor to be "0" in one of the groups, and then we can fix the intercept of the marker variable to be equal across the two groups, but not equal to "0." This strategy results in a statistically equivalent model. However, the interpretation of the parameters for the latent means changes. Using this approach, the latent mean in the reference group is always "0," and the latent means in the other groups are deviations from the latent mean in the reference group. This approach has one advantage: The Wald test for the latent mean parameter for the non-reference group provides a statistical test for the difference in the latent means across the groups. The reference latent mean is zero; however, if the latent mean for a non-reference group is statistically significantly different from "0," then there are statistically significant differences between the latent means of the two groups.

For readers who plan to use AMOS for MG-CFA, a few words of caution are in order. AMOS has a very slick "Multiple Groups Analysis" menu that theoretically tests a sequential series of increasingly constrained models with the touch of a button. We recommend that you be very cautious in your use of this option if you are planning to use MG-CFA to examine invariance in intercepts or mean structures. At the time of the writing of this book, the default for identifying the mean structure in MG-CFA is to fix the latent means in all groups to be 0 and freely estimate all of the intercepts. However, this is very problematic because it forces the latent means to be equal across all groups and then examines the invariance of item intercepts assuming that groups have the same means on the latent variables. However, we often believe that there are between group differences on the constructs, which would result in between group differences on the latent means. In fact, this is often one of our focal areas of research interest! If the groups differ in terms of their latent means, using this strategy can result in inferences that are downright wrong! Imagine two groups that differ in their latent means. Forcing the latent means to be equal across groups affects the estimates of the item intercepts. In such a scenario, at least some of the intercepts would appear to be unequal because the across group differences in the mean structure could not be reflected by differences in the latent means. For this reason, when examining the invariance of item intercepts and item means in AMOS, it is best to create the models manually using manage models and manage groups and avoid the MG Analysis entirely.

After estimating the completely unconstrained model, examine the output from this step, paying special attention to the values of the unstandardized measurement weights and the intercepts across groups. Give them the ocular test! Do they look relatively similar in magnitude? Does it seem as if imposing cross group constraints on these parameters is reasonable? Study the results of the unconstrained model closely, as this is guaranteed to be the best fitting of the increasingly constrained MG-CFA models. Imposing constraints to the MG-CFA always results in similar or worse model fit, so it is important that this unconstrained model fits reasonably well before imposing sequential constraints on the measurement weights and the intercepts. If the unconstrained model fits poorly, then additional validation work must be done prior to conducting any measurement invariance studies (After all, establishing that an instrument fits equally poorly in two populations is not exactly a reason for celebration!).

Step 2: Imposing constraints on the measurement weights

In step two, we constrain all of the measurement weights to be invariant across the two groups. The choice of marker variable is crucial! The marker variable should be the item that is most likely to be invariant across the two groups. If the measurement weight for the marker variable is not actually invariant across the two groups, but the model constrains it to be equal, then items that are actually invariant may look non-invariant. The assumption that the marker variable is invariant is necessary to test the assumption of invariance. Thus, "a circular situation exists where (a) the referent variable must be invariant, (b) invariance cannot be established without estimating a model, and (c) model estimation requires an invariant referent, which brings the process back to the original invariant referent assumption" (French and Finch 2008, p. 98). Therefore, it may be necessary to try using a few different marker variables and to compare the results of these analyses, especially if the first marker variable chosen results in partial or complete non-invariance. Rensvold and Cheung (2001) have developed a method for systematically choosing the most invariant variable; this method requires estimating a large number of models and then evaluating those models using a multistep procedure.

To compare the fit of the model with all measurement weights to be constrained to be equal to the unconstrained model using the Chi-square difference test, we compare the difference in the Chi-squares of the two models to the critical value of Chi-square with degrees of freedom equal to the difference in the degrees of freedom of the model. If the constrained model fits as well as the constrained model (i.e., the fit is not worse), then the Chi-square test should not be statistically significant. Generally, we examine the changes in the fit indices as well. The hope is that the fit indices for the constrained model look similar to those for the unconstrained model. It is quite common for some but not all of the measurement weights to be equal across the groups. This is commonly referred to as partial measurement invariance. If it is not possible to establish complete measurement invariance in step 2, it is important to conduct follow-up analyses to discover which items function differently across the groups.

There is some disagreement about the gravity of partial measurement invariance. Further, there are degrees of severity of measurement non-invariance or partial measurement invariance. For example, imagine you have a 10-item scale. If 1 of the 10 items is slightly, but statistically significantly non-invariant, this is a less severe problem than if you discover that 7 of your 10 items are moderately to severely non-invariant. In the first scenario, you have a couple of different options. First, you could remove that item from the scale and have a 9-item scale that is invariant across groups. Second, you could allow the measurement weights to differ across the two groups for that 1 item and fit what is referred to as a partially invariant measurement model. If you use such a model, you must alert readers to this decision, and caution them that one of the items appears to function somewhat differently across the two groups. However, given that 9 of the 10 items function similarly across the two groups, you may still be able to make reasonable inferences about the latent means in such a scenario. If, on the other hand, many of the items are non-invariant across the subpopulations, this is a much more serious problem, and one that does not have a "quick fix."

Step 3: Imposing constraints on the intercepts

If the measurement weights are invariant, then we can proceed to step 3, in which we impose equality constraints on all of the intercepts. Again, it is essential to use a marker variable that has the same intercept across the two groups, and we recommend using the same marker variable for both the measurement weights and the intercepts. Thus, it is advisable to conduct your preliminary analyses with a few different marker variables to ensure the invariance of the marker variable on the intercept prior to choosing the marker variable. There are two choices for estimating the model with invariant intercepts. Option 1: Constrain all intercepts to be equal to each other and constrain one of the latent means for each of the factors to be "0" in one group. Option 2: Constrain one latent intercept to be zero across the groups, constrain the other intercepts to be equal across the two groups, and estimate the factor means freely in both groups. Again, we test the difference between this model and the model with constrained measurement weights (and potentially also the unconstrained model) using the Chi-square difference test, as described in Step 2. Again, it is quite common for some but not all of the measurement intercepts to be equal across the groups, and this is also an indication of partial measurement invariance. If the model for the measurement weights exhibits partial measurement invariance, it is unnecessary to constrain the intercepts of the items that have non-invariant measurement weights. Because the slope differs across the two groups, and the location of the intercept is partially a function of the slope, we would not necessarily expect the intercept for that item to invariant. Furthermore, that item has already failed the invariance test: it is a non-invariant item whether or not the intercept can be constrained to be equal across groups. Therefore, as a general rule, we only try to constrain intercepts for items that exhibited invariant measurement weights.

Again, as in Step 2, failure to establish complete measurement invariance in Step 3 necessitates conducting follow-up analyses to discover which items function differently across the two groups and how severe your non-invariance issue is. Ideally, the models from Steps 2 and 3 fit as well as the unconstrained model. If so, then the instrument developer can argue that the instrument functions similarly across the subpopulations of interest, and researchers can move forward with the analyses of group differences in the latent means or examine questions related to whether there are structural differences in the degree to which the constructs measured by the instrument predict other outcomes.

An Illustration of Multiple Groups CFA with the Attitudes Toward Teachers/Classes Scale of the SAAS-R

To illustrate this process, we conducted a multiple groups CFA with the 7-item attitudes toward teachers and classes subscale of the *School Attitude Assessment Survey-Revised* (McCoach 2002; McCoach & Siegle 2003a, b) using a sample of 600 7–12 grade students. As a general rule, we conduct measurement invariance studies of the entire instrument simultaneously. However, for simplicity, we demonstrate the approach with one factor; the general process would be identical with a multifactor instrument. For this example, we are interested in establishing the gender invariance of the subscale. In Step 1, we ran a multiple group CFA, imposing only those constraints that were necessary for identification. The model Chi-square was 147.76 with 28 degrees of freedom. Given that there are 7 items on the scale, why are the 28 degrees of freedom? In a single group analysis with a mean structure, our knowns would include $7 * 8/2 = 28$ elements of the variance covariance matrix plus 7 means. Therefore, our total knowns are $28 + 7 = 35$. We estimate six intercepts and a latent mean, so we have a just identified mean structure. We also estimate 7 error variances, 6 measurement weights, and 1 factor variances. Therefore, our *df* in a single group model would be $35 - 7 - 7 - 6 - 1 = 14$. In an unconstrained multiple group CFA model, our *df* are exactly double the *df* for the single group model. The fit for this unconstrained model was marginally acceptable (RMSEA = 0.08, CFI = 0.96). Next we estimated the model which constrained all seven measurement weights to be equal for boys and girls. The Chi-square increased to 159.69 with 34 *df*. The Chi-square difference between the model with constrained measurement weights and the unconstrained model was 11.9 with 6 degrees of freedom ($p = 0.07$). Therefore, we concluded that it was reasonable to constrain the measurement weights to be equal for boys and girls. Next, we constrained the measurement intercepts to be equal across the two groups. The Chi-square increased to 168.16 with 40 *df*. The Chi-square difference between the model with constrained measurement weights and the unconstrained model was 8.48 with 6 degrees of freedom ($p = 0.22$). The fit of the final constrained model looks the same or slightly better than the fit of the unconstrained model, using conventional fit indices: RMSEA = 0.07, CFI = 0.96. Therefore, we concluded that it was reasonable to constrain the measurement intercepts (and the measurement weights) to be equal for boys and girls. We identified the mean structure by constraining the marker intercepts to be equal to each other and constraining the latent mean of boys to be equal to 0. Therefore, the latent mean for females represented the difference between females and males on the attitudes toward teachers/classes factor. This difference was 0.05 ($p = 0.54$), which was not statistically significant. The results of these analyses indicate that the attitudes toward teachers/classes subscale functions the same way for males and females. The items appear to have similar levels of difficulty and discrimination for boys and girls. Finally, girls and boys appear to have similar means on the underlying construct.

A Rasch Approach to Measurement Invariance

The information obtained from Rasch analyses can also contribute to the examination of construct invariance. To illustrate this, we present a construct invariance analysis carried out for one of the six constructs (i.e., Knowledge) assessed by the 26 item *Survey of Knowledge of Internet Risk and Internet Behavior—SIRIB*, an instrument developed to address the topic of cyber bullying for middle and high school students (Gable et. al. 2011; Kite et al. 2010b). The Knowledge scale contains seven items, where students offer an *agree* or *disagree* response on a two-point response scale. An example item is: *Making threats online can get me in trouble with the police*. Analysis of data for a previous sample of 1,366 grade 7–8 middle school students indicated that the 7 statements defining the Knowledge scale successfully defined a unidimensional, hierarchically ordered scale assessing knowledge of Internet risks (Gable et al. 2009). In this context, an item parameter estimate represents the "difficulty" of eliciting an *agree* response to a statement. Thus, items to which students agreed with frequently are the "easy" items (e.g., *Making threats online can get me into trouble with the police*.), and items that students tended to agree with less frequently (e.g., *An Internet predator could contact me based on what my friends have posted about me*.) were more "difficult" items.

To further examine the validity of construct interpretations for the Knowledge scale scores, we gathered data on the seven Knowledge items from a new sample of 4,215 male and female middle school and high school students. We were interested in examining the invariance of the Knowledge subscale across genders and across age groups (middle school versus high school). The Rasch model analysis used the WINSTEPS software (Wright and Linacre 1998, version 3.68.0) to generate person and item location estimates (Rasch 1960; Wright and Masters 1982) (For examples of variable maps see Gable et al. 2011; Gable et al. 1990; Gable and Wolf 1993; Ludlow et al. 2008). We generated and compared variable maps indicating person and item locations along the Knowledge continuum for the middle and high school and the male and female samples (Gable et al. 2010).

Grades 6–12

Figure 5.10 presents the structure of the Knowledge scale depicted in the Wright variable map for the total sample of 4,215 grades 6–12 students. The left side of the figure shows the location of the students on the logit "difficulty" scale. For this map, each of the # indicators shows the location for 64 students. The students are ordered from the lowest level of Knowledge (bottom of the map) to the highest level of Knowledge (top of map). The right side of the map lists the item numbers, where items toward the top are "hard" items that are "difficult" to yield a correct response (for these 7 items *agree* was correct), and the items at the bottom are the items that are "easy" to offer a correct response. The total group overall mean for the seven items is indicated by the *M* symbol located near the middle of the vertical map.

For grade 6–12 students, the listing of item difficulties for the Knowledge scale showed wide item spread with an excellent spread of the students across the entire scoring range. Starting at the bottom of the map and proceeding upward, it is easiest to *agree* with V2 (*Making threats online can get me into trouble with the police*), somewhat harder to *agree* with V7 (*An online predator could contact me using a social networking site like Myspace or Facebook if I posted my personal information on it.*), harder still to *agree* with V7 (*An online predator could contact me using a social networking site like Myspace or Facebook if I posted my* personal *information on it.),* harder still to agree with V19 and V15 *(Threats online that I carry out in school can get me into trouble; An Internet predator can easily use Internet sites such as Google earth, MSN live or other programs to locate my school and house.*), and the cluster of items V17, V12, and V25 are the hardest items to agree with (*An Internet predator could make contact with me based on the information I have posted online; With the contact information I put on Myspace or Facebook, it would be easy for an Internet predator to contact me; An Internet predator could contact me based on what my friends have posted about me.*) This cluster of "hard" items addresses the important issue of knowing that contact by an Internet predator can be made through personal information listed online. The crucial aspect of this variable map is the extent and manner in which the students and items are spread vertically across the map. The items are spread across the map indicating that we have spanned the Knowledge continuum, and the students are spread across the map, indicating that we can differentiate between high and low scorers.

Table 5.6 contains the "item statistics and misfit order" for the seven Knowledge items. Note that item V2 is identified on the far right side of the first row in the table. This item (*Making threats online can get me into trouble with the police*) displayed evidence of misfit (Outfit MNSQ = 2.61) due to large numbers of students giving a surprising *disagree* incorrect response to a relatively easy item to *agree* with. The difficulty location of item V2 is at the bottom of the variable map in Fig. 5.10 or −2.52. In Table 5.6 the −2.52 logit is listed in the 4th column from the left labeled MEASURE. This finding is consistent with the sample of 1,366 middle school students in our earlier sample (Gable et al. 2009).

Males versus Females

The Rasch model constructs invariance evidence for grade 6–12 males ($N = 2{,}115$) and females ($N = 2{,}008$) is presented in Fig. 5.11. Examination of the wide spread of student locations (males—each # is 30 students; females—each # = 34 students) and the spread of items spanning the Knowledge continuum indicates that the maps, including the mean Knowledge level listed as *M* in the map, are very similar for the gender groups and similar to the total sample

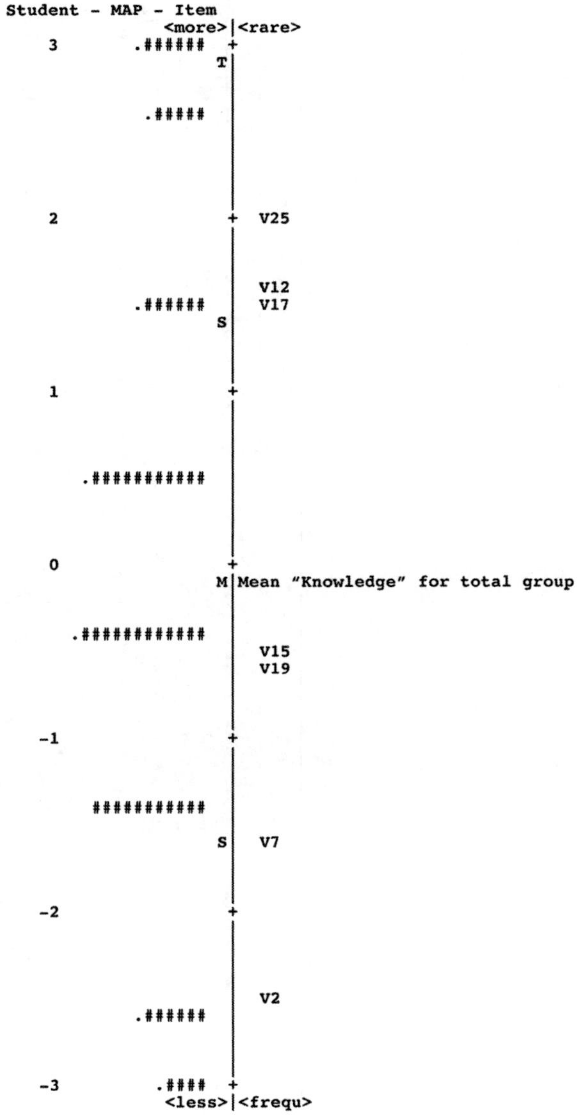

Fig. 5.10 Item-person map for the knowledge section of the survey of knowledge of Internet risk and Internet behavior instrument (SKIRIB) for the total sample

presented in Fig. 5.10. Further, the same item misfit information found for the total grade 6–12 group is present for item V2 for males (2.59) and females (2.55). Overall, these findings indicate that the structure of the Knowledge is the same for males and females.

Figure 5.12 presents a plot of the pairs of the seven item estimates for males and females. Essentially, this plot indicates the location of each item for the male/female item estimates. For example, the dot in the lower left section of Fig. 5.12 represents the male/female data for item V2, which is located at the bottom of each

Table 5.6 Knowledge scale item statistics and misfit order

Entry number	Total score	Total count	MEASURE	Model	Infit		Outfit		PT-MEASURE		Exact match		Item
				S.E.	MNSQ	ZSTD	MNSQ	ZSTD	CORR.	EXP.	OBS%	EXP%	
1	3,397	4,215	−2.52	0.05	1.15	4.8	2.61	9.9	0.49	0.56	83.3	85.4	V2
2	3,005	4,215	−1.61	0.04	0.92	−3.7	1.09	1.6	0.61	0.59	81.5	79.2	V7
3	1,210	4,215	1.61	0.05	0.96	−1.5	1.03	0.5	0.65	0.65	82.4	82.3	V12
4	2,356	4,215	−0.46	0.04	0.93	−3.7	1.00	0.1	0.64	0.63	75.7	73.5	V15
5	1,247	4,215	1.53	0.05	0.82	−7.5	0.86	−2.5	0.69	0.65	84.8	81.6	V17
6	2,411	4,215	−0.55	0.04	1.07	3.7	1.28	7.6	0.60	0.63	73.8	74.1	V19
7	1,049	4,215	2.00	0.05	0.93	−2.6	0.96	−0.5	0.66	0.64	86.2	85.1	V25
MEAN	2,096.4	4,215.0	0.00	0.05	0.97	−1.5	1.26	2.4			81.1	80.2	
S.D.	869.1	0.0	1.62	0.00	0.10	4.0	0.56	4.2			4.3	4.5	

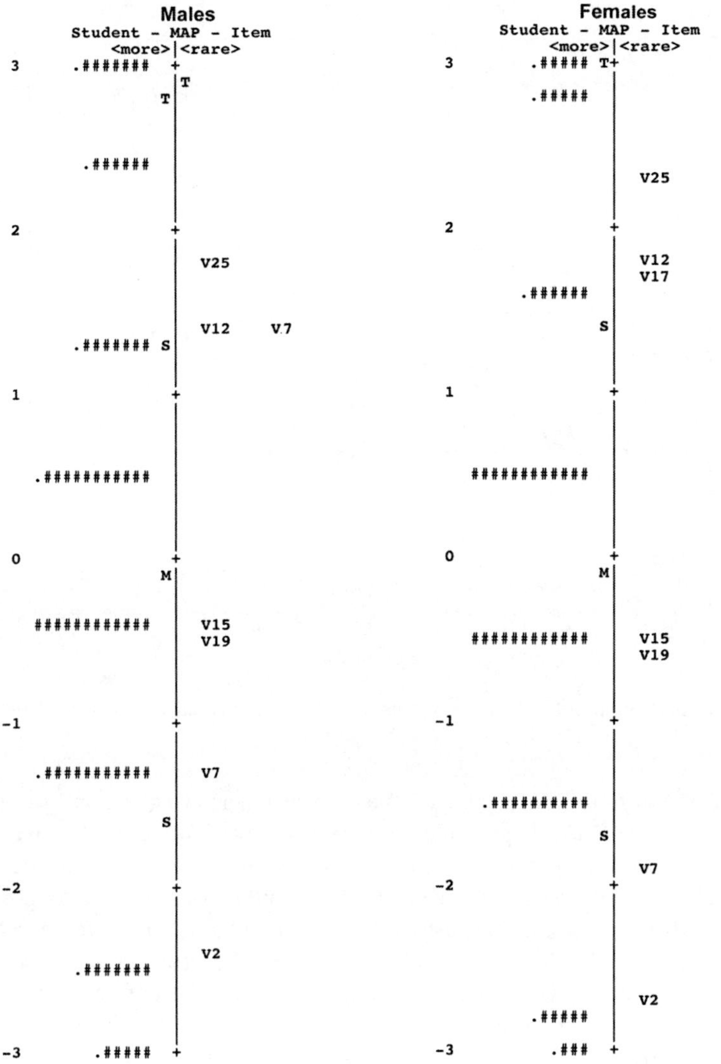

Fig. 5.11 Item-person maps for the knowledge section of the SKIRIB instrument, disaggregated by gender

variable map in Fig. 5.11. The dot for item V2 and all the other dots for the remaining six items are very close to the line is because the regression line using female item estimates to predict the male item estimates results in a near perfect relationship ($r = 0.996$, $r^2 = 0.992$). This criterion indicates that the items function in a similar way for males and females. Male estimates have a slightly smaller range than the female estimates. That is, the "hard" items are not quite as hard for the males while the "easier" items are not quite as "easy."

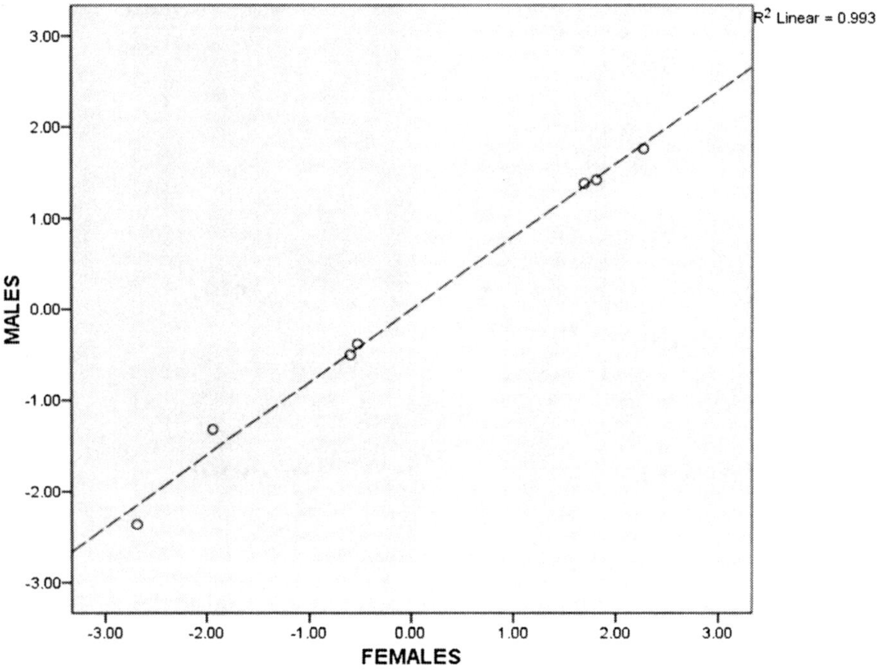

Fig. 5.12 Scatterplot of the male versus female item estimates for the knowledge scale ($R^2 = 0.993$)

In summary, the similarity of the findings across subgroups suggested the structure of the Knowledge scale/variable was invariant across gender and grade level. This method of examining invariance is quite different from the MG-CFA approach that we presented earlier in the chapter. Therefore, it is possible that using the Rasch techniques illustrated above could result in different conclusions than using the MG-CFA approach. The area of IRT provides an arsenal of techniques to evaluate DIF, which is indicative of measurement non-invariance (Holland and Wainer 1993).

Finally, the results of measurement invariance studies can provide insights that are valuable for research and evaluation within school or corporate environments. For instance, Masters and Hyde (1984) administered a 25-item attitude toward school measure to grade 3 and 4 students in 10 different schools and used the Rasch-latent-trait model to examine the invariance of item-scale values (i.e., difficulty of agreeing with a particular item) across schools. Although overall, the attitude data fit the Rasch latent trait model, two items were identified as functioning differently across the 10 schools. This finding had potential practical significance for school evaluation. For example, in a particularly disadvantaged school where special efforts were aimed at promoting self-confidence, self-esteem, and cooperation among students, a higher than expected agreement was found with the item: "I like speaking in front of the class." Across all 10 schools, this item, which was the most difficult with which to agree, turned out to have a high item-misfit statistic, probably due to the atypical response pattern found in one school in relation to the pattern expected from the latent trait model. It was also found that in one school many students found it more difficult to agree than expected with the item: "Physical education is fun." Although not causal in nature, these two examples of items with atypical response patterns could be related to aspects of school-program efforts, could contribute to program-evaluation discussions, and could be used to identify areas for potential qualitative follow-up studies.

This chapter has provided an overview and illustrations of several techniques (LCA, Rasch Models, Multiple Group CFA, and Measurement Invariance within a Rasch framework) to further elucidate the internal structure of affective instruments. In the next chapter, we turn our attention to collecting evidence of relationships among constructs and other external evidence, which helps us to buttress the argument for the validity of our inferences.

References

Akaike, H. (1987). Factor analysis and AIC. *Psychometrika, 52*(3), 317–332.

American Educational Research Association (AERA), American Psychological Association (APA), & National Council on Measurement in Education (NCME). (1999). *The standards for educational and psychological testing*. Washington, DC: American Educational Research Association.

Andrich, D. (1978a). Application of a psychometric rating model to ordered categories which are scored with successive integers. *Applied Psychological Measurement, 2*, 581–594.

Andrich, D. (1978b). Rating formulation for ordered response categories. *Psychometrika, 43*, 561–573.

Andrich, D. (1978c). Scaling attitude items constructed and scored in the Likert tradition. *Educational and Psychological Measurement, 38*, 665–680.

Beck, C. T., & Gable, R. K. (2001). Further validation of the *postpartum depression screening scale. Nursing Research, 50*, 155–164.

Boscardin, C. (2012). Profiling students for remediation using latent class analysis. *Advances in Health Sciences, 17*, 56–63.

Boscardin, C. K., Muthen, B., Francis, D. J., & Baker, E. L. (2008). Early identification of reading difficulties using heterogeneous developmental trajectories. *Journal of Educational Psychology, 100*(1), 192–208.

Bozdogan, H. (1987). Model selection and Akaike's information criteria (AIC): The general theory and its analytical extensions. *Psychometrika, 52*(3), 345–370.

Brown, T. A. (2006). *Confirmatory factor analysis for applied research*. New York: The Guilford Press.

Collins, L. M., & Lanza, S. T. (2010). *Latent class and latent transition analysis with applications in the social, behavioral, and health sciences*. Hoboken, NJ: Wiley.

Dias, J. G., & Vermunt, J. K. (2006). Bootstrap methods for measuring classification uncertainty in latent class analysis. In A. Rizzi & M. Vichi (Eds.), *Proceedings in computational statistics* (pp. 31–41). Heidelberg: Springer.

Dimitrov, D. M. (2010). Testing factorial invariance in the context of construct validation. *Measurement and Evaluation in Counseling and Development, 43*(2), 121–149.

Embretson, S. E. (1999). Issues in the measurement of cognitive abilities. In S. Embretson & S. Hershberger (Eds.), *The new rules of measurement: What every psychologist and educator should know* (pp. 1–15). Mahwah, NJ: Lawrence Erlbaum Associates.

French, B. F., & Finch, W. H. (2008). Multigroup confirmatory factor analysis: Locating the invariant reference sets. *Structural Equation Modeling: A Multidisciplinary Journal, 15*, 96–113.

Finch, W. H., & Bronk, K. C. (2011). Conducting confirmatory latent class analysis using Mplus. *Structural Equation Modeling: A Multidisciplinary Journal, 18*(1), 132–151.

Franek, M. (2005/2006). Foiling cyberbullies in the new Wild West. *Educational Leadership, 63*, 39–43.

Gable, R. K., Ludlow, L. H., Kite, S. L., McCoach, D. B., & Filippelli, L. P. (2009, April). *Development and validation of the survey of knowledge of internet risk and internet behavior.* Paper presented at the annual meeting of the American Educational Research Association, San Diego, CA.

Gable, R. K., Ludlow, L. H., McCoach, D. B., & Kite, S. L. (2010, October). *Construct invariance of the survey of knowledge of internet risk and internet behavior.* Paper presented at the Annual Conference of the Northeastern Educational Research Association, Rocky Hill, CT.

Gable, R. K., Ludlow, L. H., McCoach, D. B., & Kite, S. L. (2011). Validation of the survey of knowledge of internet risk and internet behavior. *Educational and Psychological Measurement, 71*(1), 217–230.

Gable, R. K., Ludlow, L. H., & Wolf, M. B. (1990). The use of classical and Rasch latent trait models to enhance the validity of affective measures. *Educational and Psychological Measurement, 50*(4), 869–878.

Gable, R. K., & Wolf, M. B. (1993). *Instrument development in the affective domain: Measuring attitudes and values in corporate and school settings* (2nd ed.). Boston: Kluwer-Nijhoff.

Hadzi-Pavlovic, D. (2009). Finding patterns and groupings: I. Introduction to latent class analysis. *Acta Neuropsychiatrica, 21*(6), 312–313.

Hagenaars, J. A., & McCutcheon, A. L. (2002). *Applied latent class analysis.* Cambridge: Cambridge University Press.

Hambleton, R. K., Swaminathan, H., & Rogers, H. J. (1991). *Fundamentals of item response theory.* Newbury Park, CA: Sage.

Hattie, J., Jaeger, R. M., & Bond, L. (1999). Persistent methodological questions in educational testing. *Review of Research in Education, 24*, 393–446.

Helms, B. J., & Gable, R. K. (1989). *School situation survey manual.* Palo Alto: Consulting Psychologists Press/The Mind Garden.

Holland, W., & Wainer, H. (1993). *Differential item functioning.* Mahwah, NJ: Lawrence Erlbaum Associates.

Henson, J. M., Reise, S. P., & Kim, K. H. (2007). Detecting mixtures from structural model differences using latent variable mixture modeling: A comparison of relative model fit statistics. *Structural Equation Modeling: A Multidisciplinary Journal, 14*(2), 202–226.

Johnson, W. J., Dixon, P. N., & Ryan, J. M. (1991, April). *Factorial and Rasch analysis of the Charles F. Kettering Ltd. school climate profile.* Paper presented at the Annual Meeting of the American Educational Research Association, Chicago, IL.

Kite, S. L., Gable, R. K., & Filippelli, L. P. (2010a). *Assessment of students' knowledge of Internet risk and Internet behaviors: Potential threat to bullying and contact by Internetp-Predators.* Paper presented at the Annual Meeting of the Northeastern Educational Research Association, Rocky Hill, CT.

Kite, S. L., Gable, R. K., & Filippelli, L. (2010b). Assessing middle school students' knowledge of conduct/consequences and their behaviors regarding the use of social networking sites. *The Clearing House*, 1939-912X, *83*, 158–163.

Lin, T. H., & Dayton, C. M. (1997). Model selection information criteria for non-nested latent class models. *Journal of Educational and Behavioral Statistics, 22*(3), 249–264.

Lo, Y., Mendell, N. R., & Rubin, D. B. (2001). Testing the number of components in a normal mixture. *Biometrika, 88*(3), 767–778.

Ludlow, L. H., Enterline, S., & Cochran-Smith, M. (2008). *Learning to teach for social justice-beliefs scale:* An application of Rasch measurement principles. *Measurement and Evaluation in Counseling and Development, 20*, 194–214.

Ludlow, L. H., & Haley, S. M. (1995). Rasch model logits: Interpretation, use, and transformation. *Educational and Psychological Measurement, 55*, 967–975.

Magidson, J., & Vermunt, J. K. (2004). Latent class models. In D. Kaplan (Ed.), *The Sage handbook of quantitative methodology for the social sciences* (pp. 175–198). Thousand Oaks, CA: Sage.

Masters, G. N. (1980). *A Rasch model for rating scales (Unpublished doctoral dissertation)*. Chicago, IL: University of Chicago.

Masters, G. N., & Hyde, N. H. (1984). Measuring attitude to school with a latent trait model. *Applied Psychological Measurement, 8*(1), 39–48.

McCoach, D. B. (2002). A validity study of the *school attitude assessment survey* (*SAAS*). *Measurement and Evaluation in Counseling and Development, 35*, 66–77.

McCoach, D. B., & Siegle, D. (2003a). The SAAS-R: A new instrument to identify academically able students who underachieve. *Educational and Psychological Measurement, 63*, 414–429.

McCoach, D. B., & Siegle, D. (2003b). The structure and function of academic self-concept in gifted and general education samples. *Roeper Review, 25*, 61–65.

McCutcheon, A. L. (1987). *Latent class analysis*. Newbury Park, CA: Sage.

McKenna, P. (2007). The rise of cyberbullying. *New Scientist, 195*(2613), 60.

Muthén, B., & Muthén, L. K. (2000). Integrating person-centered and variable-centered analyses: Growth mixture modeling with latent trajectory classes. *Alcoholism: Clinical and Experimental Research, 24*(6), 882–891.

Muthen, L. K., & Muthen, B. O. (2010). *MPLUS user's guide* (6th ed.). Los Angeles, CA: Muthen & Muthen.

Muthén, B. O., & Muthén, L. K. (2000). The development of heavy drinking and alcohol-related problems from ages 18 to 37 in a U.S. national sample. *Journal of Studies on Alcohol, 61*, 290–300.

Nunnally, J. C., & Bernstein, I. H. (1994). *Psychometric theory* (3rd ed.). New York: McGraw-Hill.

Nylund, K. L., Asparouhov, T., & Muthen, B. O. (2007). Deciding on the number of classes in latent class analysis and growth mixture modeling: A Monte Carlo simulation study. *Structural Equation Modeling: A Multidisciplinary Journal, 14*(4), 535–569.

Rasch, G. (1960). *Probabilistic models for some intelligence and attainment tests*. Copenhagen: Danmarks Paedogogiske Institute.

Rasch, G. (1966). An item analysis which takes individual differences into account. *British Journal of Mathematical and Statistical Psychology, 19*, 49–57.

Rensvold, R. B., & Cheung, G. W. (2001). Testing for metric invariance using structural equation models: Solving the standardization problem. In C. A. Schriesheim & L. L. Neider (Eds.), *Research in management: Equivalence in measurement* (pp. 25–50). Greenwich, CT: Information Age Publishing.

Sass, D. A. (2011). Testing measurement invariance and comparing latent factor means within a confirmatory factor analysis framework. *Journal of Psychoeducational Assessment, 29*(4), 347–363.

Schwartz, S. A. (1978). A comprehensive system for item analysis in psychological scale construction. *Journal of Educational Measurement, 15*, 117–123.

Sclove, S. L. (1987). Application of model-selection criteria to some problems in multivariate analysis [Special section]. *Psychometrika, 52*(3), 333–343.

Tormakangas, K. (2011). Advantages of the Rasch measurement model in analyzing educational tests: An applicator's reflection. *Educational Research and Evaluation: An International Journal on Theory and Practice, 17*(5), 307–320.

Tovar, E., & Simon, M. A. (2010). Factorial structure and invariance analysis in *sense of belonging scales. Measurement and Evaluation in Counseling and Development, 43*(3), 199–217.

Vermunt, J. K., & Magidson, J. (2002). Latent class cluster analysis. In J. A. Hagenaars & A. L. McCutcheon (Eds.), *Applied latent class analysis* (pp. 89–106). Cambridge: Cambridge University Press.

Vermunt, J. K., & Magidson, J. (2004). Latent class analysis. In M. S. Lewis-Beck, A. Bryman, & T. F. Liao (Eds.), *The sage encyclopedia of social sciences research methods* (pp. 549–553). Thousand Oakes, CA: Sage Publications.

Vuong, Q. H. (1989). Likelihood ratio tests for model selection and non-nested hypotheses. *Econometrica, 57*(2), 307–333.

Weiss, D. J., & Yoes, M. E. (1991). Item response theory. In R. Hambleton & J. Zaal (Eds.), *Advances in educational and psychological testing: Theory and applications* (pp. 69–95). New York, NY: Kluwer Academic/Plenum Publishers.

Wilson, M. (2005). *Constructing measures: An item response modeling approach.* New York, NY: Taylor & Francis.

Wirth, R. J., & Edwards, M. C. (2007). Item factor analysis: Current approaches and future directions. *Psychological Methods, 12*(1), 58–79.

Wright, B. D., & Linacre, M. (1998). *Winsteps*. Chicago, IL: Mesa Press.

Wright, B. D., & Masters, G. N. (1982). *Rating scale analysis*. Chicago, IL: Mesa Press.

Wright, B. D., & Stone, M. H. (1979). *Best test design*. Chicago, IL: Mesa Press.

Chapter 6
Evidence Based on Relations to Other Variables: Bolstering the Empirical Validity Arguments for Constructs

Definition

Recall that validity evidence for the instrument content argument focused on experts' judgments regarding the adequacy with which the instrument's items reflected specified categories in the content universe and evidence for the validity of the internal structure examined the degree to which the items and the dimensions conformed to our structural expectations. If the evidence that we gather to support the content and the internal structure of the instrument supports our underlying theory, then we have good reason to continue the validation process with the instrument under development. These constructs have been previously specified through the conceptual and operational definitions of the affective characteristic. The argument that the instrument actually measures the construct(s) requires that relationships among the items (operational definitions) comprising the instrument are supportive of the expected internal structure.

However, additional validity evidence is necessary to bolster the argument that the proposed scales actually reflect the constructs of interest. Another important source of validity evidence derives from analyses of the relationship of the newly created scale to external variables. External variables can include criteria that the measure is designed to predict, criteria that predict the measure, and other measures that are designed to measure the same or similar constructs (AERA, APA and NCME 1999). Thus, "evidence based on relations to other variables refers to traditional forms of criterion related evidence for validity such as correlations with external criteria relevant to the attributes measured (e.g., other test scores, grades, supervisor ratings)" (Sireci and Parker 2006, p. 28). Evidence based on relations to other variables also includes concepts such as convergent and discriminant validity, which were historically subsumed in the "construct validity" literature. This evidence may be gathered through "traditional concurrent and predictive validity studies, as well as more comprehensive investigations of the relationships among the test scores and other variables" (Sireci and Parker 2006, p. 28) using methods such as multitrait-multimethod studies, evaluation of the nomological net

D. B. McCoach et al., *Instrument Development in the Affective Domain*,
DOI: 10.1007/978-1-4614-7135-6_6,

through correlational studies and/or structural equation modeling, and validity generalization (Schmidt 1988; Sireci 2006).

It is essential that measures from the newly developed instrument demonstrate a pattern of external relationships to specified variables, scales from other known instruments, or other external criteria in a manner that is consistent with theoretical expectations. "Constructs cannot be defined only in terms of operational definitions but also must demonstrate relationships (or lack thereof) with other constructs and observable phenomena" (Raykov and Marcoulides 2011, p. 8). When these patterns exist in a manner judged to be consistent with the conceptual and operational definitions, this provides important additional validity evidence. Thus, providing evidence for the validity of constructs is an *ongoing process* of testing hypotheses regarding both internal and external response-data relationships.

The sections that follow provide suggestions for collecting and analyzing empirical evidence on the external relationships of the instrument to other variables or constructs of interest in order to bolster the case for the validity of construct interpretations.

Evidence

We gather empirical evidence of the validity of construct interpretations by administering the instrument to a representative sample of respondents for which the instrument was designed. Empirical analyses of these data should support the theoretically based logical arguments regarding the existence of meaningful constructs. This chapter describes several designs (i.e., known groups analysis, experimental studies, correlational studies) and analytical techniques for gathering validity evidence based on relations to other variables (i.e., correlation, multiple regression, logistic regression/discriminant function analysis, and structural equation modeling).

Evidence Based on Discriminant and Convergent Relations

Correlation

The most commonly employed statistical technique for examining the relationship of obtained scores to scores external to the instrument is correlation. Unfortunately, many researchers fail to appreciate the richness of this strategy because their analysis is not grounded in the theory underlying the variables. Some researchers continually list correlations between their target instrument and another instrument without including statements regarding the theoretical meaning of the observed correlation. For example, a researcher states that his new scale correlates 0.20 with another scale with no explanation of whether this magnitude of relationship is supportive of the validity of a construct interpretation on the basis of the theory underlying the two variables. Is this correlation of 0.20 indicative of a correlation between two constructs that should hypothetically be correlated? Is it indicative of a lack of relationship between two variables that should not be correlated? As an aside, in our experience, it can be difficult to build a convincing validity argument based on correlations of 0.20. Think about all of the constructs that are hypothetically correlated at 0.20! Therefore, in general, a correlation of 0.20 between your scale and some other scale or construct does not usually provide very convincing evidence that you are measuring what you claim to be measuring.

Many papers merely contain lists of correlations with other measures with no theoretical arguments supportive of validity interpretations for the construct. The instrument developer must present a compelling argument for how the theoretical construct of interest can be inferred from the various sources of evidence. When displaying such correlations, it is important to describe the *convergent* and *discriminant* evidence. *Convergent evidence* provides support that a measure is correlated with other variables that claim to measure the same (or a similar) construct. Relationships between the newly created scale and other assessments designed to measure the same or similar constructs provide convergent evidence (AERA, APA, and NCME 1999). Relationships between the newly created scale and measures of hypothetically different constructs provide discriminant evidence (AERA, APA, and NCME 1999). In other words, did the variables correlate as predicted (convergent evidence) or did they not correlate as predicted (discriminant evidence) based on the theoretical framework underlying the variables?

Simply put, all arguments for the validity of construct interpretations must be based upon theories underlying the variables in question. This amplifies the importance of developing clear conceptual definitions during the initial stages of the instrument design process. From these conceptual definitions and their theoretical base, we generate hypotheses regarding the traits measured by the instrument and those from other known instruments. Clearly, the hypotheses need to be specified in advance of gathering the data, so that the resulting data can be seen to support or fail to support the proposed relationship (see the early work of Carmines and Zeller 1979; Cronbach and Meehl 1955). Although the research was completed over 40 years ago, an example from the area of work values illustrates this point.

Example 1 Work Values Inventory

While Super's *Work Values Inventory* was in the prepublication stage, Gable (1970) revised and added selected items to the 15 *WVI* scales and studied the validity of the construct interpretations for the revised *WVI* using a sample of 503 grade 11 students from three school districts. The literature on work values was first reviewed to develop a good understanding of the work values concept and also to identify a list of "known indicators" (Cronbach 1971). These known indicators represent other well-known instruments assessing constructs theoretically related to work values. After identifying the Edwards personal preference schedule

(EPPS) (Edwards 1959), the Kuder preference record (KUD) (Kuder 1949), survey of interpersonal values (SIV) (Gordon 1960), and the study of values (SOV) (Allport et al. 1960), Gable administered normative versions of selected scales from the EPPS and SOV and the complete KUD and SIV measures. In addition, Gable examined Super's stated relationship of work values with aptitude, achievement, social class, and gender. The differential aptitude test (DAT) scores measured aptitude (Bennett et al. 1997), prior year's grades in the content areas provided measures of achievement. Finally, the researcher used the very early Warner et al. (1949) 7-point scale based on head-of-household occupation (1 = highest, 7 = lowest) to measure social class; and coded gender such that male = 1 and female = 0.

Table 6.1 illustrates the use of correlations to examine the validity of construct interpretations for one of the 15 WVI scales labeled "Altruism". Super (1970) had defined Altruism as "an orientation toward helping people". Thus, the researcher hypothesized that teachers and Peace Corps volunteers would be most likely to have high Altruism scores. Prior to gathering the actual data, the researcher generated a priori theoretically based hypotheses about the relationships among the measures. Table 6.1 contains a listing of the measures/constructs used for analysis of the Altruism scale. Each construct label is followed by a +, 0, or − sign to indicate the direction of the hypothesized relationship suggested by the appropriate theories underlying the variables; the table also contains the obtained correlations for the 503 grade 11 students. Given the large sample size, the statistical significance of the correlation coefficient provided very little useful information. Rather, the focus became the direction and magnitude of the relationships in light of theoretical expectations.

The Altruism scale correlated as predicted with several other known measures and variables. For example, people with a high score on the WVI Altruism scale tended to exhibit personality profiles with high Affiliation ($r = 0.47$) and Nurturance ($r = 0.56$) on the *EPPS,* and high interest in Social Service activities ($r = 0.53$) as measured by the *Kuder.* Further, they emphasized the interpersonal value of Benevolence ($r = 0.62$) on the SIV, exhibited a general value orientation with high emphasis in the Social ($r = 0.49$) area on the SOV, and tended to be female ($r = -0.37$). Also, as Super hypothesized, levels of Altruism tended not to be related to aptitude and achievement measures or with social class. Thus, the pattern of correlations supported the validity argument for the construct interpretations of the WVI Altruism scale. These correlations provide context and richness to the interpretation of the Altruism construct. In other words, counselors have more evidence for their understanding and interpretation of the Altruism scale because they know that people with high Altruism scores share certain personality preferences (EPPS), interests (*Kuder*), and values (SIV and SOV, as documented in Table 6.1 and described above.

Although these data represent only one sample, they become part of the ongoing process of amassing validity evidence to provide additional information for the interpretation of the WVI Altruism scores. Of course, the cumulative evidence from several validity studies using different samples of individuals and

Table 6.1 An illustration of examining construct validity using correlations

Instrument	Scale	Direction of hypothesized relationship with WVI Altruism	Correlation[a]
Edwards	Achievement	0	
Personal	Affiliation	+	0.47
Preference	Autonomy	0	
Schedule	Change	0	0.28
	Dominance	0	
	Nurturance	+	0.56
Kuder	Outdoor	0	
Preference	Mechanical	0	
Record	Computational	0	
	Scientific	0	
	Persuasive	0	
	Artistic	0	
	Literary	0	
	Social service	+	0.53
	Clerical	0	
Survey of	Conformity	0	
interpersonal	Recognition	0	
values	Independence	0	
	Benevolence	+	0.62
	Leadership	0	
Study of values	Theoretical	0	
	Economic	0	
	Esthetic	0	
	Social	+	0.49
	Political	0	
Differential	Verbal reasoning	0	
Aptitude	Numerical Reasoning	0	
Test	Abstract reasoning	0	
	Mechanical Reasoning	0	
	Space relations	0	
Achievement	English	0	0.11
	Math	0	
	Science	0	
	Social studies	0	
Social class		0	
Gender[b]		–	–0.37

[a] Only correlations greater than 0.10 have been included; decimals have been omitted
[b] Gender was coded male = 1 and female = 0

constructs permits a fuller exploration of the extent to which newly created scales appear likely to capture the essence of the constructs of interest, based on patterns of correlations within the specified nomological net.

Example 2 The Postpartum Depression Screening Scale (*PDSS*)

The Postpartum Depression Screening Scale (PDSS) (Beck and Gable 2000, 2002) provides a second example of using correlations with other known measures to examine construct validity. The *PDSS* contains 35 items: all are negative feelings to describe how a mother may feel after the birth of her baby (e.g., I felt really overwhelmed; I felt like I was losing my mind). Mothers describe their degree of disagreement or agreement with each statement on a 5-point Likert response scale ranging from 1 (*strongly disagree*) to 5 (*strongly agree*). Thus, higher scores indicate higher levels of postpartum depression. Each of the seven dimensions (i.e., Sleeping/Eating Disturbances, Anxiety/Insecurity, Emotional Lability, Cognitive Impairment, Loss of Self, and Contemplating Hurting Oneself) contains five items. The *PDSS* is designed to measure a mood disorder, postpartum depression, which mothers may experience any time during the 1 year after delivery of the child. All of the *PDSS* stems originated from actual quotes from women who had participated in Beck's (1992, 1993, 1995, 1996) qualitative research studies of postpartum depression.

In developing the *PDSS*, the authors identified a group of 150 mothers who were between 2 and 12 weeks postpartum and had no history of diagnosable depression during the pregnancy. This diagnostic sample completed three self-report depression inventories in random order: the *PDSS*, the Edinburgh Postnatal Depression Scale (Cox et al. 1987), and the *Beck Depression Inventory-II* (Beck et al. 1996). Each mother then participated in a structured interview using the Structured Clinical Interview for DSM-IV Axis I Disorders (Spitzer et al. 1978). Using the *SCID* interview, the researchers classified the mothers into one of three groups (i.e., No Depression, $N = 104$; Depressive Disorder, $N = 28$, and Major Depression, $N = 18$). Beck and Gable (2000, 2002) examined "test-criterion relationships" (i.e., the criterion was postpartum depression group membership) by computing correlations among the *PDSS* Total score, total scores from two other self-report depression inventories (the *EPDS* and the *BDI-II*), and depression diagnostic status as derived from the *SCID* interview. They found that the *PDSS* Total score was strongly correlated with *BDI-II* score ($r = 0.81$), *EPDS* score ($r = 0.79$), and *SCID* diagnostic status (i.e., depression vs. no depression; $r = 0.70$). Thus the *PDSS* was highly associated with both other established self-report depression inventories as well as depression status as ascertained by a clinical interview. Collecting evidence of convergent validity using multiple methods provides validity evidence for the *PDSS* (Beck and Gable 2002).

Multitrait-Multimethod Matrix

The multitrait-multimethod (MTMM) matrix technique (Campbell and Fiske 1959) is a classic method for systematically examining evidence of convergent and discriminant validity. MTMM is essentially a systematic way of analyzing correlation coefficients from multiple traits (constructs) using multiple methods. MTMM examines more than one trait and more than one method in an attempt to separate method-specific and trait-specific variance (Eid and Nussbeck 2009). The use of CFA techniques to analyze MTMM data has contributed to its recent resurgence as an analytic technique in validity studies. After briefly describing the rationale for the MTMM and its associated vocabulary, we briefly describe the conceptual framework for using MTMM analyses to establish evidence of validity and provide a short overview of standard CFA procedures for analyzing MTMM data.

Rationale

Campbell and Fiske (1959) employed the terms *convergent* and *discriminant* validity; however, given the current focus of the Standards for Educational and Psychological Testing (AERA, APA, and NCME 1999) on the accumulation of evidence, the current standards refer to convergent evidence and discriminant evidence. According to the *Standards*, "relationships between the test scores and other measures intended to assess similar constructs provide convergent evidence, whereas relationships between test scores and measures purportedly of different constructs provide discriminant evidence" (AERA, APA, and NCME 1999, p. 14).

To understand these terms, consider the process of validating a new instrument. The theory underlying the instrument provides guidance about how scores on the new instrument should relate to scores on other *known* instruments that measure the same or similar constructs (convergent evidence). In addition, scores should be essentially unrelated to scores from other measures that measure unrelated constructs (discriminant evidence).

For example, in the previous section we predicted that the new *Work Values Inventory (WVI)* Altruism scale should correlate positively with the *SIV* Benevolence scale (convergent validity); however, it should not correlate with the *SIV* Conformity scale (discriminant validity). In other words, a predictable pattern of high correlations and low correlations can provide evidence of construct validity.

Campbell and Fiske (1959) describe the score on a given scale as a trait-method unit. That is, the trait being measured (e.g., Altruism) is assessed by a particular method (e.g., self-report rating scale). The resulting score received on the Altruism scale then reflects variation due to the trait "Altruism" and variation due to the self-report measurement. Studying the pattern of correlations between the same and different traits (operationally defined as scales or measures) using the same and different measurement methods (e.g., self-report, teacher rating, behavioral observations, etc.) enables us to determine how much of the variation is due to the differences in the traits being measured and how much of the variance is due to using different measurement techniques to measure the same construct.

The goal of the MTMM technique is to estimate the relative contributions of the trait and method variance to the respective correlation coefficient. To achieve these goals, it is essential to measure more than one trait measured by more than one method. For example, Campbell and Fiske (1959) illustrate the technique using the traits of Courtesy, Honesty, Poise, and School Drive assessed by two different methods: peer ratings and self-report. (Readers should note that the Altruism, Benevolence, and Conformity example presented earlier illustrated the concepts of convergent and discriminant validity but does not really fit the MTMM framework, because it employed only one method, self-report). Ideally, to fully exploit MTMM, it is best to collect information on at least three different traits using at least three different methods (Marsh and Grayson 1995).

Analysis Strategy

Figure 6.1 contains a MTMM shell, used to illustrate the strategy for estimating the relative contributions of trait and method variance, along with convergent and discriminant validity. For this example, self-concept traits A, B, and C (e.g., peer relations, physical abilities, and school) are measured by methods 1 and 2 (e.g., self-report and peer rating), resulting in six variables. The intercorrelations among these six variables along with the reliabilities of each variable form the basis for the MTMM. These reliabilities can be either internal consistency or stability estimates. Figure 6.1 contains a traditional MTMM data display. The diagonal entries in parentheses are *reliability diagonals.* The reliabilities are calculated for the same trait and using the same method so the reliability diagonal contains monotrait-monomethod (MM) values. The entries in the solid triangles represent intercorrelations among different traits using the same method, so they are heterotrait-monomethod (HM) values. Further, the correlations between the same trait using different methods yield entries in the *validity diagonals*, also referred to as mono-trait heteromethod values. (These entries are, in fact, similar to the correlations we discussed in the earlier section entitled "Correlation"). Finally, the two dashed-line triangles contain correlations between different traits using different methods, which are known as heterotrait-heteromethod (HH) values.

First, the entries in the reliability diagonals should indicate that a sufficient amount of reliable variance is present in each measure. Thus, ideally, we would like the reliability diagonals to be high: usually 0.80 or greater. The reliability diagonal also places a ceiling on the magnitude of the correlations in the other portions of the MTMM matrix; the correlation of two different traits using the same method and the correlation of the same trait using two different method should not be higher than the reliability coefficient of the measure with the lowest reliability in that pair. Second, the entries in the validity diagonal indicate

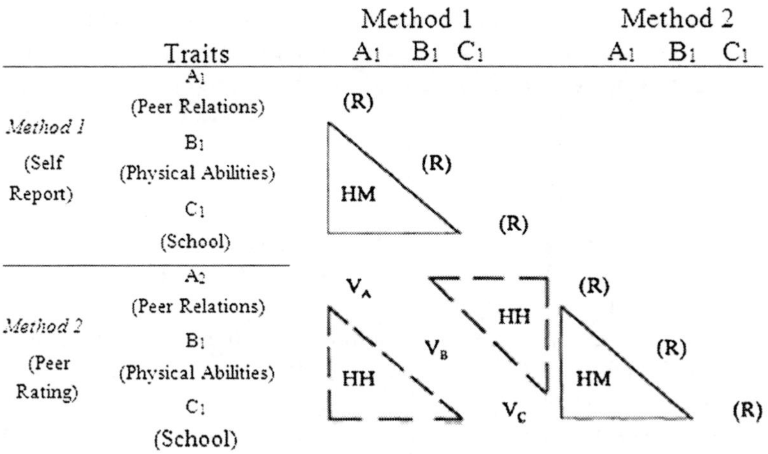

Fig. 6.1 An example of a multitrait-multimethod matrix

convergent validity; they represent the correlation of the same trait using two different methods. These entries in the validity diagonal should be reasonably high and consistent with theoretical expectations. If entries in the validity diagonal are very low, that would call into question whether the different methods were in fact measuring the same trait. Third, each respective validity diagonal value (i.e., V_A) should be higher than the correlations in the adjacent HH triangle (dashed-line triangle). That is, the A_1A_2 correlation should exceed the A_1B_2 and A_1C_2 correlations, since the B_2 and C_2 variables have neither trait nor method in common with A. When the A_1A_2 for V_A correlation is higher than the A_1B_2 and A_1C_2 values, we can say that the magnitude of the A_1A_2 validity coefficient is largely due to shared-trait variance and not to variation shared between methods 1 and 2. As noted by Campbell and Fiske (1959), this rule may seem quite obvious; however, it is often violated in the literature. Fourth, the correlation of a variable should be higher when a different method is used to measure the same trait than when the same method is used to measure different traits. Looking at the validity diagonal entry V_A and the HM solid-triangle entries A_1B_1, A_1C_1, and B_1C_1, this means that V_A, which reflects the same trait (A) and different methods (1 and 2), should have a higher value than correlations generated from any combination of variables, which reflect different traits but the same method (i.e., A_1B_1, A_1C_1, and B_1C_1). If this were not the case, this would indicate that much of the magnitude of V_A (A_1A_2) resulted from common variation due to method and not trait. A fifth guideline suggested by Campbell and Fiske (1959) is that each of the HM and HH triangles should exhibit the same pattern of relationships.

Within the traditional Campbell and Fiske approach, it is not possible to separate trait- and method-specific effects from unsystematic, random measurement error (Hovling et al. 2009). However, modern measurement approaches such as confirmatory factor analysis and generalizability theory allow for the separation of trait- and method-specific variance from measurement error (Hovling et al. 2009). Therefore, most modern MTMM research focuses simultaneously on the accumulation of evidence of convergent and discriminant validity and the separation of trait- and method-specific effects from measurement error (Hovling et al. 2009). There are several different CFA models for analyzing MTMM data. The most common are the correlated trait-correlated method model (Grimm and Widaman 2012; Hovling et al. 2009; Marsh and Grayson 1995; Widaman 1985, 1992), the correlated trait uncorrelated method model (Marsh and Grayson 1995), and the correlated trait-correlated uniqueness model (Kenny 1976; Marsh 1989; Marsh and Bailey 1991; Marsh and Grayson 1995).

The correlated trait-correlated method model specifies a latent variable (factor) for each trait in the model and a latent variable (factor) for each method in the model. All of the traits are correlated with each other, and all of the methods are correlated with each other. However, the model does not correlate traits with methods or methods with traits. Therefore, the variance in each of the observed measures is decomposed into three sources: the variance that is explained by the trait, the variance that is explained by the method, and the variance that is unexplained by either the trait or the method, which is the residual variance of the measure. Figure 6.2 depicts the correlated trait-correlated method (CTCM) model. (Note that for simplicity, the error terms for each measure are excluded from the figure). The CTCM model is the most conceptually appealing of the many MTMM models because it fully captures the conceptual framework of Campbell and Fiske's MTMM approach to the study of convergent and discriminant validity. Large trait factor loadings provide evidence of convergent validity, large method factor loadings denote method effects, and small to moderate inter-trait correlations provide evidence of discriminant validity (Marsh and Grayson 1995). Also, using the standardized solution, the sum of the squared trait factor loading, the squared method factor loading, and the error component equals 1.0. Thus these parameter estimates provide the proportion of variance for each measure that is attributable to trait, method, and other effects respectively (Marsh and Grayson 1995). As conceptually pleasing as it is, the CTCM model suffers from some serious analytic shortcomings. First, the CTCM model is notorious for producing nonconvergent and inadmissible solutions (Lance et al. 2002). In practice, the CTCM model may be empirically underidentified under a variety of conditions: small sample sizes, small numbers of traits and methods, and equal factor loadings within factors all appear to result in high rates of model failure for the CTCM model (Kenny and Kashey 1992; Lance et al. 2002; Marsh and Bailey 1991; Marsh et al. 1992).

The correlated trait uncorrelated method model (CTUM) is identical to the CTCM model except that it forces the method factors to be orthogonal to each other. Figure 6.3 depicts the CTUM. The CTUM model also frequently results in improper or non-convergent solutions (Marsh and Grayson 1995); however, it does tend to fare a bit better than the CTCM model. Therefore, if it is reasonable to assume that the method factors are uncorrelated with each other, this model is a viable alternative to the CTCM model. Also, the CTCM model and the CTUM

Fig. 6.2 MTMM: the correlated traits, correlated methods (CTCM) model

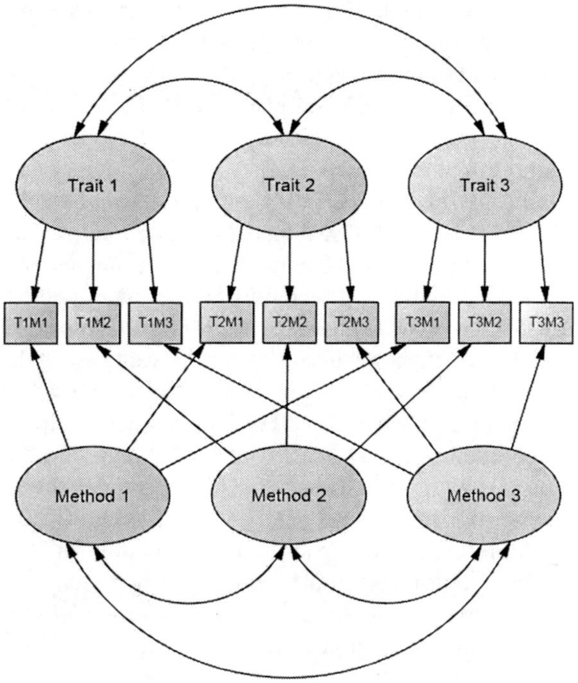

Fig. 6.3 MTMM: the correlated traits, uncorrelated methods (CTUM) model

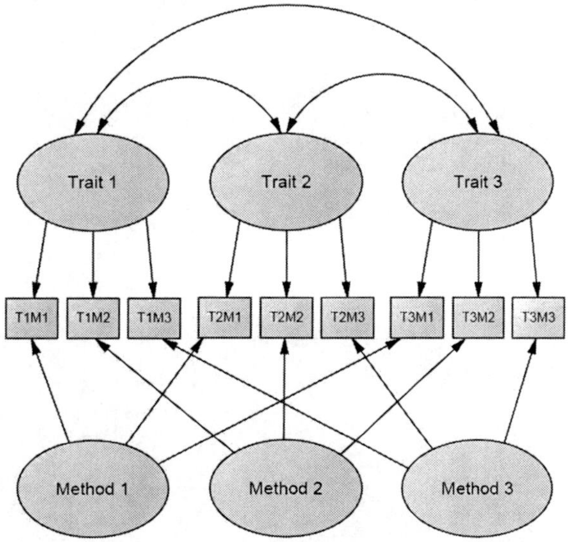

model are nested. Therefore, if both models are estimable, we can compare the fit of the two models to determine the tenability of the assumption that the method factors are uncorrelated.

Given that the CTCM and CTUM models are often inestimable, the correlated traits correlated uniquenesses (CTCU) model emerged as an alternative way to capture method effects (Kenny 1976; Lance et al. 2002; Marsh 1989; Marsh and Bailey 1991). In the CTCU model, traits are modeled as factors, as they were in the CTCM and the CTUM models. However, method effects are captured by estimating correlations among the uniquenesses (errors) of all scores (observed variables) that are collected using the same method. Figure 6.4 depicts the CTCU model. The CTCU model generally results in proper solutions (Marsh and Grayson 1995), which is a huge practical advantage of this model over the CTCM and CTUM models. However, conceptually, the CTCU model suffers from several shortcomings. First, the CTCU model can result in biased parameter estimates for the trait effects. Second, it is not possible to directly estimate the method effects in the CTCU model. Third, the CTCU model does not align with the theoretical framework of MTMM nearly as well as the CTCM model (Lance et al. 2002).

More recent approaches to estimating MTMM have also emerged. These include multilevel multitrait-multimethod analyses (Maas et al. 2009), the correlated trait-correlated method minus one model (Nussbeck et al. 2009), the direct product model (Campbell and O'Connell 1967; Marsh and Grayson 1995), and the three mode model (Oort 2009). Given the analytic complexities inherent in the estimation of these deceptively simple matrices, additional models are likely to continue to propagate within the MTMM literature.

Fig. 6.4 MTMM: the correlated traits, correlated uniqueness (CTCU) model

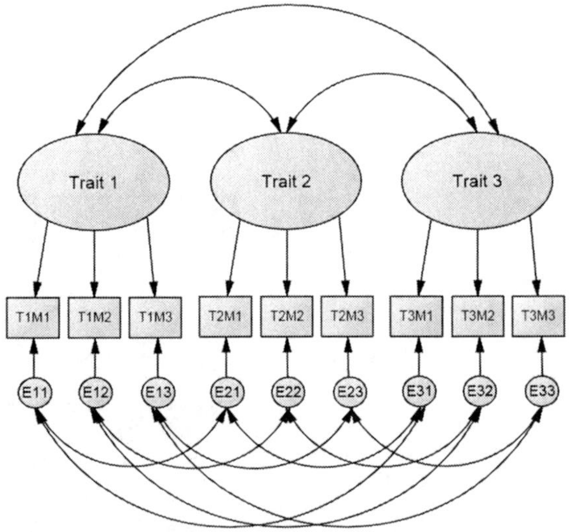

Structural Equation Modeling

Structural equation modeling (SEM) refers to a family of techniques, including path analysis, confirmatory factor analysis, structural regression models, autoregressive models, and latent change models (Raykov and Marcoulides 2006) that utilize the analysis of covariances to explore the relationships among a set of variables and to explain maximum variance within a specified model (Kline 2010). SEM is extremely versatile; it places very few restrictions on the kinds of models that can be tested (Hoyle 1995).[1] SEM has been hailed as "a more comprehensive and flexible approach to research design and data analysis than any other single statistical model in standard use by social and behavioral scientists" (Hoyle 1995, p. 15).

Over the past two decades, SEM has become an increasingly popular data analytic technique used by researchers in all fields of education, psychology, and the social sciences. What was once considered a rather burdensome and complex technique by non-methodologically oriented educational researchers has become a mainstay of many quantitative studies in the field of education. With respect to establishing evidence of relationships among constructs, SEM provides more information than that obtained from simple correlations and regressions, since it allows for the examination of a simultaneous system of multiple variables. Because SEM provides information on both the relationships between the observed variables and the constructs they represent and the relationships among the measured constructs themselves, SEM is an invaluable tool for instrument validation studies. If the results of SEM analyses demonstrate the consistency of the pattern of observed relationships with the existing body of literature, the hypothesized nomological net, and the theoretical rationale of the developer, SEM can help bolster the validity argument of the instrument developer.

Advantages of SEM

SEM offers several advantages over traditional data analytic techniques. SEM allows researchers to estimate the effects of theoretical or hypothetical constructs, commonly called latent variables (Raykov and Marcoulides 2006). In traditional analyses, researchers must confine themselves to estimating effects for measured variables. As we discussed in Chapte 4, a number of measured variables can be used to estimate the effects of a latent variable. The analysis of latent variables is both statistically and conceptually appealing. With SEM, researchers can include latent constructs such as "hope", "motivation", and "self-efficacy" in their analyses. Because SEM allows researchers to distinguish between observed and latent variables and to explicitly model both types of variables, researchers are able to test a wider variety of hypotheses than would be possible with most traditional

[1] Much of the section on Structural Equation Modeling is adapted from McCoach (2003).

statistical techniques (Kline 2010). More importantly, SEM accounts for potential errors of measurement and allows researchers to explicitly account for measurement error (Raykov and Marcoulides 2006).

The ability to separate measurement error or "error variance" from "true variance" is one of the reasons that SEM provides such powerful analyses. In multiple regression, measurement error within the predictor variables attenuates the regression weight from the predictor variable to the dependent variable (Baron and Kenny 1986). Because analyses using SEM use multiple indicators to estimate the effects of latent variables, they correct for the unreliability within the measured predictor variables, and allow for more accurate estimates of the effects of the predictor on the criterion.

In addition, as we already saw in the context of Confirmatory Factor Analysis (in Chapter 4), SEM allows researchers to specify a priori models and to assess the degree to which the data fit the specified model. SEM provides a comprehensive statistical approach to test existing hypotheses about relations among observed and latent variables (Hoyle 1995). In this way, SEM forces the researcher to think critically about the relationships among the variables of interest and the hypotheses being tested. Using SEM to test models that detail particular patterns of relationships among variables of interest can be an important aspect of compiling a validity argument (AERA, APA, and NCME 1999). Cronbach and Meehl (1955) first alluded to the importance and complexity of building argument through the use of nomological networks. In their classic paper, they stated:

> We do not first "prove" the theory, and then validate the test, nor conversely. In any probable inductive type of inference from a pattern of observations, we examine the relation between the total network of theory and observations. The system involves propositions relating test to construct, construct to other constructs, and finally relating some of these constructs to observables. In ongoing research, the chain of inference is very complicated (Cronbach and Meehl 1955, p. 294).

Further, SEM allows researchers to test competing theoretical models to determine which model best reproduces the observed variance/covariance matrix. The ability to test competing theories is invaluable in the instrument validation process, as it can provide evidence which supports or refutes theories, and this in turn can provide evidence in support of or against the validity argument.

Perhaps the most significant advantage of SEM is that it allows researchers to model the direct, indirect, and total effects of a system of variables. Therefore, SEM allows researchers to test for and model mediation within their models. A mediator variable is a "middle man", an intervening variable that explains the relationship between a predictor variable and a dependent variable (Baron and Kenny 1986). An indirect effect refers to the relationship between two variables that is mediated by one or more intervening variables (Raykov and Marcoulides 2006). "If an indirect effect does not receive proper attention, the relationship between two variables of interest may not be fully considered" (Raykov and Marcoulides 2006, p. 7). Because mediational models allow researchers to treat a single variable as both an independent variable and a dependent variable, they provide the researcher with the opportunity to test a variety of complex models. However, the use of mediational models is not without peril. Measurement error in the mediator tends to produce an underestimate of the effect of the mediator and an overestimate of the effect of the independent variable on the dependent variable when all of the path coefficients are positive (Baron and Kenny 1986). Luckily, using latent variable models to develop mediational models eliminates this problem, as SEM accounts for the measurement error in the mediator.

Although SEM models are most commonly used to examine the relationships of a system of variables, they can also be used to model effects across groups or growth across time. SEM models can be used to compare patterns of interrelationships across groups of people, using a procedure called multiple groups SEM or multisample SEM. (Recall that we discussed multiple group CFA, one type of multiple group SEM, in Chapter 5). SEM models can be used to analyze means as well as covariances. For instance, SEM models are often used to model growth over time. This procedure is commonly referred to as growth curve analysis or latent curve analysis. In addition, researchers can also use SEM techniques to model latent means, a procedure referred to as mean structure analysis.

In short, "although partial correlation, ANOVA, and multiple regression analysis can be used to isolate putative causal variables from other variables, SEM is more flexible and comprehensive than any of these approaches, providing means of controlling not only for extraneous or confounding variables but for measurement error as well" (Hoyle 1995, p. 10).

Understanding SEM

The basic building block of any structural equation model is the variance/covariance matrix. In fact, all of the information needed to perform a SEM analysis is contained in the covariance matrix.[2] Therefore, an analyst can create and analyze a SEM without the raw data file. Anytime a researcher publishes the covariance or correlation matrix, other interested researchers should be able to replicate his or her results using the published covariance or correlation matrix.[3] The heart of SEM is the covariance matrix; SEM utilizes the covariance matrix to explain complex patterns of interrelationships among variables.

---

[2] A researcher who is conducting a mean structure analysis or a growth curve analysis would need the means for all of the observed variables as well as the variance/covariance matrix. However, under normal circumstances, the variance/covariance matrix serves as the sufficient statistic for a SEM analysis.

[3] Technically, it is considered proper form to analyze a covariance matrix, but under a variety of conditions analyzing a correlation matrix will produce the same results, as a correlation matrix is simply a standardized version of a covariance matrix.

Path Diagrams

Path diagrams, visual displays of structural equation models, are perhaps the most intuitive way to conceptualize the process of developing and testing a specified model. Any multiple regression model can be reconceptualized as a path model. For example, Fig. 6.5 illustrates path diagram of a multiple regression model with three predictors and a dependent variable. The curved lines among the three predictor variables symbolize the correlations among the variables. Straight arrows connect each of the independent variables to the dependent variable. These arrows are commonly called paths. Just as in multiple regression, these paths represent a measure of the relationship between the predictor variable and the dependent variable *after controlling for* the other variables in the model. Typically, the reported value of a path is the standardized regression coefficient. Notice that all of the variables in the model are indicated by rectangles. In a path diagram, rectangles indicate observed variables. An observed variable is a variable that is actually measured. For example, a student's score on a test or a subscale is an observed variable.

In contrast, latent variables are the hypothetically existing constructs of interest in a study. Examples of latent variables include self-efficacy, peace, intelligence, and apathy. Latent variables cannot be directly measured. Rather they must be

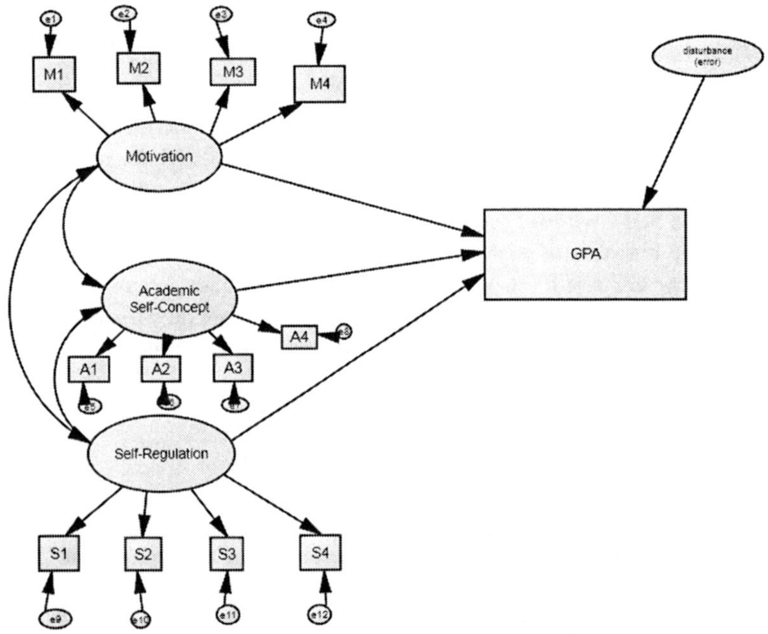

Fig. 6.5 Latent variable regression model path diagram

inferred or derived from the relationships among observed variables that are thought to be measures of the latent variable. In a path diagram, circles indicate latent variables. Generally, we use multiple observed variables as indicators of the latent variable. For example, if a researcher wants to use creativity as a latent variable in his or her model, he or she might use several observed variables including scores on a divergent thinking task, self-report measures, and peer report measures. The model posits that creativity, the latent construct, causes or predicts the responses to the multiple observed variables or indicators. The question of how many observed variables a researcher needs to adequately measure a latent variable is a very complex issue. From a technical point of view, two observed variables might be adequate if there is more than one latent variable in the model. Using three observed variables is technically adequate to estimate a latent variable. From a theoretical point of view, "constructs can differ widely in the extent to which the domain of related observable variables is (1) large or small and (2) specifically or loosely defined" (Nunnally and Bernstein 1994). In general, the more abstract and loosely defined a construct is, the more indicators are necessary to measure the latent variable adequately.

Figure 6.5 illustrates a latent variable model of achievement. Each of the three predictors: motivation, academic self-perceptions, and self-regulation, is measured using four observed variables. These observed variables could be four different subscales that each measure the latent variables. More commonly though, these observed variables are individual items or small clusters of items (sometimes referred to as item parcels) on the subscale of an instrument. The three latent variables are being used to predict GPA. In this model, there are 13 observed variables: 4 variables on each of 3 latent variables and GPA, an observed variable.

In SEM, we distinguish between exogenous and endogenous variables. Exogenous variables remain at the outside edge of the model; they are only predictors of other variables; they are not predicted by any other variables in the model. Exogenous variables may be correlated with other variables, but they never have paths (straight arrowheads) leading into them. Endogenous variables are predicted by one or more variables in the model. However, endogenous variables can also affect other endogenous variables. In a multiple regression model, the independent variables are exogenous; the dependent variable is endogenous. Every endogenous variable in the model contains an error term or residual, often referred to as a *disturbance*. The disturbance represents all other causes of the endogenous variable that are *not* explicitly specified in the model. The proportion of variance explained in an endogenous variable (R^2) is equal to 1− the disturbance variance/ the total variance. In Fig. 6.5, notice GPA, which is an endogenous variable, has a disturbance term. In addition, because each of the observed variables that is predicted by a latent variable is an endogenous variable, each has an error term.

Building a SEM Model

Specification and Identification

A researcher who plans to use SEM first specifies a hypothesized model. At this stage, it is also important to determine whether the model is identified. A model is identified if it is theoretically possible to calculate a unique estimate for every specified parameter (Kline 2010). A parameter is an unknown characteristic of the population that we are trying the estimate in the specified SEM model. In other words, there must be at least as many elements in the variance/covariance matrix[4] as there are parameters to be estimated in the model. In a SEM model, we need to estimate the variances of the exogenous variables (exogenous latent variables, exogenous observed variables, and disturbances/errors) any specified correlations among observed or latent variables, and any direct effects on endogenous variables (Kline 2010). These direct effects include the path coefficients from the latent variables to their indicators, and the path coefficients of the structural paths within the model. Therefore, these elements are the parameters in the model. Generally, we fix the paths of the errors/disturbances to 1 and estimate only their variances. In addition, we must fix one path in each of the latent variables, or fix the factor variance to be 1 in order to scale the latent variable correctly. Let us assume that we have fixed one path from each latent variable to an indicator to be 1, and count the parameters to be estimated in Fig. 6.4. We must estimate two of the three paths from each of the latent variables to its indicators, 8 paths in total. We also must estimate all 12 error variances. In addition, we must estimate the correlations among the two exogenous latent variables and the three structural paths. Finally, we must estimate the variances of the two exogenous variables and the disturbance variances of the endogenous variables. Therefore, this model contains $8 + 12 + 1 + 3 + 2 + 2 = 28$ parameters to be estimated.

For n observed variables in the model, there are $(n\ (n + 1))/2$ unique elements in the variance/covariance matrix. When there are exactly as many elements of the variance/covariance matrix as there are parameters to be estimated in a model, the model is "just identified". In this case, the model has equal numbers of estimated parameters and observations within the variance/covariance matrix. A just identified model has 0 degrees of freedom, and can perfectly reproduce the parameters from the variance/covariance matrix. Therefore, a just identified model always fits the data perfectly (Kline 2010). When a model has more elements in the variance/covariance than parameters to be estimated, the model is "overidentified". The degrees of freedom in an overidentified model equal the number of observations in the variance/covariance model minus the number of parameters to be freely estimated in the model. Although it is possible to find a unique solution for overidentified models, the solution may not perfectly reproduce the variance/

[4] If there are n observed variables in the model, there are $(n\ (n + 1))/2$ unique elements in the variance/covariance matrix.

covariance matrix (Kline 2010). Therefore, overidentified models allow researchers to test the fit of the data to the model, a procedure that is very useful for theory testing. In Fig. 6.5, there are 12 observed variables in the model; therefore, there are $[(12 \times 13)/2] = 78$ unique elements in the variance covariance matrix. How many parameters are being estimated in the model? We are estimating 2 variances (one for each of the exogenous latent variables), 2 disturbances (one for each of the endogenous variables), 3 paths, 1 correlation, 12 error variances, and 8 paths. Therefore, there are 28 parameters to be estimated in the model. Thus, there are $78 - 28 = 50$ degrees of freedom in the model depicted in Fig. 6.4.

For a SEM model to be identified, there must be at least as many elements in the variance/covariance as there are parameters to be estimated within the model. In addition, both the measurement model and the structural model must be identified in order for the entire latent variable model to be identified. However, having met this necessary condition does not ensure that the specified model is indeed identified. The issue of identification is complex, and presenting all of the rules for identification is beyond the scope of this chapter. (For a thorough treatment of identification, see Kenny et al. 1998).

Model Specification

There are two components to a structural equation model: the measurement model and the structural model. The measurement model depicts the relationships between the observed variables (also called indicators) and their underlying latent variables (Kline 2010). In Chapter 4, we provided an introduction to confirmatory factor analysis, which is a subtype of SEM that focuses on the analysis of the measurement model. The measurement model generally does not include directional linkages among the primary variables of interest. Instead measurement models focus on the measurement of the latent variables. The structural model depicts the predictive paths and consists of the structural paths between and among the latent variables and any observed variables that are not indicators of an underlying variable. In Fig. 6.6, there are three structural paths. Perhaps more interesting are the structural paths that we are constraining to 0. The model in Fig. 6.4 specifies that after controlling for motivation, the direct pathways between interest and achievement and between utility and achievement are equal to zero. We have placed these are restrictions by not estimating a pathway between the two variables. Assessing the fit of the structural model by comparing this model to the just identified structural model allows us to assess the plausibility of making these constraints.

The SEM analyst engages in a two-step modeling process (Kline 2010). Before analyzing the full structural model, the researcher examines the adequacy of the

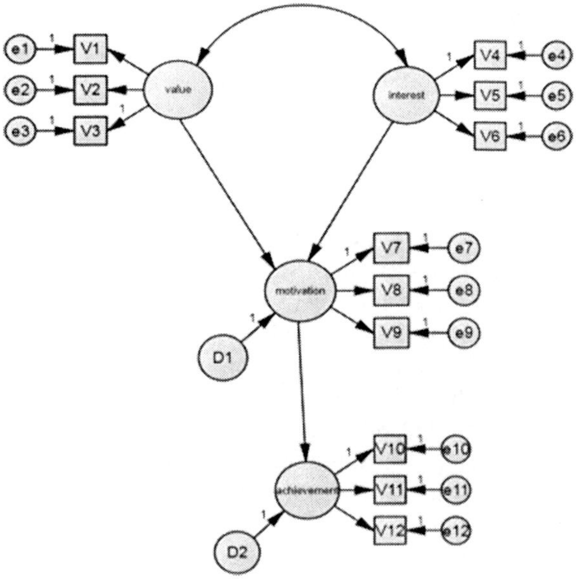

Fig. 6.6 Latent variable structural equation model

measurement model by conducting a confirmatory factor analysis of all of the latent variables and observed variables in the structural equation model and evaluates the plausibility of the measurement model. If the fit of the measurement model is unsatisfactory, the fit of the full model will also be unsatisfactory. Therefore, any problems in the measurement model should be addressed before proceeding to the structural analysis. Next, the researcher analyzes the structural model, evaluates the model fit, makes any necessary changes to the model, and evaluates the fit of the revised model (Kline 2010, pp. 49–50). Sometimes, a researcher may compare the fit of two or more competing models. At a minimum, we recommend comparing the fit of the conceptual (hypothesized) structural model to the fit of the just identified structural model. The Chi-square difference test between these two models provides an omnibus test of the deleted paths from the conceptual model. If the Chi-square difference test is statistically significant, then it is important to examine the magnitude and statistical significance of the path coefficients from the just identified model. We retain any statistically significant structural paths from the just identified model and rerun the structural model with the hypothesized paths and the non-hypothesized paths that were statistically significant in the just identified model. In our example, the two deleted paths are the pathways from the two exogenous variables (utility and interest) to achievement. Therefore, we would run a model that includes these deleted paths, and we would examine the magnitude and statistical significance of the two structural pathways that we believe to be absent, retaining structural pathways that appear warranted by the analysis.

When SEM Gives You Inadmissible Results

In addition to examining the parameter estimates, the tests of significance, and the fit indices, it is very important to examine several other areas of the output to ensure that the program ran correctly. The variances of the exogenous variables should be positive and statistically significant. The variances of the error terms and the disturbances should also be positive and statistically significant. As in multiple regression, the standardized path coefficients should be between −1.00 and +1.00. Further, the standardized error terms and disturbances should fall in the range of 0.00–1.00. Negative error variances and standardized regression weights above 1 are called Heywood cases; they indicate the presence of an *inadmissible solution*. Heywood cases can be caused by specification errors, outliers that distort the solution, a combination of small sample sizes and having only one or two indicators per factor, or extremely high or low population correlations that will result in empirical underidentifaction (Kline 2010). When any of these problems result in a Heywood case, the SEM output cannot be trusted. The analyst must try to find the cause of the Heywood case, respecify the model to fix the problem, and run the data again. It is never advisable to interpret output that contains any Heywood cases or inadmissible solutions.

Another possible problem is that the SEM program will reach the maximum number of iterations before it finds a maximum likelihood solution that minimizes the distance between the observed and model-implied covariance matrices. This problem is known as "lack of convergence". When this happens, the output should not be trusted. Large or infinite numbers of iterations can be signs of a problem such as an underidentified model, an empirically underidentified model, bad start values, extreme multicollinearity, a tolerance value approaching zero, or other specification error (Kline 2010). Some computer programs are set for a maximum number of iterations. Once the program reaches this limit, it produces output based on the last iteration. Again, do not trust the output. If the program fails to converge, it is necessary to inspect the output for possible errors or clues to the reason for the non-convergence; however, analysts should not interpret output if the computer fails to converge upon a proper solution.

Assumptions and Requirements of SEM

Normality

Many of the assumptions of SEM are similar to the assumptions of multiple linear regression. Namely, standard SEM techniques that use maximum likelihood estimation assume that the variables of interest are drawn from a continuous and multivariate normal population (Kaplan 2000). Maximum likelihood estimation performs optimally when the data are continuous and normally distributed. Much has been written on the effects of violating the assumption of normality. Generally, SEM is fairly robust to small violations of the normality assumption; however, extreme non-normality can cause problems. Newer SEM methods allow for the analysis of categorical, ordinal, and other non-normal response variables (Muthen and Muthen 1998–2007). These are especially useful for the analysis of Likert scale data, which can easily be treated as ordinal within Mplus. See Boivard and Koziol (2012) for an excellent chapter that describes measurement models for ordered categorical indicators and Edwards et al. (2012) for a chapter on using categorical data within an SEM framework.

Linearity

As in multiple regression, SEM assumes that the variables of interest are linearly related to each other. In addition, there are specialized techniques to examine nonlinear effects using SEM; however, reviewing these techniques is beyond the scope of this paper. Interested readers should consult Marsh et al. (2012) for a detailed treatment of interaction effects in SEM.

Sampling

Standard SEM assumes that the data represent a simple random sample from the population. The effects of non-independence of observations can bias the results of the analysis. Recently developed multilevel SEM models can analyze data that has been collected using multistage or cluster sampling techniques (Kaplan 2000). For more information about multilevel SEM, see Rabe-Hesketh and Skrondal (2012).

Because standard SEM techniques use maximum likelihood estimation[5] to minimize the discrepancy between the observed covariance matrix and the model-implied covariance matrix, SEM is a large sample technique. Although there are no definitive rules for a minimum sample size, there are several rules of thumb. Generally speaking, under most circumstances, sample sizes below 100 are considered to be too small to use SEM techniques (Kline 2010; Schumacker and Lomax 1996) sample sizes of at least 200 are usually recommended. Schumacker and Lomax's examination of the published SEM literature revealed that many SEM articles used sample sizes of 250–500. Generally speaking, sample sizes of 200 or more are generally considered sufficient for estimating most types of SEM models, especially if the variables are normally distributed and obtained from a simple random sample of subjects. However, very complex models may require larger sample sizes. As the ratio of the number of cases to the number of

[5] There are other estimation methods, but they are beyond the scope of this chapter. For more information about alternative estimation methods, see Kaplan (2009) or Hoyle (1995).

parameters declines, the estimates generated by SEM become more unstable (Kline 2010).

Range of Values

Because SEM is essentially a correlational technique, anything that affects the magnitudes of the covariances among the variables in the model will impact the SEM analysis. For example, restriction of range in one variable generally attenuates the covariance between that variable and any other variables in the model, resulting in small path coefficients leading to and from that variable.

Common Mistakes and Misunderstandings in SEM

Correlation Versus Causation

The purpose of path analysis is to determine if the causal inferences posited by a researcher are consistent with the data (Bollen 1989). Therefore, SEM techniques inform us about the degree of model data fit (or misfit). However, knowing that a specified model is consistent with the data says nothing about whether the model is "correct". There are several reasons that it is inappropriate to view a good-fitting structural equation model as correct, or indicative of causality. First, for every SEM that a researcher specifies, there are other equivalent models that will result in the sample Chi-square and fit indices. For example, specifying that $X \rightarrow Y$ is equivalent to specifying that $Y \rightarrow X$. For complex models, there are often several (if not dozens!) of functionally equivalent models that the researcher has not tested. Therefore, the model that is tested provides good fit to the data; however, many other equivalent models will provide equally good fit to the data, and the possibility exists that an untested model will provide even better fit to the data.

To use correlational techniques to infer that X causes Y, a researcher must meet three criteria (Kline 2010). First, X must precede Y temporally. In other words, if the two variables are measured at the same time, it is impossible to infer causality from SEM models. Therefore, it is impossible to make causal claimed based on the results of cross-sectional SEM models. Second, the direction of the causal relation must be correctly specified. The measurement of X before Y is necessary but not sufficient to prove a causal relation. For example, if high academic motivation results in high academic achievement, but the measures of academic achievement are taken prior to the measures of motivation, one could erroneously conclude that high academic achievement causes high academic motivation. In practice, it is often difficult or impossible to meet criteria 2, as it is often difficult or impossible to develop theories and gather data in a way that allows a researcher to know that the direction of the causal relation is correctly specified. Finally, the relationship between the causal variable and the criterion variable must not vanish when external causes such as common causes of both variables are partialed out (Kline 2010). This is often referred to as the omitted variable problem. A researcher may erroneously conclude that X causes Y when in reality, Z, a variable that was not included in the model causes both X and Y. For example, a researcher may assert that having high academic self-efficacy causes high academic achievement, when in fact having high academic ability causes both high academic self-efficacy and high academic achievement. Satisfying these three criteria is extremely difficult. Therefore, the ability to infer causality using SEM represents the very rare exception rather than the rule.

Multiple Groups SEM

Several specialized SEM techniques further expand the variety of research questions that can be answered using SEM. For instance, multisample or multiple groups SEM analysis involves the specification of a theoretical model with more than one sample simultaneously. Multiple groups analysis allows the researcher to compare the patterns of interrelationships among latent variables across multiple samples. Researchers can use this approach to analyze experimental, cross-sectional, or longitudinal data. We discussed using multiple groups CFA to determine measurement equivalence in Chapter 5. Multiple groups SEM includes multiple groups CFA and can be used to examine between group differences in the structural pathways. Exploring the differences in the measurement and structural relationships among key constructs can aid in our understanding of the constructs of interest.

Finally, until this point, we have talked only about modeling the covariances among variables. However, structural equation models can also include means. A mean structure analysis includes the variance/covariance matrix as well as the means of the observed variables. Using mean structure analysis allows researchers to model and test hypotheses about the means of latent variables (Kline 2010). These models provide a flexible alternative to traditional analysis of variance models (Raykov and Marcoulides 2006). Latent change (or latent growth) models represent a special class of mean structure models that allow researchers to model growth and change over time (Duncan et al. 1999). We can also examine differences in latent means to better understand between group differences on the constructs of interest.

SEM provides an extremely versatile method to model very specific hypotheses involving systems of latent variables. Researchers can use SEM to study patterns of interrelationships among variables, to compare different groups to each other, to model latent means, to study change over time, and to do many other types of sophisticated analyses. Therefore, SEM is crucial analytic technique for researchers who want to examine and test the nomological net among a series of latent and/or observed variables. SEM can be used to bolster validation, particularly if researchers are interested in measuring the variation of an attribute in response to variation in test scores (Borsboom 2005). In other words, researchers can use a SEM framework to understand how "psychological attributes relate to empirical observations" (Borsboom 2005, p. 167). A series of theoretical modeling studies into working memory and reasoning ability directly reflect this approach to validity (Süss et al. 2002; Wilhelm and Schulze 2002). Wilhelm and Schulze (2002) argue that "intelligence structure" relies heavily on measurement instruments (p. 550). As a result, their experimental approach focused on employing confirmatory factor analyses and correlational analyses to establish converging conclusions regarding speeded and unspeeded reasoning. The "clear ordering of linear relationships between mental speed and speeded and unspeeded reasoning" (p. 550) led the authors to conclude that a structural model successfully mirrored the assumptions of their theoretical view and provided a full explanation of the variability in the reasoning tests. Their supplied evidence of the relationship between these two reasoning abilities "that is not explainable only through measurement artifacts originating from timed administration of reasoning tests" (p. 550).

In a similar study of working memory, researchers selected tasks from a pool of items that had minimal overlap with other cognitive processes not associated with working memory. As a result, the researchers concluded that observed common variance between the working memory and the reasoning tests could hardly be attributed to something other than working memory capacity. The researchers tested their theoretical model and concluded that the fit of structural equation models could be improved by relating working memory and intelligence on the level of specified factors. SEM framework indicated that the paths from working memory to intelligence factors were highly specific. SEM provided a "fruitful, general framework for classifying cognitive abilities" (Süss et al. 2002, p. 284).

Test Criterion Relationships

The consideration of how well the instrument's scores predict a criterion addresses the general question: "How accurately do instrument scores predict criterion performance?" Depending upon the time frame employed in the validity inference, two types of validity studies are possible: concurrent and predictive.

Evidence of Concurrent Validity

In studying concurrent validity, the instrument is administered, and then, at *approximately the same time,* data are obtained from another instrument or through observation techniques (i.e., the criterion), so that the relationship between the instrument and the criterion can be established and analyzed with respect to the theory underlying the instrument and the criterion. The most frequent statistic employed is the simple correlation coefficient. For example, we could administer the *School Attitude Assessment Survey-Revised (SAAS-R)* to students (McCoach and Siegle 2003a). The *SAAS-R* is designed to measure factors that are related to academic underachievement: motivation/self-regulation, academic self-perceptions, goal valuation, attitudes toward teachers and classes, and attitudes toward school. Concurrently, we could gather information about the students' current grade point averages (GPA). If the *SAAS-R* measures factors related to academic achievement and underachievement, then we should be able to predict students' current GPAs at least moderately well using the *SAAS-R*. To gather evidence of the validity of the *SAAS-R* as an accurate predictor of current achievement behaviors, first we would correlate the each of students' scores on each of the subscales to their current GPA. (Alternatively, we could do this in a latent variable framework and correlate each of the five factors to GPA). The correlations between the subscales and GPA should be at least moderate. They need to be high enough to suggest some diagnostic utility for the scale.

For our next example, imagine that we want to gather information related to teaching effectiveness for a large number of teachers, and we have created a principal observation form to evaluate teachers' classroom performance. We can examine the relationship between the principal's rating of the teachers' performance and the teacher effectiveness score derived from value added measures. The higher the correlation between the two measures, the greater the evidence of validity for both measures, so each could serve as a criterion for the other. One of the most troubling issues in the assessment of teacher effectiveness is that the correlations between different measures of the teacher effectiveness are troublingly low. Readers may feel that this example provides convergent validity evidence, rather than evidence of concurrent validity, and we could certainly frame the analysis in that way. The lines between convergent validity evidence and concurrent validity evidence are often blurred. However, it is important to remember that the name that we attach to an analysis is far less important than the systematic argument that we are building for the utility of the instrument using a variety of sources of evidence.

In the context of an instrument-criterion validity study, examining the correlations between shorter instruments and other, longer standardized measures provides evidence concurrent validity, and allows us to assess the viability of substituting a quick student-rating procedure for a more time consuming procedure or assessment. For example, a test manual from an IQ measure contains a correlation of 0.90 between the long and short form administered concurrently to a sample of students. The instrument-criterion (concurrent) validity of the data from the short form is then supported as an estimate of the scores from the long form, so that practitioners can confidently use the short form in the midst of testing time constraints.

Known Groups Analysis

Providing concurrent evidence of "test-criterion relationships" can involve the examination of group differences as well as the examination of correlations. One strong source of evidence from concurrent test criterion relationships is the examination of "known groups". If groups that are known to differ on the characteristic(s) in question differ on the scale(s), this provides evidence for the validity of the instrument. Known groups analysis demonstrates that the instrument successfully distinguishes between a group of people who are known to possess a given characteristic and a group (or groups) who do not have high levels of the trait. The key to this analysis is that the existence of the trait in the groups has to be clearly documented with some external criterion. The groups are then administered the new instrument, and researchers assess how accurately the instrument is able to sort participants into their respective groups using an analysis such as a *t*-test, ANOVA, logistic regression, or discriminant function analysis. The magnitude of the observed difference between the groups should be similar to the expected difference, given the known differences between the groups. In other words, if two groups are radically different on the construct in the population, then large differences on the instrument would be supportive evidence that we are measuring the construct in question; small differences between two groups would not. In general, we have found known groups analyses to be an underutilized technique by the novice instrument developer. Often, the data needed to compare known groups is relatively easy to collect, and it can often provide compelling evidence of for the construct validity of an instrument.

Several examples should clarify the known groups technique and demonstrate its potential uses within instrument validation. Imagine that a researcher is developing a measure of criminal thinking. For such a measure to provide evidence of construct validity and to have any level of practical utility, it should be able to distinguish between criminal and non-criminal populations. One straightforward way to examine this would be to administer the instrument to incarcerated criminal populations and to college students. Although some college students may be criminals, and some inmates may be wrongly imprisoned, on average the means for the incarcerated population should be radically different from the means in the college population. If they are not, that calls into question whether the instrument is in fact actually measuring criminal thinking.

In the early development of some paper-and-pencil-anxiety measures, groups of high-anxiety and low-anxiety people took part in physiological studies. The participants' palms were wired for the skin-sweating response (i.e., galvanic skin response), and then an anxiety-provoking situation was presented so that physical levels of anxiety could be documented. The high-anxiety and low-anxiety groups then completed the anxiety instrument. If the resulting group means differed on the anxiety instrument and on the physical indicators of anxiety, the researcher could argue that the instrument measured the anxiety construct (Taylor 1953; Matarazzo et al. 1955).

In the area of personality measures, researchers have used clinical experts to diagnose a group of individuals as having a certain personality trait or different manifestations of the personality trait. A personality measure purporting to assess the same trait was then administered to the target group and to a normative group. Large differences between the groups in the predicted direction provided evidence for the construct validity of the instrument. For example, clinical research suggests that boys are more likely than girls to be both bullies and victims; however, attempts to measure differences through self-report instruments have been hampered by the apparent multidimensionality of constructs (Boulton and Smith 1994; Hawker and Boulton 2000). Using an instrument designed to measure multiple bully and victim factors (the APRI; Parada 2000) and new statistical procedures in which the many of the best features of EFA, CFA, and SEM are integrated (exploratory structural equation modeling or ESEM), researchers were able to demonstrate clear gender pattern differences in the constructs—consistent with a priori predictions (Marsh et al. 2011).

Examples of Known Groups Analyses

We provide a few short examples of known groups analyses from our own research to demonstrate the utility of the technique.

Example 3 Discriminant Function Analysis

Beck and Gable (2001) examined the accuracy of using the *PDSS* total score to assign mothers to the following three *SCID* (i.e., Structured Clinical Interview for DSM-IV Axis I Disorders; Spitzer et al. (1978) diagnosed groups: no depression, depressive disorder, and major depression using discriminant function analysis. Successful classification provides evidence for the construct validity of the *PDSS* score interpretations. They had three known groups of postpartum women: The first group consisted of 104 women who did not receive a *SCID* depression diagnosis, the second group comprised 28 women who were diagnosed with Depressive Disorder not otherwise specified (NOS), and the third group consisted of 18 women who were diagnosed with Major Depressive Disorder with Postpartum Onset. (Depressive Disorder NOS is DSM-IV terminology for significant symptoms of depression that are not severe enough to meet criteria for Major Depressive Disorder. Table 6.2 presents the results of the discriminant function analysis; the two canonical discriminant functions were significant predictors of diagnostic group membership. Overall, the procedure correctly classified 115 women (76.7% of the diagnostic sample). The accuracy rates varied across groups: The DFA correctly classified 88 of 104 women (84.6%) with no depressive diagnosis, 15 of 28 women (53.6%) with Depressive Disorder NOS, and 12 of 18 (66.7%) women with major postpartum depression. All 18 women diagnosed with major depression were classified in one of the two depression groups. This means that the *PDSS* discriminant function classification procedure yielded no false

Table 6.2 Discriminant function results of the postpartum depression screening scale

Actual group	Predicted group membership		
	No (1)	DD (2)	Major (3)
Group 1	88	16	0
No depression (N = 104)	(84.6%)	(15.4%)	(0%)
Group 2	8	15	5
Depressive disorder NOS (N = 28)	(28.6%)	(53.6%)	(17.9%)
Group 3	0	6	12
Major depression (N = 18)	(0%)	(33.3%)	(66.7%)

Note. Diagnostic sample ($N = 150$). Procedure correctly classified 76.7% of original cases, a rate which is 24% above that from chance alone. Predicted group membership variable is based on the SCID depression diagnosis

Table 6.3 Correlations between PDSS symptom content scales and canonical discriminant function

PDSS content scale	Correlation with first discriminant function
Sleeping/eating disturbances	0.63
Anxiety/insecurity	0.82
Emotional lability	0.70
Mental confusion	0.64
Loss of self	0.66
Guilt/shame	0.64
Suicidal thoughts	0.48

negatives for women with the most severe depression diagnosis, which is a highly desirable characteristic for a screening instrument (Beck and Gable 2002).

Table 6.3 presents the correlations between scores on the seven *PDSS* content scales and the first canonical discriminant function (which accounted for 92% of the variance explained by the two functions). These correlations assess the relative contributions of the content scales to the classification results. As Table 6.3 shows, all seven content scales were substantial predictors of classification. The Anxiety/Insecurity scale explained the most variance in classification and the Suicidal Thoughts scale explained the least variance in classification. The diagnostic sample was fairly homogenous on the Suicidal Thoughts variable, which may help to explain why the coefficient for that variable was relatively low (Beck and Gable 2002).

Example 4 Known Groups Analyses: Providing Validity Evidence for the *School Attitude Assessment Survey-Revised* (*SAAS-R*) Using *t*-Tests and Logistic Regression

As mentioned earlier, the *SAAS-R* purports to measure five factors that are hypothesized to be related to underachievement in academically able students: Motivation/Self-regulation, Academic Self-perceptions, Attitudes toward Teachers and Classes, Attitudes toward School, and Goal Valuation. The goal for developing the *SAAS-R* was to compare heterogeneous groups of achievers and underachievers, as well as achievers and underachievers, from a population of academically gifted students (McCoach and Siegle 2003a). Thus, if these five factors are indeed related to the underachievement of academically able students, and if the instrument adequately measures these five factors, then there should be differences between known groups of achievers and underachievers on these five factors. If a comparison of known groups of achievers and underachievers fails to find differences on any/all of these five factors, then two possibilities exist: (1) either the instrument does not actually measure the factors of interest or (2) these factors, which were identified after the extensive literature review, are not actually related to underachievement. The following information describing the known groups study designed to bolster validity evidence for the *SAAS-R* was originally published in *Educational and Psychological Measurement* (McCoach and Siegle 2003a).

To provide evidence that this instrument could help distinguish academically able achievers from academically able underachievers, McCoach and Siegle (2003a) conducted a series of *t*-tests on the mean scale scores of the five factors to explore the differences in academically able achievers' and underachievers' Academic Self-perceptions, Attitudes toward Teachers, Attitudes toward School, Goal Valuation, and Motivation/Self-regulation (see also McCoach and Siegle 2003b). The convenience sample consisted of 176 gifted high school students in grades 9 through 12 from 28 school districts across the nation. The district contact people used the following definition to identify achieving and underachieving gifted students in their districts: gifted achievers were in the top 10% of their class or had at least a 3.75 GPA. Gifted underachievers were in the bottom half of their high school class or had a GPA at or below 2.5. Both groups had an IQ score or achievement score at or above the 92 percentile. According to these criteria, the final sample contained 56 gifted underachievers and 120 gifted achievers. Although these definitions are not universally accepted, they allowed for the examination of two distinct groups of students: those who were, by conventional standards, clearly succeeding in school, and those who were not achieving at a level commensurate with their "expected" abilities. The sample consisted of 101 males, 72 females, and 3 students who did not indicate their gender. Although the gender-ratio of male to female achievers was roughly equal, there were approximately three times as many male underachievers as there were female underachievers in this sample. This is consistent with previous research on gender differences in underachievement (Peterson and Colangelo 1996; Wolfle 1991).

For each of the subscales that exhibited unequal variances, the gifted underachievers displayed greater variances than the gifted achievers. Table 6.4 shows that gifted achievers had substantially higher means than gifted underachievers on four of the five subscales: Attitudes toward Teachers, Attitudes toward School, Goal Valuation, and Motivation/Self-regulation, and the effect sizes for these differences were moderate to large ($d = 0.67$ to $d = 1.29$). Gifted achievers' scores on the Motivation/Self-regulation and the Goal Valuation scales were over one standard deviation unit above the scores of the gifted underachievers. The

Table 6.4 T-tests on each of the five subscales of the SAAS-R

Factors	(Achievers, n = 122)		(Underachievers, n = 55)		p	d
	M	SD	M	SD		
Academic self-perception	6.21	0.565	5.86	0.946	0.011	0.46
Attitude toward teachers	5.41	0.869	4.66	0.975	<0.001	0.81
Attitude toward school	5.25	1.16	4.22	1.52	0.001	0.75
Goal valuation	6.53	0.575	5.26	1.41	<0.001	1.21
Motivation/self-regulation	5.48	0.931	3.90	1.40	<0.001	1.37

mean difference of the Academic Self-perceptions subscale was not statistically significant, and this was the only subscale that demonstrated a relatively small effect size (d = 0.42). The results clearly demonstrate the ability of this instrument to differentiate between high achieving and underachieving students of high ability (McCoach and Siegle 2003a).

Then McCoach and Siegle (2003b) conducted logistic regression analyses to determine which combination of the five factors would allow us to best predict students' group membership. Logistic regression is a statistical technique that is often used to predict group membership from a set of predictor variables. Using logistic regression techniques, researchers can assess a model's ability to correctly classify cases for which group membership or outcome status is known (Tabachnik and Fidell 2001). The model with all five subscales correctly classified 81.8% of the students as either gifted achievers or gifted underachievers. Given the associations among the five factors, only two of the five factors, Motivation/Self-regulation and Goal Valuation, were statistically significant predictors of group membership. Academic Self-perceptions, Attitudes toward School, and Attitudes toward Teachers did not uniquely predict group membership after accounting for Motivation/Self-regulation and Goal Valuation. Using the Motivation/Self-regulation and Goal Valuation factors correctly classified 81.8% of the sample as either gifted achievers or gifted underachievers. The logistic regression model more accurately classified achievers (91.7% correctly classified) than gifted underachievers (60.7% correctly classified). It was more difficult to classify gifted underachievers because their responses exhibited much greater variances than those of the gifted achievers. The results of the logistic regression indicate that for every point lower a student scored on the Motivation/Self-regulation factor, he or she was over twice as likely to be an underachiever after controlling for the Goal Valuation factor. For every point lower a student scored on the Goal Valuation factor, he or she was over twice as likely to be an underachiever after controlling for the Motivation/Self-regulation factor.

The results of the t-tests and the logistic regression analyses on known groups of underachievers appeared to provide evidence for the construct validity of the *SAAS-R* score interpretations. Minimally, the results of these analyses certainly supported the legitimacy of using the *SAAS-R* in further research studies to examine the underachievement of gifted students. Additional independent research on the *SAAS-R* has demonstrated evidence of convergent and discriminant relations and criterion-related relations, as well as differences among known groups of high achieving and low achieving students (Suldo et al. 2008).

Evidence of Predictive Validity

In other situations, the instrument may be designed to *predict* a future characteristic or behavior. The instrument is administered, and then, at some later time, measures are obtained on some external criterion. Usually, predictive validity studies utilize correlational analyses (simple correlations, regression analyses, etc.); however, predictive studies can also make use of known groups analyses. Examples of potential predictive validity studies are numerous: can an instrument that measures criminal thinking be used to predict future arrests? Can a measure of motivation in graduate student populations be used to predict PhD completion? Can a measure of pre-service teachers' dedication to the profession predict teacher retention and attrition within the first 5 years of teaching?

If the prediction is successful, future users of the instrument could administer the instrument and then estimate the student's status regarding the criterion variable. Anderson et al. (2011) provide an example of establishing the instrument-criterion (predictive) validity for the data. They examined the long-term predictive validity of the *Addiction-Prone Personality (APP)* scale within a general population. They gathered self-reports of personality and alcohol use at baseline ($n = 1257$), and again after 7 years ($n = 788$). They used logistic regression to predict the incidence of new cases of alcohol abuse/dependence after 7 years, after controlling for prior drinking behavior at baseline. Their results provided evidence that the *APP* could in fact predict alcohol abuse/dependence 7 years later, even after controlling for prior drinking behavior. In addition, the *APP* scale better predicted alcohol abuse/dependence than other personality measures, which were administered for comparison purposes. They concluded that their results provided evidence for the validity of the *APP* scale, which is designed to measure personality traits that are present before the onset of problem drinking behaviors, and that the *APP* "is inherently superior to more general personality systems if one's goal is to adequately measure addiction-proneness traits using a single scale" (Anderson et al. 2011, p. 655).

Instrument-criterion validity studies are essential for cognitive instruments used in the area of personnel selection. In the personnel field, it is common for the selection measures used to assess aspects of the actual job content. Included are tasks, activities, or responsibilities needed to successfully carry out the particular job. The assessment instrument is administered as a selection measure. Thus, the hypothesis is that the people with the higher scores would perform better in the actual job. The instrument-criterion validity studies necessary to support use of the instrument in this manner are actually quite tricky because workers are not randomly assigned to jobs. Ideally, most of the applicants would be admitted to the job class so that at a later time their peers and supervisors could rate their on-the-job performance (i.e., the criterion). Then performance ratings would be correlated with scores on the selection instrument; high correlations would be supportive of the instrument-criterion (predictive) validity of the data from the instrument. In practice, it is often difficult to admit most of those tested to the job class. In this situation, the selection measure is administered to current employees in the job class so that their scores can be correlated with on-the-job performance ratings. Naturally, those already on the job are a previously selected group, which tends to restrict the range of scores on both variables. (Ideally, one would also find applicants that were not hired and administer the assessments to them as well). Thus, although these studies are sometimes used as predictive studies, they are not always accepted as good evidence of instrument-criterion validity.

An instrument-related validity study from the affective area of "interest" clearly illustrates the utility of predictive studies to provide evidence of construct validity. One measure of a successful use of an interest inventory is its ability to predict future actual job choices. In the early research to examine the predictive validity of interest inventories, researchers typically administered the interest inventory in high school, and then followed the students for a few years to find out the actual areas of their job choice. For example, the early study by Silver and Barnette (1970) reported evidence for the instrument-criterion validity of the *Minnesota Vocational Interest Inventory (MVII)* by examining job choices (e.g., building trades, electrical, and machine shop) made by high school graduates who completed the MVII in grade 9. Similarly, in the early 1970s, Campbell (1973) has presented supportive instrument-criterion (predictive) validity for the *Strong Vocational Interest Battery (SVIB)*, indicating that approximately 75% of various samples of college graduates wound up in jobs that were compatible with their high school (grade 12) SVIB profiles.

Incremental Validity

Establishing relationships between newly developed measures and existing measures or related constructs of interest is clearly an important step in the instrument validation process. However, establishing the incremental validity of a new measure over and above existing measures is an essential but often overlooked step in the development of a new measure. Haynes and Lench (2003) define incremental validity as "the degree to which a measure explains or predicts some phenomena of interest, relative to other measures" (p. 456). If time and resources are being diverted to develop a new measure, then it is incumbent on the instrument developer to demonstrate that the new measure provides utility over and above existing measures. For example, if a new measure helps to predict additional variance in a criterion variable of interest over and above traditionally used measures, then the new measure provides incremental utility or validity to the prediction of the criterion. Alternatively, if the new measure is able to predict the criterion variable equally well using a more efficient (shorter) or less costly assessment, then the utility of the new measure is easily established. Assuming that the new measure predicts a criterion variable or construct of interest, does the newly developed measure (a) predict the criterion more accurately than other measures or (b) predict the criterion of interest over and above common or more readily obtainable measures that are traditionally used to predict the criterion? (Haynes and Lench 2003). If the new measure does not add predictive utility to the arsenal of existing measures, then it should cost less than other measures, be less time consuming than other measures, or be less intrusive or onerous than other measures. Haynes and Lench describe incremental validation as "a complex and demanding addition to standard psychometric evaluations".

Incremental validity studies should compare the new measure, not just to existing measures that assess the same or similar constructs, but also to conceptually distinct constructs that have been shown to predict the criterion of interest. For example, imagine a researcher is developing self-regulation scale for college students. The theoretical rationale for the development of such a scale is that self-regulation skills help to predict college GPA over and above academic ability/achievement measures such as the *Scholastic Achievement Test (SAT)*. Therefore, the instrument is being developed for use in college environments to help college counselors identify students who would benefit self-regulation training. Given this rationale, the self-regulation instrument should be able to predict college GPA over and above *SAT* scores. If the new measure fails to explain any additional variance in GPA over and above that which is already explained by *SAT*, the new measure has failed to establish evidence of incremental validity. There are two possible reasons that could explain the lack of incremental variance explained: (1) the newly developed measure does not actually measure self-regulation accurately or adequately or (2) the theory is flawed: self-regulation skills do not actually uniquely explain college GPA over and above *SAT* scores. To determine which of the two reasons is more likely, the researcher could simultaneously collect scores on other, more established measures of self-regulation from the sample of research participants. The scores on the new measure of self-regulation should exhibit a strong pattern of correlations with the more established measures of self-regulation and adequate evidence of reliability to establish the measure as an adequate and accurate measure of self-regulation. If the more established measures of self-regulation do predict incremental variance in GPA over and above *SAT* scores, but the newly developed measure does not, this represents a serious blow to the evidence of validity for the new measure. If both the new measure and the more established measures of self-regulation fail to explain any additional variance in college GPA over and above *SAT* scores, this represents a serious blow to the underlying theory.

Often, hierarchical (sequential) linear regression analyses are used to examine the incremental validity of a new measure. For example, Wood et al. (2008) examined the incremental validity of a measure of gratitude, the *GC6*, in predicting overall satisfaction with life after controlling for the 30 facets of personality measured by the *NEO-PI-R* in a sample of 389 adults. They found that gratitude explained an additional 9% of the variance in satisfaction with life after controlling for the Big Five domains (partial $r = 0.30$) and an additional 8% after controlling for the 30 facets (partial $r = 0.28$). In addition, they found that gratitude was most related to extroversion ($r = 0.34$), and in particular, the facets of warmth ($r = 0.34$), trust ($r = 0.31$) and positive emotions ($r = 0.43$). These results suggest that the measurement of gratitude can help to explain overall life satisfaction, even after accounting for the Big Five Personality traits.

Finally, we return to Beck and Gable's (2000, 2001, 2002) development of the *PDSS* for another example of an incremental validity study. The *PDSS* total score was related to the *SCID* depression diagnostic status even after controlling for the Beck depression inventory (BDI-II) and the Edinburgh postnatal depression scale (EPDS) (Beck and Gable 2002).

Establishing Validity for Use in Different Populations

Validity evidence is tied to the purpose for the assessment. It is also tied to context within which the instrument will be administered. To what degree can the evidence of validity based on test criterion relationships be generalized to a new context without further study of the validity of the measure within that context? (AERA, APA, and NCME 1999). When a test is used to predict the same or similar criteria at different times, in different places, or for different people, the relationships between the measure and the criterion variable may vary considerably (AERA, APA, and NCME 1999). One critical aspect of the context is the population or subpopulation with whom a researcher plans to use an instrument. It is fairly common for one researcher to conduct preliminary pilot studies on an instrument with one population and publish the results of those studies. Then another researcher, seeing the results of those analyses, decides to use the instrument for his or her own research, which involves a completely different population. Instruments that appear to function well and provide useful information within one population may be completely inappropriate for use in another population. To establish the utility of an instrument for use within a given population, empirical validity evidence must be collected within that population. This point cannot be overstated.

In general, validity generalization refers to the meta-analysis of the correlations among a measure and a criterion variable of interest across a wide variety of contexts. When an assessment has been the subject of multiple validation or research studies, validity generalization can help to make predictions about test criterion relationships in new contexts that bear similarities to previously studied contexts (AERA, APA, and NCME 1999). However, most non-commercial self-report affective instruments lack the research base to effectively conduct validity generalization studies. Moreover, many of the non-commercial self-report affective instruments in the research literature lack any attention to the establishment of measurement equivalence across cultures or subpopulations or the assessment of the invariance of test criterion relationships across the subpopulations of interest. As mentioned earlier, using multiple groups SEM/CFA provides an analytic framework to aid in the understanding of between group differences, both in terms of structure and function of the instrument as well as in terms of understanding potential differences among the groups in terms of predictive or concurrent validity.

Integrating Validity Evidence

Although the various sources of validity evidence help us understand different aspects of the validity issue, "validity is a unitary concept" (AERA, APA, and NCME 1999). The task for the instrument developer is to accumulate appropriate judgmental and empirical evidence that support the meaningful interpretations of the data. Because validity is a property of the inferences that we make, not the instrument itself, understanding the purpose for the instrument and the context in which it will be administered is critical.

"A sound validity argument integrates various strands of evidence into a coherent account of the degree to which existing evidence and theory support the intended interpretation of test scores for specific users" (AERA, APA, and NCME 1999, p. 17). "Ultimately, the validity of an intended interpretation of test scores relies on all the available evidence relevant to the technical quality of a testing system" (AERA, APA, and NCME 1999, p. 17), including the evidence of careful test construction, adequate score reliability, appropriate test administration and scoring, accurate score scaling, attention to fairness for all examinees (AERA, APA, and NCME 1999). It is impossible to establish "the degree of validity" of a given instrument (Grimm and Widaman 2012, p. 639). Instead, the task of the instrument developer is to provide explicit descriptions of the entire validation process as well as interpretations of how the data gathered supports the validity of the intended interpretations of the assessment. Then test users must ultimately evaluate the evidence, especially as it relates to their particular purposes, contexts, or populations.

References

Allport, G. W., Vernon, P. E., & Gardner, L. (1960). *Study of values*. Oxford, England: Houghton Mifflin.

American Educational Research Association (AERA), American Psychological Association (APA) & National Council on Measurement in Education (NCME). (1999). *The standards for educational and psychological testing*. Washington: American Educational Research Association.

Anderson, R. E., Barnes, G. E., & Murray, R. P. (2011). Psychometric properties and long-term predictive validity of the Addiction-Prone Personality (APP) scale. *Personality and Individual Differences, 50*(5), 651–656.

Baron, R. M., & Kenny, D. A. (1986). The moderator-mediator variable distinction in social psychological research: Conceptual, strategic, and statistical considerations. *Journal of Personality and Social Psychology, 51*(6), 1173–1182.

Beck, C. T., & Gable, R. K. (2000). Postpartum depression screening scale: Development and psychometric testing. *Nursing Research, 49*, 272–282.

Beck, C. T., Gable, R. K. (2002). *Postpartum depression screening scale*. Los Angeles: Western Psychological Services.

Beck, C. T. (1992). The lived experience of postpartum depression: A phenomenological study. *Nursing Research, 41*, 166–170.

Beck, C. T. (1993). Teetering on the edge: A substantive theory of postpartum depression. *Nursing Research, 42*, 42–48.

Beck, C. T. (1995). The effects of postpartum depression on maternal-infant interaction: A meta-analysis. *Nursing Research, 44*(5), 298–304.

Beck, C. T. (1996). Postpartum depressed mothers' experiences interacting with their children. *Nursing Research, 45*, 98–104.

Beck, C. T., & Gable, R. K. (2001). Further validation of the postpartum depression screening scale. *Nursing Research, 50*, 155–164.

Beck, A. T., Steer, R. A., & Brown, G. K. (1996). *BDI-II manual*. San Antonio: The Psychological Corporation.

Bennett, G. K., Seashore, H. G., & Westman, A. G. (1997). *The differential aptitude test*. San Antonio, Texas: Psychological Corporation.

Bollen, K. A. (1989). *Structural equations with latent variables*. New York: Wiley.

Borsboom, D. (2005). *Measuring the mind: Conceptual issues in contemporary psychometrics*. Cambridge: Cambridge University Press.

Boutlton, M. J., & Smith, P. K. (1994). Bully/victim problems in middle school children: Stability, self-perceived competence, peer acceptance. *British Journal of Developmental Psychology, 12*, 315–325.

Bovaird, J. A., & Koziol, N. A. (2012). Measurement models for ordered-categorical indicators. In R. Hoyle (Ed.), *Handbook of structural equation modeling* (pp. 495–511). New York: The Guilford Press.

Campbell, D. P. (1973). The strong vocational interest blank for men. In D. G. Zytowski (Ed.), *Contemporary approaches to interest measurement*. Minneapolis: University of Minnesota Press.

Campbell, D. T., & Fiske, D. W. (1959). Convergent and discriminant validation by the multitrait-multimethod matrix. *Psychological Bulletin, 56*, 81–105.

Campbell, D. T., & O'Connell, E. J. (1967). Method factors in multitrait-multimethod matrices: Multiplicative rather than additive? *Multivariate Behavioral Research, 2*, 409–426.

Carmines, E. G., & Zeller, R. A. (1979). *Reliability and validity assessment*. Beverly Hills: Sage.

Cox, J. L., Holden, J. M., & Sagovsky, R. (1987). Detection of postnatal depression: Development of the 10-item *Edinburgh Postnatal Depression Scale*. *British Journal of Psychiatry, 150*, 782–786.

Cronbach, L. J. (1971). Test validation. In R. L. Thorndike (Ed.), *Educational measurement* (2nd ed.). Washington, DC: American Council on Education.

Cronbach, L. J., & Meehl, P. E. (1955). Construct validity in psychological tests. *Psychological Bulletin, 52*(4), 281–302.

Duncan, T. E., Duncan, S. C., Strycker, L. A., Li, F., & Alpert, A. (1999). *An introduction to latent variable growth curve modeling: Concepts, issues, and applications*. Mahwah: Erlbaum.

Edwards, A. L. (1959). *Edwards personal preference schedule manual*. New York: Psychological Corp.

Edwards, M. C., Wirth, R. J., Houts, C. R., & Xi, N. (2012). Categorical data in the structural equation modeling framework. In R. Hoyle (Ed.), *Handbook of structural equation modeling* (pp. 195–208). New York: Guilford Press.

Eid, M., & Nussbeck, F. W. (2009). The multitrait-multimethod matrix at 50! *Methodology: European Journal of Research Methods for the Behavioral and Social Sciences, 5*(3), 71.

Gable, R. K. (1970). A multivariate study of work value orientations. *Unpublished doctoral dissertation*, State University of New York at Albany.

Gordon, L. V. (1960). *Survey of interpersonal values*. Chicago: Science Research Associates.

Grimm, K. J., & Widaman, K. F. (2012). Construct validity. In H. Cooper (Ed.), *APA handbook of research methods in psychology*. Washington, DC: APA.

Hawker, D. S., & Boulton, M. J. (2000). Twenty years' research on peer victimization and psychosocial maladjustment: A meta-analytic review of cross-sectional studies. *Journal of Child Psychology and Psychiatry, 41*, 441–455.

Haynes, S. N., & Lench, H. C. (2003). Incremental validity of new clinical assessment measures. *Psychological Assessment, 15*(4), 456–466.

Hovling, V., Schermelleh-Engel, K., & Moosbrugger, H. (2009). Analyzing multitrait-multimethod data: A comparison of three approaches. *Methodology: European Journal of Research Methods for the Behavioral and Social Sciences, 5*(3), 99–111.

Hoyle, R. H. (Ed.). (1995). *Structural equation modeling: Concepts, issues, and applications.* Thousand Oaks: Sage Publications.

Kaplan, D. (2000). *Structural Equation Modeling: Foundations and Extensions*. Newbury Park, CA: Sage.

Kaplan, D. (2009). *Structural equation modeling: Foundations and extensions* (2nd ed.). New York: Sage Publications.

Kenny, D. A. (1976). An empirical application of confirmatory factor analysis to the multitrait-multimethod matrix. *Journal of Experimental Social Psychology, 65*, 507–516.

Kenny, D. A., & Kashy, D. A. (1992). Analysis of the multitrait-multimethod matrix by confirmatory factor analysis. *Psychological Bulletin, 112*, 165–172.

Kenny, D. A., Kashy, D. A., & Bolger, N. (1998). Data analysis in social psychology. In D. T. Gilbert, S. T. Fiske, & G. Lindzey (Eds.), *Handbook of social psychology* (4th ed., pp. 233–265). New York: McGraw Hill.

Kline, R. B. (2010). *Principles and practice of structural equation modeling* (3rd ed.). New York: The Guilford Press.

Kuder, G. F. (1949). *Manual for the Kuder preference record (personal)*. Chicago: Science Research Associates.

Lance, C. E., Noble, C. L., & Scullen, S. E. (2002). A critique of the correlated trait-correlated method and correlated uniqueness models for multitrait-multimethod data. *Psychological Methods, 7*(2), 228–244.

Maas, C. J. M., Lensvelt-Mulders, G. J. L. M., & Hox, J. J. (2009). A multilevel multitrait-multimethod analysis. *Methodology, 5*, 72–77.

Marsh, H. W. (1989). Confirmatory factor analysis of multitrait-multimethod data: Many problems and a few solutions. *Applied Psychological Measurement, 12*, 335–361.

Marsh, H. W., & Bailey, M. (1991). Confirmatory factor analysis of multitrait-multimethod data: A comparison of the behavior of alternative models. *Applied Psychological Measurement, 15*, 47–70.

Marsh, H. W., Byrne, B. M., & Craven, R. (1992). Overcoming problems in confirmatory factor analysis of MTMM data: The correlated uniqueness model and factorial invariance. *Multivariate Behavioral Research, 27*, 489–507.

Marsh, H. W., & Grayson, D. (1995). Latent variable models of multitrait-multimethod data. In R. Hoyle (Ed.), *Structural equation modeling* (pp. 177–198). Thousand Oaks, CA: Sage.

Marsh, H. W., Nagengast, B., Morin, A. J. S., Parada, R. H., Craven, R. G., & Hamilton, L. R. (2011). Construct validity of the multidimensional structure of bullying and victimization: An application of exploratory structural equation modeling. *Journal of Educational Psychology, 103*(3), 701–732.

Marsh, H. W., Wen, Z., Nagengast, B., & Hau, K. (2012). *Handbook of structural equation modeling* (pp. 436–455). New York: The Guilford Press.

Matarazzo, J. D., Guze, S. B., & Matarazzo, R. G. (1955). An approach to the validity of the *Taylor Anxiety Scale*: Scores of medical and psychiatric patients. *The Journal of Abnormal and Social Psychiatry, 51*(2), 276–280.

McCoach, D. B. (2003). SEM isn't just the school wide enrichment model anymore: structural equation modeling (SEM) in gifted education. *Journal for the Education of the Gifted, 27*, 36–61.

McCoach, D. B., & Siegle, D. (2003a). The *school attitude assessment survey-revised*: A new instrument to identify academically able students who underachieve. *Educational and Psychological Measurement, 63*(3), 414–429.

McCoach, D. B., & Siegle, D. (2003b). Factors that differentiate underachieving gifted students from high-achieving gifted students. *Gifted Child Quarterly, 47*(2), 144–154.

Muthen, L. K., & Muthen, B. O. (1998–2007). *Mplus Users Guide* (4th Ed.). Los Angeles: Muthen & Muthen.

Nunnally, J. C., & Bernstein, I. H. (1994). *Psychometric theory* (3rd ed.). New York: McGraw-Hill.

Nussbeck, F. W., Eid, M., Geiser, C., Courvoisier, D. S., & Lischetzke, T. (2009). A CTC(M-1) model for different types of raters. *Methodology, 5*, 88–98.

Oort, F. J. (2009). Three-mode models for multitrait-multimethod data. *Methodology: European Journal of Research Methods for the Behavioral and Social Sciences, 5*(3), 78–87.

Parada, R. (2000). *Adolescent Peer Relations Instrument: A theoretical and empirical basis for the measurement of participant roles in bullying and victimization of adolescence: An interim test manual and a research monograph: A test manual.* Publication Unit, Self-concept Enhancement and Learning Facilitation (SELF) Research Centre, University of Western Sydney.

Peterson, J. S., & Colangelo, N. (1996). Gifted achievers and underachievers: A comparison of patterns found in school files. *Journal of Counseling and Development, 74*, 399–406.

Rabe-Hesketh, S., & Skrondal, A. (2012). Multilevel and longitudinal modeling using stata (3rd edn). College Station, TX: Stata Press.

Raykov, T., & Marcoulides, G. A. (2011). *Introduction to psychometric theory*. New York: Routledge.

Raykov, T., & Marcoulides, G. A. (2006). *A first course in structural equation modeling* (2nd ed.). Mahway: Lawrence Erlbaum Associates, Inc.

Silver, H. A., & Barnette, W. L. (1970). Predictive and concurrent validity of the Minnesota vocational interest inventory. *Journal of Applied Psychology, 54*(5), 436–440.

Sireci, S. G. (2006). Content validity. In N. J. Salkind (Ed.) *Encyclopedia ofmeasurement and statistics*. Thousand Oaks, CA: Sage.

Sireci, S. G., & Parker, P. (2006). Validity on trial: Psychometric and legal conceptualizations of validity. *Educational Measurement: Issues and Practice, 25*(3), 27–34.

Schmidt, F. L. (1988). The problem of group differences in ability scores in employment selection. *Journal of Vocational Behavior, 33*, 272–292.

Schumacker, R. E., & Lomax, R. G. (1996). *A beginner's guide to structural equation modeling*. Mahwah: Lawrence Erlbaum Associates.

Spitzer, R. L., Endicott, J., & Robins, E. (1978). Research diagnostic criteria: Rationale and reliability. *Archives of General Psychiatry, 35*(6), 773–782.

Suldo, S. M., Shaffer, E. J., & Shaunessy, E. (2008). An independent investigation of the validity of the *School Attitude Assessment Survey–Revised. Journal of Psychoeducational Assessment, 26*(1), 69–82.

Süss, H.-M., Oberauer, K., Wittmann, W. W., Wilhelm, O., & Schulze, R. (2002). Working-memory capacity explains reasoning ability—And a little bit more. *Intelligence, 30*, 261–288.

Super, D. E. (1970). *Work values inventory manual*. Boston, MA: Houghton Mifflin Company.

Tabachnick, B. G., & Fidell, L. S. (2001). *Using multivariate statistics*. New York: Harper Collins.

Taylor, J. (1953). A personality scale of manifest anxiety. *The Journal of Abnormal and Social Psychology, 48*(2), 285–290.

Warner, W. L., Meeker, M., & Eells, K. (1949). *Social class in America; a manual of procedure for the measurement of social status*. Oxford, England: Science Research Associates.

Widaman, K. F. (1985). Hierarchically nested covariance structure models for multitrait-multimethod data. *Applied Psychological Measurement, 9*, 1–26.

Widaman, K. F. (1992). Multitrait-multimethod models in aging research. *Experimental Aging Research, 18*, 185–201.

Wilhelm, O., & Schulze, R. (2002). The relation of speeded and unspeeded reasoning with mental speed. *Intelligence, 30*, 537–554.
Wolfle, J. A. (1991). Underachieving gifted males: Are we missing the boat? *Roeper Review, 13*, 181–184.
Wood, A. M., Joseph, S., & Maltby, J. (2008). Gratitude uniquely predicts satisfaction with life: Incremental validity above the domains and facets of the five factor model. *Personality and Individual Differences, 45*(1), 49–54.

Chapter 7
The Reliability of Scores from Affective Instruments

In previous chapters, we focused on the accumulation of evidence of validity to make particular inferences using the instrument that we have developed. We now turn to the issue of score reliability, which is an indication of the consistency, stability, or precision of scores. Conceptually, reliability is an indication of the accuracy of the scores. Score reliability is prerequisite to the establishment of validity: if scores are not accurate, then it is not possible to make meaningful inferences from them. For example, imagine that you had an old bathroom scale, and every time you stepped on the scale, it registered a completely different weight. As you stepped on and off multiple times, the scale registered "20 lbs," "240 lbs," "89 lbs," "167 lbs," "110 lbs." Given the imprecision and inaccuracy in the scale's measurement of your weight, it is not possible for the scale to provide you with the information that you need to make a valid inference about your weight (Thompson 2002).

Thus, at its crux, reliability is concerned with the question: "How accurate are the scores?" Accuracy (or precision) and error are inversely related. The more error there is in our measurement, the less reliable the scores are. There are several different types of errors of measurement, and each type of measurement error corresponds to a reliability estimate. In the context of our work in affective instrument design, when we talk about accuracy of scores, we are generally most concerned with establishing that scores that are *internally consistent* upon one administration of the instrument, as well as *stable* over time, given two or more administrations (see Stanley 1971). Thus, we focus on the two types of measurement errors and their corresponding reliability estimates: measurement error within the set of questions, which is quantified using internal consistency reliability estimates; and measurement error across occasions, which is quantified using test–retest reliability estimates.

In this chapter, we briefly present a conceptual introduction to the measurement theory underlying reliability and the evidence needed to support its internal consistency and stability. Following this, we discuss several factors affecting the level of reliability and explore the relationship between reliability and validity. Finally, we conclude the chapter with a presentation of an internal consistency reliability

D. B. McCoach et al., *Instrument Development in the Affective Domain*,

DOI: 10.1007/978-1-4614-7135-6_7, © Springer Science+Business Media New York 2013

analysis of a subscale from the School Value Assessment Scale (McCoach 2002). We cannot overstate the importance of employing instruments that demonstrate adequate reliability. Unfortunately, some researchers do not take the issue of reliability seriously enough and later find the results of their study to be confusing and disappointing.

Reliability Theory

After administering an affective instrument, we obtain scores on all the items contained in the instrument. However, rather than analyzing the results at the item-level, we wish to create subscales that we can use to measure the constructs of interest. Therefore, we generally create mean scores for each of the clusters of items that were identified in the factor analysis. These are the means of the responses to a set of items that have been written to operationally define the affective characteristic. Using these mean scores allows us to make inferences back to the original conceptual definition of the characteristic. However, these mean scores contain some amount of error or imprecision. How much error is there in the mean score as a measure of the construct of interest? In other words, how reliable are these scores? Although scores that are highly reliable may or may not measure the constructs that they are intended to measure, scores that are highly unreliable measure very little at all. Therefore, establishing the reliability of scores is necessary but not sufficient condition for establishing the validity of the inferences that can be made from the instrument. As such, collecting evidence of adequate score reliability is a critical step in the creation of an affective instrument.

Classical True Score Theory

Stated differently, the inferences that we make about constructs of interest are as good as the amount of true score variance in the observed score. In classical true score theory (CTT), a test score, X, is the sum of the true score, T, and error, E. In other words, any individual's observed total score (X_{total}) consists of a true score component (X_{true}) and an error component (X_{error}) such that

$$X_{\text{total}} = X_{\text{true}} + X_{\text{error}} \tag{7.1}$$

The first part, X_{total}, reflects the portion of the individual's total score that is associated with the "true score." The true score itself is a hypothetical component, since it reflects the individual's score obtained by a perfect measurement instrument under perfect conditions. Conceptually, this score can be considered as the mean of the individual's scores under repeated administrations, assuming no learning has taken place (Kerlinger 1973). Therefore, the true score is "a latent, unobserved score on the underlying dimension of actual interest, which is free from random measurement error" (Raykov and Marcoulides 2011, p. 120). Quite obviously, we can never actually observe an individual's true score; we can only *estimate* the portion of the total score that is attributable to the true score. At the same time, each individual's total score includes an error component (X_{error}), which reflects the portion of the total score that is not attributable to the true score. The raw score formula can also be written in terms of variance components as

$$\text{Var}_{\text{Tot}} = \text{Var}_{\text{True}} + \text{Var}_{\text{Error}} \tag{7.2}$$

In other words, the total variance on a measure can be decomposed into two parts: the true score variance and the error variance. Of course, our goal is to measure affective characteristics with precise measurement tools; however, all the instruments we use have some error of measurement. In assessing the reliability of an instrument, we attempt to estimate the amount of error in the scores so that we can estimate the amount of true variance in the total score—the less error involved, the more reliable the measurement is

The reliability coefficient is the proportion of the "true" variance to the total (observed) variance (Kerlinger 1973).

$$\rho = \frac{\text{Var(True)}}{\text{Var(Total)}} \tag{7.3}$$

As such, the reliability coefficient is actually in an R^2 metric (Thompson 2002). The reliability coefficient is also defined as the squared correlation between the true score and the observed score (Raykov and Marcoulides 2011). Given formula (7.2), reliability is also the proportion of error variance to the total obtained variance yielded by a measuring instrument subtracted from 1.00, the index 1.00 indicating perfect reliability, as shown in Eq. (7.4).

$$\rho = 1 - \frac{\text{Var(Err)}}{\text{Var(True)}} \tag{7.4}$$

Formula (7.3) is theoretical because we never actually measure the true variance directly. Formula (7.4) provides a practical strategy for estimating reliability: the ratio of error variance to total variance tells us about "unreliability". Therefore, 1—this ratio captures the reliability of the scores.

Nunnally and Bernstein (1994) present a description of this measurement error in the context of a domain-sampling model. This model is consistent with the view that the items on a given instrument represent a sample of items from a well-defined domain or universe of content. According to Nunnally and Bernstein (1994), an individual's true score is the score the person would hypothetically obtain over the entire domain of items. Thus, reliability can be conceptualized in several ways. First, it is the proportion of the total variance in a scale that is explained by the true score (DeVellis 1991; Pett et al. 2003). Therefore, the correlation between the scale and the true score is the square root of the reliability coefficient. This term, shown in Eq. (7.5) is sometimes referred to as the reliability index.

$$\rho_{x,T} = \frac{\sigma_T}{\sigma_X} \tag{7.5}$$

The reliability index, the square root of the reliability coefficient, represents the correlation between the observed score and the true score. [This unfortunate choice of terminology sometimes leads to confusion when reading descriptions of reliability: the term reliability usually (but not always) refers to the reliability coefficient].

Second, the reliability coefficient is the correlation between two parallel tests. Parallel tests have equal reliabilities and equal error variances. Imagine that the correlation between test 1 and the true score is the reliability index shown above. Given that the tests are parallel, the correlation between test 2 and the true score is also the reliability index shown above. Using the tracing rule, the correlation between the two tests is the product of their paths (Loehlin 2004). Squaring formula (7.5) produces formula (7.3), which is the formula for the reliability coefficient. "The reliability coefficient cannot exceed the reliability index- the correlation between two fallible measures (r_{12}) cannot be higher than the correlation between a fallible measure and the true score (r_{1t})" (Nunnally and Bernstein 1994, p. 221). And of course, given that correlations cannot exceed 1.0, when the reliability index, which is the correlation between the measure and the true score, is squared, the resulting reliability coefficient must indeed be smaller.

How does the reliability coefficient relate to a given individual item? Under the assumption that the items are all equally correlated with each other, and therefore all are equally correlated with both the observed total score and the true score, the correlation between an item and the true score equals the square root of the average intercorrelation of that item with all of the other items (j) in the domain (Nunnally and Bernstein 1994):

$$r_{1\text{true}} = \sqrt{\bar{r}_j} \tag{7.6}$$

Because the average correlation of an item with all the other items in the domain is the reliability coefficient, then the square root of the reliability coefficient equals the correlation of the item with true scores in the domain (i.e., the sum of all items in the domain) such that

$$r_{1\text{true}} = \sqrt{\rho} = \sqrt{\text{rel}} \tag{7.7}$$

By squaring both sides of Eq. (5.6), we can also state that the reliability coefficient equals the squared correlation between an item and the true score.

$$r^2_{1\text{true}} = \rho \tag{7.8}$$

Recalling that squared correlations indicate the proportion of shared variance, we can extend this to a cluster of items defining a scale on an instrument and state that, conceptually, the reliability coefficient indicates the percentage of variance in the scale scores that can be considered "true" variance. For example, if the reliability of a scale is 0.90, then we estimate that 90% of the total variance in the scale scores is true variance; 10% of the total variance in the scale represents error variance or noise.

Sources of Error: Generalizability Theory

The previous section described the theory underlying reliability and related reliability to measure error. This section explores possible sources of error in the context of selecting appropriate procedures for establishing reliability.

We know that an instrument that produces more reliable scores also exhibits less measurement error. But what is measurement error? Where do errors of measurement come from? Measurement error is not a monolithic construct. Instead, there are several different sources of potential error depending on the nature of the instrument and how it is employed. According to Nunnally and Bernstein (1994), one major source of error within an instrument is due to inadequate sampling of items from the content domain. Instability across time represents another source of error. Administration of the same instrument ton the same group of people on two different occasions provides information about the stability of the scores across time. In the absence of intervention, most affective characteristics are fairly stable across a relatively brief time period of, say, approximately 3 weeks. If we administer the same instrument to a sample of individuals and find that their scores are not stable across time, the variability in individual responses over time indicates a degree of unreliability in scores.

Parallel forms of an instrument may introduce some degree of error into the measurement of people's scores. Therefore, when developing parallel forms of an instrument, it is essential to quantify the extent to which the items on both forms assess the same concepts, the degree of error within each of the two forms, and the degree of correspondence in scores across the parallel forms. Although this source of measurement error is indeed important, such parallel forms are relatively rare for most affective measures, especially those that are non-commercially developed.

If multiple raters are asked to rate the same set of behaviors or characteristics, variability across raters in terms of their perceptions of the attribute represents another source of error. This is an important source of error in teacher rating scales or in employee and managerial evaluations.

In addition, several other sources of error exist. For instruments measuring affective characteristics, these situational factors include (a) individual response variation due to fatigue, mood, or motivation, which could lead to random or careless responses; (b) variation in administration procedures (i.e., across time for two administrations or across settings during one administration), (c) physical factors such as temperature and noise, (d) psychological factors such as unclear instructions or lack of test time pressures; and, (e) errors in scoring or data entry (Isaac and Michael 1981, p. 126).

Akin to validity, reliability is a generic term that refers to different research questions and types of evidence. When reporting estimates of score reliability, researchers must clearly state the type of reliability addressed and the sources of error being studied. For most affective measurement applications, the first two sources of error, *items* and *occasions*, are the most important to assess. CTT allows us to quantify the sources of error one at a time (Brennan 1992; Shavelson and Webb 1991; Shavelson et al. 1989; Webb et al. 1988). Thus, Cronbach's coefficient alpha provides information regarding internal consistency reliability and item-sampling, but provides no information about the stability of the assessment instrument across time. To determine the reliability of scores across time, we would need to administer the instrument to a matched group of participants on a second occasion and examine the error due to occasion. By considering only one definition and source of error at a time, the researcher cannot simultaneously examine the relative importance of various sources of error. In fact, it can be quite puzzling if one of the separately generated reliability coefficients is high and the other is quite low. This could happen if the stability of test scores across time is quite high but the internal consistency of the items is low. Conversely, the internal consistency of scores on the scale could be low, but the stability of scores could be high. How could the instrument developer or user make sense of such seemingly contradictory results?

Generalizability theory (G-theory) allows us to estimate the magnitude of these multiple sources of error simultaneously. Using G-theory, we could simultaneously examine the homogeneity of the items and the stability of the responses over time, as well as the interaction of these two sources of error. The classical and most common approach to G-theory "estimates sources of variation among scores within an analysis of variance framework" (Cardinet et al. 2010, p. viii). Using ANOVA allows for the partitioning of variance into multiple sources, which can either be crossed or nested. Although the topic of G-theory is incredibly important to the study of score reliability, providing a full treatment of the analytic technique is beyond the scope of this book. Readers should consult Brennan (2001), Cardinet et al. (2010), Meyer (2010), and Shavelson and Webb (1991), all of which provide thorough introductions to the technique.

We will now turn to the two major types of reliability evidence that are of most concern for the affective instrument developer: internal consistency and stability.

Types of Reliability Coefficients

Internal Consistency Reliability

The most commonly used estimate of internal consistency reliability is Cronbach's (1951) coefficient alpha. The formula for Cronbach's alpha internal consistency reliability coefficient is

$$\rho_\alpha = \frac{k}{k-1}\left(1 - \frac{\sum_1^k \sigma_k^2}{\sigma_{\text{Total}}^2}\right) \tag{7.9}$$

where k = the number of items, $\sum \sigma_k^2$ = the sum of the item variances, and σ_{Total}^2 = the variance of the total (scale) scores. The total variance in a scale is equal to the sum of the elements in the item variance covariance matrix. Therefore, the formula for Cronbach's alpha can be reexpressed as

$$\rho_\alpha = \frac{k}{k-1}\left(\frac{\sum_i \sum_j \sigma_{ij}^2}{\sigma_{\text{Total}}^2}\right), \ (i, j = 1, 2, \ldots, k; i \neq j) \tag{7.10}$$

where $\sum_i \sum_j \sigma_{ij}^2; (i, j = 1, 2, \ldots, k; i \neq j)$ indicates that all of the covariance elements of a given matrix are summed (Cronbach 1951). The sum of the elements a variance covariance matrix is equal to the sum of the variances plus 2 times the sum of all of the unique covariances. The sum of the covariances is multiplied by 2 because each of the unique covariances appears twice in the covariance matrix. Therefore, Cronbach's alpha is $k/(k-l)$ times the ratio of inter-item covariances to total variance of the scale. Given that there are $k(k-1)$ covariances and only k variances on a scale with k items, the multiplier $k/(k-1)$ takes into account that the number of elements of the covariance matrix is less than the total number of elements in the variance/covariance matrix by a factor of $(k-1)/k$.

Imagine two extreme scenarios. If none of the items on a scale are correlated with each other at all, then the sum of the item covariances equals 0 and 2* the sum of the item covariances also equals 0. In such a scenario, the sum of the item variances equals the scale score variance, therefore, the ratio in Eq. (7.9) equals 1 and 1 minus that ratio equals 0. Alternatively, using formula (7.10), the sum of the item covariances equals 0; therefore, the Cronbach's alpha estimate equals 0. In that scenario, the reliability of the scale will equal 0, no matter how many items are on the scale. Imagine another extreme scenario. Imagine that all of the items were correlated at 1.0. In other words, all of the variance in each item is also captured in the covariances among items. In such an extreme scenario, the covariances would all be equal to each other and to the variances. Therefore, using formula (7.10), we can substitute X for each of the variance and covariance elements. In such a scenario,

$$\rho_\alpha = \frac{k}{k-1}\left(\frac{k \cdot (k-1) \cdot X}{k \cdot X + [k \cdot (k-1) \cdot X]}\right) \tag{7.11}$$

Factoring $k * X$ out of the numerator and the denominator of the expression within parentheses results in

$$\rho_\alpha = \frac{k}{k-1}\left(\frac{(k-1)}{1+(k-1)}\right) = \frac{k}{k-1}\left(\frac{k-1}{k}\right) = 1 \tag{7.12}$$

Obviously, this demonstrates that if all items are perfectly correlated with each other, Cronbach's alpha will equal 1.0. This also helps to illustrate the purpose for the $\frac{k}{k-1}$ term, which accounts for the difference in the number of elements that are used to compute the numerator and the denominator of the expression.

Why does increasing the number of items increase Cronbach's alpha? What may not be obvious from the formulas above is why the magnitude of Cronbach's alpha is so dependent on the number of items. To demonstrate this, let us imagine a scenario in which the variances of all items are equal to each other and the covariances of all the items are equal to each other and are some factor r of the magnitude of the variances. In such a scenario, formula (7.10) reduces to

$$\rho_{\alpha} = \frac{k}{k-1}\left(\frac{k(k-1)\cdot rV}{k(k-1)\cdot rV + kV}\right) = \frac{k}{k-1}\left(\frac{(k-1)r}{(k-1)r+1}\right) = \frac{k\cdot r}{1+(k-1)\cdot r} \tag{7.13}$$

As k gets larger, the ratio of $\frac{k\cdot r}{1+(k-1)\cdot r}$ gets smaller for any positive value of r. The formula that we have just derived, $\frac{k\cdot r}{1+(k-1)\cdot r}$, is actually the Spearman-Brown prophecy formula, which we return to shortly. Clearly, the number of items plays a role in the reliability estimate. The number of items, which determines k, has an impact on the ratio of the number of covariances to the number of variances.

We can easily compute the number of unique off-diagonal elements in an inter-item correlation (IIC) or covariance matrix. Conceptually, this is the number of combinations of k items things taken two at a time, which can be expressed as

$$\frac{k!}{2!\,(k-2)!}$$

where k represents the number of items, and 2 indicates that we are correlating two items at a time.[1]

Because $\frac{k!}{(k-2)!}$ simplifies to $k(k-1)$ and 2! Simplifies to 2, we can re-express this formula as

$$\frac{k(k-1)}{2}$$

Therefore, the total number of off-diagonal elements in the variance covariance matrix is $k(k-1)$. The number of variances is equal to the number of items, k. Given that the number of covariances in a variance/covariance matrix equals $k(k-1)$ and the number of variances equals k, the ratio of the number of covariances to the number of variances is $k-1{:}1$. For example, with 3 items, there are three variances and six covariances (there are only three unique covariances, but there are six elements in the off-diagonal portion of the matrix). However, with 30 items, there are 30 variances and 870 covariances.

[1] The symbol ! indicates "factorial." For example, $4! = 4 \times 3 \times 2 \times 1$.

Because the reliability gets larger as the ratio of the item covariances to the item variances and covariances gets larger, all other things being equal, adding items increases reliability. Therefore, given the same average inter-item correlation, increasing the number of items increases the reliability coefficient. However, this relationship is not linear. Increasing a scale by one or two items has a very large effect when the number of items on the scale is small and a very small effect when the number of items is large. Figure 7.1 illustrates the relationship between the average inter-item correlation, the number of items, and the internal consistency reliability coefficient.

Figure 7.1 illustrates a few important points about Cronbach's alpha. First, higher average inter-item correlations result in higher Cronbach's alpha values, holding the number of items constant. Increasing the number of items also increases alpha. So there are many ways to obtain a high Cronbach's alpha coefficient. Scores from a scale with low or modest average inter-item correlations can have a high Cronbach's alpha given enough items. Conversely, when the average inter-item correlation is high, it takes very few items to produce a high Cronbach's alpha, and additional items do not add much value in terms of increasing the reliability coefficient. This leads to a concrete and pragmatic recommendation regarding the recommended number of items for an affective scale. If the construct or dimension of interest is narrowly bound and defined, the IICs are usually high, and such a narrowly defined construct can be reliably measured with only a few items. If, on the other hand, the construct is diffuse and broadly defined, the IICs are often fairly low. In such a scenario, to reliably measure the construct requires a large number of items. From a domain-sampling approach, this also makes sense, as it would require a larger number of items to adequately

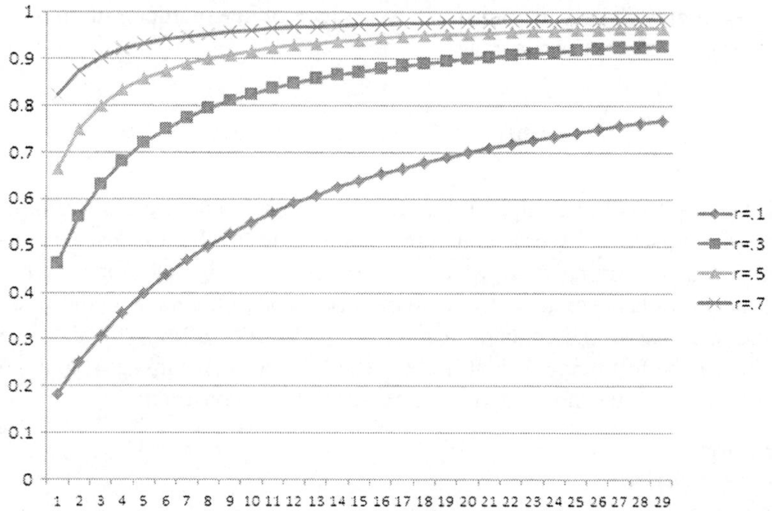

Fig. 7.1 Reliability as a function of the number of items and the average inter-item correlation

sample from a large, diffuse domain than it would to adequately sample from a tightly constrained, narrowly defined domain.

Assume for a moment that all items on the scale have equal variances and covariances, and thus equal correlations. In such a scenario, calculating the average of the IICs estimates the reliability of an one-item scale. Therefore, we can use the formula that we derived in Eq. (7.13) to estimate the reliability of a scale with k items using the Spearman-Brown Prophecy Formula:

$$\frac{k \cdot \bar{r}}{1 + (k - 1) \cdot \bar{r}} \tag{7.14}$$

where k represents the number of items on the scale, and $\bar{r}$ represents the average inter-item correlation. For example, inserting $k = 5$ and $r = 0.25$ into the formula

$$\frac{k \cdot \bar{r}}{1 + (k - 1) \cdot \bar{r}} = \frac{5 \cdot 0.25}{1 + (5 - 1) \cdot 0.25} = \frac{1.25}{2.0} = 0.625$$

yields an expected alpha of 0.625. Using the same average inter-item correlation of 0.25 with a 10-item scale produces an expected coefficient alpha of 0.77, as shown below.

$$\frac{k \cdot r}{1 + (k - 1) \cdot r} = \frac{10 \cdot 0.25}{1 + (10 - 1) \cdot 0.25} = \frac{2.5}{3.25} = 0.77$$

Finally, a 20-item scale with an average inter-item correlation of 0.25 produces an expected coefficient alpha of 0.87, as shown below.

$$\frac{k \cdot r}{1 + (k - 1) \cdot r} = \frac{20 \cdot 0.25}{1 + (20 - 1) \cdot 0.25} = \frac{5}{5.75} = 0.87$$

These examples clearly demonstrate the effect of the number of items on the estimate of coefficient alpha.

Small Numeric Example of Cronbach's Alpha

The ideal way to generate alpha reliabilities is to use a statistical software package, which also generates several other item- and scale-level statistics. However, we can also estimate alpha quite quickly using a hand calculator or a spreadsheet, using the formulas provided above. We work through a simple numeric example by hand to illustrate the concept of internal consistency of individuals' responses.

Consider the following four attitude-toward-school items taken from a larger set of items—(Note that this is a very narrowly defined construct):

I like school.
School is really fun.
I enjoy going to school.
School makes me happy.

Assume that 200 grade-6 students responded to these four items on a 5-point Likert scale ranging from *strongly disagree*, (1) to *strongly agree* (5). Rather than utilizing the applicable variances specified in Eq. (7.9) or (7.10), the coefficient alpha reliability can be estimated by using the IICs using the Spearman-Brown prophecy formula from formula (7.14) (Cronbach 1951).

Table 7.1 contains hypothetical IICs. To generate the alpha reliability coefficient, first calculate the average inter-item correlation by taking the mean of all off-diagonal elements in the correlation matrix. In this example, that results in an average inter-item correlation of 0.47. Once we know the average inter-item correlation, we can use the Spearman-Brown prophecy formula from formula (7.14) to estimate the alpha reliability coefficient of the scale.

$$\frac{k \cdot \bar{r}}{1 + (k - 1) \cdot \bar{r}} = \frac{4 \cdot 0.47}{1 + (4 - 1) \cdot 0.47} = \frac{1.88}{2.41} = 0.78$$

Based upon this reliability coefficient, we can then say that 78% of the variance in the scale scores (i.e., sum of four items) can be considered true score variance and about 22% of the scale variance is attributable to error. The estimated correlation of the scale with the true score is the square root of 0.78 or 0.88 [see Eq. (7.7)].

In essence, calculating the average of the IICs estimates the reliability of an one-item scale. Therefore, we can also reexpress of the Spearman-Brown Prophecy Formula as follows:

$$\frac{L \cdot \text{rel}}{1 + (L - 1) \cdot \text{rel}} \tag{7.15}$$

where L represents the number of times one wishes to increase the length of the instrument, and rel represents the reliability of the scale at its current length. Recall that our 4-item scale had an average inter-item correlation of 0.47, yielding an alpha of 0.78. What would be the estimated reliability if we doubled the length of the scale? We can use formula (7.15) to compute the reliability if we doubled the number of items in the scale:

$$\frac{L \cdot \text{rel}}{1 + (L - 1) \cdot \text{rel}} = \frac{2 \cdot (0.78)}{1 + (2 - 1) \cdot 0.78} = 0.876$$

Table 7.1 Inter-item correlations for attitude toward school items

		1	2	3	4
Items	1	–			
	2	0.40	–		
	3	0.50	0.55	–	
	4	0.55	0.40	0.40	–

This formula is equivalent to (7.14). Doubling the length of the scale means that we increase the scale from 4 to 8 items. Therefore, we can use formula (7.14) to estimate the reliability coefficient for an 8-item scale:

$$\frac{k \cdot \bar{r}}{1 + (k - 1) \cdot \bar{r}} = \frac{8 \cdot (0.47)}{1 + (8 - 1) \cdot 0.47} = \frac{3.76}{4.29} = 0.876$$

As we mentioned earlier, the number of items on a scale relates to the reliability of the scale. Furthermore, having larger numbers of items on a scale allows us to more adequately sample from the universe of content. It also helps to increase variability in the resulting scale scores. Therefore, one way to increase the reliability of a subscale is to increase the number of items on the scale. To determine the number of items needed on a scale to generate a given internal consistency reliability estimate, we can use Eq. (7.16):

$$L = \frac{\rho_{\text{desired}}(1 - \rho_{\text{current}})}{\rho_{\text{current}}(1 - \rho_{\text{desired}})} \tag{7.16}$$

where ρ_{desired} is the desired reliability (i.e., 0.80), ρ_{current} is the current estimate of reliability, and L is the factor by which the scale needs to be increased to yield the desired reliability. A common error in using this formula is to conclude that L represents the number of items to add to the scale. Note carefully that L represents the factor by which the original number of items should be multiplied to lengthen the original scale.

This formula is useful in that it allows one to calculate directly the number of items needed. For example, if we have a 3-item scale with a reliability of 0.60, and we wished to know how long the scale would need to yield an alpha reliability of 0.80, we would calculate L as follows:

$$L = \frac{\rho_{\text{desired}}(1 - \rho_{\text{current}})}{\rho_{\text{current}}(1 - \rho_{\text{desired}})} = \frac{0.80\,(1 - 0.60)}{0.60\,(1 - 0.80)} = \frac{0.80\,(0.40)}{0.60\,(0.20)} = 2.6667$$

Therefore, the 3-item scale would have to be increased by a factor of 2.6667 to yield a reliability of 0.80. Therefore, the scale would need to contain 3 * 2.6667 = 8 items; therefore, 5 new items would need to be developed for the scale. Of course, this assumes that the average inter-item correlation remains constant after the addition of the 5 new items. If the new items were generally less homogeneous (less inter-correlated) than the original items, the average inter-item correlation would decrease, and the 8-item scale would have a reliability estimate below 0.80. This version of the Spearman-Brown prophecy formula is very helpful as it allows us to determine how many items we need to add to a scale (holding the average inter-item correlation constant) to reach our desired level of internal consistency.

In this section, we have illustrated the procedure suggested by Cronbach (1951) to estimate an alpha reliability based upon IICs. A final example using the four attitude-toward-school items listed earlier should further clarify the concept of internal consistency. Just what is it about individual response patterns that lead to high alpha internal consistency reliabilities? We answer this question by considering the two small hypothetical data sets contained in Table 7.2. Example 1, on the left hand side of the table, illustrates internally consistent responses across the four items defining the scale. Note that some of the individuals tend to consistently "agree" with the items—i.e., they like school—while other students appear not to like school—they consistently "disagree" with the items. Picture two hypothetical students who really do like school (e.g., individuals A and D). When these individuals processed these four item stems, they perceived content similarities so that they responded in a similar and consistent manner by tending to "agree" with the statements. In contrast, individual "C" does not like school. Therefore, he disagrees or strongly disagrees with all four of the items. The internal consistency responses provides some evidence of reliability of scores.

Example 2, on the right hand side of Table 7.2, illustrates response patterns that are not internally consistent across the four items. When processing these four item stems, some individuals (e.g., B and C) did not perceive similar meaning and thus supplied inconsistent responses. For example, individual C "strongly agreed" with the item "I like school," but "strongly disagreed" with the item "School is really fun." Given this inconsistent response pattern, it is difficult to predict how these individuals will answer any given item based on their responses to the other items

Table 7.2 Response patterns leading to high and low alpha reliabilities

		Example 1-high				Example 2-low			
		Items				Items			
		1	2	3	4	1	2	3	4
Individuals	A	5	4	4	5	2	2	1	2
	B	2	1	2	3	4	1	4	1
	C	1	1	2	1	5	1	4	3
	D	4	5	5	4	2	4	3	2
	E	5	5	5	5	2	4	1	2
	F	5	3	4	5	4	5	4	5
	G	2	3	1	2	2	1	5	2
	H	3	2	4	1	1	2	5	2
	I	5	2	2	5	4	3	3	1
	J	2	5	5	4	2	2	5	2

Item stems
1. I like school
2. School is really fun
3. I enjoy going to school
4. School makes me happy

Response format
5 = Strongly agree
4 = Agree
3 = Undecided
2 = Disagree
1 = Strongly disagree

Table 7.3 Inter-item correlations and estimated alpha reliabilities

	Example 1					Example 2				
	Item					Item				
		1	2	3	4		1	2	3	4
Inter-item correlations	1	–	0.43	0.44	0.81	1	–	−0.06.	0.06	−0.12
	2		–	0.77	0.57	2		–	−0.39	0.30
	3			–	0.45	3			–	0.33
	4					4				–
Estimated alpha	0.85					0.08				

on the subscale. What is the effect of internally inconsistent response patterns on alpha reliability?

Table 7.3 contains the IICs and the estimated Cronbach's alpha reliability estimates for each of the example datasets. The average inter-item correlation ($r = 0.58$) is higher for Example 1: students agree with any given item tend to agree with the other items on the subscale. In Example 2, the lower average inter-item correlation ($r = 0.02$) indicates that responses to the items on the scale are unrelated to each other: knowing the response to a given item does not help to predict responses to other items. Given that the estimate of alpha reliability is a function of the number of items and the average inter-item correlation, the Cronbach's alpha reliability estimate for Example 2 is much lower (alpha = 0.08) than the estimate for Example 1 (alpha = 0.85). If the items and data from Example 2 were part of a pilot test of a new instrument, we could only say that 8% of the observed variance in the attitudes toward school scale can be considered true variance; 92% of the variance would be attributed to error. The estimated correlation between scale scores formed from these items and true scores is 0.28 ($\sqrt{0.08}$). Given the low internal consistency among the items, results resembling those in Example 2 would suggest that we need to return to step 1 of the validation process, reanalyze the operational definitions of the content domain, and conduct a new content- validity study. Why? The four items are not measuring any one common thing. Scores that do not measure any one thing do not measure anything, and scores that do not measure anything cannot possibly be measuring what we had intended to measure. Hence evidence of reliability is prerequisite to that of validity. Using the formula (7.16) serves to illustrate the issue quite dramatically. Given a 4-item scale with a reliability of 0.08, we can solve for *L*.

$$L = \frac{\rho_{\text{desired}}(1 - \rho_{\text{current}})}{\rho_{\text{current}}(1 - \rho_{\text{desired}})} = \frac{0.80\,(1 - 0.08)}{0.08\,(1 - 0.80)} = \frac{0.80\,(0.92)}{0.08\,(0.20)} = 46 \qquad (7.17)$$

Therefore, we would need to increase the number of items by a factor of 46 to achieve an alpha reliability of 0.80. Given that our scale has 4 items, the new scale would need to contain 46 * 4 = 184 items to achieve a reliability of 0.80. Clearly, this is not feasible or practical.

Split-Half Estimates of Reliability

The *split-half* technique has also been used to examine internal consistency reliability. This procedure randomly splits the scale into two equivalent sets of items which represent two samples of items from the content domain. The correlation of the scores from the two halves is then entered into the special form of the Spearman-Brown Prophecy Formula presented in Eq. (7.15), to generate the reliability of the whole instrument as follows:

$$\frac{2 \cdot r_{12}}{1 + (2 - 1) \cdot r_{12}} = \frac{2 \cdot r_{12}}{1 + r_{12}} \tag{7.18}$$

where 2 = the factor that indicates that the instrument is really twice as long, and r_{12} = the correlation between the two half-instruments. This technique depends on obtaining a proper split of the whole instrument on the basis of item content. Given that computer programs can readily produce Cronbach's alpha, which conceptually represents the average of *all possible splits* of the instrument, it is rare that one would use the split-half technique to estimate reliability.

Assumptions of Cronbach's Alpha

Cronbach's alpha as an estimate of internal consistency reliability is predicated on several assumptions. First, the items for which Cronbach's alpha id being computed are assumed to be unidimensional. Therefore, we compute Cronbach's alpha estimates separately for each subscale. We never compute Cronbach's alpha for an entire instrument if it contains multiple factors or dimensions. Performing a factor analysis prior to the computation of Cronbach's alpha can assist in the assessment of unidimensionality. Cronbach's alpha provides a good estimate of internal consistency reliability when used for congeneric measures (Raykov and Marcoulides 2011). In a congeneric measure, all of the items are equally related to a common factor and there are no correlated uniquenesses among the items. Therefore, when a factor analysis reveals that all items have similar loadings and none of the items are more correlated with each other than the factor structure would suggest, then Cronbach's alpha is a good estimate of internal consistency reliability. Unfortunately, we do not always meet these fairly strict assumptions. Therefore, other estimates of reliability have been developed to estimate reliability within a factor analytic framework. Raykov and Marcoulides provide an excellent introduction to this alternative method to estimating internal consistency reliability. At the time of writing this book, these more nuanced (and more correct) approaches to the estimation of reliability within a latent variable modeling framework tend to be reported within the SEM literature. However, Cronbach's alpha remains the most commonly reported measure of reliability within the affective instrument design literature.

Factors Affecting Internal Consistency Reliability

The reliability of a set of items is affected by several factors, including the homogeneity of the item content, the number of items, the response format, and the characteristics of the sample. It is essential that instrument developers understand how these areas potentially affect the reliability of a set of items. In this section, we discuss each area, noting that they are not independent, but most likely interact with each other to affect reliability estimates, especially estimates of internal consistency reliability.

Negatively Worded or Reverse Scored Items

The most common error in the computation of internal reliability coefficients is forgetting to reverse score-negative item stems prior to generating the correlations. The computation of Cronbach's alpha assumes that all IICs are positive. Therefore, if one-item is negatively related to the other items on the scale (whether by design or by fluke), it is essential to reverse score that item prior to conducting the reliability analyzes. Failure to do this results in negative correlations that appear to lower the alpha reliability. Reverse scoring all negatively worded items in the beginning of the analysis should alleviate the problem of having negative inter-item correlations. However, occasionally, items that seem like they should be positively correlated with the other items on the scale are actually negatively correlated with rest of the scale. For this reason, we recommend examining the correlation matrix for each subscale prior to computing reliability coefficients. Ideally, there should be no negative correlations within the matrix. Certainly, any item that is negatively correlated with most or all of the other items on the subscale needs to be reverse scored prior to conducting the reliability analyzes.

Homogeneity of Item Content

During the process of establishing content validity, we operationalize the conceptual definitions by developing several item stems that hail from a domain of content and are indicators of a particular underlying construct. Of course, it is the degree of interrelationship that the respondents perceive among the items that drives the alpha internal consistency reliability. If the items assigned to a particular scale are very homogeneous in content, it is more likely that the item/scale correlations and IICs will be higher, which in turn will lead to higher alpha reliabilities. Having said that, from a validity standpoint, it is certainly possible for a set of items to be too homogeneous. If items are simply restatements of the same basic item stem, then although scores on a scale may exhibit very high internal consistency reliability, the scale is so narrowly defined that it may not capture the entire domain of the construct as the developer had originally intended. Therefore, in general, we strive to maintain IICs in the 0.30–0.60 range for items that measure the same subscale, and item-total score correlations of 0.30–0.60 are ideal for affective instruments.

Variability in the Inter-Item Correlations

Both the average magnitude of average inter-item correlations and the variability in their magnitudes provide us with important information about the scale. Ideally, the average inter-item correlation should be neither too low nor too high. Very low or near zero IICs indicate that respondents' responses to the two items are virtually unrelated to each other. In other words, knowing how someone responded to one of the questions would not help to predict their responses to another other question. Such results could reflect a high incidence of error in the sampling of items from the domain of content, the possible existence of situational factors that would influence the responses to the items, or other issues that need to be addressed in the revision of the instrument. Very high IICs (above 0.80) are also troubling. Two items that are too highly correlated with each other are likely to be redundant: they are often restatements of the exact same stem using slightly different wording. Having two very highly correlated items on a scale will boost the Cronbach's alpha reliability coefficient. However, from a domain-sampling perspective, the instrument oversamples from one small space in the content domain. Therefore, the set of items is not really a representative sample from the universe of items. In general, most affective instruments have average inter-item correlations in the 0.30–0.60 range. Ideally, the individual IICs should cluster fairly tightly around the average inter-item correlations: we prefer not to have a great deal of variability in the magnitudes of the IICs for a given scale. Why? If some items on the subscale are highly correlated with each other and some are virtually uncorrelated with each other, this could be indicative of multidimensionality. In such a scenario, it is likely that not all items are measuring the same construct. At the very least, not all items are measuring the construct equally well. To assess the degree of variability in the IICs, we can compute the variance and the standard deviation of the inter-item correlation. Ideally, the variance of the IIC should be below 0.01, which translates into a standard deviation of the IIC of 0.10. SPSS provides the variance of the IICs. Taking the square root of this estimate provides the standard deviation of the inter-item correlations.

Sample Characteristics

In pilot testing a set of items, the selection of the sample is crucial. The goal is to select a pilot sample that exhibits the same level of variability in the affective characteristic as that which exists in the target population. For example, to validate a school attitude questionnaire with high-school students, the pilot sample should reflect the entire high-school population. Administering these items to four easily available grade 9–12 honors classes would be problematic. Because the honors students would exhibit more positive and more homogeneous attitudes, the variance in their responses would be smaller than the variance for the total high-school population.

Decreasing the variance in either or both variables involved in the computation of a correlation necessarily reduces the size of the correlation. Therefore, although two items on the scale may be strongly conceptually related, the sample characteristics have, in effect, put a ceiling on the level of correlation. As a result, if the variances of the items are restricted, the average inter-item correlations for the set of items will be lower, which results in a lower estimate of the alpha internal consistency reliability for those scores. The developer might erroneously conclude that the sampling of items from the universe of items is inadequate, when in fact the sampling of items was quite adequate, but the sampling of people was inadequate. Pilot samples should always include representative individuals who will produce variability in responses similar to that in the target population.

This lack of variability also occurs when respondents tend to exhibit extreme responses which result in either high or low means. Items with very high or low means and associated low variability will contribute little to the internal consistency estimate of reliability for the set of items. Also, items with extreme means and low variances do not fare well in factor analyzes because the factor analysis model is also based upon correlations and shared variance among items. Again, items with little to no variance cannot and will not exhibit much shared variance with other items. We caution the readers to be wary of writing items that are hard to disagree with (e.g., "I feel sad sometimes") or hard to disagree with ("I have never felt envious of one of my friends"). Without variability in response patterns, items cannot contribute to the reliability estimates, and they cannot help to distinguish among people who differ on the latent trait of interest.

A final comment regarding how the sample relates to sample size is in order. In general, we favor large samples for instrumentation studies. However, large samples are not necessarily representative samples. For example, imagine that a hotel chain wants to develop an instrument to measure brand-name loyalty and satisfaction. The company decides to pilot the instrument with their elite rewards members because they have easy access to the email addresses for their elite members. Although the company surveys over a million elite members, this sample is likely to be more positively disposed toward the chain and more homogeneous in their responses than a randomly drawn sample of people. For this reason, low response rates can also be problematic. For example, imagine that a company emails a large sample of adults to ask about consumer preferences but only 5% of the target population responds to the survey. It is likely that the 5% of people who took the time to complete the survey are systematically different from the 95% of people who ignored the survey. Thus, their responses are likely to be more homogeneous than the responses of the population at large. Therefore, although pilot studies do not require a random sample of participants from the target population, sampling and data collection should be conducted in a manner that attempts to capture full range of variability in the population as well as possible.

Stability Reliability

The measures of internal consistency discussed in the previous section do not address an important source of measurement error—error due to fluctuations in individual responses over time. When using an affective instrument in a pre/post program-evaluation model or to document changes over time, it is critical to collect evidence for the stability of scores across time. Why? When we observe differences in scores across time, we would like to assume that the differences between the pre- and post-scores are due to a treatment effect and not due to a lack of stability reliability in the instrument. Thus, we need to first theoretically establish that the trait should be stable for, say, a three- week period in the absence of a treatment designed to change the trait. Then we administer the instrument to the same sample at two different times and correlate the test/retest scores to estimate the degree stability reliability in the scores.

There are some cautions for planning a stability reliability study. First, we need to be aware that high stability reliability does not address the item-sampling issue from the domain-sampling model (see Nunnally 1978, Ch. 7). That is, an inadequate sample of items could result in an average inter-item correlation near zero, which would yield a very low alpha internal consistency reliability, as we demonstrated above. These same items, though, could be found to have a very high stability reliability. This may seem contradictory, but the two types of reliability address different sources of error. Thus, it is important to first establish the alpha reliability and then, if appropriate, generate the stability reliability coefficient. Scores with a low Cronbach's alpha and a high stability reliability should not be considered reliable.

A second caution pertains to the effect of learning from the first test or remembering previously reported responses. It is important to carefully think through the nature of the concept measured by the particular operational definitions (items) selected. If the time between the test and retest is too short (i.e., a few days), respondents may merely repeat their recalled responses. Third, the tendency to respond with extreme ratings (*strongly agree*) for many items, or attempts to fake or give socially desired responses, can yield stable response patterns.

It is important to consider the nature of the construct when assessing and evaluating stability reliability. Traits should be quite stable across time. However, states, such as moods, are by definition, fleeting. Therefore, high estimates of stability reliability are necessary to adequately measure traits. However, high estimates of stability reliability could actually call into question whether one is adequately capturing the measurement of a state.

A final, more general caution is in order. Reliability is a generic term: different methods of generating reliability evidence account for different sources of error. Clearly designed and labeled reliability evidence should be present prior to using any instrument. Researchers often report reliability estimates from journal articles or test manuals without carefully thinking through and defending the nature of the reliability evidence needed for their particular use of the instrument. They may report reliability data for samples that have little in common with the samples to be employed in the proposed research. Reliability is a property of scores, not instruments, and tools that produce reliable scores in one context may not produce reliable scores in a different setting or with a different group of participants. Therefore, even when using a previously created instrument, researchers should compute reliability estimates for their samples and report those reliability estimates. In addition, general statements such as "the test is reliable" are not acceptable (AERA, APA and NCME 1999).

Acceptable Levels of Reliability

How high should the estimates of score reliability be? According to the Standards for Educational and Psychological Testing (AERA, APA and NCME 1999), it is the responsibility of the test user to determine "whether or not scores are sufficiently trustworthy to justify anticipated uses and interpretations" (p. 31). They also discourage instrument developers from making assertions such that a test is reliable or that it demonstrates sufficient reliability to permit interpretations of individual scores. Having said that, both instrument designers and consumers seek guidance on minimal acceptable levels of reliability. Given that "the level of a score's reliability places limits on its unique contribution to validity for all purposes" (p. 31), scores must meet some minimal threshold in terms of consistency and replicability to have utility. Generally, rules of thumb regarding acceptable levels of reliability depend in part on the use for which the instrument is intended. In general, affective measures have slightly lower reliability levels than do cognitive measures. Cognitive skills tend to be more consistent and stable than most affective characteristics. In addition, cognitive measures generally contain more items and have undergone a far more rigorous validation process. Thus, it is typical for thoughtfully developed cognitive measures to have alpha and stability reliabilities in the 1990s, whereas published affective instruments frequently report reliabilities as low as 0.70.

The difference in the reliability-criterion level also reflects the nature of the decisions to be made based upon the obtained scores. Obviously, the higher the stakes of the decisions that are being made using an assessment, the higher the reliability of the instrument needs to be. Several crucial programming decisions (e.g., special-education placement and college admissions) are often based upon the results of cognitive achievement measures. Thus, it is essential that those scores exhibit a very high degree of reliability.

On the other hand, researchers generally tolerate lower reliability estimates for data resulting from affective measures that are being used for research purposes. Because the scores are not being used to make individual diagnoses or decisions, researchers often argue that reliability estimates at or above 0.70 are reasonable for research purposes. We feel that in general, higher levels of score reliability are desirable, even for research studies. For example, imagine that a researcher compared two methods of teaching social studies on the dependent variable "attitude toward social studies," measured by an instrument with a reliability of the data at 0.70. Employing a *t* test, the researcher found no differences between the groups. Given that 30% of the variance was error variance, this greatly increased the estimated error in the sampling distribution of mean differences (i.e., the denominator of the *t* test). This could conceal a treatment effect that was really present. Thus, using affective instruments that produce unreliable scores as dependent variables in a program-evaluation study could readily result in what statisticians call a "Type II error"—failure to reject a false null hypothesis (i.e., the program really worked and you say it did not). Consider also a similar problem encountered in the use of affective measures regression analysis. In regression and the analysis of covariance, we actually make the assumption that all independent variables are measured with perfect reliability. Unreliability in the independent variable or covariate can produce biased parameter estimates. In mediational models, we assume that the mediator is estimated without error. Again, unreliability in the mediator results in biased parameter estimates of the direct and indirect effects. In short, many of our analyzes depend on reliably estimated scores. Therefore, when conducting research, we must be certain that the scores exhibit a high degree of reliability; otherwise, our inferences from the operational to the conceptual definitions of the affective characteristics are likely to be inaccurate and our research conclusions may be wrong.

The Relationship of Reliability to Validity

In this chapter, we have depicted reliability as an indication of the proportion of variation in test score that is true variance as opposed to error variance. Further, we noted that score reliability can take many forms, including the internal consistency of responses upon one testing or the stability of scores across time. Does reliability of scores ensure validity of inferences? The answer is clearly no!

It is commonly stated that "reliability is a necessary but not a sufficient condition for validity." This statement implies that it is clearly possible for scores to exhibit high internal consistency and stability reliability without actually capturing the essence of the construct that we sought to measure. For example, we could administer a set of items to a sample of students and find that the internal consistency and stability (upon a retest) reliability of the responses were quite high. The validity of the instrument depends upon what we claim that set of items measures and the inferences that we wish to make from the scores on that scale. If we claim that the items reflect attitudes toward school, can we offer validity evidence to support this claim? An instrument that produces reliable scores may or may not allow us to make valid inferences. But an instrument that demonstrates adequate evidence of validity generally produces reasonably reliable scores. Why? if an instrument is carefully developed so that (1) clear judgmental evidence exists to support the correspondence of the operational and conceptual definitions and (2) the empirical evidence based upon the internal structure of the instrument, and the relations of the constructs with other known measures, then the scores from the instrument should demonstrate at least some minimal level of consistency. If the scales on the instrument contained a large portion of error variance, the responses would fluctuate erratically. Under such conditions, the correlations with other known instruments would not be high nor would the analyzes of the internal structure yield coherent and meaningful results. In other words, meaningful correlations during the study of construct-validity should occur when only when scores have some degree of consistency. Thus, gathering evidence of reliability is important in instrument development; it is a necessary but not a sufficient condition for validity.

Finally, consider how reliability sets a ceiling on the magnitude of the validity coefficient, which is defined as the correlation between two measures:

$$r_{ab} = \sqrt{\rho_a \cdot \rho_b} \tag{7.19}$$

Suppose that we have a new scale (a) and a known scale or criterion measure (b). If the reliability of both instruments is 0.80, the maximum possible correlation between the two scales is also 0.80. If the reliability of scale a is 0.60 and the reliability of scale b is 0.80, the maximum correlation between the two scales is 0.69. Therefore, a lower than theoretically expected correlation with a known measure may be influenced by unreliability in one or both sets of scores. Conversely, we would generally not consider correlations of 0.60 or 0.70 between two scales to be indicative of discriminant validity issues. However, if the reliability estimates of the two scales are 0.70, then the correlation between the two scales cannot be greater than 0.70. Therefore, a correlation above 0.60 between two scales with reliability estimates of 0.70 could indeed indicate discriminant validity issues.

In this section we have discussed the relationship between reliability and validity. Some instrument manuals present the more easily obtained evidence of score reliability and then try and argue that "validity" follows. Meaningful evidence of validity may be somewhat more difficult to obtain; however, such evidence must be present in all technical manuals before users can hope to make meaningful score interpretations.

Table 7.4 Items on the utility value subscale of the SVA

	Mean	Std. deviation	N
16. School is necessary for achieving my future goals	6.44	1.00	181
17. School has many "real world" applications	5.23	1.40	181
18. The content of my classes is useful	5.09	1.40	181
19. Doing well in school will hep me with my future goals	6.24	1.17	181
20. I am learning valuable information in school	5.34	1.38	181
21. I will definitely use the information taught in my courses	5.07	1.46	181
22. School will help to "get me where I want to go"	6.03	1.22	181

Computer Output: Cronbach's Alpha Internal Consistency

In this chapter we have emphasized the importance of the alpha internal-consistency reliability coefficient. In light of its importance, we have attempted to develop an understanding of the concept of internal consistency by illustrating how responses were internally consistent and how to estimate alpha using IICs. In the process of developing a new instrument or studying an existing one, much more statistical information is needed in addition to the actual alpha coefficient. Basically, this information reflects item-level statistics which contribute to the level of alpha. In this section, we illustrate how reliability can be estimated using SPSS. For this illustration, we use the data gathered from 181 secondary students responding to the 7-item utility value subscale listed in Table 7.4. The scale is designed to measure how useful students believe that school is for achieving their goals.

Descriptive Statistics

Table 7.4 contains the item-level means and standard deviations for the seven items on the utility value scale. Extremely high or low means, especially in conjunction with low standard deviations would indicate potential problems with restricted variance at the item-level. The most problematic item in this regard is item 16: "School is necessary for achieving my future goals." The mean of this item is 6.44 on a 7-scale and the standard deviation is 1.0. However, a standard deviation of 1.0 is not problematic. As a general rule, when using a 7-point scale, we flag for further examination all items with standard deviations that are less than 1.0 and all means that are 0.50 or less away from the floor or ceiling of the response scale. In addition, we examine the frequency distribution of all items to get a sense of the shape of the item distribution.

Correlations

Table 7.5 contains the item-level inter-correlations. These are particularly important: alpha reliability and the adequacy of the sampling of item content in the domain-sampling theory (see Sources of Error discussion earlier in this chapter) are based upon the magnitude of the average inter-item correlations. For these items, we observe that all of the correlations are positive and range from 0.35 to 0.73 in magnitude. As a result, the average inter-item correlation of 0.51 (see Table 7.6) is quite high. Table 7.6 contains the variance of the IICs, which is 0.012. We take the square root of 0.012 to calculate the standard deviation of the inter-item correlations, which is 0.11. Ideally, we would like the standard deviation of the inter-item correlations to be below 0.10; however, 0.11 is not troubling.

Reliability Statistics

First, two values of alpha are presented in Table 7.7. The first value labeled "alpha" is the alpha reliability coefficient generated using Eq. (7.9) or (7.10). The second alpha labeled "standardized item alpha" represents the estimate of alpha generated through the correlation technique as specified in Eq. (7.13). This technique standardizes each item by dividing it by its respective standard deviation found during the correlation process. The resulting two alpha values are generally quite similar; most researchers report the unstandardized Cronbach's alpha from Eq. (7.10). The Cronbach's alpha estimate of 0.874 indicates a high degree of internal consistency. This is not surprising, given the average inter-item correlation of 0.51.

The next section of the output presents the item- and scale-level reliability statistics, as shown in Table 7.8. The *scale mean if item deleted* column contains the scale mean that would result if the particular item were deleted from the scale. The *scale variance if item deleted* column indicates the amount of variance the scale would have if the particular item were deleted. The next column labeled *corrected item-total correlation* provides the correlation of an item with the remaining items on the scale. This is different from an "item-total correlation," which provides the correlation of the item with the subscale, including the item itself. Items correlating less than 0.20 with their respective scale should be targeted for review. The *squared multiple correlation* column contains the correlation between the particular item and a linear composite of the remaining items defining the scale. This value is calculated using multiple regression where the target item is the criterion and the remaining items are the predictors. The final column, *alpha if item deleted* indicates the estimate of alpha reliability if that particular item were deleted from the scale. Generally speaking, any item that has a higher alpha if item deleted than the current estimate of Cronbach's alpha should be considered for potential deletion. After all, such a result suggests that decreasing the scale by one-item actually produce scale scores with higher internal consistency reliability. In such a scenario, that particular item

Table 7.5 Inter-item correlations of the unity value subscale items of the SVA

	16. School is necessary for achieving my future goals	17. School has many "real world" applications	18. The content of my classes is useful	19. Doing well in school will help me with my future goals	20. I am learning valuable information in school	21. I will definitely use the information taught in my courses	22. School will help to "get me where I want to go"
16. School is necessary for achieving my future goals	1.000	0.356	0.347	0.667	0.452	0.364	0.542
17. School has many "real world" applications	0.356	1.000	0.534	0.413	0.494	0.398	0.385
18. The content of my classes is useful	0.347	0.534	1.000	0.514	0.661	0.588	0.497
19. Doing well in school will help me with my future goals	0.667	0.413	0.514	1.000	0.566	0.438	0.729
20. I am learning valuable information in school	0.452	0.494	0.661	0.566	1.000	0.637	0.503
21. I will definitely use the information taught in my courses	0.364	0.398	0.588	0.438	0.637	1.000	0.525
22. School will help to "get me where I want to go"	0.542	0.385	0.497	0.729	0.503	0.525	1.000

Table 7.6 Summary item statistics for the utility value subscale of the SVA

	Mean	Minimum	Maximum	Range	Maximum/ minimum	Variance	N of items
Item means	5.635	5.072	6.442	1.370	1.270	0.339	7
Item variances	1.686	0.992	2.134	1.141	2.150	0.168	7
Inter-item covariances	0.840	0.483	1.281	0.798	2.652	0.054	7
Inter-item correlations	0.505	0.347	0.729	0.382	2.099	0.012	7

Table 7.7 Cronbach's alpha of the utility value subscale of the SVA

Cronbach's alpha	Cronbach's alpha based on standardized items	N of items
0.874	0.877	7

Table 7.8 Values of the unity value subscale if individual items removed from the SVA

	Scale mean if item deleted	Scale variance if item deleted	Corrected item-total correlation	Squared multiple correlation	Cronbach's alpha if item deleted
16. School is necessary for achieving my future goals	33.00	38.97	0.57	0.47	0.87
17. School has many "real world" applications	34.21	35.82	0.55	0.34	0.87
18. The content of my classes is useful	34.35	33.77	0.70	0.55	0.85
19. Doing well in school will help me with my future goals	33.20	35.72	0.72	0.67	0.85
20. I am learning valuable information in school	34.10	33.43	0.74	0.59	0.84
21. I will definitely use the information taught in my courses.	34.37	33.93	0.65	0.50	0.86
22. School will help to "get me where I want to go"	33.41	35.61	0.69	0.59	0.85

exhibits lower IICs with all of the other items on the scale, and the corrected item-total correlation for that item is substantially lower than the corrected item-total correlation for the other items. In this example, all of the *Cronbach's alpha if item deleted* estimates are lower than our Cronbach's alpha.

In Table 7.9, the average measures intraclass correlation coefficient is equal to the Cronbach's alpha estimate. However, Table 7.9 also provides the upper and lower limits of the 95% confidence interval for Cronbach's alpha. The confidence interval provides an estimate of the precision of alpha, and it is dependent on the sample size. In our example, we are 95% confident that the population value for alpha lies between 0.84 and 0.90. If this interval is very wide, it means that we cannot be as confident about our point estimate of alpha, given the sampling error inherent in its estimation.

Table 7.9 Intraclass correlations of the unity value subscale of the SVA

	Intraclass correlation	95% confidence interval	
		Lower bound	Upper bound
Single measures	0.498	0.436	0.564
Average measures	0.874	0.844	0.900

When examining the reliability output:

1. Check the overall alpha reliability. (We are hoping for an alpha of 0.80 or above for all of our subscales.)
2. Examine the means and standard deviations for relatively high or low means and associated low standard deviations. Also run a separate program to get frequency distributions for all items outside the reliability program.
3. Examine the item intercorrelations to ascertain if you have any low or negatively correlated items. Also, look to see if any items are too highly correlated with each other. For affective scales, we generally would like correlations in the 0.30–0.60 range.
4. Examine the variability in the IICs by computing the standard deviation of the inter-item correlation. Ideally, we would like the standard deviation of the inter-item correlation to be below 0.10
5. In Table 7.8, focus on the columns labeled *corrected item-total (scale) correlation* and *alpha if item deleted.* These two columns are loaded with crucial information regarding which items may be pulling down the Cronbach's alpha reliability estimate. In general, deleting items with the lower item/scale correlations will enhance the alpha level.
6. Examine the confidence interval around alpha from Table 7.9. When the sample size is large, this confidence interval around the point estimate is fairly small.

Computing Scale Scores

Ultimately, the goal of designing an instrument is to be able to create scale scores for use in substantive research analyzes. Therefore, the final step in the instrument creation process is to compute scale scores. There are multiple methods for computing scale scores: the most common include mean scores, sum scores, and factor scores. We recommend creating mean scores for each of the subscales. Mean scores possess several advantages over sum scores. First, using mean scores maintains the scale score in the same metric as the original response scale. Therefore, the mean score is more easily interpreted than the sum score. In addition, if a respondent misses one of the items on a subscale, the mean score can easily be computed with the remaining items on the subscale. After computing the means for each of the subscales on the instrument, we recommend reporting simple subscale level descriptive statistics including means and standard deviations for all of the subscales. We also recommend reporting a table of correlations among the subscales.

Finally, the instrument developer names the subscales and describes what it means to have a high or low score on the subscale. These subscales then provide the foundation for the future substantive research studies.

In this chapter, we described the basic principles of reliability, illustrated the analysis of reliability using SPSS, and discussed the computation of scale scores. The next chapter reviews the steps in the instrument design process.

References

American Educational Research Association (AERA), American Psychological Association (APA), & National Council on Measurement in Education (NCME). (1999). *The standards for educational and psychological testing*. Washington, DC: American Educational Research Association.

Brennan, R. L. (1992). Generalizability theory. *Educational Measurement: Issues and Practice, 11*(4), 27–34.

Brennan, R. L. (2001). *Generalizability theory*. New York, NY: Springer.

Cardinet, J., Johnson, S., & Pini, G. (2010). *Applying generalizability theory using EduG*. New York, NY: Taylor and Francis.

Cronbach, L. J. (1951). Coefficient alpha and the internal structure of tests. *Psychometrika, 16*(3), 297–334.

DeVellis, R. F. (1991). *Scale development: Theory and applications*. Newbury Park, CA: Sage.

Isaac, S., & Michael, W. B. (1981). *Handbook in research and evaluation* (2nd ed.). San Diego, CA: Edits publishers.

Kerlinger, F. N. (1973). *Foundations of Behavioral Research* (2nd ed.). New York: Holt, Rinehart and Winston.

Loehlin, J. C. (2004). *Latent variable models: An introduction to factor, path and structural analysis* (4th ed.). Hillsdale: Erlbaum.

McCoach, D. B. (2002). A validity study of the School Attitude Assessment Survey (SAAS). *Measurement and Evaluation in Counseling and Development, 35*, 66–77.

Meyer, P. (2010). *Reliability: Understanding statistics measurement*. New York: Oxford University Press.

Nunnally, J. C. (1978). *Psychometric theory* (2nd ed.). New York: McGraw-Hill.

Nunnally, J. C., & Bernstein, I. H. (1994). *Psychometric theory* (3rd ed.). New York: McGraw-Hill.

Pett, M. A., Lackey, N. R., & Sullivan, J. J. (2003). *Making sense of factor analysis: The use of factor analysis for instrument development in health care research*. Thousand Oaks, CA: Sage.

Raykov, T., & Marcoulides, G. A. (2011). *Introduction to psychometric theory*. New York: Taylor and Francis Group.

Shavelson, R. J., & Webb, N. M. (1991). *Generalizability theory*. Newbury Park, CA: Sage.

Shavelson, R. J., Webb, N. M., & Rowley, G. L. (1989). Generalizability theory. *American Psychologist, 44*(6), 922–932.

Stanley, J. C. (1971). Reliability. In R. L. Thorndike (Ed.), *Educational measurement* (2nd ed., pp. 356–442). Washington, DC: American Council on Education.

Thompson, B. (2002). *Score reliability: Contemporary thinking on reliability issues*. Thousand Oaks, California: Sage Publications.

Webb, N. M., Rowley, G. L., & Shavelson, R. J. (1988). Using generalizability theory in counseling and development. *Measurement and Evaluation in Counseling and Development, 21*, 81–90.

Chapter 8
Review of the Steps for Designing an Instrument

In this chapter, we briefly review the steps for developing an instrument to measure affective characteristics. Table 8.1 lays out the basic steps in the instrument design process and provides a reference to the chapter that describes the step in greater detail. Following the table, we provide a brief summary of the steps. Because some of the steps occur virtually in tandem, we present the steps in blocks.

Major Steps in the Instrument Development Process

Step 1: Specify the Purpose of the Instrument.
Step 2: Confirm that There are No Existing Instruments that will Adequately Serve Your Purpose.

Before even venturing into the world of instrument development, it is important to have a clear purpose or goal in mind for the proposed instrument and ensure that no other currently available instruments could serve that purpose. Instrument development is a lengthy and potentially costly process, so if there is already a suitable instrument out there somewhere, you should use it. In addition, if there is an existing measure that is routinely used, you need to be able to justify your use of your own instrument and explain how it is more appropriate than the existing measure for your particular research study.

Step 3: Describe the Constructs and Provide Preliminary Conceptual Definitions.
Step 4: Specify the Dimensions (Facets) of the Construct.
Step 5: Develop Final Conceptual Definitions for Each Dimension Based on a Thorough Literature Review.

The first step in the development of any instrument is to conduct a comprehensive review of the literature, in order to develop conceptual definitions of the affective characteristic. This is a crucial step in the process because the development or selection of a conceptual definition for the affective characteristic provides the

D. B. McCoach et al., *Instrument Development in the Affective Domain*,
DOI: 10.1007/978-1-4614-7135-6_8, © Springer Science+Business Media New York 2013

Table 8.1 Basic steps in the instrument design process

Step	Chapter
1. Specify the purpose of the instrument	2
2. Confirm that there are no existing instruments that will adequately serve your purpose	2
3. Describe the constructs and provide preliminary conceptual definitions	2, 3
4. Specify the dimensions of the construct(s)	2, 3
5. Develop final conceptual definitions for each dimension based on a thorough literature review	2, 3
6. Generate operational definitions—generate/select items for each of the dimensions	2, 3
7. Select a scaling technique, select/generate response scales	2
8. Match items back to dimensions, ensuring adequate content representation of each dimension	2, 3
9. Conduct a judgmental review of the items	3
10. Develop directions for responding; create final version of survey (including formatting, demographic questions, etc.)	3
11. Pre-pilot instrument with a small number of respondents from the target group. Make any necessary revisions based on their feedback	3
12. Gather pilot data from a sample that is as representative as possible of your target population	4
13. Conduct EFA, reliability analyses, initial examination of item and scale properties	4, 7
14. Revise the instrument based on the initial pilot data analyses	4
15. Conduct a second pilot study followed by CFA, reliability analyses, additional examination of item and scale properties; preliminary evidence of external relationships with other scales, constructs etc.	5, 6, 7
16. Prepare test manual and/or manuscript based on results of steps 1–15	1, 2, 3, 4, 5, 6, 7

important theoretical base underlying the instrument. There is an iterative process across steps 3–5. The delineation of what you want to measure determines the path of your literature review; however, your literature review also helps to shape the conceptual definitions for the constructs and dimensions that you wish to measure.

Step 6: Develop Operational Definitions.
Step 7: Select a Scaling Technique.
Step 8: Match Items Back to the Dimensions/Constructs, Ensuring Adequate Content Representation on Each Dimension.

After careful consideration of the literature review and the conceptual definitions, the next step is to develop operational definitions. Recall, these are the affective statements to be used in the instrument. The scaling technique needs to be selected quite early in the process. Thus steps 7 and 8 often occur virtually simultaneously. The selection of a technique has implications for how the remaining steps are conducted. The Likert (1932) *Summated Rating* technique is the most common scaling method for affective scales. Likert Scaling requires statements that are clearly favorable (i.e., positive) or unfavorable (i.e., negative) in direction.

However, neutral statements do not fit the Likert technique. Why? Disagreeing with a neutral item could indicate *either* a high-level (i.e., School is not OK, it is great!) or a low-level (i.e., School is not OK, it is horrible!) on the trait being measured.

After creating the operational definitions, it is important to match the items back to the dimensions, ensuring adequate content coverage on each of the dimensions. Sometimes it is much easier to write item stems for certain dimensions or certain aspects of a dimension. However, it is important to ensure that the items that you have developed span the entire domain of content and capture some range in intensity. Also, the proportions of questions for each of the dimensions or subdimensions should be roughly proportional to the importance of that concept in the definition of the overall dimension or construct.

Step 9: Conduct a Judgmental Review of Items.

Step 9 marks the beginning of the formal validation process. We begin by collecting evidence based on test content. Content experts review all of the statements both qualitatively and quantitatively. Generally, content experts provide feedback on the adequacy of content coverage, the clarity of the content coverage (Is it clear which items are designed to measure each of the dimensions?), the relevance of the item content for the proposed instrument, the wording and structure of the items, and the appropriateness of the response scale. Generally, in addition to soliciting qualitative feedback, we design a quantitative judgmental rating task that asks the content experts to categorize the items into the correct dimension and to rate the extent to which the statements reflect the stated conceptual definition. Remember, all Likert scaled agree–disagree items should be clearly positive or negative in nature.

The instrument developer should consider conducting a formal readability analysis. Procedures available examine word difficulty and the complexity of the sentence structure. Word difficulty is usually based upon the number of syllables in a word and comparisons with known word lists. There are a variety of ways to compute readability or reading level. See Dale and Chall (1948) for grade 4 and up; Spache (1953) for early elementary grades, or Kincaid et al. (1975) for the formula that is currently employed in Microsoft Word).

Step 10: Develop Directions for Responding; Create Final Version of Survey (Including Formatting, Demographic Questions, etc.).

The directions are a crucial but often overlooked part of the instrument. Respondents, especially young children or adults with limited reading ability, should never be confused by incomplete or vague instructions. Carefully develop instructions that explain the procedures for responding to the statements as well as the meaning of anchor points on the continuum. Be sure to ask both colleagues and members of the target group to review the directions for completeness and clarity.

It is important that the final version of the pilot instrument looks professional. The survey should be pleasing to the eye, have plenty of white space, and be easy to read. The clearer and crisper the formatting is, the easier and faster the task of completing the instrument will be for your respondents. People are far more likely to start and far more likely to complete a questionnaire that is easy to read and pleasing to the eye. Sloppy, ugly surveys are actually somewhat insulting to the target population. The presentation of your survey conveys a message about your level of respect for your participants. Do not cut corners on the layout or formatting. If you are not skilled with layout, you may want to consider enlisting the help of a professional or a more highly skilled colleague. In some cases you can use online software such Survey Monkey or Zoomerang to create your survey.

It is inadvisable to ask too many demographic or non-pilot related questions on the initial version of the survey. If the survey gets too long, people are far less likely to complete it. However, a few quick demographic or other survey type questions can help you to describe the pilot sample and may also help to provide some very preliminary evidence of validity based on relations to other variables. We recommend limiting the demographic and other questions to one side of one page. Do not use open-ended questions or responses. Respondents are most likely to skip open-ended questions, even when they can be answered simply (i.e., What is your age?).

Step 11: Pre-Pilot Instrument with a Small Number of Respondents from the Target Group. Make Any Necessary Revisions Based on Their Feedback.

First, show the instrument to two or three appropriate colleagues for final review of such areas as clarity of directions, readability, and ease of responding. Then, administer the instrument to a representative sample of 5–10 people from the target population and watch them complete the form. Following the session, discuss the form with them and obtain their reactions to the clarity of the directions and the item stems, the appropriateness of the response scales. Ask them to identify any items that were confusing or unclear. Listen well and take good notes; a few perceptive comments from members of the target group could be of immense importance to the success of your project.

Step 12: Gather Pilot Data from a Sample that is as Representative as Possible of Your Target Population.

Once the instrument has been produced, it is time to gather data for a pilot study. Locate a representative sample of people from your target population. Ideally, the size of your sample should contain 10 times as many people as there are statements on the instrument (e.g., for a 40-item instrument, 400 people is a good target sample size). This may seem like a large sample for only a pilot study; however, keep in mind that this sample provides the empirical basis for the assessment of the internal structure of the instrument, a key aspect of the validation process. This is the sample that you use to decide the structure of the instrument (i.e., which items appeared to work well, which items were problematic) and compute a first estimate of internal consistency reliability of the data. Of course, it is possible to use fewer people than specified above and still run the various item analysis, reliability, correlation, and factor analysis procedures. There are two key issues with using small samples. First, the results may be idiosyncratic. One or two outliers or aberrant responders can have much more of an impact in a small sample. Second, the ratio of the number of people to the number of estimated parameters is smaller, which can lead to overfitting of the data. At least as important as the sample size are the variability and representativeness of the response patterns compared to those of the larger target population. Restricting the variation in responses lowers the covariations and the correlations among the items on the instrument, which adversely affects the results of the factor analyses and the internal consistency reliability analyses, both of which utilize the correlations/covariances among items. Also, if the sample respondents do not produce response patterns similar to those of the population, the factor structure of the pilot data may not be stable across future groups of respondents. It is common to use convenient samples to pilot new instruments. However, if you pilot the instrument in one school or company, be sure that the sample resembles your target population. For example, if you were piloting an attitudes toward school measure, you should sample heterogeneous groups with respect to ability, gender, and grade level in several types of schools (e.g., rural, urban, and suburban).

Finally, be aware that the factor structure of the affective characteristic may not be the same across different sub populations. Often, in school-based research, different age levels may respond to the survey differently. A common error is to examine the factor structure and calculate the alpha reliability on a middle school grades 6–8 sample and then use the instrument for different grade levels, such as grades 3–5. Consideration of the formation of attitudes at the lower grades and the readability of the items may reveal that the instrument does not adequately assess the constructs of interest at the lower grade levels.

Step 13: Analyze Pilot Data.

Generally, analyses of the initial pilot data employ factor analysis, item analysis, and reliability analysis, which we describe extensively in Chapters 4 and 7.

Factor Analysis

Exploratory factor analysis helps us to determine the factor structure of the instrument. This provides insight into which factors best explain the variation among the items on the instrument. These empirically derived constructs are then compared with the judgmentally developed categories reviewed previously. If the empirically derived constructs and the judgmentally created categories do not correspond, the conceptual and operational definitions of the affective characteristic should be reviewed in light of the characteristics of the target group of people. Put simply, if the results of the EFA do not support the theoretical structure, it may be necessary to go back to the beginning of the instrument design process (Chapter 4).

Item Analysis

An item analysis can be conducted along with or even prior to the factor analysis. It is always helpful to examine item frequencies, percentages, means, and standard deviations. Items associated with either high or low means and low standard deviations should be reviewed and considered for deletion. Also, examine the pattern of correlations of items within a given scale. Items should also correlate with the subscale score (total score) defined by the cluster of items that hang together on a given dimension/subscale (Chapters 4 and 7).

Reliability

The final analysis of the pilot data consists of examining the internal consistency reliability of the data from the item clusters defining each subscale (Chapter 7). In addition, create subscale scores by taking the means of each subscale, and compute the means and standard deviations of each of the subscales as well as the correlations among all of the subscales. You may also wish to use your demographic and survey questions to look for between group differences on the subscales.

Step 14: Revise the Instrument Based on the Initial Pilot Data Analyses.

Based on the information obtained from the prior steps, it is virtually always necessary to conduct revisions of the instrument. Items can be added, deleted, or revised to enhance clarity of the items and the structure of the instrument. The goal of instrument revision is to produce a scale that produces scores that are internally consistent and stable across time. In addition, these scores should allow us to make inferences about the constructs of interest within our target population.

Step 15: Conduct a Second Pilot Validation Study Followed by CFA, Reliability Analyses, Additional Examination of Item and Scale Properties; Preliminary Evidence of External Relationships with Other Scales, Constructs etc.

If very substantial changes are made to the instrument, after collecting additional pilot data, you should repeat step 13 by conducting an additional exploratory factor analysis. If you have made only minor modifications to the instrument in step 14, then you can proceed to step 15. This second pilot study is generally a bit more involved than the first pilot study. In step 15, it is important to collect enough data to conduct a confirmatory factor analysis (CFA). (Generally, for a CFA, it is best to have at least 200 people and 5–10 times as many people as items.) In addition, Rasch (or other IRT analyses) may aid in the interpretation of item difficulty and in the assessment of person-model fit.

In addition to reexamining internal consistency reliability, we recommend that you also collect data to examine the test–retest reliability of the instrument. Of course, examination of stability reliability requires administering the instrument to the same group of people on two separate occasions. Additionally, you must be able to match respondents' scores across the two administrations. We also recommend that you gather additional evidence of validity, especially validity evidence gathered from relations with other variables. Chapter 6 described appropriate procedures to be considered here—these include correlations with other known measures, multitrait-multimethod matrix analyses, known groups analyses, regression analyses, and structural equation modeling. These types of information will be necessary for a meaningful interpretation of scores obtained from the new affective instrument. Such analyses may require that you collect data from other previously validated instruments and/or from other outcome variables.

Step 16: Prepare a Test Manual or a Manuscript.

The final step in the process of instrument development is to share your work with other professionals who would be interested in using the newly created instrument. At the end of this lengthy process, it is quite helpful to prepare a short manual, documenting such areas as theoretical rationale, the process followed to develop the instrument, scoring procedures, validity, reliability, and score interpretation. Readers are encouraged to consult the APA publication entitled *Standards for Educational and Psychological Tests* (AERA, APA, and NCME 1999) for guidelines in preparing such a manual. Alternatively, the results of this research may be synthesized for a journal article, describing the instrument and the validation process. Some journals, such as *Measurement and Evaluation in Counseling and Development*, publish the results of instrument validation studies relatively routinely. Other journals, such as *Journal of Educational Research*, have a policy against the publication of such pieces. Therefore, it is best to inquire about the journal's policy on publishing validation studies prior to submitting a manuscript to a journal. Pett et al. (2003) devote an entire chapter on reporting the results of instrument development projects, and we highly recommend consulting their chapter as you prepare your results for publication. It is also helpful to find examples of other published validation papers from well-respected journals such as *Educational and Psychological Measurement*. Then try to follow the exemplar article in both form and content.

Final Thoughts

In closing, developing an affective instrument properly requires a great deal of hard work. Realistically, the instrument development process can take years. Trying to cut corners generally results in an inferior instrument at the end of the validation process. We hope that this book has provided you with a fundamental understanding of the instrument design process. However, entire book has been written about many of the topics and techniques that we have introduced in this text. Therefore, we hope that our guided tour of this landscape will inspire you to delve into these topics in more depth as the need arises.

References

American Educational Research Association (AERA), American Psychological Association (APA), & National Council on Measurement in Education (NCME). (1999). *The standards for educational and psychological testing*. Washington, DC: American Educational Research Association.

Dale, E., & Chall, J. (1948, January). A formula for predicting reliability. *Educational Research Bulletin, 27*, 11–20.

Kincaid, J. P., Fishburne, R. P., Rogers, R. L., & Chissom, B. S. (1975). *Derivation of New Readability Formulas (Automated Readability Index, Fog Count, and Flesch Reading Ease formula) for Navy Enlisted Personnel*. Research Branch Report 8–75. Chief of Naval Technical Training: Naval Air Station Memphis.

Likert, R. (1932). A technique for the measurement of attitudes. *Archives of Psychology, 140*, 152.

Pett, M. A., Lackey, N. R., & Sullivan, J. J. (2003). *Making sense of factor analysis: The use of factor analysis for instrument development in health care research*. Thousand Oaks, CA: Sage.

Spache, G. (1953). A new readability formula for primary grade reading materials. *Elementary School Journal, 53*, 410–413.

Permissions

The work reported herein was supported under the Educational Research and Development Centers Program, PR/Award Number R305A060044 as administered by the Institute of Education Sciences, U.S. Department of Education. The findings and opinions expressed in this report do not reflect the position or policies of the Institute of Education Sciences or the U.S. Department of Education.

DOI: 10.1007/978-1-4614-7135-6, © Springer Science+Business Media New York 2013

Appendix A: Content Validation: Baslanti and McCoach

An important phase in the development of any instrument is that of content validation. By offering your expertize, you are contributing to the development of an instrument that is content valid. Your assistance in this phase of instrument development is sincerely appreciated. Thanks in advance for your time and help.

Instructions: Each of the following items is being considered for inclusion in a new underachievement inventory that Ugur Baslanti and Betsy McCoach are developing. You will be providing three ratings for each item. The conceptual definitions of the constructs these items are supposed to reflect are listed below. The rating tasks are listed on the next page.

Construct		Conceptual definition
I	Alienation	This factor measures the degree to which students feel alienated, alone, and unhappy at school.
II	Negative academic self-perception	This factor measures students' negative perceptions about their academic/scholastic ability
III	Negative attitudes toward teachers and school	This factor measures the degree to which students feel negatively about school, classes, and teachers
IV	Low motivation/self-regulation	This factor measures students' negative perceptions about their ability to regulate effort to complete academic tasks effectively
V	Low goal valuation	This factor measures the degree to which students report not caring about school or grades and not valuing the goals of school
VI	None of the above	If an item does not fit into any of the categories, then

D. B. McCoach et al., *Instrument Development in the Affective Domain*,
DOI: 10.1007/978-1-4614-7135-6,

Rating Tasks

Please detach this sheet for use as a reference in examining the proposed item stems. You will rate each item stem in regard to the following aspects:

A. **Category**

Please indicate the construct that each item best fits into by circling the appropriate numeral. (Items not fitting any category should be placed in Category VI)

I. Alienation
II. Negative Academic Self-Perceptions
III. Negative Attitudes Toward Teachers/School
IV. Low Motivation/self-regulation
V. Low Goal Valuation

B. **Certaity**

Please indicate how certain you feel about your placement of the item into the construct by circling the appropriate number as follows:

1. Completely Unsure
2. Unsure
3. Pretty Sure
4. Very Sure

C. **Relevance**

Please indicate how relevant you feel each item is to the construct.

1. Completely Irrelevant
2. Somewhat Relevant
3. Highly Relevant

Please Note:

Feel free to write comments regarding item stems directly on the stem. (These comments could regard suggested changes in wording or if you feel the item should be eliminated).

Item	Category						Certainty				Relevance		
1. Getting A's is very difficult for me	I	II	III	IV	V	VI	1	2	3	4	1	2	3
2. I feel alienated at school	I	II	III	IV	V	**VI**	1	2	3	4	1	2	3
3. I am not motivated to study for exams	I	II	III	IV	V	**VI**	1	2	3	4	1	2	3
4. I dislike my courses	I	II	III	IV	V	**VI**	1	2	3	4	1	2	3
5. School is of no value to me	I	II	III	IV	V	**VI**	1	2	3	4	1	2	3
6. I wish that I went to a different school	I	II	III	IV	V	**VI**	1	2	3	4	1	2	3
7. I feel socially isolated at school	I	II	III	IV	V	**VI**	1	2	3	4	1	2	3
8. I put forth minimal effort on my schoolwork	I	II	III	IV	V	**VI**	1	2	3	4	1	2	3
9. Most teachers here are poor teachers	I	II	III	IV	V	**VI**	1	2	3	4	1	2	3
10. I do not feel like I belong at this school	I	II	III	IV	V	**VI**	1	2	3	4	1	2	3
11. I have trouble keeping track of my assignments	I	II	III	IV	V	**VI**	1	2	3	4	1	2	3
12. I hate school	I	II	III	IV	V	**VI**	1	2	3	4	1	2	3
13. I feel powerless at school	I	II	III	IV	V	**VI**	1	2	3	4	1	2	3
14. I have trouble keeping track of my school supplies	I	II	III	IV	V	**VI**	1	2	3	4	1	2	3
15. People say that I am a lazy student	I	II	III	IV	V	**VI**	1	2	3	4	1	2	3
16. Nobody at this school cares about me	I	II	III	IV	V	**VI**	1	2	3	4	1	2	3
17. I feel depressed when I am at school	I	II	III	IV	V	**VI**	1	2	3	4	1	2	3
18. I am much happier when I am not in school	I	II	III	IV	V	**VI**	1	2	3	4	1	2	3
19. I withdraw at school	I	II	III	IV	V	**VI**	1	2	3	4	1	2	3
20. People think that I am smarter than I actually am	I	II	III	IV	V	**VI**	1	2	3	4	1	2	3
21. I have problems in concentrating on my schoolwork	I	II	III	IV	V	**VI**	1	2	3	4	1	2	3
22. My teachers have negative attitudes toward me	I	II	III	IV	V	**VI**	1	2	3	4	1	2	3
23. I have no plans for the future	I	II	III	IV	V	**VI**	1	2	3	4	1	2	3
24. I am unable to do well in school	I	II	III	IV	V	**VI**	1	2	3	4	1	2	3
25. I feel alone at school	I	II	III	IV	V	**VI**	1	2	3	4	1	2	3
26. I have problems with time management	I	II	III	IV	V	**VI**	1	2	3	4	1	2	3
27. My teachers' grading practices are not fair	I	II	III	IV	V	**VI**	1	2	3	4	1	2	3
28. I do not care how I do at school	I	II	III	IV	V	**VI**	1	2	3	4	1	2	3
29. I need help to do assignments	I	II	III	IV	V	**VI**	1	2	3	4	1	2	3
30. No one at school understands me	I	II	III	IV	V	**VI**	1	2	3	4	1	2	3
31. I hate the way courses are taught at this school	I	II	III	IV	V	**VI**	1	2	3	4	1	2	3
32. I have problems staying organized	I	II	III	IV	V	**VI**	1	2	3	4	1	2	3
33. Grades do not mean anything to me	I	II	III	IV	V	**VI**	1	2	3	4	1	2	3
34. I mostly keep to myself at school	I	II	III	IV	V	**VI**	1	2	3	4	1	2	3
35. I need help to understand many topics in my classes	I	II	III	IV	V	**VI**	1	2	3	4	1	2	3
36. I do not know how to study effectively	I	II	III	IV	V	**VI**	1	2	3	4	1	2	3
37. I have bad relationships with my teachers	I	II	III	IV	V	**VI**	1	2	3	4	1	2	3
38. I see no purpose to school	I	II	III	IV	V	**VI**	1	2	3	4	1	2	3

(continued)

(continued)

Item	Category						Certainty				Relevance		
39. I am not as smart as most other students in my classes	I	II	III	IV	V	**VI**	1	2	3	4	1	2	3
40. I am quiet at school	I	II	III	IV	V	**VI**	1	2	3	4	1	2	3
41. I have trouble concentrating on my schoolwork	I	II	III	IV	V	**VI**	1	2	3	4	1	2	3
42. My teachers do not expect much from me	I	II	III	IV	V	**VI**	1	2	3	4	1	2	3
43. My classes are pointless	I	II	III	IV	V	**VI**	1	2	3	4	1	2	3
44. I am a passive learner at school	I	II	III	IV	V	**VI**	1	2	3	4	1	2	3
45. I consider myself an academic failure	I	II	III	IV	V	**VI**	1	2	3	4	1	2	3
46. I dislike my teachers	I	II	III	IV	V	**VI**	1	2	3	4	1	2	3
47. I procrastinate when it comes to schoolwork	I	II	III	IV	V	**VI**	1	2	3	4	1	2	3
48. School is useless	I	II	III	IV	V	**VI**	1	2	3	4	1	2	3
49. I cannot seem to get good grades in school	I	II	III	IV	V	**VI**	1	2	3	4	1	2	3
50. I feel discriminated against at school	I	II	III	IV	V	**VI**	1	2	3	4	1	2	3
51. I do not have regular study routines	I	II	III	IV	V	**VI**	1	2	3	4	1	2	3
52. Most teachers here are not very bright	I	II	III	IV	V	**VI**	1	2	3	4	1	2	3
53. School will not help me with my future plans	I	II	III	IV	V	**VI**	1	2	3	4	1	2	3
54. I do not feel like I am part of the school community	I	II	III	IV	V	**VI**	1	2	3	4	1	2	3
55. I am not smart in school	I	II	III	IV	V	**VI**	1	2	3	4	1	2	3
56. I have poor study habits	I	II	III	IV	V	**VI**	1	2	3	4	1	2	3
57. Most teachers here are ineffective	I	II	III	IV	V	**VI**	1	2	3	4	1	2	3

Appendix B: Full AMOS Output for CFA Example (Chapter 4)

Notes for Model (With no correlated errors)

Computation of degrees of freedom (With no correlated errors)

Number of distinct sample moments	171
Number of distinct parameters to be estimated	37
Degrees of freedom (171– 37)	134

Result (With no correlated errors)

Minimum was achieved
Chi-square = 635.481
Degrees of freedom = 134
Probability level = 0.000

Estimates (Group number 1—With no correlated errors)

Scalar estimates (Group number 1—With no correlated errors)

D. B. McCoach et al., *Instrument Development in the Affective Domain*,
DOI: 10.1007/978-1-4614-7135-6,

Maximum likelihood Estimates

Regression weights (Group number 1—With no correlated errors)

			Estimate	S.E.	C.R.	P	Label
SQ10	<—	TEACHA	1.000				
SQ9	<—	TEACHA	1.299	0.097	13.378	***	
SQ8	<—	TEACHA	0.827	0.081	10.251	***	
SQ7	<—	TEACHA	1.233	0.086	14.387	***	
SQ6	<—	TEACHA	1.285	0.101	12.699	***	
SQ5	<—	TEACHA	0.844	0.067	12.588	***	
SQ3	<—	TEACHA	1.100	0.079	13.883	***	
SQ1	<—	GENA	1.000				
SQ2	<—	GENA	0.901	0.065	13.793	***	
SQ4	<—	GENA	0.934	0.061	15.402	***	
SQ11	<—	GENA	1.114	0.078	14.341	***	
SQ12	<—	GENA	1.186	0.066	17.924	***	
SQ13	<—	GENA	0.866	0.052	16.528	***	
SQ14	<—	GENA	0.988	0.069	14.413	***	
SQ15	<—	GENA	1.127	0.068	16.531	***	
SQ16	<—	GENA	0.901	0.053	16.893	***	
SQ17	<—	GENA	0.974	0.065	15.040	***	
SQ18	<—	GENA	1.127	0.063	17.790	***	
SQ1	<—	TEACHA	0.000				

Standardized Regression Weights: (Group number 1—With no correlated errors)

			Estimate
SQ10	<—	TEACHA	0.628
SQ9	<—	TEACHA	0.632
SQ8	<—	TEACHA	0.458
SQ7	<—	TEACHA	0.698
SQ6	<—	TEACHA	0.591
SQ5	<—	TEACHA	0.585
SQ3	<—	TEACHA	0.665
SQ1	<—	GENA	0.622
SQ2	<—	GENA	0.600
SQ4	<—	GENA	0.689
SQ11	<—	GENA	0.629
SQ12	<—	GENA	0.847
SQ13	<—	GENA	0.756
SQ14	<—	GENA	0.633
SQ15	<—	GENA	0.756

(continued)

(continued)

			Estimate
SQ16	<—	GENA	0.779
SQ17	<—	GENA	0.668
SQ18	<—	GENA	0.838
SQ1	<—	TEACHA	0.000

Covariances: (Group number 1—With no correlated errors)

			Estimate
TEACHA	<->	GENA	0.644
e14	<->	e15	0.000
e5	<->	e3	0.000
e2	<->	e14	0.000
e15	<->	e16	0.000

Correlations: (Group number 1—With no correlated errors)

			Estimate	S.E.	C.R.	P	Label
TEACHA	<->	GENA	0.235	0.024	9.608	***	
e14	<->	e15	0.000				
e5	<->	e3	0.000				
e2	<->	e14	0.000				
e15	<->	e16	0.000				

Variances: (Group number 1—With no correlated errors)

	Estimate	S.E.	C.R.	P	Label
TEACHA	0.241	0.029	8.449	***	
GENA	0.555	0.063	8.844	***	
e10	0.369	0.023	16.131	***	
e9	0.610	0.038	16.076	***	
e8	0.622	0.035	17.588	***	
e7	0.384	0.026	14.994	***	
e6	0.740	0.045	16.563	***	
e5	0.330	0.020	16.630	***	
e3	0.368	0.024	15.606	***	
e1	0.878	0.050	17.722	***	
e2	0.802	0.045	17.817	***	
e4	0.536	0.031	17.356	***	
e11	1.050	0.059	17.690	***	
e12	0.308	0.020	15.138	***	
e13	0.312	0.019	16.772	***	

(continued)

(continued)

	Estimate	S.E.	C.R.	P	Label
e14	0.809	0.046	17.672	***	
e15	0.529	0.032	16.769	***	
e16	0.293	0.018	16.489	***	
e17	0.653	0.037	17.487	***	
e18	0.300	0.020	15.386	***	

Squared Multiple Correlations: (Group number 1—With no correlated errors)

	Estimate
SQ18	0.701
SQ17	0.446
SQ16	0.606
SQ15	0.572
SQ14	0.401
SQ13	0.571
SQ12	0.717
SQ11	0.396
SQ4	0.474
SQ2	0.360
SQ1	0.387
SQ3	0.442
SQ5	0.342
SQ6	0.350
SQ7	0.488
SQ8	0.209
SQ9	0.400
SQ10	0.395

Residual Covariances (Group number 1—With no correlated errors)

	SQ18	SQ17	SQ16	SQ15	SQ14	SQ13	SQ12	SQ11	SQ4	SQ2	SQ1	SQ3	SQ5	SQ6	SQ7	SQ8	SQ9	SQ10
SQ18	0.000																	
SQ17	0.044	0.000																
SQ16	−0.013	0.007	0.000															
SQ15	−0.031	−0.070	0.091	0.000														
SQ14	−0.067	−0.021	0.048	0.193	0.000													
SQ13	0.007	0.023	−0.011	−0.056	−0.038	0.000												
SQ12	0.028	−0.020	−0.027	−0.033	−0.079	0.045	0.000											
SQ11	−0.004	0.032	−0.046	−0.019	−0.028	−0.006	0.025	0.000										
SQ4	0.019	0.035	−0.036	−0.061	−0.028	0.015	0.005	0.062	0.000									
SQ2	−0.039	−0.042	0.022	0.081	0.214	−0.046	−0.024	−0.048	−0.059	0.000								
SQ1	0.067	−0.009	−0.037	0.034	−0.057	−0.039	0.013	0.060	−0.003	0.064	0.000							
SQ3	−0.055	−0.053	−0.019	−0.046	−0.053	−0.002	−0.003	−0.071	0.085	−0.038	−0.084	0.000						
SQ5	−0.028	−0.009	−0.003	−0.024	−0.012	0.005	0.013	−0.043	0.090	−0.013	−0.054	0.082	0.000					
SQ6	−0.091	−0.047	0.012	−0.063	0.046	0.027	−0.042	−0.075	−0.047	0.008	−0.219	−0.030	−0.026	0.000				
SQ7	−0.051	−0.053	0.044	0.032	0.080	0.027	−0.007	−0.007	0.026	0.048	−0.115	−0.012	−0.044	0.072	0.000			
SQ8	−0.023	−0.011	−0.004	−0.016	−0.026	0.033	0.008	0.000	0.058	−0.030	−0.104	−0.010	0.051	−0.031	0.002	0.000		
SQ9	0.003	0.034	0.044	−0.068	0.034	0.054	0.040	0.019	0.048	−0.039	−0.144	−0.033	−0.049	0.091	0.017	0.002	0.000	
SQ10	0.010	0.029	0.076	0.081	0.048	0.033	0.076	0.088	0.051	0.042	−0.036	0.011	−0.005	−0.046	−0.007	−0.018	−0.009	0.000

Standardized Residual Covariances (Group number 1—With no correlated errors)

	SQ18	SQ17	SQ16	SQ15	SQ14	SQ13	SQ12	SQ11	SQ4	SQ2	SQ1	SQ3	SQ5	SQ6	SQ7	SQ8	SQ9	SQ10
SQ18	0.000																	
SQ17	0.934	0.000																
SQ16	−0.324	0.177	0.000															
SQ15	−0.608	−1.364	2.151	0.000														
SQ14	−1.332	−0.410	1.118	3.550	0.000													
SQ13	0.172	0.574	−0.350	−1.356	−0.901	0.000												
SQ12	0.566	−0.408	−0.651	−0.624	−1.515	1.109	0.000											
SQ11	−0.063	0.547	−0.950	−0.310	−0.440	−0.128	0.428	0.000										
SQ4	0.417	0.755	−0.947	−1.272	−0.583	0.413	0.110	1.123	0.000									
SQ2	−0.808	−0.835	0.555	1.566	4.032	−1.141	−0.475	−0.795	−1.274	0.000								
SQ1	1.297	−0.172	−0.848	0.603	−1.007	−0.909	0.246	0.934	−0.050	1.185	0.000							
SQ3	−1.659	−1.525	−0.659	−1.263	−1.430	−0.066	−0.100	−1.673	2.601	−1.058	−2.195	0.000						
SQ5	−1.004	−0.288	−0.106	−0.774	−0.359	0.211	0.447	−1.166	3.192	−0.433	−1.640	3.508	0.000					
SQ6	−2.138	−1.032	0.317	−1.346	0.947	0.760	−0.944	−1.359	−1.117	0.168	−4.380	−0.846	−0.855	0.000				
SQ7	−1.445	−1.411	1.453	0.820	2.009	0.909	−0.183	−0.158	0.755	1.253	−2.804	−0.422	−1.750	1.902	0.000			
SQ8	−0.664	−0.284	−0.123	−0.406	−0.646	1.110	0.212	0.010	1.680	−0.769	−2.534	−0.339	2.079	−0.826	0.058	0.000		
SQ9	0.065	0.791	1.270	−1.530	0.743	1.575	0.939	0.356	1.199	−0.877	−3.040	−0.972	−1.681	2.092	0.455	0.065	0.000	
SQ10	0.319	0.856	2.835	2.333	1.351	1.253	2.324	2.176	1.621	1.219	−0.978	0.415	−0.220	−1.368	−0.231	−0.642	−0.280	0.000

Modification Indices (Group number 1—With no correlated errors)

Covariances: (Group number 1—With no correlated errors)

			M.I.	Par change
e18	<->	TEACHA	13.324	−0.037
e17	<->	e18	8.609	0.055
e16	<->	TEACHA	6.480	0.025
e15	<->	e18	5.151	−0.039
e15	<->	e17	11.319	−0.081
e15	<->	e16	44.721	0.110
e14	<->	e18	15.604	−0.082
e14	<->	e16	7.656	0.055
e14	<->	e15	69.013	0.221
e13	<->	TEACHA	5.870	0.024
e13	<->	e15	15.802	−0.067
e12	<->	e18	7.867	0.038
e12	<->	e16	7.128	−0.035
e12	<->	e15	5.836	−0.042
e12	<->	e14	21.682	−0.099
e12	<->	e13	18.532	0.058
e11	<->	e16	5.442	−0.053
e4	<->	GENA	5.059	−0.041
e4	<->	TEACHA	13.996	0.048
e4	<->	e16	6.553	−0.042
e4	<->	e15	10.562	−0.071
e4	<->	e11	5.237	0.069
e2	<->	e18	5.216	−0.047
e2	<->	e15	12.256	0.093
e2	<->	e14	52.595	0.232
e2	<->	e13	6.473	−0.052
e2	<->	e4	6.210	−0.065
e1	<->	GENA	13.286	0.085
e1	<->	TEACHA	36.803	−0.100
e1	<->	e18	14.373	0.082
e3	<->	e14	5.784	−0.055
e3	<->	e4	20.979	0.086
e5	<->	e4	19.916	0.077
e5	<->	e3	47.829	0.102
e6	<->	e14	5.468	0.074
e6	<->	e13	5.129	0.045
e6	<->	e4	6.259	−0.065
e6	<->	e1	11.779	−0.113
e7	<->	e18	5.519	−0.036
e7	<->	e17	5.446	−0.050

(continued)

(continued)

			M.I.	Par change
e7	<->	e15	6.240	0.049
e7	<->	e14	10.980	0.078
e7	<->	e2	5.842	0.057
e7	<->	e5	13.478	−0.056
e7	<->	e6	16.292	0.093
e8	<->	e5	10.143	0.059
e9	<->	e15	13.855	−0.089
e9	<->	e1	7.081	−0.080
e9	<->	e5	9.848	−0.059
e9	<->	e6	15.585	0.112
e10	<->	GENA	13.667	0.058
e10	<->	TEACHA	6.299	−0.027
e10	<->	e15	6.980	0.049
e10	<->	e11	5.143	0.058
e10	<->	e6	6.544	−0.056

Regression weights: (Group number 1—With no correlated errors)

			M.I.	Par change
SQ18	<—	TEACHA	6.564	−0.130
SQ18	<—	SQ14	9.020	−0.059
SQ18	<—	SQ1	8.487	0.055
SQ18	<—	SQ6	6.487	−0.054
SQ18	<—	SQ7	10.092	−0.083
SQ18	<—	SQ10	5.962	−0.071
SQ16	<—	SQ15	17.612	0.082
SQ16	<—	SQ7	6.300	0.063
SQ16	<—	SQ10	6.530	0.071
SQ15	<—	SQ17	5.971	−0.065
SQ15	<—	SQ16	15.937	0.134
SQ15	<—	SQ14	39.629	0.157
SQ15	<—	SQ13	6.238	−0.085
SQ15	<—	SQ4	5.257	−0.066
SQ15	<—	SQ2	7.567	0.071
SQ15	<—	SQ9	9.092	−0.087
SQ14	<—	SQ15	27.012	0.164
SQ14	<—	SQ12	5.149	−0.076
SQ14	<—	SQ2	32.435	0.178
SQ14	<—	SQ6	5.064	0.074
SQ14	<—	SQ7	7.334	0.110
SQ13	<—	SQ15	6.232	−0.050
SQ13	<—	SQ6	7.062	0.056

(continued)

(continued)

			M.I.	Par change
SQ12	<—	SQ14	12.541	−0.071
SQ12	<—	SQ13	7.360	0.074
SQ4	<—	TEACHA	6.841	0.168
SQ4	<—	SQ3	22.819	0.169
SQ4	<—	SQ5	23.588	0.197
SQ4	<—	SQ8	6.718	0.084
SQ2	<—	SQ14	30.121	0.164
SQ1	<—	TEACHA	18.014	−0.345
SQ1	<—	SQ6	24.333	−0.169
SQ1	<—	SQ7	14.779	−0.162
SQ1	<—	SQ8	10.430	−0.133
SQ1	<—	SQ9	19.313	−0.159
SQ1	<—	SQ10	7.997	−0.132
SQ3	<—	SQ14	7.156	−0.057
SQ3	<—	SQ4	5.231	0.056
SQ3	<—	SQ5	29.118	0.189
SQ5	<—	SQ4	8.888	0.068
SQ5	<—	SQ3	23.497	0.137
SQ5	<—	SQ7	5.928	−0.064
SQ5	<—	SQ8	7.688	0.072
SQ5	<—	SQ9	5.330	−0.052
SQ6	<—	SQ4	7.773	−0.095
SQ6	<—	SQ1	12.671	−0.102
SQ6	<—	SQ7	7.133	0.106
SQ6	<—	SQ9	8.399	0.099
SQ7	<—	SQ14	6.573	0.057
SQ7	<—	SQ5	8.267	−0.104
SQ7	<—	SQ6	9.800	0.076
SQ8	<—	SQ5	6.113	0.107
SQ9	<—	SQ5	6.004	−0.109
SQ9	<—	SQ6	9.321	0.090
SQ10	<—	GENA	6.893	0.089
SQ10	<—	SQ16	10.335	0.091
SQ10	<—	SQ15	12.721	0.079
SQ10	<—	SQ12	8.643	0.069
SQ10	<—	SQ11	11.014	0.062

Model Fit Summary

CMIN

Model	NPAR	CMIN	DF	P	CMIN/DF
With correlated errors and double loading	42	372.916	129	0.000	2.891
With correlated errors	41	415.850	130	0.000	3.199
With no correlated errors	37	635.481	134	0.000	4.742
Saturated model	171	0.000	0		
Independence model	18	5924.073	153	0.000	38.719

RMR, GFI

Model	RMR	GFI	AGFI	PGFI
With correlated errors and double loading	0.039	0.940	0.921	0.709
With correlated errors	0.046	0.933	0.912	0.709
With no correlated errors	0.052	0.897	0.868	0.703
Saturated model	0.000	1.000		
Independence model	0.385	0.274	0.189	0.245

Baseline Comparisons

Model	NFI Delta1	RFI rho1	IFI Delta2	TLI rho2	CFI
With correlated errors and double loading	0.937	0.925	0.958	0.950	0.958
With correlated errors	0.930	0.917	0.951	0.942	0.950
With no correlated errors	0.893	0.878	0.913	0.901	0.913
Saturated model	1.000		1.000		1.000
Independence model	0.000	0.000	0.000	0.000	0.000

Parsimony-Adjusted Measures

Model	PRATIO	PNFI	PCFI
With correlated errors and double loading	0.843	0.790	0.808
With correlated errors	0.850	0.790	0.808
With no correlated errors	0.876	0.782	0.800
Saturated model	0.000	0.000	0.000
Independence model	1.000	0.000	0.000

NCP

Model	NCP	LO 90	HI 90
With correlated errors and double loading	243.916	189.920	305.554
With correlated errors	285.850	227.994	351.318
With no correlated errors	501.481	426.769	583.720
Saturated model	0.000	0.000	0.000
Independence model	5771.073	5522.689	6025.790

FMIN

Model	FMIN	F0	LO 90	HI 90
With correlated errors and double loading	0.540	0.354	0.275	0.443
With correlated errors	0.603	0.414	0.330	0.509
With no correlated errors	0.921	0.727	0.619	0.846
Saturated model	0.000	0.000	0.000	0.000
Independence model	8.586	8.364	8.004	8.733

RMSEA

Model	RMSEA	LO 90	HI 90	PCLOSE
With correlated errors and double loading	0.052	0.046	0.059	0.259
With correlated errors	0.056	0.050	0.063	0.040
With no correlated errors	0.074	0.068	0.079	0.000
Independence model	0.234	0.229	0.239	0.000

AIC

Model	AIC	BCC	BIC	CAIC
With correlated errors and double loading	456.916	459.295	647.518	689.518
With correlated errors	497.850	500.172	683.914	724.914
With no correlated errors	709.481	711.576	877.392	914.392
Saturated model	342.000	351.684	1118.022	1289.022
Independence model	5960.073	5961.092	6041.759	6059.759

ECVI

Model	ECVI	LO 90	HI 90	MECVI
With correlated errors and double loading	0.662	0.584	0.752	0.666
With correlated errors	0.722	0.638	0.816	0.725
With no correlated errors	1.028	0.920	1.147	1.031
Saturated model	0.496	0.496	0.496	0.510
Independence model	8.638	8.278	9.007	8.639

HOELTER

Model	HOELTER 0.05	HOELTER 0.01
With correlated errors and double loading	290	314
With correlated errors	262	283
With no correlated errors	176	191
Independence model	22	23

Nested Model Comparisons

Assuming model with correlated errors and double loading to be correct:

Model	DF	CMIN	P	NFI Delta-1	IFI Delta-2	RFI rho-1	TLI rho2
With correlated errors	1	42.934	0.000	0.007	0.007	0.008	0.008
With no correlated errors	5	262.564	0.000	0.044	0.045	0.048	0.049

Assuming model with correlated errors to be correct:

Model	DF	CMIN	P	NFI Delta-1	IFI Delta-2	RFI rho-1	TLI rho2
With no correlated errors	4	219.631	0.000	0.037	0.038	0.040	0.041

Execution time summary

Minimization	0.019
Miscellaneous	0.606
Bootstrap	0.000
Total	0.625

Nested Model Comparisons

Assuming model with correlated errors and double loading to be correct:

Model	DF	CMIN	P	NFI Delta-1	IFI Delta-2	RFI rho-1	TLI rho2
With correlated errors	1	42.934	0.000	0.007	0.007	0.008	0.008
With no correlated errors	5	262.564	0.000	0.044	0.045	0.048	0.049

Assuming model with correlated errors to be correct:

Model	DF	CMIN	P	NFI Delta-1	IFI Delta-2	RFI rho-1	TLI rho2
With no correlated errors	4	219.631	0.000	0.037	0.038	0.040	0.041

Execution time summary

Minimization	0.019
Miscellaneous	0.606
Bootstrap	0.000
Total	0.625

Index

D. B. McCoach et al., *Instrument Development in the Affective Domain*,
DOI: 10.1007/978-1-4614-7135-6,

CPSIA information can be obtained at www.ICGtesting.com
Printed in the USA
LVOW100140180513

334421LV00008B/71/P

9 781461 471349